NORMS WITHOUT THE GREAT POWERS

Norms without the Great Powers

International Law and Changing Social Standards in World Politics

ADAM BOWER

OXFORD
UNIVERSITY PRESS

OXFORD
UNIVERSITY PRESS

Great Clarendon Street, Oxford, OX2 6DP,
United Kingdom

Oxford University Press is a department of the University of Oxford.
It furthers the University's objective of excellence in research, scholarship,
and education by publishing worldwide. Oxford is a registered trade mark of
Oxford University Press in the UK and in certain other countries

First Edition published in 2017
Impression: 2

Published in the United States of America by Oxford University Press
198 Madison Avenue, New York, NY 10016, United States of America

British Library Cataloguing in Publication Data
Data available

Library of Congress Control Number: 2016945278

ISBN 978–0–19–878987–1

Printed and bound by CPI Group (UK) Ltd, Croydon, CR0 4YY

For Magdalena:
I love you ~ Ti amo ~ Kocham Cię

Preface

This book is about the prospects for global governance without the great powers. More specifically, it concerns the consequences of pursuing international legal rules and more broadly, norms, in situations where the most powerful states in the international system do not support the rule-making efforts. The question of whether the international community should seek to develop new international standards without the buy-in of global leaders like the United States and China is a matter of no small importance. Indeed, despite the renewed talk of multilateralism that has characterized the Obama presidency, the United States retains an ambivalent relationship toward international institutions, whether concerning the laws of war ('targeted killing' programmes in the War on Terror), human rights (detention and treatment of terrorist suspects), or global climate change and environmental protection to name but a few prominent examples. Yet these and other subjects of global import do not recede in the face of resistance from leading states—if anything, they only become more intractable and challenging. Hence the need for serious thinking concerning when and how international cooperation might be possible—and desirable—under such testing conditions.

Yet International Relations as a scholarly discipline has comparatively little directly to say about these questions, since prominent theories assume that successful multilateral initiatives require the stewardship of the leading states. This notion of a special role—and commensurate responsibilities—for great powers also resonates with policymakers and the general public. For these reasons, the *absence* of the United States and other great powers from international institutions deserves detailed analysis.

This book aims to evaluate the promise, and limits, of multilateralism without the great powers in light of its purported costs. My interest in this topic dates back to the commencement of my doctoral studies, and a series of conversations with my subsequent dissertation supervisor Richard Price. Dick's observation, articulated in his 2004 *International Journal* article titled 'Hegemony and Multilateralism', was that actors seeking to generate new institutions contrary to the wishes of dominant states face a strategic choice with three principal options: (a) proceed despite great power opposition, resulting in a stronger agreement but without key participants (in the hopes that membership can be expanded later); (b) grant concessions to great power demands, leading to a weaker treaty but with broader initial buy-in; or (c) abandon formal multilateralism altogether, and instead seek non-binding understandings or nothing at all. A corollary of this calculation is the question: under what circumstances is a particular approach advisable?

Norms without the Great Powers seeks to contribute to the debate over the future of multilateralism and global governance by providing an in-depth assessment of two archetypal examples of the first of these strategic options—that is, creating global institutions without great power support. To do so the book seeks to answer two fundamental questions, one of which is primarily theoretical in nature, the other empirical. First, how might treaties generate broadly influential norms without the military, economic, and diplomatic resources frequently associated with predominantly powerful states? Second, has this potential been realized in practice: have the Antipersonnel Mine Ban Treaty and International Criminal Court engendered new social expectations and policy change in line with their core obligations, and what variance can be observed between the treaties and across the system of states? As will become apparent, this book takes as its central focus the 'so what?'—or 'what next?'—problem that follows from the successful negotiation of a multilateral treaty. The creation of a binding legal agreement thus serves as the starting point for this study, which attends instead to the subsequent experience of implementation and actor change.

In its application of academic concerns for theory and empirical evidence to practical questions of contemporary global governance, it is hoped that this book will appeal to a wide range of readers. International Relations scholars will, I believe, regard this a worthy subject of inquiry and a productive analytical approach, for reasons I laid out briefly above and elaborate upon in the chapters to come. It is also my sincere wish that diplomats and civil society practitioners involved in disarmament, international criminal justice, and human rights will find much that resonates with their own experiences and assessments, and that the evaluation of the cases will contribute in some small way to future discussions concerning the prospects for additional norm-building in times of great power ambivalence. Finally, I hope that the central concerns of this book will equally appeal to those in the wider public who retain a commitment to the pursuit of an (even modestly) less violent world.

Even a book-length study must necessarily exclude important lines of inquiry, and the present work is no exception. Readers will notice that the proceeding analysis is primarily directed towards the experiences of *states* in adopting, contesting, and implementing the treaties and associated norms that are the object of this study. For this reason, other actors of consequence receive comparatively less attention. Any comprehensive assessment of legal and normative developments in world politics would have to encompass the increasingly important roles played by non-state entities, a list that would include non-state armed groups; transnational civil society actors; intergovernmental organizations, secretariats, and bureaucracies; multinational corporations; and private military companies to name but a few of the most relevant. The particular objectives of this project, and the resulting demands of research design and data collection aimed at demonstrating the extent of change with and among states, pointed to a more bounded focus. However, the book does detail the crucial agency of transnational civil society—especially the International Campaign to Ban Landmines, International Committee of the Red Cross, and Coalition for the International Criminal Court—in promoting implementation and addressing non-compliance in the treaty cases, and in this respect takes seriously their vital influence in the still-evolving status of these institutions.

The decision to largely forego a systematic assessment of non-state armed groups in the development of the Mine Ban Treaty and International Criminal Court, in particular, was not made lightly. After all, non-state armed groups are prominent participants in contemporary armed conflict and as such contribute to the promotion of, and resistance to, international norms concerning the regulation of armed violence and criminal accountability. However, further broadening the scope of the study would come at the cost of analytic depth, as one of the virtues of the current presentation is the wealth of detailed data with which to assess the relative success in changing social expectations within and between states. Other scholars have recently provided sophisticated accounts of the increasing engagement of non-state armed groups with international humanitarian law (e.g. Jo 2015) and interested readers would do well to consult these sources. Insofar as this book does not presume to offer the last word on the subject, therefore, my hope is that it will provide impetus for further research on the contemporary status and trajectories of non-great power institutions which can—and should—include a number of productive avenues of inquiry.

Adam Bower

Edinburgh
13 May 2016

Acknowledgements

A project of this size, compiled over a period of years and several iterations, accrues a great many personal debts. The present book began as a doctoral dissertation at the University of British Columbia (UBC), and my first thanks must therefore go to the vibrant community of scholars in the Department of Political Science. My fellow graduate students Nathan Allen, Shane Barter, Michael Cohen, Elise Leclerc-Gagné, Clare McGovern, and Chris Tenove offered probing critiques and genuine encouragement through the many ups and downs of research and writing. Ryder McKeown has read and commented on various aspects of this and related projects, and remains a valued interlocutor.

The members of my doctoral dissertation committee, Richard Price, Michael Byers, and Katharina Coleman, deserve special thanks for their prodigious efforts. Each of these impressive scholars contributed to my understanding of international politics, challenged me to further sharpen my arguments, and provided guidance for which I remain grateful. Steven Bernstein of the University of Toronto offered insightful critiques as the dissertation external examiner. My greatest intellectual debt is owed to my doctoral supervisor and long-time mentor, Richard Price. As an enthusiastic and impressionable UBC undergraduate, Dick's senior seminar introduced me to the intersections between international politics and law that would come to be my overriding intellectual interest. Later as my doctoral supervisor, he provided the initial inspiration for my eventual dissertation topic, and has been endlessly supportive through this project's long trajectory, offering wise counsel and a model of academic integrity. It is a great honour to now be able to consider Dick a colleague.

The revised text presented herein was written during a wonderful two-year postdoctoral fellowship at the University of Oxford, funded by the Social Sciences and Humanities Research Council of Canada. In Oxford I was hosted by the Department of Politics and International Relations and Nuffield College. Special thanks go to Andrew Hurrell, Neil MacFarlane, Yuen Foong Khong, Duncan Snidal, Ben Ansell, and the staff at DPIR and Nuffield for welcoming me so graciously. My colleagues Christina Cook, Sarah Garding, Sukriti Issar, Beverley Loke, Amy Nivette, Noel Pereyra-Johnston, Anna Ross, Lorenzo Rotunno, Henning Tamm, Henry Thomson, and Jesse Tomalty all provided feedback on aspects of this project and more generally offered their friendship and encouragement. My new colleagues in the School of International Relations, University of St Andrews also have my appreciation for the warm welcome they have extended to me.

My thanks also go to the editorial team at Oxford University Press and three anonymous reviewers whose suggestions and critiques substantially improved the final manuscript. Dominic Byatt, Sarah Parker, and Olivia Wells have provided patient and helpful assistance in the editorial and production process. Dominic's belief in the book's potential, in particular, has been greatly appreciated.

Prior to my time at Oxford I spent a blissfully diverting and productive year as a Max Weber Postdoctoral Fellow at the European University Institute in Florence, Italy. I would like to place on record my thanks to the Max Weber Programme team and my academic mentor Christian Reus-Smit for all their efforts. My Max Weber Programme colleagues Gregorio Bettiza, Julia Cordero, James Cross, Brad Epperly, Mathew Hoye, Simon Jackson, Aidan Regan, Brandon Restrepo, Michalis Rousakis, and Laura Sudulich deserve special mention for their social and intellectual contributions.

One of the great pleasures of this research has been the opportunity to meet committed professionals working in the fields of international disarmament, criminal justice, and human rights. Over fifty NGO representatives, diplomats, legal experts, and treaty officials—in Geneva, Kampala, New York, Ottawa, Sarajevo, The Hague, and elsewhere—kindly took time from their busy schedules to share their first-hand knowledge and answer my many questions. While only a limited number are cited in this study—either due to the sensitivity of our discussions or the evolution of the research focus—each interviewee enriched this research in important ways. I would particularly like to acknowledge the assistance of the Coalition for the International Criminal Court (CICC), International Campaign to Ban Landmines (ICBL), and Implementation Support Unit of the Antipersonnel Mine Ban Treaty (ISU). In addition to facilitating interviews, the CICC and ICBL kindly allowed me to attend treaty meetings as part of their delegations, while the ISU provided access to its archives. Any remaining errors and omissions, of course, are my responsibility alone. A list of interviewees cited in the text is included as an Appendix.

I gratefully acknowledge the following groups and agencies that provided generous financial support for this research: the Department of Political Science, UBC; the Liu Institute for Global Issues, UBC; the International Security Research and Outreach Programme, Foreign Affairs Canada; the Security and Defence Forum, Department of National Defence Canada; the Simons Foundation for Disarmament and Non-Proliferation Research; the Social Sciences and Humanities Research Council of Canada; the Max Weber Postdoctoral Fellowship Programme and European University Institute; and the Department of Politics and International Relations and Nuffield College, University of Oxford.

Some arguments and evidence presented in this book appeared in an earlier form in the following publications: 'Norms without the Great Powers:

International Law, Nested Social Structures, and the Ban on Antipersonnel Mines', *International Studies Review* 17.3 (2015): 347–73; and 'Arguing with Law: Strategic Legal Argumentation, US Diplomacy, and Debates over the International Criminal Court', *Review of International Studies* 41.2 (2015): 337–60. The right to reprint these passages is acknowledged and greatly appreciated.

The support of family and friends—whom, I am fortunate to say, are too numerous to adequately name here—has been invaluable during the many years in which this work has taken shape. The Rance, Lachance, Wosk, and Watt families have taken the time to inquire about my progress and have invariably had the decency to listen to my often long-winded replies. The Moś family have welcomed me into their fold with uncommon generosity, providing space to work when necessary and, more importantly, the benefit of a new culture to share in. *Dziękuję*. To my most immediate family I owe a great and unanswerable debt of gratitude for their ceaseless support. My father, Stephen Bower, was a man of great integrity and courage, who set a model for conduct before his untimely passing. My sister, Margot Bower Watt and brother-in-law, Michael Watt are cherished long-distance partners-in-crime. Undoubtedly the most profound influence on my moral and intellectual development has been my mother, Holly Bower. Mom made it possible for me to pursue an academic career even before I realized I was doing so, while her compassion and open-mindedness set an example that has shaped my interest in humanitarian endeavours. For that, as for so much else, she has my unending appreciation.

The most transformative event of these past few years has been meeting my wife, Magdalena Moś. This coincided with the beginning of my postdoctoral fellowship in Florence, and as such Magdalena has been party to this book's evolution as my ultimate sounding board and most trusted confidante. She has remained ever-patient in the face of the late nights and bouts of uncertainty that are the inevitable by-product of writing, and has contributed to this project in more ways than she knows. I am grateful beyond measure for her constant love, sharp intelligence, and boundless support, and can imagine no better partner in life. This book is dedicated to her, with sincere thanks for joining me on this amazing adventure.

[illegible]

Contents

List of Figures and Table

List of Abbreviations

ANC	African National Congress
AP	antipersonnel (mine)
APIC	Agreement on Privileges and Immunities of the International Criminal Court
APII	Amended Protocol II, Convention on Certain Conventional Weapons
ASP	Assembly of States Parties
ASPA	American Service Members' Protection Act (United States of America)
ATT	Arms Trade Treaty
AU	African Union
BIA	Bilateral Immunity Agreement (United States of America)
BTWC	Biological and Toxin Weapons Convention
CAHWCA	Crimes Against Humanity and War Crimes Act (Canada)
CAR	Central African Republic
CAT	Convention against Torture
CCM	Convention on Cluster Munitions
CCW	Convention on Certain Conventional Weapons
CICC	Coalition for the International Criminal Court
CM	cluster munitions
CPA	Comprehensive Peace Agreement (Nepal)
DRC	Democratic Republic of the Congo
ERW	explosive remnants of war
EU	European Union
GoU	Government of Uganda
IANSA	International Action Network on Small Arms
ICBL	International Campaign to Ban Landmines
ICC	International Criminal Court
ICCPR	International Convention on Civil and Political Rights
ICRC	International Committee of the Red Cross
ICTY	International Criminal Tribunal for the Former Yugoslavia
IHL	international humanitarian law
IR	International Relations
KP	Kyoto Protocol
LRA	Lord's Resistance Army

MBT	(antipersonnel) Mine Ban Treaty
MNC	multinational corporation
NATO	North Atlantic Treaty Organization
NGO	non-governmental organization
NSAG	non-state armed group
OTP	Office of the Prosecutor, International Criminal Court
PoA	Programme of Action to Prevent, Combat and Eradicate the Illicit Trade in Small Arms and Light Weapons in All Its Aspects
SALW	small arms and light weapons
SPLM/A	Sudanese People's Liberation Movement/Army
TCS	transnational civil society
UK	United Kingdom of Great Britain and Northern Ireland
UN	United Nations
UNCLOS	United Nations Convention on the Law of the Sea
UNGA	United Nations General Assembly
UNSC	United Nations Security Council
US	United States
USCBL	United States Campaign to Ban Landmines

1

Introduction

Non-Great Power Treaties in International Relations

SETTING THE SCENE

In the early hours of 18 July 1998, in a large plenary hall of the United Nations Food and Agriculture Organization in Rome, delegates to the UN Diplomatic Conference of Plenipotentiaries on the Establishment of an International Criminal Court convened for the final vote on the draft Rome Statute. This was the culmination of years of painstaking negotiations, and at many points it appeared that the long-held dream of a permanent global court would fall victim of competing visions that pitted the vast majority of states seeking a genuinely autonomous court against a minority of powerful states demanding a more limited institution. Even at this late hour, the final outcome remained uncertain:

> The committee of the whole assembled at first in the Red Room…In this cramped and inconvenient space with too few seats, representatives of NGOs and governments alike thronged the aisles and sides. India and the United States asked for votes on their proposed amendments to the complete draft text of the statute for the international criminal court, which Chairman Philippe Kirsch of Canada had introduced. Following a scenario carefully choreographed by the bureau of the UN Secretariat, Norway's delegation and other speakers addressed the conference before the vote was taken. They pronounced the chairman's text a delicately balanced and painfully achieved package and claimed that—if any element of it were to be changed—the package would fall apart. When India's amendment was defeated by 114 votes out of 148 cast an exuberant uproar ensued. It was a celebration that the package had held with the support of a majority that would give it legitimacy.
>
> In the biggest and most emotional demonstration of the evening, cheering, hugging, weeping, and rhythmic applause followed the similar defeat (by 113 votes) of the U.S. amendments. The intense reaction reflected a fear many participants had harbored: that even at the last minute the strenuous diplomacy of the United States in Rome and its blunt bilateral maneuvers around the world

> would succeed either in putting the conference in impasse or in rendering largely impotent the eventual court. (Benedetti and Washburn 1999, 26–7)

A final vote on the complete draft Statute ensued, and electronic scoreboards displayed the outcome: 120 states in favour, with seven states voting against, and twenty-one abstentions.[1] In this way the International Criminal Court (ICC) was born, an achievement that followed only a year after the successful conclusion, in Ottawa, of a comprehensive ban on antipersonnel (AP) mines in strikingly similar conditions. Yet even in the midst of the initial exuberance, both treaties faced significant challenges, most notably the fact that prominent global powers like China, India, the Russian Federation, and the United States of America had strenuously opposed the new institutions, calling into question their prospective efficacy.

This book seeks to understand the problems and prospects for global governance under conditions of great power ambivalence. More specifically, it concerns the possibility, and limits, of generating strong international social standards—norms—in instances where the most materially powerful states do not support new multilateral initiatives. This has become a key subject for the international community. In the past two decades, a series of major treaties have emerged through processes that challenged the prerogatives of dominant states. In issue areas including security, human rights, and the environment, coalitions of middle power states[2] and their civil society allies successfully negotiated binding legal rules that were more stringent than leading states were willing to accept (Brem and Stiles 2009; Cooper, English, and Thakur 2003; Fehl 2012). These instances of 'non-great power' law-making reflect a deliberate attempt on the part of less materially powerful actors to use multilateral legal institutions to generate new standards of appropriate behaviour that could prospectively bear on all states regardless of their formal endorsement of the treaty. The decision to proceed without the great powers was thus not an accident of diplomacy but rather the product of a calculation that these particular global governance challenges could be more effectively addressed via strong rules with incomplete membership that may be expanded over time, rather than by weaker agreements that from the outset include all of the allegedly most vital actors. To do so, supporters of more rigorous treaties created ad hoc diplomatic fora intended to blunt the traditional dominance of leading states and pushed

[1] Though no official record was made public, it is widely understood that the seven negative votes were cast by China, Iraq, Israel, Libya, Qatar, the United States of America, and Yemen (Wippman 2004, 152).

[2] Bolton and Nash (2010, 173) define middle powers as 'relatively wealthy, small to medium-sized states, with no nuclear weapons and no permanent seat on the UN Security Council'. Prominent examples include Austria, Australia, Belgium, Canada, Chile, Denmark, Ireland, Mexico, the Netherlands, New Zealand, Norway, South Africa, and Sweden.

ahead with negotiations even once it was clear that these actors would not support the resulting institutions.

This strategy poses an important puzzle for International Relations (IR) as a scholarly discipline, since it is widely held that successful global governance efforts must be directed by, or at least encompass, the most materially powerful states. The notion that the international system requires concerted management from a predominant power or powers also resonates with a popular view of international politics held by policymakers and the general public (Ferguson 2005; Mandelbaum 2005). Critics therefore regard the 'new diplomacy' that typified the mine ban and ICC processes as naïve because it fails to account for the critical role for great powers in the promotion and enforcement of international cooperation. The result, in this view, will be weak and ineffective institutions; more seriously, by excluding key actors, these diplomatic processes could spur a withdrawal of great power (and especially US) participation in international governance efforts, leading to worse humanitarian outcomes than in the previous status quo (Goldsmith 2003; Lietzau 2001; Morgan 2002; Smidt 2001).

The present book evaluates the consequences of multilateralism without the great powers in light of these perceived challenges. The field of IR has long been concerned with how the unequal concentration of material power shapes the patterns and prospects of governance in the international system (Byers and Nolte 2003; Foot, MacFarlane, and Mastanduno 2003; Ikenberry 2011; Ikenberry, Mastanduno, and Wohlforth 2011b). But amongst this diverse literature, less attention has been given to the similarly important issue of how the international community should address resistance from the United States and other powers to new governance efforts (Price 2004b). Yet this study is not concerned with explaining the impetus towards cooperation or the negotiation processes, since these issues have been extensively addressed already. Rather, it aims to evaluate the subsequent outcomes of institutional creation, and specifically the success (or not) of formal multilateral treaties in instantiating globally respected norms. In my view, existing scholarship lacks a convincing answer as to whether the strategy of developing treaties in the absence of great power support has proven worthwhile given the drawbacks, and what this may mean for the prospects of similar efforts in the future. In grappling with this subject, this book seeks to answer two fundamental questions. First, how might treaties influence the conduct of global politics in the absence of the coercive, instrumental, and legitimating agency typically associated with predominantly powerful states? Second, to what extent has this potential been realized: have the legal institutions generated new social expectations as evidenced by systematic changes in behaviour and practice, and what variance can be observed among the treaties and across the system of states? While both questions have received some modest treatment before, more systematic thinking concerning non-great power governance is needed.

This motivation provides the basis for four central contributions of the following study. The first is theoretical as I build on recent constructivist theorizing to offer a new account for how treaties may defy the wishes of preponderantly powerful actors to become independent sources of authority in the international system. Prevailing treatments are excessively wedded to a notion of law that is both exclusively voluntaristic and contractual, and a reflection of distributions of material power. These assumptions result in an overly narrow view of what law is and how it functions. Constructivist scholars, by contrast, have persuasively argued for a conception of international law that is deeply social in its origins and operation (Brunnée and Toope 2010; Finnemore and Toope 2001; Kratochwil 2014; Reus-Smit 2003). Rather than a strictly regulative constraint that responds to already identified problems, international law derives its legitimacy as an intersubjective social practice that constitutes actors—who gets to 'count'—and defines the content of appropriate action in the international system, thereby informing interests and subsequent behaviours. International law is not simply politics by other means, therefore, but a separate and distinctly legitimate source to which actors can appeal in justifying and adjudicating their policies. This social account of international law's development and impact, I contend, opens up productive space for exploring how legal institutions may be employed as a means of generating change in the absence of the material power resources that are so often emphasized.

A second contribution of this study is to generate extensive new empirical evidence by which to systematically evaluate these theoretical claims. To do so I engage in in-depth analysis of two archetypal examples of non-great power treaties, the AP Mine Ban Treaty (MBT) and Rome Statute of the ICC. A number of excellent studies have already illuminated the processes by which these treaties were concluded through concerted campaigns among a coalition of middle power states and transnational civil society actors (Benedetti and Washburn 1999; Cameron, Lawson, and Tomlin 1998; Deitelhoff 2009a; Deitelhoff 2009b; Price 1998; Rutherford 2009; Schiff 2008; Struett 2008). I focus instead on the comparatively under-addressed question of subsequent implementation: whether and to what extent the respective treaties have succeeded in changing the expectations and behaviours of states across the international system, even in the face of objections of certain powerful states. There has been some important work in this respect already (Bower and Price 2013; Nouwen 2013; Price 2004a), but existing treatments are selective in their analysis and lack a comparative assessment between treaties. By combining measures of compliance and state discourse, I am able to marshal a wealth of within- and cross-case comparative data from which to make more rigorous assessments concerning the relative impact of the treaties in light of their apparent limitations.

Third, this book aims to contribute to wider policy debates concerning the appropriate response to great power intransigence in global governance. Governments and civil society participants contemplating new international institutions without the United States and other leading states face a trade-off between inclusion and depth: either concede to the demands of predominantly powerful states for various exceptions and exemptions during negotiations—resulting in weaker rules—or proceed without them and face increased challenges concerning the enforcement and universalization of the resulting agreement. Alternatively, the international community may decide to simply abandon formal multilateral processes altogether, in favour of less binding 'soft law' solutions or nothing at all (Price 2004b). What option offers the best chance of achieving strong norms and effective policy outcomes, and under what circumstances? Case analysis, rooted in theory and buttressed by detailed evidence, provides a sound basis for considering the conditions under which non-great power efforts may succeed, and when they should be avoided in favour of more traditional diplomatic strategies. I return to this wider question in the final section of the book, by outlining a research agenda that expands the current focus to issue areas such as global finance and trade, human rights, and the environment. It is therefore hoped that the present study will serve as a stimulant for further work in these directions.

Fourth and finally, the book aims to offer additional insights into long-running debates concerning the interaction of law and politics in international relations (Byers and Nolte 2003; Dunoff and Pollack 2013; Reus-Smit 2004b). A central contention of this study is that material capabilities are not determinative on their own, but exist only in the context of a broader web of intersubjective meaning that is largely structured by international laws and norms. States typically pursue their interests through international institutions, and being seen to be 'law-abiding' is thus a potent source of status in the contemporary international system. In engaging with law, actors are inducted into dense webs of collective expectations and practices that profoundly shape the scope of acceptable behaviour. This bears on all states in ways that are difficult to fully manipulate, such that even powerful actors may find themselves constrained by legal structures they do not formally recognize. Most fundamentally, then, this book is about power in world politics, and is concerned with further explicating the *social* dimensions of power as the capacity to shape how actors think about the world by demonstrating its application in a legalized context (Barnett and Duvall 2005). The resort to law channels and moderates the raw application of military and economic power while simultaneously opening avenues for less materially powerful actors to influence the composition and conduct of global politics. In other words, institutions exist within and are shaped by power politics, and vice versa.

NON-GREAT POWER TREATIES AND GLOBAL GOVERNANCE

Great Powers and the Rest

This section lays out the main phenomena that motivate this study. I employ the term 'non-great power treaties' throughout this book as the core subject of interest. This has two operative components, the latter of which is the more straightforward. I restrict my analysis to multilateral treaties, meaning formally promulgated and binding legal agreements negotiated between three or more states.[3] The particular subjects of this study are also global in scope since they are open to universal membership among recognized sovereign states. The book thus does not directly address other forms that international law may take, such as bilateral treaties, various forms of 'soft law', or customary international law—though I do draw reference to the last of these as an analogue for studying the effects of legal norms (Byers 1999).

More particularly, I am interested in instances where such treaties were negotiated and entered into force in the face of opposition from the great powers, by which I mean the limited group of states possessing the military, economic, and diplomatic resources and political interests to seriously influence the operation and order of the international system (Hurrell 2006, 1–2; Kennedy 1989, xv–xxv; Wight 2004, 41–53).[4] The United States is the natural starting point in this endeavour since there remains widespread acceptance that it stands alone as the sole genuinely global power.[5] 'No other great power has enjoyed such advantages in material capabilities—military, economic, technological, and geographical. Other states rival the United States in one area or another, but the multifaceted character of American power places it in a category of its own' (Ikenberry, Mastanduno, and Wohlforth 2011a, 1). These empirical assessments pervade scholarly and popular accounts of America's place in the world. The IR literature has emphasized US agency in underwriting the liberal international order, beginning with the post-World War II

[3] This follows the definition enshrined in the Vienna Convention on the Law of Treaties, Article 2(1)(a). https://treaties.un.org/doc/Publication/UNTS/Volume%201155/volume-1155-I-18232-English.pdf.

[4] As Martin Wight (2004, 41) long ago pointed out, however, it is usually easier to identify the great powers of a given historical period—since there is usually general agreement on their identities—than provide a concise definition.

[5] For various treatments and measures of US primacy see Brooks and Wohlforth (2008); Brown et al. (2009); Ikenberry (2002); Ikenberry, Mastanduno, and Wohlforth (2011a; 2011b). There are, however, significant disagreements concerning the degree, scope, and substance of US power, and more fundamentally of the concept of hegemony itself (Clark 2011; Hopf 2013). I do not engage substantively in these debates, but am rather interested in the consequences of multilateralism in instances characterized by the formal absence of preponderantly powerful states.

settlement that included the United Nations, International Monetary Fund and World Bank, General Agreement of Tariffs and Trade, and the North Atlantic Treaty Organization (NATO). This leading role has continued in areas as diverse as arms control, environmental protection, and global finance and trade (Foot, MacFarlane, and Mastanduno 2003; Ikenberry 2011; Malone and Khong 2003). There is consequently a widely held expectation among academics and policymakers that these disproportionate capacities bestow special responsibilities upon the United States for the maintenance of the international order (Bukovansky et al. 2012).

At the same time, this period of dominance has also witnessed a frequent resistance to the notion of subjecting American power to international constraints (Brooks and Wohlforth 2008; Krisch 2005). The United States is expected to serve as the guarantor of international order but it is also in many cases the most vociferous opponent of new multilateral initiatives that it regards as injurious to American interests. This is particularly so in the cases under examination here. While the United States is among the most active participants in international diplomacy, therefore, it also remains the most willing to publicize its objections when negotiations diverge from its basic demands, and thus serves as the focal point of debates concerning the viability of recent non-great power treaties.

Yet this book also adopts a broader conceptual lens in two respects. On the one hand, it is interested in resistance not only from the United States, but also from other established and emerging great powers—principally China, India, and the Russian Federation—as well as prominent regional actors such as Iran and Israel. In particular, the rise of the so-called BRICS countries has generated extensive debate concerning the existence, nature, and extent of a shift in the global balance of power to encompass new great powers, and what this may mean for the future of global governance (Cai 2013; Destradi 2010; Hurrell 2006). All of these states have an abiding interest in the development of international legal institutions, and all have opposed the specific treaties under consideration. Their views and behaviour are therefore consequential to a more holistic assessment of legal impact and norm diffusion. Indeed, for a sceptical reader, extending the expectations of diplomatic resistance to other prominent states only serves to further undermine the prospective viability of such initiatives. By the same token, however, a core contention of this study is that official opposition often masks a more nuanced, ambivalent relationship with legal institutions, as great powers experience forms of gradual accommodation to new international social expectations.

On the other hand, the concern is not just with opponents of new institutions, but equally with the much larger group of states that have agreed to binding rules in the absence of these notable outliers. Many of the leading proponents of the AP mine ban and ICC—such as Canada, Norway, and emerging powers like Brazil and South Africa—have sought political influence through the endorsement and promotion of these initiatives. While the impetus for this study is found in the *formal* absence of the great powers, therefore, my focus is ultimately on the broader question of whether and how treaties created under these conditions can nonetheless influence the full range of states in the international system.

Defining Non-Great Power Diplomacy

This question is made especially pertinent by the particular conditions of non-great power multilateralism. The MBT and ICC are the most prominent manifestations of a so-called new diplomacy that emerged in the late 1990s in response to the end of the Cold War and an impatience with the continuing slow pace of international change despite apparent new opportunities (Axworthy 1998; Behringer 2005; Cooper, English, and Thakur 2003; Davenport 2002). As such, the treaties share three key features. First, the diplomacy was directed by coalitions of middle power states and transnational civil society actors[6] rather than by the more typical leadership of the great powers. These actors were united by their commitment to a set of objectives—a comprehensive ban on AP mines and a permanent global criminal court independent from powerful state control, respectively—that served as a precondition for membership in the informal yet tightly connected groups that drove the processes. Second and relatedly, these actors maintained control over the diplomatic agenda by circumventing the entrenched dominance of great powers in traditional consensus-based diplomatic venues. To achieve this, the leaders of the mine ban and ICC processes shifted negotiations into new ad hoc fora that featured less formal decision rules and the prominent participation of non-governmental organizations. The usual diplomatic procedures and protocols—typified by lengthy technical discussions among specialists and private political wrangling far away from the public eye—were thus upended in favour of a more open and fast-paced diplomacy that featured direct engagements between civil society and state representatives and the extensive use of new information technologies.

Third and most obviously, the resulting treaties were concluded over the active opposition of the United States and other powers. While these states did achieve a number of important concessions, they were unable to steer the negotiations to an outcome they could accept, and consequently refused to

[6] Following Price (2003, 580), I adopt a broad definition of transnational civil society as 'self-organized advocacy groups that undertake voluntary collective action across state borders in pursuit of what they deem the wider public interest'. In the context of this study this most especially encompasses non-governmental organizations; private individuals such as lawyers, aid workers, and peace activists; and international organizations such the International Committee of the Red Cross.

join the final agreements. Most fundamentally, therefore, 'new diplomacy' is characterized by a willingness to eschew compromise with powerful states in the pursuit of effective international governance. Leaders of the Ottawa Process that led to the MBT believed that an absolute ban on AP mines without exceptions (permitting self-deactivating mines), exemptions (a release clause in times of war), or geographic exclusions (especially for US forces in the Korean peninsula) would result in a more authoritative stigmatization of the weapons, and thus better address their humanitarian impacts even in the absence of key AP mine users and producers (Cameron 1999, 89). State and NGO advocates for the ICC similarly assumed that a strongly independent Court and Prosecutor would constitute a more legitimate and effective mechanism for promoting international justice than one in which great powers were granted special authority—via UN Security Council (UNSC) control of Court cases—in exchange for their participation (Deitelhoff 2009a; Fehl 2004; Schabas 2004). Moreover, neither treaty permits formal reservations, a diplomatic tool that has been frequently employed elsewhere as a means of facilitating membership by acknowledging concerns that would otherwise hinder ratification.[7] Ruth Wedgwood, for example, has warned that 'all-or-nothing packages will predictably make it harder to gain ratification in countries that would like nothing better than to be the treaty regime's strongest supporters' (Wedgwood 1999, 107). Yet this too was a deliberate decision on the part of treaty proponents to bolster the new institutions by reducing the scope for differential application of rules.

Negotiators in both cases therefore avoided compromise solutions that were perceived to water down the scope and depth of the treaties, and proceeded even when it was clear that the United States and others would not support, and might seek to disrupt, the final agreements. This strategic calculation provides the impetus for the present study. The decision to seek new international norms and legal rules without the great powers is interesting in part because it is relatively unusual: policymakers have instead tended to pursue gradual, lowest common denominator agreements that include the widest range of participants on the assumption that excluding major states will doom an agreement to failure.[8] Indeed, as will be shown in a moment, IR scholars—and the public imagination more generally—are by and large quite pessimistic in their approach to international law. Has this choice proven to be worth it in light of the well-recognized risks and if so, how? After all, both negotiations were highly perilous and contingent endeavours, vulnerable to

[7] My thanks to Richard Price for stressing this point in our previous conversations.

[8] This pattern is often reflected in the sphere of environmental governance, for example, whereby broad framework agreements are created to maximize inclusivity, with subsequent protocols negotiated in the hopes of strengthening the agreement over time (Miles et al. 2002, xiii).

any number of potential spoilers: 'the odds were very long, the obstacles immense, the process fragile, and the outcome extremely uncertain throughout' (Goose, Wareham, and Williams 2008, 1). This fact is often lost in analyses that take the creation of the treaties for granted either as unproblematic 'easy' cases of institutional development or uninteresting examples of marginal cooperation among unimportant states. Yet neither perspective is sufficient, while both leave unanswered the question of what happens after the creation of a new treaty. I seek to rectify this gap by attempting to better understand whether, and how, the preference for strong rules over more inclusive membership can provide an effective means of generating new social expectations that transform global politics.

An Explanatory Gap: Expectations of Great Power Leadership

This prospect is not well accounted for by prevailing IR approaches that have long emphasized the contributions of predominant states in creating and stewarding international institutions. Broadly speaking, three logics of great power agency can be identified within the contemporary IR literature. The first, typical of various forms of realism, expects that preponderantly powerful states will promote laws, norms, and organizational forms that reflect their particular interests and thereby extend their dominance of the international system (Glennon 2001; Goldsmith and Posner 2005; Mearsheimer 1994; Steinberg 2013). The condition of anarchy severely constrains the possibility of non-exploitative cooperation in the international system; governance is consequently brittle, and requires the continued deployment of coercive power to sustain it. To overcome this, hegemons and other leading states offer inducements (such as security alliances, aid, or preferential trade agreements) and threats (including sanctions or military intervention) in order to gain support for their preferred policies and compel compliance with international rules (Schneider and Urpelainen 2013; Thompson 2013). Preponderantly powerful states are consequently essential to the creation and maintenance of a rule-governed order, yet they do not face the same constraints on their own action. Great powers may therefore selectively interpret—and, if necessary, violate—ostensibly binding rules and norms, even as they rhetorically uphold the standards and demand adherence from others (Glennon 2001; Krasner 1999).

In sum, international law does not provide a meaningful constraint on the behaviour of powerful actors, but merely reflects and amplifies existing distributions of capabilities. Realists recognize that efforts at political control are often directed through formal intergovernmental organizations like the UNSC or International Monetary Fund, but regard this as merely a convenient mode of domination, rather than evidence of the independent influence of institutions (Thompson 2006). International law can make states better off on aggregate—producing better outcomes than would occur without resort to cooperative governance—but law is ultimately the product of powerful states and hence merely a tool through which they enact their control over weaker actors (Mearsheimer 1994).

A second major approach generally associated with liberal and institutionalist theories regards international law as a functional tool for coordinating a complex international political and economic system. Here again there is broad agreement that materially powerful states are particularly consequential to the design and operation of institutions that provide public goods. This diverse literature has long argued that institutions facilitate cooperation by improving transparency and information exchange (increasing the efficiency of transactions), acting as focal points for coordination among participants (stabilizing expectations), making commitments credible (improving reciprocity), and enforcing contracts (extending the shadow of the future) (Abbott and Snidal 1998; Guzman 2008; Koremenos 2013a). Because of their emphasis on the instrumental motivations and benefits of cooperation, scholars of the 'rational design' school (Koremenos, Lipson, and Snidal 2001) in particular have been criticized for underplaying the extent to which differential material and ideational resources shape the processes of institutional creation, for example by bestowing some actors with expansive capacities to choose their preferred cooperative venue and privileging particular institutional forms as dominant solutions to multifaceted problems (Byers 2008; Hurrell 2005, 37–41). The question of choice in institutional design is never a politically neutral response to prevailing incentives, but is rather profoundly shaped by geopolitical realities.

Yet while often left implicit, power clearly matters in institutionalist accounts, principally because compliance is assumed to rely on a self-interested assessment of value rather than a normative compulsion towards rule-following; consequently, states will cheat from their obligations without suitable positive and negative inducements. Great powers are in a superior position to deploy sanctions, side payments, and issue linkage needed to ensure adherence, and are therefore instrumental in underwriting the distributive and organizational gains that underpin collective action (Abbott and Snidal 1998, 8; Koremenos, Lipson, and Snidal 2001, 792). At the same time, if great powers are presumed to set the rules, they should also have a heightened role in demonstrating what counts as good behaviour; in other words, they should be especially relevant as a reference point in informing the content of reputational concerns that animate some rational choice accounts of legal compliance (Guzman 2008). The need to ensure a (more or less) smoothly functioning international system thus trumps equality concerns in the design of institutions: 'anarchy matters, and power asymmetries can explain why more powerful actors get more favorable terms' (Koremenos 2013a, 63). At the same time, by locking in an international order that privileges established leaders, institutionalization helps extend this predominance even as a great power's relative position declines vis-à-vis others (Keohane 1984; Norrlof 2010). Authors like John Ikenberry therefore argue that great powers will practice 'strategic restraint' in developing rule-governed institutions that place limits on their own freedom of action in order to gain support for a system of rights and responsibilities that ratify existing power imbalances (Ikenberry 2001; Ikenberry 2011). The provision of public goods is thus a potent means of extending dominance, but it relies on a willingness to subordinate absolute power to external restraints as a means of securing the acceptance or acquiescence of weaker states.

A third literature has highlighted the fact that great powers exert important influence through the propagation of ideas and norms (Atkinson 2006; de Nevers 2007; Fordham and Asal 2007; Ikenberry and Kupchan 1990). While not a fundamental theoretical commitment, constructivists have suggested that materially powerful states enjoy disproportionate—though not always decisive—resources by which they may generate new intersubjective social standards via persuasion, emulation, and social pressure. As a result, 'because norms are geopolitically constructed, their specific content and application will tend to reflect the broad interests of powerful states in international society over time' (Thomas 2001, 31). This proposition is reinforced by historical examples including the abolition of the Atlantic slave trade and apartheid; bans on assassination, piracy, and mercenaries; the emergence of humanitarian intervention; and the evolution of constraints on warfare (Kern 2004; Klotz 1993; Percy 2007b; Sandholtz and Stiles 2008; Sandholtz 2007; Thomas 2000).

Yet even preponderantly powerful actors cannot dictate norms unilaterally, but must seek to promote their vision by negotiating with other members of the international community. Writing from the English School perspective, Ian Clark (2011, 4) persuasively contends that hegemony—or material and political preponderance more generally—is enacted as a 'legitimate social arrangement' that must be conferred upon a prospective hegemon by other members of the society of states. In this reading, rather than a descriptive fact, superordinate power relations are necessarily intersubjective and therefore always limited by the need to recruit 'followers'. While less overtly coercive, this form of influence is not benign: 'critical' constructivists like Sinclair (2010) or Acharya (2011) suggest that much of the mainstream literature implicitly accepts a narrative of the triumph of Western liberal norms that fails to grapple with the deeper structural forms of power that impede alternative norms and challenges to the status quo. Hence the capacity to shape ostensibly universal values remains a potent form of power, even if it is not openly sustained by force.

Despite their notable differences, what unites these various theoretical lenses is a belief that attempts to fashion collective responses to global challenges are generally more effective to the extent that they encompass the most powerful actors of the period. Yet if the United States and other powers are typically regarded as so important to the prospects for multilateralism, their *absence* from such initiatives should also warrant close attention. A few recent studies have sought to provide theoretically informed accounts of this phenomenon; yet they have focused on the creation of agreements rather than their subsequent implementation, and have emphasized the non-participation of the United States to the exclusion of other great powers (Fehl 2012, 39–53; Stiles 2009, 4–14). As such, we do not yet have a suitable understanding of whether and how treaties may succeed in the face of opposition from the leading states, and what, precisely, such success would entail.

THE ARGUMENT IN BRIEF: TREATIES AS VECTORS FOR INTERNATIONAL SOCIAL CHANGE

How can the strategic bet made by proponents of non-great power treaties—that authoritative social standards can be developed without the initial endorsement of the most powerful states—be realized in practice? In Chapter 2, I present a theory of legal efficacy that draws on constructivist accounts of international law as a distinctive type of social practice (Brunnée and Toope 2010; Finnemore and Toope 2001; Reus-Smit 2003; Reus-Smit 2004b). My most fundamental argument is that legal institutions possess greater capacity to reshape international affairs than sceptics allow, due to the pre-eminent role that law plays in defining acceptable behaviour in the international system. While multilateral treaties by no means exhaust the range of forms that international law can take, they are an especially potent means of generating new social expectations that can prospectively bear upon all states, regardless of their formal acceptance (or not) of the legal instrument.

The Relationship between Norms and Law

The starting point for this account is to conceptualize treaties as focal points in the development of international norms, which I define conventionally as standards of appropriate behaviour that describe what types of actions are permissible (or impermissible) for actors in a particular context. Norms often lack codification in an explicit written text but nonetheless exert important influence in defining the acceptable type and range of actor behaviours and, more fundamentally, contribute to the constitution of their identities and interests. The notion that law is underpinned by more fundamental normative commitments is not in itself revelatory: it is generally recognized that particular systems of rules necessarily rely upon more fundamental principles and rules for their creation, interpretation, and modification (Hart 1994). At the same time, there is a sense that some necessary distinction can be drawn between the broader universe of social or moral norms and those that have taken on a legal form. Sandholtz and Stiles (2008, 1) for example contend that international law represents 'the most codified, formal subset of norms'. Similarly, for Cortell and Davis (1996, 452) legal rules 'constitute specific applications of norms to particular situations'. Yet despite this acknowledgement, existing accounts—especially in the field of IR—have been less interested in examining differences in the form or operation of legal and non-legal norms, and have often used the two interchangeably (Finnemore 2000, 701–2; Reus-Smit 2004a, 4; Sandholtz and Stiles 2008, 1, n. 1). For this reason, the linkages between norms and rules, and the consequences for the potency of intersubjective social standards when transitioning to a legal form, could be made more explicit.

Chapter 2 argues that while norms and laws both articulate standards of behaviour, international law is distinguished by its distinctive form of creation, argumentation, and regeneration that contributes to its obligatory status (Brunnée and Toope 2010, 16; Finnemore and Toope 2001, 750; Percy 2007b, 18). Law's essence is rooted in a principled justificatory discourse in which actors debate the meaning and application of rules, in reference to previously articulated standards. These repertoires of ideas, behaviours, and language aggregate over time as precedents that structure international legal practice. In other words, law is defined *both* 'as a body of rules [and] a process of decision-making' (Wippman 2004, 153). As a number of authors have observed, international law provides a dominant vocabulary and grammar for articulating forms of acceptable and unacceptable action in the international system: it offers a language for describing certain types of activities in relation to existing law—as 'legal' or 'illegal'—and defining criteria by which ideas and actions may be presented—in effect, 'tell[ing] us which constructions are permissible' (Borgen 2009, 2; Kratochwil 2014, 1; Krisch 2005, 377). Law is therefore not merely a regulatory device, but also serves as an especially potent means of creating authoritative intersubjective conceptions of appropriate behaviour and legitimate political agency in the international system. By the same token, this is not a closed system, as legal rules and wider norms are always subject to interpretation and modification—contestation is thus a fundamental aspect of legal reasoning and development.

The Social Power of Treaties

Thinking of treaties as normative structures brings to bear the well-developed constructivist IR literature on the nature and impact of norms in international politics. Yet I also draw on fruitful insights from rationalist scholars by examining the ways that norms inform the content of actor interests and pursuit of strategic goals (Abbott and Snidal 2013; Fearon and Wendt 2002). In doing so, I advance two core theoretical claims to account for how treaties can succeed in the face of great power resistance. On the one hand, the creation of a binding legal text translates general standards of appropriate behaviour into a set of more specific prescriptive and proscriptive rules that are bound up in the wider practices of law. The treaty-making process thus helps to clarify the content and scope of these emergent standards; once established, legal institutions further provide a structure through which existing norms may be progressively elaborated, contested, or replaced via accepted legal practices.[9] The translation of norms into a legal form thus contributes to subsequent institutional efficacy by increasing the authority of these social standards. On the other hand, treaties are not isolated islands of legal commitment floating freely in the international system, but rather exist as part of a much larger network of principles, norms, and rules that structure international practice. These include prior constitutive norms like sovereign statehood, the commitment to observe consensual rules (*pacta sunt servanda*), and the practices of modern diplomacy. Actors consequently evaluate and interact with specific institutions in the context of this wider social environment. This quality of embeddedness—what I term the 'nested' social structure of international law—is a key reason why international law is regarded as a 'prime source of legitimacy' in international affairs (Krisch 2005, 377), and helps explain how particular treaties can transcend particular configurations of material power to shape international politics.

This social account of international legal efficacy in turn leads to two principal expectations concerning institutional impact. First, international law is sustained by conceptions of appropriateness rather than ongoing enforcement, and for this reason treaties may generate communities of legal obligation among their members even in the absence of the agency provided by predominantly powerful actors. This challenges the realist contention that international law does not exert a distinctive influence independent of the coercive power of leading states (Mearsheimer 1994; Thompson 2013). Second, because they instantiate norms that are linked to pre-existing and more fundamental institutions, treaties may generate informal compliance and adaptation among non-party states—including great powers—even as these actors remain outside the formal legal agreement. That is, even expressions of resistance such as the non-ratification of treaties and continuing violation of some of their core rules often contain forms of accommodation

[9] Of course, the content of relevant norms does not always match the existing international law in a given issue area, and norms may be more or less permissive than the formal legal strictures (Percy 2007b; Thomas 2001, 42–3).

that are missed by conventional positivist accounts of international law. This can be seen, for example, in the (sometimes grudging) acknowledgement of underlying norms by ambivalent states or in the various ways that new social expectations may circumscribe policy choices even as non-compliance continues in other ways. This latter claim thus challenges the view that sovereign states (and especially powerful ones) can largely ignore new institutional developments not to their liking (Glennon 2001; Wohlforth 2012), and is especially surprising for the preponderance of scholars who regard voluntary consent as the basis of international legal impact.

Demonstrating these complex manifestations of institutional influence also requires a method for identifying relevant evidence. This book adopts a particular account of institutional effectiveness that emphasizes the propagation of widely endorsed norms rather than the mitigation of collective action problems such as the reduction in AP mine casualties or the deterrence of grave international crimes. An effective treaty will generate new social expectations that shape state policy and hence the conduct of international politics. I undertake this assessment by evaluating the extent of global compliance with treaty obligations and contextualizing these patterns through a close study of official state discourse concerning the treaties' legal and normative status. This dual approach provides a richer view of how institutions may influence state policy by relating evidence of what states say to what they do, and explicitly includes the possibility of informal adaptation by non-parties.

CASE SELECTION: NON-GREAT POWER TREATIES AND THEIR ALTERNATIVES

Options for Great Power Engagement

The shadow of power politics hangs over this study, especially as the substantive subject matter is identified by its deviation from anticipated patterns. In many instances great powers do successfully employ their predominant status and resources to shape the terms of multilateral diplomacy and entrench unequal rights and responsibilities in international law (Byers and Nolte 2003; Krisch 2005). This can take a number of forms. First, great powers have historically built in preferential rights in the design of new global institutions, so as to safeguard their interests. This can be seen in the creation of the post-World War II institutions, with the inclusion of a veto at the UNSC, disproportionate vote share in the World Bank and International Monetary Fund, and consensus rules at the World Trade Organization and NATO. Predominant states thus typically condition their participation in negotiations on an expectation that their demands will be reflected in the treaty text.

As a consequence, the international community frequently incorporates a variety of concessions to facilitate great power engagement, thereby limiting the scope of legally binding rules. This has been the experience, for example, in the long-term efforts to regulate small arms and light weapons that recently culminated in the Arms Trade Treaty (ATT). The same underlying dynamics mean that powerful states can derail undesired progress through the use of formal institutional rules—requiring consensus decision-making, for example—or deference. Notably, work at the United Nations Conference on Disarmament has stalled for more than a decade, due to a variety of substantive and procedural objections from the United States and other delegations. In other cases, the United States and other leading powers may exit multilateral processes and seek more preferable arrangements via bilateral or ad hoc agreements that introduce greater flexibility in terms of the strength of obligations or the more limited number of parties they encompass. The US shift to informal 'coalitions of the willing' in prosecuting the so-called War on Terror is an exemplar of this strategy. In situations where subordination, institutional control, or forum shopping do not achieve desired ends, a withdrawal of support is often enough to block incipient cooperative efforts. For example, a proposed verification protocol for the Biological and Toxin Weapons Convention was abandoned in 2002 when US negotiators indicated that they would not support the draft proposal. In other instances, the refusal to ratify *existing* agreements—such as the Comprehensive Test Ban Treaty in the case of China and the United States—has meant that they cannot enter into force even for other states.

Finally, great powers may publicly reject new governance initiatives proposed by less powerful actors, yet fail to prevent the creation of institutions. This more limited occurrence is the subject of this study. When great powers do not achieve rules that they find acceptable, they typically seek to isolate the regimes and insulate themselves against these new constraints (Krisch 2003; Vagts 2001). Great power intransigence, however, must be distinguished from a more common failure to formally join treaties. There are a variety of bureaucratic reasons relating to domestic political and legal structures that may delay the ratification of agreements over potentially long periods of time. The United States, for example, has not ratified a number of major agreements—such as the Convention on the Elimination of All Forms of Discrimination against Women, the revised UN Convention on the Law of the Sea, and the Convention on the Rights of the Child—owing to procedural obstacles in gaining formal Senate approval rather than deep principled objections within successive administrations. For these reasons, ratification statistics in isolation are not a reliable means of distinguishing genuinely non-great power initiatives of the kind I am interested in from a more numerous set of treaties that lack the official participation of great powers (Simmons 2010, 274–5).

This book focuses on two core multilateral treaties, rather than attempting to systematically compare these examples against other ostensibly similar cases or the variety of potential scenarios of great power engagement. In the first instance, then, cases are chosen for their fit with the core concern of this study rather than on criteria that would maximize variation in the outcome of the initial diplomatic effort (George and Bennett 2005, 83 and 112–13; Klotz 2009, 44–5). As a first cut I reviewed the histories of major global treaties created since 1945, looking for evidence of opposition from the United States (and less frequently, other great powers) during negotiations and, crucially, to the final agreed treaty text (Table 1.1).[10] Alternatively, a treaty was included if none of the five permanent members of the UNSC (P5) joined the agreement, suggesting that leadership in its creation came from other, less powerful actors.

These results suggest a wider universe of cases, albeit one that still constitutes only a small fraction of the total number of multilateral agreements. Detailed analysis of their impact is beyond the scope of this chapter, but a few trends are readily apparent. First, the seventeen treaties included here exhibit wide variation in membership characteristics. Of the sixteen that are currently active, the average length of time between creation (the conclusion of negotiations resulting in an agreed text) and entry-into-force is 5.75 years, but ranges between one year and eighteen years. There is a similar diversity of membership, with an average of 107 states parties between a low of fifteen and high of 192. On both of these measures the MBT and Rome Statute compare favourably, with entry-into-force after two and four years and 162 and 123 members, respectively. Finally, membership among permanent members of the UNSC also varies both in terms of quantity and timing. Perhaps unsurprisingly, France and the United Kingdom are the most frequent P5 participants, and are members of eleven and ten of the treaties, respectively (China has joined six, Russia/Soviet Union five, and the United States none). For those P5 states that did join, the average time from treaty creation to ratification was roughly eight years. This latter finding hints at a key theme of this study, which concerns the prospects for gradual adaptation as actors become increasingly familiar and comfortable with new norms over time.

There is also great variance with respect to the implementation of non-great power treaties. Some appear to have generated broadly respected norms despite opposition from powerful states. The UN Convention on the Law of the Sea (UNCLOS), for example, is recognized as the primary legal institution

[10] As Caroline Fehl (2012, 11) points out, however, 'the detailed information about individual negotiation processes that would be needed to reliably identify . . . instances of [great power] opposition to stringent commitments in the negotiation phase, is much harder to come by'. The brief discussion presented in this section is thus suggestive only, and in highlighting the most important global instances of non-great power treaty-making does not claim to provide a comprehensive accounting of all potential cases across time and subject matter.

Table 1.1. Non-great power treaties, 1945–2015

Name	Created	EIF	Parties	P5 Members
International Convention on the Suppression and Punishment of the Crime of Apartheid	1973	1976	109	China (1983), USSR/Russia (1975)
Protocol Additional to the Geneva Conventions of 12 August 1949, and relating to the Protection of Victims of International Armed Conflicts (Protocol I)	1977	1978	174	China (1983), France (2001), USSR/Russia (1989), United Kingdom (1998)
Protocol Additional to the Geneva Conventions of 12 August 1949, and relating to the Protection of Victims of Non-International Armed Conflicts (Protocol II)	1977	1978	168	China (1983), France (1984), USSR/Russia (1989), United Kingdom (1998)
Vienna Convention on Succession of States in Respect of Treaties	1978	1996	22	*none*
Agreement Governing the Activities of States on the Moon and Other Celestial Bodies	1979	1984	16	*none*
Convention on the Elimination of All Forms of Discrimination against Women	1979	1981	189	China (1980), France (1983), USSR/Russia (1981), United Kingdom (1986)
UN Convention on the Law of the Sea	1982	1994	167	China (1996), France (1996), USSR/Russia (1997), United Kingdom (1997)
United Nations Convention on Conditions for Registration of Ships	1986	NIF	15	*none*
Second Optional Protocol to the International Covenant on Civil and Political Rights, aiming at the abolition of the death penalty	1989	1991	81	France (2007), United Kingdom (1999)
International Convention against the Recruitment, Use, Financing and Training of Mercenaries	1989	2001	34	*none*
International Convention on the Protection of the Rights of All Migrant Workers and Members of Their Families	1990	2003	48	*none*
Convention on the Prohibition of the Use, Stockpiling, Production and Transfer of Anti-Personnel Mines and on their Destruction (antipersonnel Mine Ban Treaty)	1997	1999	162	France (1998), United Kingdom (1998)

(*continued*)

Table 1.1. Continued

Name	Created	EIF	Parties	P5 Members
Kyoto Protocol to the United Nations Framework Convention on Climate Change	1997	2005	192	China (2002), France (2002), Russia (2004), United Kingdom (2002)
Rome Statute of the International Criminal Court	1998	2002	123	France (2000), United Kingdom (2001)
Cartagena Protocol on Biosafety to the Convention on Biological Diversity	2000	2003	170	China (2005), France (2003), United Kingdom (2003)
International Convention for the Protection of All Persons from Enforced Disappearance	2006	2010	51	France (2008)
Convention on Cluster Munitions	2008	2010	100	France (2009), United Kingdom (2010)

Note: The columns are as follows. The first column gives the acronym and year of signature for each treaty. The second column provides the year of entry into force (if applicable); 'NIF' denotes that the treaty has not yet entered into force. The third column lists the total number of states parties (as of May 2016), while the fourth column notes parties from the Permanent Five members of the UNSC, along with the year of ratification/accession.

governing the oceans. The majority of treaty provisions are accepted as customary international law, including by the United States. Indeed, while the United States raised a series of principled concerns during the negotiations and has yet to ratify the Convention, it has largely adopted the demands of UNCLOS, including by accepting the mandated 12-mile territorial sea limit.[11] The global spread of the UNCLOS and its norms, therefore, has not been appreciably derailed by official US opposition, which has itself substantially receded with the passage of time.[12] In a similar vein, substantial portions of Additional Protocols I and II to the 1949 Geneva Conventions are now regarded as customary international law, meaning that they impose obligations on all states regardless of their formal acceptance of the treaties (Henckaerts 2005, 187–8). Many (but not all) of the rules have been widely incorporated into national military manuals and legal systems—including by non-parties like the United States—and have shaped international discourse over appropriate conduct in warfare (Meron 1994, 681–2). Yet compliance with these rules in combat situations is both highly uneven and difficult to measure, so the impact of the Additional Protocols is harder to establish. Sceptics charge that controversial aspects of Protocol I have been rejected by

[11] I am grateful to one of the anonymous reviewers for drawing my attention to this point.

[12] In 2007, President Bush indicated his support for ratification and the Senate Foreign Relations Committee voted overwhelmingly to send the treaty to the full Senate for a ratification vote (Drawbaugh 2007).

powerful states like the United States, are widely ignored in practice, and as a result have done little to restrain armed conflict (Dinstein 1997; Feith 1985).

Other non-great power treaties have clearly been rendered ineffectual by their political circumstances. The Kyoto Protocol (KP), for example, has 192 members—the largest number in this list—but is widely regarded as a failure, as noted in Chapter 9 (Fehl 2012, 112–39). Sarah Percy has convincingly demonstrated that the International Convention against the Recruitment, Use, Financing and Training of Mercenaries has proven less efficacious than more widely endorsed norm that preceded it (Percy 2007a). Others like the Vienna Convention on Succession of States in Respect of Treaties or the Agreement Governing the Activities of States on the Moon and Other Celestial Bodies are largely irrelevant due to limited state interest that is presumably dictated in large part by the non-participation of great powers.

Answering the question of whether non-great power multilateralism is advisable in relation to other possible diplomatic strategies first requires a thorough assessment of the current status of actually existing treaties. Yet the limited metrics presented above only provide a partial snapshot of the wider picture. What this brief discussion demonstrates most of all, therefore, is that rendering convincing judgements concerning the status and efficacy of international institutions demands detailed empirical evidence drawn from diverse sources. This, in turn, justifies the focus on a few exemplary cases adopted in this book. The analytical bet, to put it simply, is that more can be learned about the prospects and pitfalls of non-great power treaty-making through the qualitative examination of a few core cases rather than seeking broad empirical patterns via large-*n* statistical analysis or the comparison of a wide array of cases. At the same time, the present focus on non-great power multilateralism risks giving the—incorrect—impression that attempts to bypass great power resistance have always produced the desired institutional result, leading to biased conclusions concerning the likelihood of achieving similar results in other issue areas. The final chapters (Chapter 8 and 9) take a wider view of the subject matter with this concern in mind, as described more fully in a moment. Taken together, this approach thus provides the first essential step in rendering more holistic judgements concerning the promise and limits of similar efforts in the future.

The Mine Ban Treaty and Rome Statute of the ICC as Archetypal Cases

As noted already, the MBT and Rome Statute of the ICC are the most prominent examples of a so-called new diplomacy that emerged in the mid 1990s and sought to bypass resistance from leading states in creating new multilateral legal institutions. The considerable attention—both hopeful support and scepticism—both have received in academic and policy circles warrants a thorough accounting of their subsequent implementation. Case selection is further justified by the concern for maintaining conceptual coherence. Despite their differing focus and intentions, the MBT and ICC are fundamentally directed towards constraining the use of organized violence, whether individually or collectively. The particular dynamics associated with banning military weapons and punishing acts of grave criminality are sufficiently distinct as to justify their exclusive attention instead of in combination with other issue areas such as global trade or environmental protection. The case studies also provide extensive variation on the key dependent variable—the status of core treaty norms as evidenced by behavioural and discursive change. Indeed, as demonstrated in Chapters 4–7, the MBT has generated greater norm development than the ICC, for reasons that are considered in Chapter 8. Focusing on treaties with broadly similar subject matter removes one source of variation that would otherwise be very difficult to control for in the context of a study with only two core cases, while still allowing for important variation in outcomes.

The ban on AP mines and the creation of a permanent international criminal court are also hard cases for generating strong international rules and norms and thus especially valuable in assessing the utility of the theoretical argument. As I explain in Chapter 3, both treaties seek to impose new and potentially costly obligations that proscribe the internal and external powers of the state in areas—security and domestic powers of policing and justice—that are most jealously guarded by governments (Price 2003, 598). The MBT places limits on the scope of military operations and thus represents a direct intervention in the war-fighting capacity of the state, as was clearly recognized at the time of its negotiation. Just as significantly, the ban belies the common assertion that weapons are only eliminated once they are no longer useful: the prohibition was instead proposed at a time when the weapons were in frequent use and widely regarded as valuable instruments of military arsenals (Gard, Jr 1998; Maslen 2005, 1:1–13). The ICC for its part seeks to fundamentally restructure international expectations concerning the punishment of grave crimes, via an expansive and potentially invasive supranational oversight mechanism. As David Wippman (2004, 152) notes, however, 'States wishing to maximize their freedom of action internally and internationally in general have an interest in insulating their conduct from any authoritative external review and assessment.' The Court is, therefore, a major innovation that holds substantial implications for the practice of state sovereignty. Evidence of substantial actor change in matters of fundamental global concern and under such challenging circumstances would bolster my theoretical claim that international legal structures can exert meaningful independent influence in world politics.

Finally, while the AP mine ban and ICC deserve attention on their own merits, a careful evaluation of their contemporary status also holds implications for other existing or potential institutions not directly considered here. Detailed, comparative consideration of the implementation of these important cases, and the reasons for their diverging impact, can provide insights as to when the strategy of pursuing binding legal rules without great power support may offer an effective vector for norm development in other issues of global concern. Indeed, the theory presented in Chapter 2 is specifically oriented towards the phenomenon of non-great power law-making, but the underlying conception of international law as fundamentally *social* and *normative* in its development and operation applies much more broadly. Moreover, the extensive involvement of non-state actors—most especially secretariats and transnational civil society—is a widespread feature of many contemporary treaty regimes. While the partnership between motivated states and non-state actors has proven critical to the MBT and ICC, therefore, this dynamic is by no means unique to the present cases. For this reason, the processes described in this book may also feature in other instances of actual or prospective norm development either with or without the great powers. Understanding when, and to what extent, the conclusions concerning the present treaties may be applicable more widely is the objective of the final section of the book (Chapters 8 and 9).

THE PLAN FOR THE BOOK

The book is divided into three main parts. Chapter 2 develops a theoretical account of the prospects for non-great power law, while Chapter 3 then presents a set of methodological tools for evaluating this potential. My basic claim here is that multilateral treaties should be understood as distillations of normative reasoning and as such, concepts and methods developed by constructivist IR scholars for studying international norms are most appropriate for the task of assessing treaty impact. The next section (Chapters 4–7) applies this approach to the core cases, with dedicated attention paid to States Parties and non-parties for each treaty. Each chapter follows a similar structure to aid in subsequent comparison, but with important allowances for the unique conditions of each case.

In the final section I return to the question of whether the strategic choice associated with losing the support of the great powers was justified in light of the empirical record and the potential alternatives. A few authors have tentatively engaged this subject already (Malanczuk 2000; Price 2004b); my aim is to provide a more systematic basis upon which to render such judgements. Chapter 8 evaluates the chief patterns uncovered in the preceding analysis, and draws some comparative conclusions regarding the depth of change attributable to each treaty. I then propose a series of hypotheses drawn from the IR literature that can help explain this observed variation. Understanding what is working—and not—in the core case studies can provide analytic leverage in identifying the conditions under which non-great power diplomacy may prove successful, and when such a strategy is to be avoided. This exercise thus serves as the first step in identifying features of a conditional theory of non-great power legal efficacy.

The concluding chapter (Chapter 9) begins the process of thinking beyond the present focus. It first sets the earlier findings against a counterfactual consideration of how the principal institutional alternatives—treaties that sufficiently incorporated great power demands or no institutions at all—might have addressed the policy challenges that motivated the diplomacy in the first place. This seeks to broaden the implications of the previous chapters by explicitly accounting for the most likely consequences of including the United States and other powerful states. Would such treaties have generated stronger norms and greater state change? For a variety of reasons, I believe the most reasonable answer is no: substantial concessions would have resulted in weaker standards and less, rather than more, international governance capacity. At the same time, focusing only on those limited cases of non-great power treaties ignores a large universe of real and potential examples that did, or could have, developed differently. I therefore briefly apply the conditional hypotheses developed in Chapter 8 to other instances of non-great power treaty-making—notably the implementation mechanism for the KP and ban on cluster munitions—and a wider range of governance scenarios where great power engagement appears to have been more decisive in facilitating or impeding cooperation. The chapter, and book, concludes by proposing avenues for future research prompted by this study.

2

A Social Theory of Treaty Influence

This chapter sets out a theoretical account of how multilateral treaties may shape international affairs under conditions of great power ambivalence. The question of international law's relationship to wider social, economic, and political forces is of central importance to the study of international relations because 'the language and conduct of politics has become increasingly legalised' (Sinclair 2010, 1):

> Law now provides in large part the vocabulary for contemporary politics. Whether we discuss the 'legality' of the second Gulf War, address human rights, the (in)admissibility of certain means of 'enhanced interrogation,' or trade and development issues, legal concepts figure prominently in all arguments and are made by all sorts of people, be they decision-makers, journalists, public intellectuals, or the proverbial men (and women) in the street. (Kratochwil 2014, 1)

Law is thus deeply embedded in the practice of international relations (Abbott and Snidal 2013; Abbott et al. 2000; Brunnée and Toope 2010; Byers and Nolte 2003; Dunoff and Pollack 2013; Finnemore and Toope 2001; Glennon 2001; Hafner-Burton, Victor, and Lupu 2012; Reus-Smit 2003; Reus-Smit 2004b; Scott and Ambler 2007; Slaughter, Tulumello, and Wood 1998). Yet as Chapter 1 indicated, many prominent theories are sceptical that international law can independently influence the conduct of international affairs, principally because institutions are understood as reflections of, and subordinate to, the interests of the (typically powerful) states that create them.

In the following pages I present an alternative account that builds on the rich constructivist scholarship concerning the social structure of international law and its place in the wider international system. This chapter is therefore principally oriented towards offering a more specific application of this diverse literature to the problem of non-great power treaties. My purpose is not to engage in a 'three-cornered fight' in order to pit competing theories against one another and prove the superiority of my preferred lens to all domains. Rather, I seek to demonstrate how constructivism's explicit attention to the social origins and dynamics of international law can widen law's potential impact and thereby address some of the apparent challenges noted in Chapter 1. In essence, I contend that proponents of non-great power institutions deliberately use the language of international law to introduce new international social expectations because the structure and procedural legitimacy of law makes it an especially effective vehicle for changing norms. In so doing I also incorporate insights from rationalist theories in those many areas of shared interest where distinctions between theoretical approaches are more a matter of emphasis and degree than wholesale disagreement (Fearon and Wendt 2002, 52). Most especially, I am interested in how the employment of law—through its development, promotion, interpretation, and contestation—is bound up in the creation of new standards of appropriate behaviour that shape actor identities and interests and how, in turn, these processes inform the strategic pursuit of policy goals. My more particular focus should therefore also hold implications for broader discussions concerning the nature and consequences of law and norms in IR.

I first briefly introduce some key claims of the prominent rationalist view of legal influence that raise questions about the prospects for developing effective institutions without the great powers, and outline the main features of a constructivist alternative. In contrast to realist and institutionalist accounts in which the status of law is dependent upon its continued enforced observance, constructivists contend that legal obligation derives from the internal procedures of law as an intersubjective practice that generates collective meaning (Brunnée and Toope 2010; Reus-Smit 2003; Reus-Smit 2011). This implies a different basis for compliance, and greater potential for international law to influence state conduct. The chapter then transitions to the more specific account concerning the potential of non-great power law. Multilateral treaties constitute a particular form of normative reasoning in that they crystallize emergent social standards in a publicly articulated text that offers some—often greatly varied—degree of clarity and precision in the context of the particular procedural legitimacy law enjoys. Treaties are not the only form that law may take, and nor should the creation of binding legal instruments be regarded as the necessary end point of all norm-building efforts. Yet due to their emergence through collective negotiations and their more detailed content, treaties represent an especially productive way by which new norms may be instantiated in the international system.

Hence a central contention of this book is that the process of legalization[1] matters to the development of international social standards and the subsequent efficacy of institutions, as rationalist theories have long contended (Abbott and Snidal 2000; Abbott et al. 2000; Koremenos 2013b). Yet the approach favoured here also diverges from 'hard law' accounts in important ways, particularly by emphasizing the social structure of international law. Legal institutions are not isolated entities, but are embedded within a broader international system

[1] Following Abbott and Snidal (2013, 34), I understand 'legalization' here as 'the dynamic process through which law changes and develops, whereas law consists of the rules and institutions that result from the cumulation of legalization at any point in time'.

composed of overlapping legal and non-legal principles, norms, and rules that structure international practice by constituting actors and regulating (prescribing and proscribing) their actions. It is this nested quality that is the ultimate source of law's legitimate authority, and explains how particular institutions may generate new social expectations without recourse to forms of great power agency. Coming to grips with the relationship between international law and wider normative architecture of the international system is therefore of great importance; I address this issue at some length below.

I then draw out the implications of these theoretical moves for two constituencies of states. The obligatory status of law is predicated on notions of appropriate action rather than exertions of raw material power and for this reason, treaty parties may develop communities of legal obligation in the absence of leading powers. This account also suggests more diffuse sources of agency in promoting legal norms, to include 'middle power' states, civil society actors, and treaty bureaucracies. At the same time, treaties may alter the policy choices even among those states that resist the binding legal commitments, mainly because they inculcate a type of legalized norms that are connected to a web of pre-existing—and more fundamental—standards that have received wider endorsement, including among treaty hold-outs. While materially powerful states possess greater latitude to selectively interpret and challenge new legal developments, they are still implicated in the broader complex of values from which a treaty derives. This fact can simultaneously impose social pressures towards accommodation with new institutions while limiting the scope for effective contestation, even as actors continue to maintain their formal opposition. This latter possibility is unanticipated by accounts that emphasize the consensual basis of law.

Conceiving of multilateral treaties as key vectors for the development of globally relevant norms challenges sceptical assumptions regarding the prospective influence of non-great power institutions by refocusing attention away from law solely as a constraint. Processes of socialization that operated during institutional creation—so well addressed by constructivist scholars already—continue to exert influence during the ensuing implementation phase (Betts and Orchard 2014; Risse, Ropp, and Sikkink 2013). In this respect, the creation of a treaty is not the end point of norm development process, but rather marks the transition to a new phase in which questions of adherence and contestation take on a new, legalized form.

THREE PROBLEMS FOR NON-GREAT POWER LAW

For IR studies of international law, a central concern is whether legal institutions can be said to operate at least partially independently of the political and economic forces that are more typically thought to shape state action. This is especially important in the context of the present study since effective non-great power treaties would have to generate changes in international outcomes without the support of leading states. Rationalist theories of IR—broadly encompassing realist and institutionalist approaches—are particularly sceptical of the prospects for such influence because they regard the exclusion of predominant actors as contrary to the exigencies of the anarchical international system in which material capabilities should shape the contours of cooperation.[2] Rationalist accounts adopt an instrumental, positivist conception of law as a set of articulated rules made effectual by the application of sanction, either via centralized enforcement or more diffuse forms of mutual monitoring (Abbott et al. 2000, 402–3; O'Connell 2008). Ruggie (1998) has termed these 'utilitarian' theories, in that they regard international law as a set of agreed constraints that respond to pre-existing interests and do not themselves alter the content of state identities or their resulting policy preferences (Goldsmith and Posner 2005; Guzman 2008). States are self-interested, utility-maximizing actors that resort to cooperation only when it is valuable either in providing an additional means of exerting control in the international system (Glennon 2001; Mearsheimer 1994; Steinberg 2013), or in facilitating mutual gain through the coordination of expectations and the distribution of cooperative goods (Abbott and Snidal 1998; Koremenos 2013a; Koremenos, Lipson, and Snidal 2001). Many rationalist scholars do recognize that institutions gradually influence state preferences by 'changing the context within which states make decisions based on self-interests' (Keohane 1984, 13). But in the near term, the identities and interests that motivate institution building and compliance are assumed to be largely static.

A theory of treaty impact under conditions of great power ambivalence must therefore confront three more particular challenges stemming from this account. First, following the dominant view in international legal scholarship, rationalist theories adopt a voluntaristic account of legal obligation in which commitments may only accrue via consent (Abbott et al. 2000; Goldsmith and Posner 2005). The acceptance of legal rights and duties occurs via formal processes of ratification and accession while adherence to rules is taken as the benchmark for identifying the status of legal obligation (Glennon 2005, 940). In the positivist-voluntarist conception, therefore, treaties cannot bind non-parties and should have little if any influence over the behaviour of defiant states, especially powerful states that possess the material and diplomatic resources to resist outside pressures.

Second, institutions are understood as subordinate to the already established goals of the states that create them. Habitual observance—high rates of compliance—is then an unsurprising by-product of the fact that law simply codifies these mutually held interests. Von Stein (2005) has argued that since

[2] For further discussion, see Chapter 1, pages 10–13.

states self-select into joining treaties, this screening effect dramatically reduces the independent impact on subsequent behaviour that can be attributed to the institutions themselves. Legal institutions are therefore expected to offer only a weak constraint on the practice of even those states that voluntarily adhere to their dictates, since 'most treaties require states to make only modest departures from what they would have done in the absence of an agreement' (Downs, Rocke, and Barsoom 1996, 380). Yet even voluntary submission to the law may be a tenuous basis upon which to build a rule-governed order if it does not encompass the most important actors. Indeed, for realists genuine legal obligation can only derive from hierarchical enforcement as in a domestic society—a condition that is notably absent in the international system. Thus for Morgenthau (1940, 276), 'an alleged rule, the violation of which is not followed by such a sanction, is a mere idea, a wish, a suggestion, but not a valid rule.' Institutionalist theories are more optimistic in this regard, since they increasingly emphasize the potential for decentralized monitoring and enforcement among members via mechanisms like reputation and reciprocity (Guzman 2008; Morrow 2007). But these theories still regard compliance as emanating from the ability of an institution to ensure a more or less consistent stream of goods—order or material gains—rather than an 'internal' sense of obligation to the law itself.

Both realist and institutionalist accounts thus assume that agreements must be supervised so as to deter cheating and maintain the smooth operation of transactions and, as Chapter 1 made clear, great powers are thought to be the most potent agents for discharging such responsibilities. Hence a third problem with non-great power institutions is that they fail to encompass dominant political actors that can generate the conditions necessary for cooperation at the international level. When taken together, these expectations would seem to severely restrict the scope of legal authority available to the kind of institutions under study here. Indeed, treaties concluded without great power support should be particularly ineffectual since they will only entrench the existing goals of a limited subset of less important states, and leave out the vital constituency of states that are most able to ensure subsequent compliance and broader social change.

THE SOCIAL STRUCTURE OF INTERNATIONAL LAW AND ITS CONSEQUENCES

Constructivism and International Law: Language, Legitimacy, and Obligation

While undoubtedly capturing important trends, the positivist view also elides significant sources of meaning and change in the international system.

Empirically, the expectation of great power leadership marginalizes instances of law-making among other actors, and thus leaves scholars unable to persuasively account for real-world instances of governance such as the subjects of the present study. Theoretically, rationalist/instrumental accounts of law ignore more fundamentally transformative effects of norms and laws in shaping state identities and subsequent policy preferences. Previous scholarship has demonstrated that even ultimately supportive states underwent transformations—spurred by social processes of persuasion and emulation—through which their prior interests shifted in favour of an independent international court and a comprehensive ban on antipersonnel (AP) mines (Deitelhoff 2009b; Price 1998). A central contention of this book is that similar processes may also bear on states that formally reject new legal rules.

In recent decades, constructivist IR scholars have developed a potent alternative to the rationalist account of international legal emergence and impact. Constructivism takes as its starting point the belief that the foundational structures of the international system are social rather than material since they are created and sustained through the interaction of human collectives—they are 'social facts' in that they require intersubjective agreement to exist and influence outcomes (Ruggie 1998, 856; Wendt 1999). International law is a prominent location for intersubjective processes of creating meaning and developing collective social standards. Most fundamentally, law can be thought of as a generative language—indeed, *the* language—for articulating forms of appropriate and inappropriate action in the international system:

> International law is a vocabulary in that it defines the words that can or cannot be used in diplomatic discourse, the terminology that is or is not acceptable... Similarly, international law provides a grammar for international relations by setting the rules by which words fit together—essentially, how ideas can be expressed... It tells us which constructions are permissible. (Borgen 2009, 2)

International law is, in other words, a social construct that human societies employ to generate order, yet with particular features that distinguish it from other, non-legal, forms of interaction.

For constructivists, law is not delimited by the formal criteria of rationalist 'hard law' approaches, but rather encompasses a distinctive mode of practice based in precedent:

> Actors assume the existence of a set of socially sanctioned rules, but international law 'lives' in the way in which they reason argumentatively about the form of these rules, what they prescribe or proscribe, what their jurisdictional reach is, what new rules should be enacted, how these relate to established rules, and about whether a certain action or inaction is covered by a given rule. (Reus-Smit 2004d, 41)

International law's essence is rooted in this principled justificatory discourse that channels present debates over the meaning and scope of law through reference to previously articulated rules and procedures (Finnemore and Toope 2001; Johnstone 2011; Ratner 2013). International law is never static, therefore, but is constantly evolving through the purposive and at times inadvertent actions of actors mediated by past experience and existing institutions (Sandholtz and Stiles 2008). These processes inform the re-creation of successive practices that structure subsequent interactions and behaviour. This dynamic feature is intrinsic to the nature of international law, but is missed in rationalist accounts that regard legal institutions as strictly regulative devices that respond to pre-existing cooperation challenges. Rather, international law is properly conceived as both a device for regulating behaviour—by articulating permissive and prohibitionary rules that stipulate what can and cannot be done in particular domains—and 'defin[ing] the set of practices that make up a particular class of consciously organized social activity—that is to say, they specify what counts as that activity' (Ruggie 1998, 871; Finnemore and Toope 2001, 745).

A key insight from recent constructivist theorizing, therefore, is that international law is deeply embedded within the wider international social system. The international legal order is stratified, as specific institutions emerge out of a set of prior ordering principles that define legitimate actors (who gets to participate in the system) and structure subsequent efforts to develop frameworks for appropriate conduct, shaping dominant institutional forms and conceptions of rightful action. In Reus-Smit's account, for example, each iteration of international society is rooted in a set of constitutional structures—concerning the moral purpose of the state, sovereign status of constituent actors, and a concept of procedural justice (how to develop rules of international conduct)—that have varied across time to generate distinctive fundamental institutions that constitute the 'elementary rules of practice that states formulate to solve the coordination and collaboration problems associated with coexistence under anarchy' (Reus-Smit 1997, 557). In the modern international system, these encompass a conception of territorially based sovereign statehood, contractual international law, the sanctity of commitments (*pacta sunt servanda*) and multilateral diplomacy (Reus-Smit 1997; Ruggie 1993). These are 'generic' structural features of the international system in the sense that 'they provide the basic framework for cooperative interaction between states, and institutional practices transcend shifts in the balance of power and the configuration of interests, even if these practices' density and efficacy vary' (Reus-Smit 1999, 4; Ruggie 1993, 11).[3] Here there is a similarity with H. L. A. Hart's influential conception of 'secondary rules' that

[3] They are further mirrored in the development of customary legal norms relating to (for example) the legal personality and consequent responsibilities of states and other actors, the notional inviolability of borders, human rights, and the use of force (Byers 1999; Finnemore and Toope 2001, 746).

contextualize and make possible the development, articulation, promotion, contestation, and modification of so-called 'primary rules' that impose direct obligations on actors (Hart 1994, 94).[4] Taken together, fundamental institutions operate both as a precondition for membership in the system (since adhering to them is necessary for recognition) and the foundational rules of the game through which actors pursue their policy goals.

The enactment of international law thus shapes the very composition of the international system by demarcating the constituent units and constituting the identities of these actors by articulating the features of 'responsible' statehood. For example, 'one of the requirements for being a "civilized" state is participation in the regulation of warfare,' an activity that has become progressively more legalized over time (Tannenwald 1999, 437). The exercise of restraint—as with the taboos surrounding assassination, the use of chemical and nuclear weapons, or the employment of mercenaries—has been shown to derive from a desire to conform to new social standards that regard certain behaviours as outside the boundaries of accepted practice for legitimate members of the community of states (Percy 2007b; Price and Tannenwald 1996; Thomas 2000). Actors possess agency in shaping institutions through their interactions, yet social structures have a powerful reciprocal impact in informing their interests and policy objectives and hence enabling and constraining subsequent behaviours (Brunnée and Toope 2010, 14). As will be shown in a moment, such processes gain particular potency and 'take a distinctive form when conducted within the realm of legal reasoning and practice' (Reus-Smit 2004d, 14).

This social density explains why actors regard law as an especially legitimate means of ordering the world and, consequently, how a generalized obligation towards the law develops.[5] States and other actors observe legal rules and norms because they regard the more particular features as emerging from their own intersubjective practices and corresponding to the underlying normative structure of the system as a whole (Brunnée and Toope 2010; Franck 1990; Reus-Smit 2003; Reus-Smit 2011). Hence, acting through international law generates shared understandings and imbues particular rules with collective social sanction that reciprocally leads actors to seek further recourse in legal institutions to govern their behaviour. Put differently, law possesses a distinctive type of procedural legitimacy that is socially constructed through reiteration: 'only through social interaction, and the participation in shared practices, can actors develop an "internal commitment" to observe the law'

[4] This notion of an international system rooted in higher-order or temporally prior principles is not unique to constructivist thought, as both rationalist (Abbott et al. 2000, 403, 409) and English School scholars (Bull 2012) have made similar observations.

[5] Following Hurd (1999, 381), I conceive of legitimacy as entailing 'the normative belief by an actor that a rule or institution ought to be obeyed'.

(Reus-Smit 2011, 342–3). Legal institutions—both specific rules and broader norms—are thus to be obeyed not simply because they are deemed valid or useful in isolation, but because they are inextricably linked to the constitutive features of the international system and thereby with legitimate social order.

It is in this sense that Reus-Smit (Reus-Smit 2003, 613) speaks of constructivism as offering an 'anterior conception of international legal obligation' that precedes and informs the rational pursuit of self-interest via law. While compliance is undoubtedly driven in part by the desire of state actors to advance individualistic goals like improving organizational efficiency, bolstering their reputation or avoiding sanctions, these considerations are given meaning by a pre-existing belief that legal systems are worthy of adherence. This is why compliance is generally the default presumption and the standard against which any deviations must be justified. More specifically, the attention to the social basis of obligation addresses two foundational claims of rationalist scholars. First, law is not binding because it enjoys a reliable means of enforcement; rather, states seek to ensure respect for rules because they a priori regard legal commitments as generically obligatory, which amounts to a reversal of the causal arrow. Second, the possibility of a pre-existing collective conception of obligation offers a deeper logic to status-based instrumental models of compliance (Guzman 2008), since it explains why international law should be intersubjectively valued in the first place, and hence why individual actors should be motivated to conform to norms and rules as a means of fulfilling the expectations of other actors. In both cases this sense of obligation endures irrespective of the existence of immediate sanctions or expectations of reciprocity (Reus-Smit 2003, 597–8).

Law, Power, and Ideology

At the same time, law emerges and is transformed through political processes, as actors create and interpret legal institutions in the pursuit of their own egoistic policy preferences. In this way the international system conditions the means by which institutions are promoted and adjudicated, in particular by privileging powerful states in their (re)creation (Byers and Nolte 2003; Krisch 2005). Critical legal scholars have pointed out that the development of modern international law is intimately bound up in political processes of inclusion and exclusion, most especially through discourses that divided actors between a privileged 'civilized' minority and 'uncivilized' or (more recently) 'outlaw' states (Anghie 2007; Koskenniemi 2002; Simpson 2004). Asymmetries of material and cultural power thus operate in the background even if overt coercion is not always visible.

Though profoundly shaped by these realities, a transition to a legal forum channels moderates these forces through a particular type of social practice that is generally regarded as more legitimate in its form of argumentation and adjudication. Politics and law are inextricably linked, yet actors view the international legal realm (ideally) as a distinctive field in which policies are evaluated through the application of widely accepted principles, rules, and discourses rather than brute material facts. This is the essence of what Judith Shklar termed 'legalism', that is, the view that 'politics is regarded not only as something apart from law, but as inferior to law... Law aims at justice, while politics looks only to expediency. The former is neutral and objective, the latter the uncontrolled child of competing interests and ideologies' (Shklar 1964, 110). Shirley Scott (1994) has therefore pointed to an underlying 'ideology' of international law wherein states behave *as if* outcomes should be determined on the merits of claims rather than a purely political calculus driven by particularistic self-interest and the distribution of power. When states invoke international law in seeking to coordinate their actions, assert their rights, or resolve disputes, therefore, they are simultaneously pursuing their own interests within a distinctive social context and set of constraints, and contributing to the further reification of legal criteria and processes as the highest standard of justification. While law is ultimately manifest in 'the interlocking of authority with power' (Higgins 1994, 4) and is therefore necessarily *of* politics, international law is also discursively presented as being *above* politics and especially particular configurations of political power. In these respects the resort to law is not just 'cheap talk', but profoundly influences the construction and conduct of international relations.

THE PROMISE OF NON-GREAT POWER LAW

The remainder of this chapter applies these insights to the more particular, and less well studied, problem of legal development and policy change without the great powers, via three theoretical moves. I first briefly explore the relationship between legal and non-legal institutions by way of an argument concerning the role that formal multilateral agreements play in generating international norms. The transition to a legal context is important, since it inculcates norms with a distinctive status derived from law's particular mode of reasoning and justification. The second step further elaborates upon the notion of a stratified international system by demonstrating how this social structure opens up greater potential for institutional impact. Individual treaties do not float freely in the international system, but are embedded within a much larger web of principles, norms, and rules, and these connections to prior constitutive structures provide treaties with their social power. The third step applies this nested account to formal treaty members and those states—including predominantly powerful states—that have refused to officially endorse a given legal agreement. It is here that the social power of international law becomes most apparent; I therefore draw out the principal observable implications of this theory that can be assessed in subsequent chapters.

Multilateral Treaties and the Development of International Norms

The insight that law is a particular type of human activity is by no means unique to constructivism, as institutionalist IR theories (among others) have long made this case (Abbott and Snidal 2013; Abbott et al. 2000). Yet my account diverges from the legal positivism of rationalist accounts by explicitly emphasizing the intersubjective foundations of law; these internal procedural features of legal genesis and change, not descriptive formality, are its defining characteristic (Finnemore and Toope 2001). This account thus shares insights with scholarship on customary international law since both emphasize the social dynamics at the heart of legal development and contestation, and the potential this creates for the accrual of international obligations in the absence of explicit endorsement by states (Byers 1999; Price 2004a).

My most fundamental claim is that the transition to a legal form marks a turning point in the ontological status of a norm that invests a social standard with the distinctive affirmation of legal process and, consequently, a greater obligatory status. This is true of many forms that international law may take, though this study focuses on the role of multilateral treaties in consolidating norms. The creation of a legal text translates general standards of appropriate behaviour into a set of more specific rules and associated legal procedures that together constitute a new legalized norm. In this sense, a treaty serves as a 'public declaration' that further articulates prior values and expresses the views of the international community concerning acceptable and unacceptable behaviour and, with it, the social status of actors in the community in light of their standing vis-à-vis the agreement (Hathaway 2002, 2005; Percy 2007a, 387). The fact that a law is written down matters here because it creates a structure of repetition for legal language that is key to solidifying social expectations over time. As Byers (1999, 125) has noted, treaty-making is relevant to the development of international norms 'partly because of the legitimate expectations which are created—to the effect that States will subsequently behave in a manner which is consistent with those treaties' provisions'.[6] The move to a legal form thereby invests a norm with a particular 'rational-legal' authority that is regarded as more legitimate and binding

[6] In the context of his rational choice theory of compliance, Guzman similarly argues that 'treaties represent a more serious commitment and a greater pledge of reputational capital, all else equal, than do other agreements' (Guzman 2008, 212–13).

than non-legalized standards (Finnemore 2000, 703–5). This occurs in two specific ways.

First, multilateral negotiations serve as focal points in the progressive crystallization of emergent norms (Brunnée and Toope 2010, 48; Coleman 2013). Diplomatic processes, especially when conducted in an inclusive fashion open to all states and (potentially) non-state actors, encompass a diverse array of views in the international system, and take on a quasi-legislative status in promoting new social understandings and shaping responses to global challenges. 'When actors create institutions, they are almost always engaged in the simultaneous construction of social identities, definition and validation of individual and collective interests, deliberation on the good and the just, and the strategic pursuit of instrumental objectives' (Reus-Smit 2004d, 30). Multilateral negotiations are therefore a key setting through which constitutive social processes may play out via the deployment of bargaining, argumentation, and persuasion and social influence that shape both the content of norms, and the prospects for their adoption (Risse 2000; Schimmelfennig 2001; Zürn and Checkel 2005). Exposure to diplomatic processes can exert pressures on state actors to endorse new ways of thinking with respect to matters of cause and effect (e.g. the humanitarian impact of AP mines as outweighing concerns for military utility) or rights and responsibilities (e.g. the legitimacy of an independent supranational criminal court capable of superseding domestic legal processes) in the international system. Once concluded, legal institutions can further offer a venue for the diffusion of new norms among members and, potentially, other associated actors (Greenhill 2010; Johnston 2001), meaning that many of the same processes that featured in the negotiation phase should be evident during implementation.

A second way that treaties transform norms is through the addition of greater precision to existing or emergent social standards, thereby aiding in their consolidation (Abbott et al. 2000; Brunnée and Toope 2010). Treaties translate social norms into a set of prescriptive and proscriptive rules that clarify the content of a norm and specify its application to a particular context.[7] Embedding norms in a legal text provides greater certainty in terms of the scope

[7] Jutta Brunnée and Stephen Toope have elaborated on this insight to propose a set of criteria that distinguish law from other forms of order: 'generality, promulgation, non-retroactivity, clarity, non-contradiction, not asking the impossible, constancy, and congruence between rules and official action' (Brunnée and Toope 2010, 6–7). The strict differentiation between social and legal types is often difficult to sustain in practice, not least because any criteria are bound to be criticized either for being overly broad (and thus lacking descriptive power), or excessive narrow in their content or historical scope. Christian Reus-Smit, for example, has criticized Brunnée and Toope for 'naturalizing' the criteria of legality and in so doing failing to account for fundamental changes in legal practices over time (Reus-Smit 2011, 344–6). This study consequently does not seek to enumerate a definitive set of conditions that uniquely characterize law, but is rather concerned with the more general matter of how international law both reflects and transforms social norms.

and limits of obligation, and provides an institutional context for subsequent discursive efforts aimed at applying, contesting, or further refining the law. This, in turn, can have salutary effects on compliance, since the relative precision of a legal text narrows—though by no means eliminates—the scope for disputes regarding permissible behaviour in a given situation (Hafner-Burton, Victor, and Lupu 2012, 54; Simmons 2010, 277).

Two caveats to this general contention are necessary. First, the transition to a legal form may not, in and of itself, strengthen an underlying social norm. Sarah Percy (Percy 2007a) has argued, for example, that the greater precision provided by the UN Convention Against Mercenaries generated loopholes that states could exploit in avoiding their binding commitments. A strong social norm against mercenaries did not transfer into effective law—because its terms were not easily translated into a suitable legal format—and legalization in turn did not motivate a more expansive acceptance of the prior norm. In some circumstances, therefore, the principled, moral basis of many norms may exert a compelling pull on state action irrespective of, and indeed more forcefully than, their legal status per se (Finnemore 2000, 702). Second and relatedly, legal codification does not necessarily result in an obvious consensus over the meaning of rules. Treaties frequently contain extensive ambiguity, and interpretations cannot be determinatively derived from the legal text or associated rulings or stated precedent. Rather, the law—like politics more generally—necessarily involves contestation in settings of unequal power (Klabbers 2006; Sinclair 2010, 37–60; Wiener 2008). For this reason, the creation of a treaty is not the end point of norm development, but rather marks a new phase of implementation (Betts and Orchard 2014).

While a legal text does not decisively settle debates over the content and scope of norms, the structure of law gives coherence to intersubjective processes of deliberation that in turn enhance the social legitimacy of rules. The shift to a legal mode engages an agreed framework for interactions defined by a principled—ostensibly impartial and technocratic—form of reasoning and justification and more robust expectations concerning the nature of obligation. In this sense, international law functions as a language that expresses common understandings and informs the pursuit of policy goals. Appreciation for this productive role adds greater nuance to institutionalist accounts of negotiations as instrumental responses to acknowledged collective action problems *and* constructivist concerns for the conditions of norm development. In his assessment of the negotiations of the Rome Statute, for example, David Wippman has argued that important aspects of the new court could not be resolved by merely invoking existing legal standards in isolation, and political interests were necessarily part of the calculus; but by the same token, established instituions *did* inform a great deal of the ICC's content:

> Because international law has its own 'language of justification', much of the negotiations in Rome took the form of legal arguments. These arguments were

> deployed in support of the interests of the particular actors making the arguments, but the process of invoking and pursuing legal argumentation in turn helped shape the range of possibilities viewed as permissible and the content of the final agreement in particular and distinctive ways. Moreover, these legal arguments were also shaped by competing general conceptions of what legal institutions and rules should look like and what role international law and institutions should play in international affairs. (Wippman 2004, 153–4)

All diplomacy is informed by a combination of these normative and instrumental considerations. The legalization of norms matters to these processes, principally, by offering cognitive and discursive resources for articulating and adjudicating debates over appropriate action. These features, in turn, provide an architecture around which new or existing standards may be promoted, challenged, and replaced. Law is never fully stable, therefore, but neither is it wholly capricious, as 'legal norms are built, maintained, and sometimes destroyed through a continuing practice of legality' (Brunnée and Toope 2010, 15). For these reasons, a number of scholars have argued that codification and associated processes of institutionalization results in enhanced authority, thereby giving legal norms greater power to constitute actor identities and interests, and influence consequent behaviours (Brunnée and Toope 2010; Percy 2007b, 26; Reus-Smit 2004a, 3).

Nested Legal Structures and the Social Power of Treaties

Rather than seeing international law as fully set apart from other institutional forms, the particular influence of treaties is due to the way in which they are embedded within the wider international social system. As we have seen, constructivist scholars contend that international law is made, revised, and given collective sanction through iterative intersubjective engagements structured by the distinctive procedures of law and associated diplomatic practice. Specific institutions are linked to these processes in two ways. On the one hand, treaties emerge from the same fundamental institutions of sovereign statehood, contractual law, and multilateral diplomacy and thus share a common legal heritage that represents the accepted means for generating binding obligations. The hierarchical linkage to these foundational ground rules of the system provides resources of inherited legitimacy that sustain and give obligatory force to new legal developments. Treaties are also horizontally connected to established rules and organizational forms in other issue areas in ways that are frequently reflected in their founding texts. This web of deliberate associations—what I term the nested social structure of international law—is the key in entrenching discrete legal institutions within the wider international order.

Legal—and more broadly, normative—change thus proceeds via analogy, as new claims are linked to already existing standards at differing levels of generality. Studies have demonstrated the complex ways in which the international abolition of slavery was deeply influenced by changing notions of individual human dignity and equality (Ray 1989), for example, while others have shown how norms of sovereignty and human rights informed the decolonization and anti-apartheid movements more than a century later (Crawford 2002; Klotz 1993). Sandholtz and Stiles (2008) have found similar processes at work in a variety of cases of norm change including prohibitions on piracy and territorial conquest and more contemporary shifts in the treatment of refugees and the promotion of democracy. Institutions evolve in the shadow of prior social structures that define the range of design options that actors regard as possible or desirable. Hence the successful introduction of new norms in one arena can lead to pressures for further institutional development in related areas.

Conceiving of law as part of an interconnected international social system helps explain how non-great power treaties may defy the wishes of powerful actors to promote authoritative legal commitments and norms. The above account has suggested that international law is rendered powerful by the way in which legal institutions—including multilateral treaties that are the subject of this study—both crystallize new norms and simultaneously draw upon prior and more fundamental social standards for justification. The dense interconnections that result provide actors with a wealth of ideational resources by which to promote, validate, or contest a new legal entity, thereby replicating and reinforcing the social legitimacy of legal process. This structural enmeshment, in other words, provides opportunities for normative development and imposes important constraints on the design of new institutions, since the legitimacy of international law depends on its continued accordance with more fundamental 'social background understandings' that underpin the international system (Brunnée and Toope 2010, 76; Reus-Smit 1997). These linkages are not automatic, however, but must be cultivated: 'legal claims are legitimate and persuasive only if they are rooted in reasoned argument that creates analogies to past practice, demonstrate congruence with the overall systemic logic of existing law, and attend to contemporary social aspirations and the larger moral fabric of society' (Finnemore and Toope 2001, 749). Richard Price has therefore suggested that efforts to develop new social standards are more likely to succeed to the extent that entrepreneurs are able to 'graft' the incipient standard onto norms and practices that enjoy widespread acceptance (Price 2003, 584, 596). This, in turn, represents a vital source of authority that can transcend configurations of material power to generate potent new standards of appropriate behaviour in the international system.

The nested social structure does not imply that all legal development will be complementary. Norms make demands on actors, and this opens the possibility for competition among differing standards. The emergence of a new norm (such as a commitment to national self-determination) may conflict with earlier beliefs (such as the right to imperial conquest) leading to a cognitive dissonance that must be resolved if the actor is to make decisive judgements about future action in a given area. The adoption of a new norm can therefore push actors to abandon previous beliefs and behaviours, or more modestly may force them to defend their prior position via alternative, and perhaps less persuasive, means (Percy 2007b, 30). The existence of norm conflict can also work against a legal innovation if actors regard the newer norm or rule as transgressing a more resonant standard. The processes of legal and normative development are therefore necessarily recursive, as changes in one area may generate additional pressures towards further adaptation in other social structures. This can either generate sources of support for a new multilateral initiatives or can serve to undercut legal developments, as the emerging literature on contestation has recognized (Wiener 2004; Wiener 2008). In either potential scenario, the particular normative quality of international law holds implications for the manner in which multilateral treaties may influence international practice, both in respect of those states that have joined a given treaty, and for those resistant parties that remain outside of the formal legal agreement. As subsequent chapters will demonstrate, such processes of normative expansion and resistance are of fundamental importance in understanding the emergence and impact of the AP mine ban and International Criminal Court.

States Parties: Building a Legal Community without Great Powers

An effective treaty must first be able to transform social expectations and generate obedience among its members; yet non-great power treaties must do so without the support provided by materially powerful states. This is possible because, as argued at length already, international law is sustained by a set of collective practices underpinned by a prior generic conception of obligation (Reus-Smit 2003). Parties to a treaty have agreed to a set of specific commitments structured by a powerful belief concerning the legitimacy of law and its observation. Membership matters, therefore, because it informs intersubjective determinations of status that increase incentives towards adherence—and magnify the costs of violations—beyond what can be provided by coercion or material inducements alone.

Yet actors do not enter legal processes with their views fully formed; instead, participation in diplomatic negotiations exposes actors to beliefs concerning the nature of governance challenges and appropriate responses that can in turn generate fundamental changes in identities and interests. When undertaken in a legal environment, these processes are further invested with the spectre of legal practice and obligation.[8] As I show in Chapters 4 and 6, this form of socialization via law has played a critical role in the two core case studies of this book. Diplomacy in both instances was not merely concerned with the establishment of institutional structures, but more fundamentally with the introduction of new social standards that substantially recast the existing status quo understandings. Quite in contrast to the view that the ban on AP landmines and the creation of a permanent international criminal court were 'easy', therefore, the decision to join the treaties was often substantially more complex than the widespread ratifications would suggest. A great many states faced considerable resistance from key domestic constituencies, most frequently the military and civilian bureaucratic structures concerned with how the treaties would constrain their operational conduct and ability to participate in coalitions with non-parties, most notably the United States. In both cases, proponents of more expansive legal commitments were able to harness the social power of law to overcome these forms of opposition (Deitelhoff 2009b; Price 1998).

Adaptation to new legal norms carries over to the subsequent phase of implementing a new treaty, which is the particular focus of this book. Treaty regimes are organized around regular meetings in which state representatives interact on the basis of sovereign equality—while not enjoying similar parity in terms of capabilities or status—and which frequently include the direct participation of civil society actors. These structures foster the density of interaction necessary for communities of practice to interpret and apply the law (Adler and Pouliot 2011; Johnstone 2011). In this way, institutions act as environments facilitating diffuse forms of agency to promote compliance with and internalization of social standards. This may occur via persuasive appeals to the legitimate status of the law, argumentation and contestation over the meaning and scope of rules, the use of social pressure (such as status, sense of belonging, shame, and exclusion), acculturation (motivations to conform or assimilate with a referent standard or group), and finally the deployment of material resources to support or coerce implementation (Checkel 2001; Checkel 2005; Goodman and Jinks 2013; Johnston 2001; Ratner 2013; Risse 2000; Schimmelfennig 2005).

This book does not set out to trace these various processes—or assess their relative merits—upon the socialization of individuals or groups, but rather seeks theoretically informed evidence of behavioural change across the entire international system. It therefore offers a macro-structural account of legal and normative impact rather than a micro-level investigation of specific mechanisms. In general terms, the processes of promoting legal rules and

[8] In rationalist terms, Simmons and Hopkins (2005) have contended that treaties may both 'screen' (respond to existing preferences) and 'constrain' states (by generating incentives toward anticipatory compliance before joining an agreement) at the same time.

assessing and in some cases challenging their scope reinforce the intersubjective social legitimacy of law. This can initially work to constrain state behaviour by associating particular acts with the support for, or deviation from, collective expectations. Indeed, as I show in proceeding chapters, member states frequently frame instances of compliance and non-compliance in the explicit context of specific treaty commitments and in light of parallel norms and rules and a generalized belief that agreements must be kept. Over time, these engagements can generate greater affinity with and internalization of legal norms leading to the reconstruction of actor identities and interests. In this latter sense, the rules and norms of a given treaty may acquire a taken-for-granted status, such that violations are no longer considered, and compliance is thus non-instrumental (Kratochwil 2000, 58).

This account does not, however, assume that treaty members must deeply identify with constituent obligations from the outset. States may initially join a treaty for self-interested reasons such as an attempt to defuse criticism or gain material benefits. Yet in an environment governed by expectations of fidelity to legal commitments, such a position ultimately reifies the law as the proper arbiter of acceptable action, narrowing the scope for justification and interpretation. Continued participation in a treaty regime can expose deviant states to forms of social pressure in which their ostensible acceptance of new norms and rules leads to rhetorical entrapment, in turn pushing them towards greater conformance and, potentially, the internalization of norms over time (Risse, Ropp, and Sikkink 2013; Schimmelfennig 2001). Concerned parties can assess the actions of other actors on the basis of established legal injunctions and in a social setting in which violations are understood to be qualitatively different from other types of antisocial behaviour in non-legalized environments. Heather Smith-Cannoy, for example, has found that governments often sign human rights treaties in order to placate domestic constituencies and secure international economic goods, yet these instrumental incentives nonetheless provide avenues for individuals and groups to apply these new legal commitments in holding their governments to account (Smith-Cannoy 2012). By the same token, however, other scholars have found that ratification of legal instruments often does little to improve—and may be negatively correlated with—human rights performance (Hafner-Burton and Tsutsui 2007; Hathaway 2002; Simmons 2010, 288–92). It is therefore important to distinguish between degrees of compliance and their various motivations: for example, non-conformance that stems from a lack of technical capacity would seem less damaging to the health of a legal institution than instances in which a state actively disputed its application or legitimacy. I elaborate on this issue in the discussion of research methodology in Chapter 3.

This social view of international law offers an alternative basis for the emergence of a legal community from rationalist theories that variously emphasize coercion, material inducements, reciprocity, or concern for reputational gains as the basis for effective law. On the one hand, it suggests that social density can generate powerful collective expectations for rule following in lieu of a continual threat of sanction, thereby mitigating a principal realist critique. On the other hand, exposure to diplomatic processes of norm negotiation and the subsequent participation in a legal community can alter underlying interests—and hence incentive structures—in favour of adherence as the socially appropriate response, illuminating the sources of legitimacy that underpin rational choice accounts of strategic action (Guzman 2008; Morrow 2007). Legal practices contribute to the social construction of actors and in this way may generate pulls towards compliance that are independent of these various instrumental motivations.

Non-Party States: Social Pressure and Informal Adaptation

A legal community can exist amongst a more limited group of states, but the full impact of a multilateral agreement can only be realized by encompassing all states within its sphere. Yet the prevailing emphasis on voluntary consent as the basis for legal obligation would suggest that exerting meaningful influence over non-parties is impossible since they have explicitly chosen not to accept these commitments. The social account of international law presented here offers a way out of this apparent impasse. Most fundamentally, it challenges us to think of specific legal institutions not as isolated entities, but rather as nodes in the much larger network of beliefs and practices that make up the international system. All states are situated within the same international legal order that helps to construct their identities and interests and thereby imposes important constraints on the range of acceptable policy options. It is in this respect of changing broader social expectations regarding legitimate behaviour that a treaty may influence even those states that reject binding obligations stemming from the formal agreement. While materially powerful states possess greater latitude to selectively interpret and challenge new institutional developments, they are still deeply embedded within these structures and are thus implicated in the complex web of practices from which a treaty derives (Krisch 2005, 374).

These pressures operate from two directions simultaneously. On the one hand, treaties are linked to fundamental institutions and the density of these arrangements holds important consequences for the ability of states to resist unwelcome legal developments in a particular issue area. As constituent actors of the system, states cannot exempt themselves from foundational norms of statehood, multilateralism, or diplomatic conventions since to do so would fundamentally transgress a basic component of their identity and obviate their ability to participate in the state system. To the extent that a new treaty is legitimately created via these universal values and processes and shares the basic features of accepted legal form, it is difficult to disregard as entirely irrelevant. On the other hand, legal institutions typically draw inspiration from existing norms and rules in related issue areas through forms of horizontal linkage. In this way, the prior acceptance of *other* relevant institutions—such as the laws of war or principles of criminal jurisprudence—can generate further pressures towards recognition of a new treaty even by those states that do not accept the *legal* authority of a given treaty.

For these reasons, non-parties—including great powers—frequently participate in formal treaty settings as observers and seek to influence the subsequent implementation of new legal institutions. A common strategy is thus for resistant states to acknowledge broad principles animating a treaty while resisting formal binding restraints. In Chapter 5 I argue that the widespread endorsement of a norm of 'humanitarian effect' has led prominent non-parties to a partial accommodation with the Mine Ban Treaty. Similarly, while the United States and others openly reject various institutional features of the ICC, they generally do not contest the underlying—and pre-existing—legal principle that individuals should be subject to criminal prosecution for grave violations of international humanitarian and human rights law, nor indeed the vast majority of the constituent crimes and legal procedures covered by the Court (Chapter 7). In this way, non-parties attempt to selectively invoke the language of new legal norms and rules to pursue their own, often contrary, policy goals. Yet it is difficult for states to fully anticipate or control the outcomes of such engagements, and through their participation non-parties may be subject to the same types of socialization processes as States Parties discussed earlier. Risse, Ropp and Sikkink (1999; 2013) have demonstrated that hypocrisy—expressing support for a norm while continuing with contrary behaviours—can provide openings for interventions from third parties in which non-compliant actors are challenged to close the gap between their stated ambitions and particular acts. Even apparently cynical attempts to 'use' the law can therefore have lasting consequences for the development of norms, by further reinforcing the social legitimacy of the particular institution as the arbiter of acceptable behaviour.

Contestation thus often contains the seeds of greater accommodation in ways that might initially be unforeseen by non-parties. This can occur informally, as exposure to a legal institution initially changes cost–benefit calculations with respect to compliance. Resistant states may then partially observe treaty rules, ending some prohibited behaviour or engaging in new proactive efforts. In such cases, treaty norms can have the effect of foreclosing previously unexceptional acts while simultaneously increasing their perceived importance, rendering any policy reversal a more substantial political issue than it would have been in the absence of a legal institution. The US decision to abandon research and development of all new types of AP mines—including so-called 'smart' mines that it maintains should not be subject to a global prohibition—along with formal moratoria on production and transfer by a number of prominent non-parties are important examples of this phenomenon (Chapter 5). These behavioural adaptations may be mirrored in changes in state discourse that reflect a rejection of certain rhetorical strategies due to a sensitivity to the social expectations fostered by a treaty. From this perspective, the decision by China, Russia, and the United States not to oppose the United Nations Security Council referrals with respect to Darfur and Libya represents a substantial development in the expansion of ICC legitimacy, as examined in Chapter 7.

While great powers play a dominant role in the creation and maintenance of international law, therefore, they are not immune from developments that emerge outside of their own agency. This important point would be lost were we to focus on voluntary consent to the exclusion of other, more informal means through which legal institutions may generate a sense of fidelity or, more simply, a social expectation towards observance (Price 2004a, 122–3). Hence forms of resistance and accommodation are important to the extent that they reflect various manifestations of principled and instrumental reasoning, providing important sources of empirical evidence concerning the impact of law on the subtle and gradual evolution of state practice. This accords with established scholarship on customary international law, which makes clear that the development and refinement of international norms is not limited to the purposive actions of consenting states, and can occur through acquiescence or the unintentional recognition of a given norm or rule (Byers 1999). These processes may lead, over time, to further engagement by non-parties with the treaty, perhaps leading to full membership and a change in interests to correspond with treaty obligations. On the other hand, non-parties, and especially powerful ones, may succeed in challenging new norms in ways that undermine respect for the law rather than bolster it. A key issue for the subsequent analysis is thus determining the extent of non-party contestation, whether completely rejecting the applicability of law to the domain in question, or more specifically challenging the application of a legal rule under discrete circumstances.

CONCLUSION

Treating multilateral agreements as normative structures provides an account of how States Parties may build a community of legal obligation in the absence of great powers, and equally, suggests informal processes through which non-parties may come to be implicated by legal innovations they officially reject. The key point is that social standards are constructed by the actions and reactions of all actors within the international system. To the extent that compliance with and, more deeply, fidelity to international law may emerge from these social processes, they offer an alternative means of generating international change that does not primarily rely on the continual enforcement of rules. The creation of legal structures that promote alternative conceptions of appropriate behaviour is thus a potent way that less traditionally powerful actors—small and middle power states and members of transnational civil society including lawyers, peace activists, national and international bureaucrats, and judges—can influence global politics. These theorized processes leave observable residues in the behaviours and discourse of actors that can be traced in the empirical record, a subject taken up in Chapter 3.

3

Assessing Treaty Impact

CONCEPTUALIZING INSTITUTIONAL EFFECTIVENESS

A central claim of this study is that legal institutions are not just instruments for coordinating among existing preferences, but more fundamentally are a means by which actors can introduce new ideas about appropriate behaviour into international affairs. My primary concern is therefore in determining whether, and to what extent, the Mine Ban Treaty (MBT) and International Criminal Court (ICC) have achieved this more expansive aim to transform international politics in light of their particular origins and associated challenges. This is important not only in gaining an appreciation for whether the particular diplomatic initiatives were worth the risks, but equally in providing a baseline against which other existing or potential governance efforts can be evaluated.

This book does not test competing theories of legal influence, but rather employs case studies to generate detailed empirical observations concerning the implementation of two archetypal non-great power treaties. The assessment of institutions is most broadly concerned with their effects: we are seeking to understand how, if at all, multilateral treaties alter outcomes in the international system, and how much of these observable changes can be attributed to the institutions themselves rather than other exogenous forces such as the distribution of material power. As Keohane (1993, 31) points out, however, this is no simple task, as 'we do not have a hypothetical institution-free baseline from which to measure the impact of actual institutions on state capabilities.' There are a variety of approaches for addressing this challenge, and a veritable cottage industry—particularly in the field of environmental governance—has emerged that addresses the effectiveness problematique (Helm and Sprinz 2000; Hovi, Sprinz, and Underdal 2003; Miles, Andresen, Carlin, Skjaerseth, and Underdal 2002). Most generally, however, effectiveness relates to the capacity of an institution to shift the status quo ante in an intended direction (Alter 2014, 6, n. 2). This is typically assessed in relation to the degree to which institutions generate changes in behaviour that either

(a) achieve the goals or purpose of the rule; or (b) lead to improvement in the original problem to which the rule is addressed.[1] The present study adopts the first of these framings as the primary point of reference, as I explain below.

As argued at length in Chapter 2, multilateral treaties—as a sub-set of international law—are fundamentally normative institutions in that they aim to instantiate widely respected norms that re-shape identities and interests in the international system. This understanding implies that the most foundational measure of effectiveness is the extent to which a treaty generates systematic changes in social expectations across the range of relevant actors in the international system. More specifically, for non-great power treaties to prove broadly effective, they must first be able to claim obedience among their formal members without the coercive and legitimating assistance provided by materially powerful states. At the same time, a treaty is only fully successful when the policies and actions of all relevant actors—including non-parties to the agreement—reflect adherence to its norms and rules. Yet as noted already, this goal, and especially the latter part, is antithetical to the way scholars have typically thought of the genesis and expansion of legal authority.

The next section discusses some challenges involved in the study of norms, and lays out a set of interactive metrics for evaluating institutional influence in world politics. This approach takes the text of the treaty as its starting point in that it represents the legal expression of the wider norm. The second half of the chapter then identifies the principal features of my two core treaty cases as the basis for the subsequent empirical evaluation. In this regard I am most concerned with the *political* consequences of these legal developments—in shifting how states conceptualize appropriate conduct and the impact this has on patterns of behaviour—rather than in comprehensively assessing the treaties in terms of the mitigation of global humanitarian problems. My assessment of the MBT therefore focuses first and foremost on the core prohibitions with respect to the weapon itself and not on the consequent impact on the rate of civilian or military casualties or in international and domestic amelioration of the many needs of mine victims and their families (Bailey and Channareth 2008; Eaton 2008). Equally, my study of the ICC is principally preoccupied with evaluating national responses to this new global legal institution, rather than its internal administrative and procedural development measured in terms of the number of centralized ICC cases or more diffuse considerations for the Court's potential role as a deterrent in reducing grave violations of human rights. These other important institutional outcomes have been well addressed by other authors, while in my view the wider

[1] While the two metrics are potentially related, they must also be kept conceptually distinct. For example, a treaty could set unambitious targets or entrench weak commitments, in which case even full compliance would not satisfactorily address the underlying governance challenge that ostensibly motivated the agreement in the first place.

transformations in international affairs occasioned (or not) by these treaties has received inadequate attention.

TREATIES, NORMS, AND OUTCOMES

How do we know when a treaty has achieved widespread influence in the international system? Constructivist IR theory offers a rich toolkit for conceptualizing the impact of norms and developing methods for their assessment (Kurki 2006; Lupovici 2009; Pouliot 2007; Price 2006; Wendt 1998). I also draw on insights from the study of customary international law, which attends to the processes by which actor behaviour and discourse may come to reflect a 'generalized consensus' concerning the content of the obligatory status of law in the absence of specific codification or explicit state consent (Byers 1999; D'Amato 1971; Roberts 2001) While I limit my attention to formal multilateral treaties, the study of legal custom is relevant for how it highlights the normative underpinnings of international law—with legal developments potentially influencing the policies even of resistant actors—and the ways that both purposive and unintended actions can further shape the development of law.

How Norms Matter: Logics of Action and the Problem of Causality

Despite extensive attention, scholars of international relations and law do not agree on a single method for identifying a strong norm when they see one (Price 2006, 252–3). The challenges of assessment stem most fundamentally from the nature of norms as intersubjective phenomena: norms are sustained through social interactions and therefore do not exist independent of the agency of actors but are rather inherently bound up in 'the mutually constitutive and recursive nature of the relationship among norms, interests, and power' (Thomas 2001, 20). Norms—including those formalized through law—are not static properties operating in a binary 'on/off' fashion, but dynamic social constructions subject to continual re-interpretation. Consequently, norms can exert varying degrees and types of influence on actors, and can strengthen or weaken, or be replaced altogether, through subsequent iterations. For these reasons, norms are not well suited to assessment by exclusively positivist methods, insofar as they fail to correspond to the basic notion of causality that the presence or absence of a variable can be said to produce a given outcome (Kurki 2006, 194; Price 2006, 257). Moreover, if actors and structures are co-constituted as constructivists insist, then clearly identifying causal agency and direction is fundamentally impossible, because the impact of norms on subsequent actions is subsumed within prior changes in the composition of actor identities and interests. To the extent that norms inform the content of strategic decision-making, therefore, the distinction between ideational and instrumental action is largely collapsed (Fearon and Wendt 2002).

These features not only make it difficult to isolate particular causal processes, but more fundamentally raise important questions concerning the appropriateness of treating norms as *causes* of actions in the first place. This study, by contrast, regards legal norms as *logics* or *reasons* that inform action by providing guidance or justifications concerning the proper response in a given social setting:

> Norms may 'guide' behavior, they may 'inspire' behavior, they may 'rationalize' or 'justify' behavior, they may express 'mutual expectations' about behavior, or they may be ignored. But they do not effect cause in the sense that a bullet through the heart causes death or an uncontrolled surge in the money supply causes price inflation. (Kratochwil and Ruggie 1986, 767)

Because of their intersubjective nature and the consequent reliance on interpretation, norms can both constrain and enable actions and thus have meaningful impact on outcomes even though they cannot be said to be fully temporally prior to, or independent of, the actors being influenced. This insight highlights the need for a broader conception of causality that is not restricted to mechanistic metaphors, but is rather rooted in the 'conceptual explanation of the variety of forces that bring about regularities of observables' (Kurki 2006, 210).[2]

Adjudicating the often contentious debates between positivists and post-positivists is beyond the scope of this study. I adopt a middle ground position between treating norms and legal institutions as exclusively stable structures that states respond to, or as completely fluid properties of agency. This conceptual framing is appropriate to my primary interest in the implementation of non-great power treaties rather than a 'critical' focus that would attempt to recover the meaning of norms within their diverse social settings (Wiener and Puetter 2009; Wiener 2008). For my purposes, legal norms—as articulated in a treaty as binding rules—can be studied *as if* they are more or less coherent social standards that inform the decision-making of actors at a moment in time. In order to exert any influence on current or future behaviour, legal institutions must possess some measure of stability (Byers 1999, 49). I therefore take the legal text as the formal expression of the broader social standard, and the baseline against which to measure norm adoption and resistance (Raustiala and Slaughter 2002, 538). At the same time, it is

[2] For discussions of the relationship between causal and constitutive theory, see Elder-Vass (2010); Kurki (2006); Wendt (1998).

important to recognize that actor conduct—whether supportive or confrontational, overt or covert, intentional or inadvertent—does have consequences for the status and efficacy of institutions. Indeed, the conception of law as a fundamentally social construct demands an appreciation for the ways that actors in turn shape the meaning of legal rules and norms through their interpretations, actions, and discursive justifications. As Ward Thomas points out, any assessment must therefore account for the inherently intersubjective nature of normative development: 'because they are collective understandings and not abstract principles… norms derive their strength from the degree of consensus they enjoy and the level of commitment they engender' (Thomas 2001, 30).

In the most general sense, a legal institution can be said to affect international politics to the extent that it 'induces states to engage in practices they would not otherwise perform' (Price 2004a, 114). This influence is posited as a counterfactual in that observed behaviours (both adherence and contestation) are assumed to differ in important ways from those which would have occurred absent the given treaty and its attendant norms (Martin 2013, 605). But precisely because they are social constructions and not raw material facts, norms may shape the range of acceptable options open to actors in complex and often subtle ways. First, norms may be conditionally held, and thus internalized only in the shallow sense that they make some actions more or less desirable and provide some constraint on actor calculations. In such instances norms can act as 'ethical speed bumps' (Thomas 2001, 39) in that they spur actors to consider their actions in light of a new standard regardless of whether the actor ultimately follows the norm or not. More substantially, norms may become 'highly valued but not unconditionally taken for granted' in that they may be violated under extreme circumstances, though the threshold for noncompliance is raised substantially (Thomas 2001, 38). Finally, a deeply internalized norm may become so fundamental to an actor's identity that it is accepted in a subconscious sense, foreclosing certain behavioural options before they can be considered. Under these conditions, violations are essentially unthinkable and contrary practices never enter the policymaking process—the effect of the norm is thus non-instrumental in its impact. Problematizing the sources of actor change in this way can help to account for what might otherwise be regarded as anomalous policy shifts if we were to assume that the relevant actors possess fixed identities and interests (Finnemore 1996, 7–13).

This perspective requires more nuanced measures that are able to account for inherent contingency in the development and impact of legal norms. While no decisive standard exists, scholars of IR and customary international law do agree that any assessment must take into account the interaction of two types of contextual evidence. On the one hand, actor behaviour must generally accord with the norm or rule(s) in question—though this can vary in important ways as discussed below. On the other hand, actors must express a belief that the relevant standards are legally applicable (in the case of States Parties) and more broadly constitute a compelling standard of appropriateness—what is termed *opinio juris* in the more specific context of customary international law.[3] Without this latter feature, any observed compliance could be epiphenomenal. Behavioural and discursive data are most valuable, therefore, when they are employed in concert rather than separately (Kirgis 1987) (Figure 3.3).

Behavioural Adaptation and Compliance

Evidence of legal influence is on the one hand derived by comparing observable patterns of behaviour against core treaty obligations expressed as legal injunctions and (for non-parties) broader norms (Simmons 1998; Simmons 2010). By compliance I simply mean 'a state of conformity...between an actor's behaviour and a specified rule' (Raustiala and Slaughter 2002, 539). Rule-following is crucial for both practical and symbolic reasons: the efficacy of international law relies on the willingness and capacity of states and other actors to observe their commitments, while widespread adherence reinforces the perceived legitimacy of legal constraints among an intersubjective community. The health of legal instruments—and norms more generally—is therefore assessed largely in relation to 'the relative degree of supporting as compared to opposing practice' (Byers 1999, 162), though there is no single formula for determining how much rule-following among what percentage of states is necessary (Price 2006, 260). While possessing formal sovereign equality, states are nonetheless highly *unequal* in terms of their material power and social status within the international system, both of which influence their capacity to contribute to the development of international law (Byers 1999, 36–7). The rejection of a norm by an especially important state —measured by military and economic power or diplomatic prestige—or otherwise 'specially affected' states—those that are particularly implicated by the emergence of new rules—would thus be more consequential than similar behaviour on the part of a small, peripheral state.

Ratification of a legal instrument is an important indicator of a widening acceptance of a new social standard embodied in a treaty, as it signals the formal political recognition of legal obligations. However, ratification on its own is neither a necessary or sufficient condition for behavioural adaptation and norm internalization. The adoption of treaties may not result in greater

[3] As Byers points out, *opinio juris* is fundamentally based in an interpretative judgement concerning 'those shared understandings which enable States to distinguish between legally relevant and legally irrelevant State practice' (Byers 1999, 148–9; Price 2006, 261–3).

alignment with relevant norms, either because states lack the capacity to implement mandated reforms (despite a sincere desire to comply) or because they aim to use membership as a means to shield their contrary behaviours behind a veil of official adherence (Chayes and Chayes 1993; Hafner-Burton and Tsutsui 2007). Inversely, the failure to formally join a multilateral agreement does not necessarily represent a fundamental rejection of its objectives, since a variety of procedural and bureaucratic challenges may impede ratification. This leaves open the internalization of norms that would then be manifest in other forms of engagement and adaptation. Finally, in some circumstances even states with substantive objections to a new legal instrument may begin to align themselves with legal rules and norms, thus demonstrating the impact of new social expectations despite official resistance. Focusing strictly on formal adherence would miss these important forms of treaty influence; this study, by contrast, dedicates considerable attention to such possibilities.

Beyond questions of formal membership, other forms of conduct also directly bear on the status of an institution. Most critically, frequent violations would indicate a weak and ineffective institution which, if they persist for long enough, would result in its decline and eventual abandonment (Glennon 2005). For example, if the empirical record demonstrated that antipersonnel (AP) mines were being used as (or more) frequently as before the advent of the MBT, we would rightly conclude that the treaty itself has had no discernible positive impact on actor conduct. The same could be said about the ICC if we observed little or no change in domestic capacity or willingness to investigate and prosecute grave international crimes, or support the Court in its own operations. Widespread non-compliance among treaty members would be especially damaging to the health of an institution, since these actors have made explicit commitments to observe the rules. Evidence of extensive violations by non-parties is also relevant to the evaluation of a legal norm, since it would strongly suggest that the treaty has not succeeded in transforming the wider social environment beyond the confines of formal institutional membership, an explicit goal of the proponents of non-great power treaties.

Yet political change is a gradual process and and rules are rarely if ever observed with perfect regularity. A key insight from the constructivist literature is that norms are 'counterfactually valid', in that they may continue to assert authority in the face of some contrary behaviours (Kratochwil and Ruggie 1986). In determining this threshold, the nature and degree of challenges are

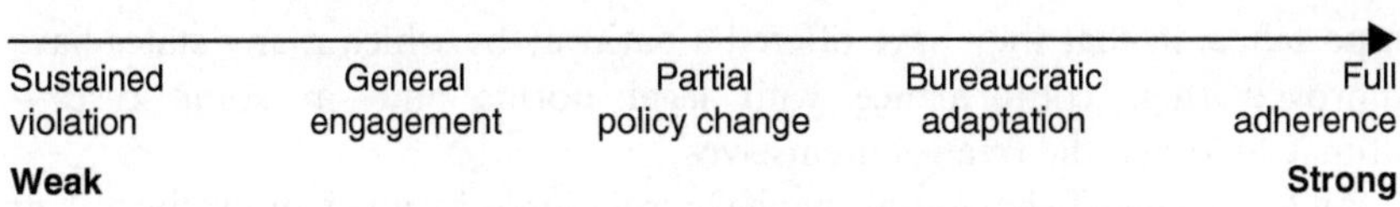

Figure 3.1. Spectrum of behavioural indicators and norm strength

important, since they inform an assessment of whether 'there is general acceptance of the central validity claims of the norms' (Price 2004a, 114). Are violations becoming less frequent over time, either by particular offenders or on aggregate? Just as importantly, are the conditions for continued violations of the norm—discussed more fully below—becoming more proscribed? This can provide initial indications that social expectations are shifting.

Compliance exists along a continuum, and a holistic account must therefore take into account a wider range of policy changes that can be spurred by the introduction of a new legal instrument and associated norm. Figure 3.1 outlines forms of progressively stronger evidence of state adaptation and institutional impact. First, states may adopt a position of general recognition and engagement, for example by attending treaty meetings; this can include resistant states participating as observers. These gestures may initially appear to be of limited symbolic value; yet a key claim of my theory is that exposure to diplomatic processes can stimulate greater comfort with norms, potentially leading to more substantial adherence over time. This prospect is addressed in detail in Chapters 5 and 7. Moving further towards the 'strong' end of the spectrum, states may undertake incremental policy changes—abandoning certain behaviours that contravene particular aspects of the treaty, or inversely taking actions that conform to these commitments—even while failing to fully observe the agreement. Prominent non-parties like the United States, China, and Russia have shown increasing willingness to cooperate with ICC operations, most notably by authorizing UN Security Council (UNSC) referrals of the Darfur and Libya situations to the ICC Prosecutor and (in the case of the US) providing material support for efforts to arrest suspects (Chapter 7). And, as Chapter 5 details, the United States has not employed AP mines since 1991, despite its leading role in a number of armed conflicts in which the weapons may have proven highly useful. These forms of behavioural change offer partial, though increasingly important, evidence suggesting a gradual recognition of new social expectations.

Finally, both member and non-party states may undertake bureaucratic changes to facilitate greater compliance with core treaty requirements. A number of states have revised their domestic laws to facilitate cooperation with the ICC (Chapter 6) or altered their training and operational planning to reflect a removal of AP mines from military doctrine. Some MBT non-parties have enacted formal moratoria on the production and transfer of AP mines, even while reserving the right to use weapons in some circumstances (Chapter 5). These forms of incremental adaptation can have great cumulative importance, in that they have offered a pathway by which many states have improved their conformance with legal norms and—in some cases—ultimately joined the treaties themselves.

But focusing on behavioural change in isolation is insufficient for the task of assessing the status of legal norms. Emphasizing regulative effects on their own suggests that these are the only ways that legal institutions matter, thus missing other critical aspects of law's normative power. Relatedly, measures of behavioural change imply that the interaction between actors and 'the law' is unidirectional, thereby downplaying the vital roles that capacity, interpretation, and contestation play in the development of legal meaning. States may lack the resources to meet international commitments regardless of their dispositions toward a treaty, while there might also be genuine ambiguity concerning the scope of a norm or rule. Identifying instances of individual or aggregate behavioural change is part of the story, therefore, but such measures still lack an appreciation for the *motivations* that inspired observed (non-) compliance.

State Discourse and the Status of Treaty Norms

Integrating an analysis of state behaviour with attention to the ways in which actors define and defend their actions can provide the context necessary for a richer view of treaty influence. The constructivist IR literature recognizes that discursive justifications shape the development of intersubjectively valid meaning and, similarly, scholars of customary international law have demonstrated that *opinio juris* constitutes a crucial source of customary legal obligation. Hence, the manner in which states and other actors interpret their obligations, articulate their rights and responsibilities, and justify their policy choices all contribute to the formulation of international law and its reciprocal impact on outcomes. More specifically, attention to the use of language can help to further unpack the challenging question of whether institutions are themselves influencing observed behaviours, by suggesting whether compliance stems from a sense of fidelity to a treaty or more general recognition of the social status of given standards rather than solely exogenous factors like coercion or instrumental benefit. 'Because norms by definition embody a quality of "oughtness" and shared moral assessment, norms prompt justifications for action and leave an extensive trail of communication among actors that we can study' (Finnemore and Sikkink 1998, 892). As Chapter 2 made clear, legal discourse[4] involves a particular language of justification that differs in important ways from moral and especially political claims. These distinctions should be apparent in the public record of official diplomatic statements and policy positions of state representatives (Figure 3.2).

The clearest indication of treaty influence comes through a convergence of types of practice, wherein norm-confirming behaviour is mirrored by statements that make specific reference to the treaty as a source of obligation.

[4] By discourse I simply a 'cohesive ensemble of ideas, concepts, and categorizations' expressed in writing or speech (Epstein 2008, 2).

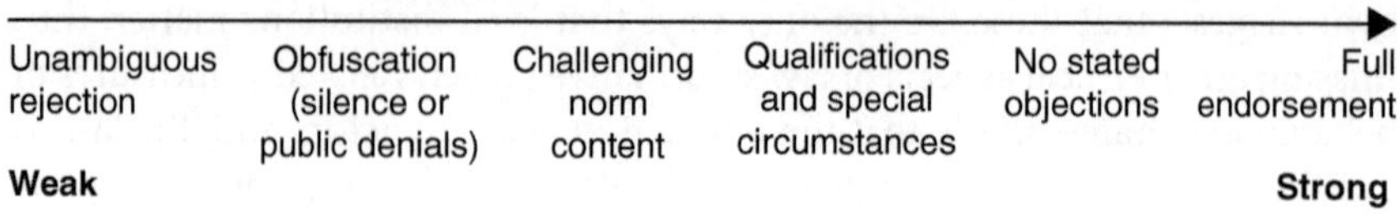

Figure 3.2. Spectrum of discursive indicators and norm strength

However, discourse can reveal important evidence for the influence of legal norms even in the absence of parallel behavioural change.[5] The interpretive context is key here, since different rhetorical strategies have the potential to impact the status of norms in varying ways: are 'challenges or rejections of the norm directed at the central validity claim of the norm per se, or are they directed at the definitional margins?' (Price 2006, 262).

Most critically, states may simply reject the authority of the legal instrument and norm and, in so doing, assert that their own practices—whether involving explicit violations or not—are uncontroversial. Until recently, states like Myanmar and the Russian Federation have made no attempt to excuse their continued use of AP mines as part of regular military operations (Chapter 5). Similarly, the United States under the first administration of George W. Bush aggressively voiced its wholesale opposition to the ICC in its public diplomacy. With a similarly provocative approach the government of Sudan has actively flouted the ICC indictment of President Omar al-Bashir, both rhetorically and through its actions (including Mr Bashir's public travel outside of Sudan) (Chapter 7).

Yet such overt challenges—at least in the cases under study here—are quite rare, since the international community tends to regard open hostility as excessive and, in a word, undiplomatic. A more frequent tactic for states accused of norm violations—whether formal treaty parties or not—is to obfuscate, either by saying nothing or publicly denying the alleged acts. Such efforts offer a modest but potentially important indication of how normative concerns can influence instrumental calculations, as the attempt to avoid critique signals an emerging recognition of the cost of non-conformance in light of a salient social standard. The customary prohibition of torture is an instructive example of this phenomenon: while abuse undoubtedly occurs with regrettable frequency, state agents go to great lengths to conceal these activities, suggesting that grave abuses cannot be dismissed as unproblematic in the contemporary international system.[6] Covert non-compliance does not

[5] This analysis is particularly indebted to the framework previously advanced by Richard Price (2006, 261–3).

[6] The debate concerning so-called enhanced interrogation techniques employed during the administration of George W. Bush would seem to challenge the robustness of the anti-torture norm both in terms of the practices employed, and the semantic games deployed by senior administration officials. Nevertheless, US leaders were unwilling to openly declare 'torture' to be

directly undermine the status of legal norms, in other words, but rather suggests that the norm has gained sufficiently widespread support that non-compliance implies an unpalatable political cost to an actor's reputation. This is a key mechanism in many rationalist accounts of legal compliance (Guzman 2008). The subsequent confirmation of violations would then become even more significant, since they would be assessed in the context of previous denials and bring into play considerations of the state's good faith standing. Previous studies have demonstrated that hypocrisy can be politically significant, since it offers opportunities for external actors to reinforce the status of a legal rule or norm as the relevant social standard and pressure deviant actors towards greater adherence (Risse, Ropp, and Sikkink 1999; Risse, Ropp, and Sikkink 2013; Smith-Cannoy 2012). Even when detached from actual practice, therefore, efforts to ignore or repudiate allegations represent a form of de facto rhetorical support for a norm or legal rule (D'Amato 1988, 469), providing even stronger evidence of a growing sensitivity to community expectations.

Moving towards the middle of the spectrum, actors often raise disputes concerning the meaning or implications of norms. This, too, can have internal gradations that bear on the relative impact of such actions. Just as with international law more broadly, treaties contain an implicit internal hierarchy whereby some features are understood to be more fundamental than others and their acceptance or rejection is viewed as more consequential. More seriously, actors may dispute core features of an institution and in so doing seek to challenge its legitimacy. A number of African states have rejected the ICC indictments of Sudanese President al-Bashir and Kenyan President Kenyatta on the grounds (among other claims) that Article 27 of the Rome Statute is incompatible with the pre-existing and foundational norm of Head of States immunity, as discussed later in this chapter and examined at length in Chapters 6 and 7. Less problematically, states—whether formal parties to a treaty or not—may challenge the content or application of discrete rules while upholding the wider purpose of a treaty. Particularistic claims of this kind do not necessarily substantially undermine the status of a legal norm, but can instead indicate a serious engagement with the consequences of legal institutions. Indeed, were it not for the standard established by the treaty, there would be little reason to justify contrary behaviours in the first place, since such actions would not appear to be extraordinary or problematic.

Alternatively, actors may seek to qualify their non-compliance as the product of exceptional circumstances that do not challenge the general authority of the treaty. For example, States Parties to the MBT have cited technical challenges—relating to the high cost and complex logistics—in

permissible, and indeed went to great lengths to re-frame their activities as constituting a different, and less problematic, form of behaviour (Brunnée and Toope 2010, 220–70; McKeown 2009).

explaining their failure to meet legally binding deadlines for destroying their AP mine stockpiles (Chapter 4). More broadly, many of the remaining users of AP mines have substantially narrowed their justification from one of general utility (mines as unproblematic weapons) to extreme instances where vital national security interests are at stake. Making these kinds of claims can bolster the perceived legitimacy of the treaty, by reinforcing the view that contrary actions are *normally* unacceptable:

> Even if the justification appears to be no more than a lip-service pronouncement totally divorced from the facts of state action, if the state must pay lip-service to the norm it demonstrates that the state believes the norm to be important enough so that it must be acknowledged. If the norm were wholly without importance, surely the state would not use normative language to justify its action.
>
> (Percy 2007b, 37)

Non-parties may similarly accept the general principles enshrined in an agreement while resisting its specific legal restrictions, often because the aforementioned treaty is deemed unsuitable *under present conditions*. This position has been widely adopted by sceptics of the MBT and ICC, as will be shown later. Importantly, such a framing leaves open the possibility of formal adherence should these conditions change. Though the invocation of special circumstances offers a seemingly cost-free means of indicating general support while avoiding binding constraints, therefore, this strategy equally provides a rhetorical opening for other actors to exploit in pressing for more fulsome change.

Importantly, I do not claim that public discourse constitutes a faithful representation of the complete diplomatic position of the state—with its complex array of policy actors—or the private psychological dispositions of the myriad human beings that make up bureaucracies. My focus is on the global adoption or contestation of legal norms, and so I do not systematically inquire into the socialization of discrete individuals and groups, which is where the internalization of norms ultimately occurs (Brunnée and Toope 2010, 61). Yet public discourse is one prominent way in which states recreate their social environment, and is therefore consequential to the assessment of legal norms. States seek to influence the development of legal structures through their interpretations, and *opinio juris* is best understood as comprising 'statements of belief [about the legality of a given action] rather than actual beliefs' (Roberts 2001, 758). These articulations may accurately represent state views concerning the legal status of a given rule or norm (or more broadly their relationship to fundamental principles of law), or may instead be the product of instrumental efforts to shape diplomacy by justifying actions, delegitimizing opponents, or deflecting criticism (Bower 2015; Krebs and Jackson 2007). But since international law is created and modified through publicly expressed views, even disingenuous or cynical statements have the

STRONG ↑

	Unambiguous rejection	Obfuscation (silence or public denials)	Challenging norm content	Qualifications and special circumstances	No stated objections	Full endorsement
Full adherence					De facto compliance without policy change (e.g. small states with no AP mines)	MBT and ICC members without compliance issues
Bureaucratic adaptation			US AP mine policy review (2009–14)	AP mine production and export moratoria by MBT non-parties US acceptance of MBT obligations with exception of Korean peninsula (2014)	Domestic legislative and institutional change by States Parties or non-parties in advance of ratification/accession Submission of mandated annual transparency reports (MBT) Incorporation of Rome Statute crimes and procedures	
Partial policy change			US shift to 'smart mines' (2004) Acceptance by China, Russia, United States of UNSC referrals re. Darfur and Libya (2009 and 2012)	US non-use of AP mines (1991–) Non-party cooperation with ICC situations		
General engagement			Non-party state attendance at MBT and ICC meetings			De facto compliance by non-parties (e.g. states with no AP mines)
Sustained violation	Use of AP mines by some non-party states Sudan re. ICC Bashir indictment	Syrian government AP mine use Allegations of AP mine use against MBT States Parties	African state responses to al Bashir, Kenyatta, and Ruto indictments	MBT State Party missed stockpile destruction deadlines		

WEAK → STRONG

Figure 3.3. Combined indicators of norm strength

potential to contribute to the reproduction of legal norms and their solidification as social facts. For this reason, official discourse constitutes highly relevant evidence concerning the effect of legal institutions irrespective of any judgement concerning the underlying sincerity of a claim.

Since norms are intersubjective phenomena, the communicative process also implicates the agency of *other* actors in assessing and responding to claims. Moments of apparent crisis, involving alleged or confirmed violations, offer productive opportunities in which to clarify the content of a treaty and identify deviations as unacceptable practices and thereby reinforce the intersubjective validity of the norm as an important standard of appropriate behaviour. States and civil society representatives thus have a range of options in how they engage deviant actors, and may highlight transgressions and engage in public condemnation or choose to downplay the violations or disputes and pursue non-confrontational, cooperative solutions.

Behavioural and discursive indicators should therefore properly be seen as interactive sources of evidence of treaty impact, in that each complements, qualifies, and contextualizes the other. This integrated approach to assessing treaty influence also helps to address the contingency inherent in the development of international institutions. Norms and laws are deeply influenced by social and political forces, and therefore do not advance along a unidirectional trajectory but instead reside in an ongoing cycle of development, interpretation, and dispute, potentially leading to their reformulation or even abandonment. This in turn permits more nuanced assessment of the incomplete and at times contradictory patterns of change within and among actors. Evidence of these processes is thus important both in assessing the relative influence of the treaties in question, and in appreciating the reciprocal impact that state actions have on the status of international rules and norms.

THE NORMATIVE STRUCTURE OF THE MINE BAN TREATY AND ROME STATUTE OF THE ICC

An analysis of the MBT and Rome Statute must first come to grips with their principal features, since the content of the respective treaties is centrally relevant to the subsequent evaluation of their efficacy. I also briefly draw attention to the diplomatic choices that facilitated the creation of the legal agreements in the absence of support from great powers. This discussion is important as it identifies the key innovations of each treaty, and hence the principal points at which compliance and non-compliance, endorsement and contestation take place.

The Antipersonnel Mine Ban Treaty

A prohibition on AP mines, under all circumstances and conditions, constitutes the foundational norm in the MBT.[7] In this aim the MBT draws inspiration from a broader principle of humanitarianism, as the preamble (paragraph 1) makes clear:

> Determined to put an end to the suffering and casualties caused by anti-personnel mines, that kill or maim hundreds of people every week, mostly innocent and defenceless civilians and especially children, obstruct economic development and reconstruction, inhibit the repatriation of refugees and internally displaced persons, and have other severe consequences for years after emplacement.

Indeed, as subsequent paragraphs demonstrate, the treaty is consciously rooted in a long tradition of international humanitarian law (IHL), found most particularly in reference to the notion that the right to choose the methods of warfare is not unlimited, commands against superfluous injury and unnecessary suffering, and an articulation of the twin principles of distinction and discrimination (Maslen 2005, 1:66–71). The reference to existing legal standards is important, because it provides the particular rationale for prohibition. Proponents of a comprehensive ban have long contended that the inherent characteristics of AP mines—most especially concerning their persistence once deployed and inability to distinguish between legitimate military targets and civilians—mean that they cannot be employed in a way that would sufficiently respect established legal principles (International Committee of the Red Cross 1997; Price 1998, 627–31). Leaders of the mine ban movement thus asserted that their use in any conceivable scenario was de facto already illegal, and the MBT was thus merely redressing an ambiguity in existing law.

Most fundamentally, therefore, the MBT seeks to overturn a well-established international social standard that regarded AP mines as largely unproblematic tools of war, in the same category as other conventional military technologies like artillery, rockets, and firearms. The claim that AP mines intrinsically violate the basic standards of IHL amounts to a fundamental reversal of the burden of proof that has typically given benefit of the doubt to the security needs of the state in the first instance over concerns for humanitarian impact. As Richard Price explains, in endorsing the ban norm 'many states have decided not that mines are not at all useful, but that their military utility is outweighed by their humanitarian costs, thus introducing a moral calculus into the definition of national interest' (Price

[7] Overviews of the negotiation process can be found in Dolan and Hunt (1998); Maslen and Herby (1998).

1998, 614).[8] In this respect, the MBT is a more recent expression of a long-term, if intermittent, effort at restricting the means and consequences of war.

This prohibitionary approach sits uneasily with prior expectations concerning the legitimate conduct of warfare. AP mines were a prominent feature in armed conflict during the second half of the twentieth century: it is estimated that between two-and-a-half and four million AP mines were emplaced annually in the 1970s, 1980s, and 1990s, and by the time of the MBT's negotiation over seventy countries were infested with a total of 60–70 million mines (Department of State, United States of America 1998; International Campaign to Ban Landmines 1999, 4–5; Vines 1998). Hence, contrary to the claim that treaties only reflect existing interests (Downs, Rocke, and Barsoom 1996; von Stein 2005), I contend that the mine ban constitutes a dramatic change in the international status quo regarding the practice and limits of national defence—an area in which states are least likely to accept onerous restrictions on their freedom of action.

Moreover, the treaty seeks to implement this new social expectation in the face of concerted resistance from the largest military powers. The United States, China, India, and Russia (among others) have long maintained that the deleterious humanitarian effects of AP mines can be addressed through the existing parameters of IHL governing conventional weapons (Morgan 2002). In particular, these prominent opponents argued that the core concerns of the pro-ban constituency stemmed from the irresponsible use of AP mines by poorly trained armed forces and rebel groups and not from the legitimate operations of modern militaries. These states therefore supported an alternative legal framework that further regulated, but did not eliminate, the use AP mines, codified in Amended Protocol II (APII) to the Convention on Certain Conventional Weapons (CCW) (Maslen 2005, 1:18–22; Rutherford 2009, 125–8).[9] It was widely understood at the time that this partial restriction was as much as could be achieved via consensus voting rules that included great powers resistant to a more far-reaching prohibition.

It is particularly significant, then, that the process leading to the MBT was precipitated by widespread dissatisfaction with the outcome of negotiations on APII, which was regarded by many states and civil society groups as 'overly

[8] A 1997 report by the International Committee of the Red Cross thus concluded that 'the limited military utility of AP mines is far outweighed by the appalling humanitarian consequences of their use in actual conflicts' (International Committee of the Red Cross 1997, 73). Similar conclusions were reinforced in a subsequent review conducted for the ICRC by senior (retired) military officers (International Committee of the Red Cross 2004). For a concise review of arguments concerning the utility of AP mines, see Gard, Jr (1998); Maslen (2005, 1:2–14).

[9] Protocol on Prohibitions or Restrictions on the Use of Mines, Booby-Traps and Other Devices as amended on 3 May 1996 (Amended Protocol II to the 1980 CCW) http://www.icrc.org/ihl/INTRO/575. Most pertinently, Article 5(2) of the treaty permits the use of AP mines that contain self-destruct or self-deactivation mechanisms, or in instances where the minefields are fenced and actively patrolled.

complex and insufficiently stringent to deal with the extent of the humanitarian crisis [caused by AP mines]' (Maslen 2005, 1:22). Ban proponents therefore felt that the immediacy and depth of the humanitarian threat posed by AP mines required an aggressive and unconventional approach to diplomacy, typified by the creation of an ad hoc negotiating forum to bypass typical consensus-based decision rules that favoured powerful states and a close partnership between a committed 'core group' of governments[10] and transnational civil society actors under the umbrella of the International Campaign to Ban Landmines (ICBL) (Cameron, Lawson, and Tomlin 1998). The objective was not to find the lowest common denominator that all states would willingly accept, but inversely to establish a firm legally binding standard that actors would be encouraged to adopt (Maslen 2005, 1:40–2). In this respect, the Ottawa Process differs from the experience of most major arms control and disarmament treaties in eschewing consensus—and especially the support of powerful states—as a baseline for new legal initiatives.

The final treaty text entrenches a series of obligations designed to address the adverse humanitarian effects associated with AP mines. First and most centrally, the treaty requires that States Parties *cease using* these weapons unconditionally (Article 1.1(a)). To supplement and give further effect to this obligation, the MBT also includes a further set of prohibitions concerning the *production* and *transfer* of AP mines, as well as positive commitments to *destroy all stockpiles* and *clear all mined areas* on territory under a state's control (Articles 1.1(b), 4, and 5). These behavioural injunctions are understood to comprise the core features of the mine ban norm (Herby and Lawand 2008, 205).[11] Finally, the treaty incorporates incipient norms regarding mine action and victim assistance. The MBT does not itself codify industrial standards for humanitarian demining, but rather provides an institutional context in which such standards have further evolved. In a similar vein, the treaty also contains positive obligations to provide assistance to mine survivors within

[10] The initial members of the Core Group—which later expanded during the negotiation process—were Austria, Belgium, Canada, Ireland, Mexico, Netherlands, Norway, the Philippines, South Africa, and Switzerland (Maslen 2005, 1:27 and n. 143).

[11] While the core obligations are phrased as absolute injunctions, there are some limited exceptions, concerning for example the right to retain a small number of AP mines for training in mine detection and clearance. For detail concerning the definition of 'antipersonnel mine', see Maslen (2005, 1:100–31). The MBT also outlines a set of expectations concerning the domestic implementation of legal obligations. Most notably, States Parties are required to 'take all appropriate legal, administrative and other measures, including the imposition of penal sanctions, to prevent and suppress any activity prohibited to a State Party under this Convention undertaken by persons or on territory under its jurisdiction or control' (Article 9). This has been interpreted as requiring the creation of national laws criminalizing violations of the treaty and, arguably, the establishment of a national authority to oversee implementation issues. Additionally, the MBT requires the submission of annual transparency reports detailing progress in the national implementation of treaty mandates. These commitments highlight the political dimensions of treaty compliance, but are not studied systematically in this book.

one's own country, as well as to other mine-affected states, as articulated in Article 6 (Brinkert 2006).[12] However, given obligations relating to mine action and victim assistance remain largely un-codified as precise commitments in the MBT, these particular norms are largely excluded from the proceeding analysis. Instead, I focus my attention on the positive and negative obligations contained in Articles 1 to 5 as the core legal elements to the prohibition on AP mines. This decision does not imply a judgement concerning their relative ethical merit, but simply reflects an effort to keep the study within manageable limits.

The MBT thus aims to reshape international practice via the introduction of a new constitutive standard of appropriate behaviour, and regulative rules governing the particular scope of these commitments. Yet in contrast to earlier diplomatic experiences, the Ottawa Process was animated by a calculation that a global stigmatization of AP mines would be most effectively achieved via an uncompromising prohibition that permitted no exemptions, rather than through a more modest agreement that included concessions to military powers. This is significant, as powerful non-party states have focused much of their diplomatic energy in challenging the absoluteness of the mine ban norm. This process was already apparent during the negotiations:

> The United States participated in the [Mine Ban] Treaty final drafting conference in Oslo, but its delegation came with a series of requests that they wanted to incorporate into the treaty. The demands were presented in a take-it-or-leave-it package consisting of five interlocking components: exception for landmine use in Korea; deferral of the treaty's entry-into-force date; changes in the definition of an anti-personnel landmine [to exclude anti-tampering devices on US anti-tank mines]; more intensive verification measures; and a withdrawal clause from the treaty in cases of national emergency. (Rutherford 1999, 40)

US officials indicated that these demands were a necessary precondition for formal US membership since, in its current configuration, the MBT placed undue burdens on the exercise of the United States's global military responsibilities (United States of America 1997a; United States of America 1997b; Wareham 1998). Other delegations—notably those of China, India, Israel, and the Russian Federation—were even more hostile to the aims of the negotiations. Despite intense pressure from the United States and these other states, the pro-ban contingency refused to weaken the treaty via exceptions or the possibility of reservations. This strategic choice was crucial to maintaining the unity of the pro-ban coalition, though it also provides the basis for non-party contestation. Most fundamentally, prominent opponents continue to contend,

[12] These broad commitments have been further clarified in subsequent documents, most notably the Action Plans of the treaty Review Conferences in 2004 (Nairobi), 2009 (Cartagena), and 2014 (Maputo). Documents are available at http://www.apminebanconvention.org/review-conferences/.

often vociferously, that AP mines remain legitimate and useful weapons in modern military doctrine. At the heart of my assessment, therefore, is the question of whether, and to what extent, the MBT has realized widespread adherence to its particular obligations, in light of these substantial challenges.

The Rome Statute of the International Criminal Court

Compared to the relatively confined initiative to ban a particular weapon system, the ICC constitutes an even more complex and wide-ranging intervention in international politics.[13] Indeed, as David Bosco (2014, 2) has noted, the ICC, 'represents a remarkable transfer of authority from sovereign states to an international institution. The investigation and prosecution of individuals, particularly senior military, political, and security officials, is a sensitive function even for countries with strong and stable domestic institutions. In the context of internal or external conflict, that sensitivity increases markedly.' The Rome Statute codifies an extensive set of international humanitarian, criminal, and jurisprudential rules drawn from an array of treaty and customary sources, and creates a new institution for enforcing this resulting legal order. Yet its origins as part of the 'new diplomacy' are strikingly similar to the MBT discussed above, as the Rome Statute was negotiated via an ad hoc diplomatic model that emphasized cooperative engagement among a motivated group of 'like-minded' middle power states[14] and civil society groups under the banner of the Coalition for the International Criminal Court (CICC), and avoided more traditional venues within the United Nations system where great powers are better able to control proceedings. And, as with the mine ban process, sceptical great powers (most especially the United States) were heavily involved in the negotiations, and made substantial contributions to the draft text despite their ultimate inability to gain sufficient concessions to enable formal membership (Scheffer 1999a).

At its most fundamental level, the purpose of the Court is 'to try persons alleged to be responsible for the most serious crimes affecting the entire community as well as the peace, security, and well-being of the world' (Bourgon 2002, 559)—in effect, to promote the rule of law and end impunity for grave crimes at the international and domestic levels. In so doing, the Statute embeds a social expectation that judicial process and penal sanction constitute an appropriate response to grave international crimes (*Rome*

[13] This book cannot hope to comprehensively review the drafting and legal content of the Rome Statute. A number of excellent volumes have undertaken this task, including Benedetti, Bonneau, and Washburn (2013); Cassese, Gaeta, and Jones (2002); Schabas (2010); Stahn (2015).

[14] For a full list of members, see The Parliament of the Commonwealth of Australia, Joint Standing Committee on Treaties (2002, 100).

Statute of the International Criminal Court 1998, preamble para. 4; Drumbl 2007). The ICC is the first permanent international court charged with trying individual human beings for grievous crimes, and thus reinforces a recent expansion of international law to include individuals as subjects of criminal responsibility and punishment (Bass 2001; Dupuy 2002; Sikkink 2011). Yet this general mandate can imply very different configurations of rights and responsibilities, and the particular structure of the Rome Statute and resulting Court represents one of a variety of potential responses to the challenge of how to address international criminality considered during negotiations (Struett 2008, 24–5).[15] As will be argued below, the particular institutional solution embodied in the Rome Statute represents both its foundational normative commitment and contains the principal points of contestation.

A primary consideration in the construction of the Rome regime was the scope of its mandate, concerning what acts and actors should properly fall under the aegis of the Court. The ICC has jurisdiction over genocide, crimes against humanity, war crimes, and—at some point after 2017—the crime of aggression (*Rome Statute of the International Criminal Court* 1998, Art. 5–8).[16] These *core crimes* are understood as the most serious forms of organized violence in the international system, to be distinguished from other types of international criminal activity like piracy, drug trafficking, and terrorism. Moreover, the distinct intentionality, scale, and context of the constituent acts—like murder, rape, and kidnapping—means that they should be regarded as a particularly egregious class of behaviours and not treated as simply more expansive instances of 'common' crimes under existing domestic laws (Drumbl 2007, 4). The inclusion of certain crimes, with the necessary exclusion of others, thus elevates these acts and invests them with particular opprobrium. These decisions were not especially innovative or controversial on the aggregate, since the Statute for the most part reflects established international customary and statutory law as well as the practice of recent ad hoc criminal tribunals.[17] The acts constituting genocide, crimes against

[15] Indeed, despite the extensive work by the Preparatory Committee in preparing a draft treaty text, the document under discussion at Rome 'was riddled with some fourteen hundred square brackets, i.e., points of disagreement, surrounding partial and complete provisions, with any number of alternative texts' (Kirsch and Holmes 1999, 3).

[16] An amendment to the Rome Statute operationalizing the crime of aggression was adopted at the Review Conference in Kampala, Uganda (Assembly of States Parties 2010b). This issue is addressed in Chapter 7.

[17] Especially the Geneva Conventions of 1949, Additional Protocols of 1977, and the Genocide Convention, in the case of the former, and the International Criminal Tribunals for Rwanda and the Former Yugoslavia in the latter. The Rome Statute represents a compromise solution and is thus less progressive on some matters than existing statutory and customary international law. At the same time, the Statute also advances the law in some important respects, as with gender and sexual violence crimes and the rights of victims in legal proceedings (Glasius 2005, 77–93). For a good brief discussion of differences between the Rome Statute and other international

humanity, and war crimes (though notably not aggression) and the related modes of responsibility were therefore largely settled by the time of the 1998 Rome Conference and consequently were generally accepted even among sceptical delegations. One of the significant contributions of the Statute is thus to bring together disparate strands of international law under a single legal architecture. In so doing, the Rome Statute helps to consolidate international legal practice both by reaffirming the special status of these crimes and adding greater precision to their substantive definitions.

The revolutionary nature of the ICC is therefore primarily found in its specific solution to the problem of how to enforce compliance with the grave crimes regime. To address this challenge the Rome Statute creates a new norm of internationalized procedural justice: while national authorities retain the primary responsibility for investigating and prosecuting atrocity crimes, they must do so via internationally agreed standards of criminal law and with the oversight of a supranational legal body that is able to step in when national authorities are unwilling or unable to act. This configuration 'represents a sharp contrast to the earlier normative solution' in which the responsibility for enforcing international criminal law rested solely with the domestic legal processes of sovereign states (Deitelhoff 2009a, 151). The institutional architecture for this new international expectation comes in four principal parts, concerning the *scope of criminal accountability*, 'fundamental implementing obligations' of *cooperation* and *complementarity* (Amnesty International 2010, 5), and the *modalities* by which the Court can assert its authority in the international system.

First, the institutional structure of the ICC is predicated on an assertion that all perpetrators—no matter their official role—must be held accountable for the serious crimes under the Court's purview. To that end, the Rome Statute deviates from previous practice by rejecting legal immunity for Heads of States and other political figures, thereby reversing prior diplomatic norms concerning the special legal status of certain high officials (*Rome Statute of the International Criminal Court* 1998, Art. 27; Gaeta 2002). This innovation is complicated by the fact that the Statute also accommodates established international obligations *between states* concerning these same forms of legal exemption, meaning that the status of immunities under the ICC remains contentious, as will be shown extensively in Chapters 6 and 7 (*Rome Statute of the International Criminal Court* 1998, Art. 98; Akande 2004). The Statute also adopts well-accepted modalities of jurisdiction and applies to acts either committed on the territory of a States Party (even if committed by nationals from a non-party) or by the national of a States Party on any territory (*Rome Statute of the International Criminal Court* 1998, Art. 12.2; Bourgon 2002).

criminal law sources, particularly concerning the definition of crimes, jurisdiction, and modes of liability, see Amnesty International (2010, 7–16).

This does not include a more expansive assertion of authority via 'universal jurisdiction', a decision that negotiators believed would increase the acceptability of the resulting Statute by retaining a more modest reach for the new institution.

Second, the Statute entrenches an expectation that states—primarily parties to the Rome Statute but also all UN members in instances of a Security Council referral—have a legal obligation to 'cooperate fully with the Court in its investigation and prosecution of crimes within the jurisdiction of the Court' (*Rome Statute of the International Criminal Court* 1998, Art. 86). This involves a host of more specific expectations including on matters of arresting and surrendering suspects, providing evidence and documentation, enforcing sentences, and other means of support (*Rome Statute of the International Criminal Court* 1998, Art. 86–111; Ciampi 2002). Since the Court does not possess its own police force, the enforcement of international criminal law necessarily relies on the active assistance of states.

Third, the substantial limits on the ICC's capacity to investigate and prosecute crimes mean that the majority of criminal processes will be undertaken by national-level entities. To organize this division of labour, the Rome Statute creates a new principle of complementarity whereby the Court shall defer to states 'unless the States is unwilling or unable genuinely to carry out the investigation or prosecution' (*Rome Statute of the International Criminal Court* 1998, Art. 17.1(a); Stahn and El Zeidy 2011). The preference for national legal processes is based on a normative expectation in which all states have a duty to investigate, prosecute, and punish grave crimes through their own domestic criminal procedures, conditioned by a potentially invasive form of oversight from an international body. The assumption is that justice can best be realized by transforming national criminal systems, and not by centralizing legal activity within the ICC (Terracino 2007). To facilitate this, and to avoid an intervention from the Court, states must ensure that their national laws address all relevant aspects of the criminal law regime set out in the Rome Statute, particularly by adopting ICC crimes and jurisdiction, eliminating immunities for all national figures, and implementing appropriate criminal law procedures, including forms of criminal liability, fair trial standards, and specific modalities of criminal investigation and prosecution (*Rome Statute of the International Criminal Court* 1998, Art. 22–33, 62–7, and 86–102). The broader purpose of the ICC is thus to facilitate the application of international criminal law to domestic jurisdictions and thereby create a homogenous global legal regime. This produces a strong incentive towards legal standardization:

> The more a national legal process approximates that of the ICC . . . the greater the likelihood that this process will be palatable and pass muster. This, in turn, suggests that . . . national institutions will model themselves along the lines of the ICC in order to maximize their jurisdiction. Complementarity, therefore, may encourage heterogeneity in terms of the number of institutions adjudicating

> international crimes, but homogeneity in terms of the process they follow and the punishment they mete out. (Drumbl 2007, 143; Cryer 2005, 148–9, 171–2)[18]

For this reason, domestic legal transformation via the incorporation of the Rome Statute in national law provides one valuable metric—in addition to other behavioural measures—by which norm adoption can be assessed (Amnesty International 2010; Human Rights Watch 2001a; International Centre for Criminal Law Reform and Criminal Justice Policy 2008).

Fourth and most fundamentally, debates over the content and structure of the ICC ultimately revolve around competing visions for the legal and political independence of the Court, and concomitant assessments concerning how this might relate to its subsequent effectiveness. From the outset, proponents of a strong court were convinced that ICC could only achieve its stated aims if it was constituted as an autonomous legal entity. On the one hand, as noted already, the Court will be able to consider alleged violations that occurred either on the territory of a state party or committed by the national(s) of a party, leaving open the possibility that nationals from non-member states may be subject to ICC prosecution even though their governments do not accept the Court's authority. This jurisdictional structure was strongly resisted by many prominent opponents on the grounds that it violates the foundational principle of voluntary state consent in international law (Lietzau 2001, 125–30; Wedgwood 1999, 99–102). The United States took the lead in pushing for a more modest institution, by insisting that *both* the territorial state *and* the state of nationality must consent to an ICC investigation (Scheffer 1999a, 20). The US delegation made clear that this was a deal-breaker, and that failure to address their concerns could push the US to a position of active hostility towards the new court. Despite this threat, the majority of states involved in the negotiations did not accept the legal validity of the US interpretation; moreover, they contended that the proposed limits on the court's jurisdiction would substantially impede its capacity to deliver genuinely impartial justice for crimes of global concern (Wippman 2004, 155 and 170–4).

On the other hand, the Rome Statute also gives the Prosecutor the power to initiate investigations *proprio motu*—that is, under his or her own initiative—a much broader form of discretionary power than some key states wanted. The permanent members of the UNSC (including, initially, France and the United Kingdom) demanded that in the absence of a self-referral by a party to the Statute, the sole right to launch proceedings would be vested with the UNSC (Schabas 2004). The United States was the most vocal proponent of the view that international organizations needed to conform to the prevailing political

[18] For a critique of how complementarity may lead to over-standardization of legal codes, by demanding 'identical' rather than 'equivalent' domestic standards that do not necessarily improve state capacity to respond to grave abuses, see Mégret (2011).

realities of the international system in which the UNSC retained the ultimate responsibility for ensuring peace and security; a permanent international court must therefore remain subordinate to this higher authority (Wedgwood 1999, 96–8; Wippman 2004, 175). The majority of states, by contrast, regarded this position as a deliberate attempt to 'politicize' international justice by giving the five permanent members of the UNSC the ability to block any inconvenient ICC investigations.

These dual requirements were regarded by a number of powerful states as a threat to their predominant position in the international system which, among other things, has permitted a considerable degree of discretion in selectively interpreting and in some cases ignoring the application of international rules. The United States in particular feared that an independent court would become an instrument for states and civil society groups to constrain the use of US military power through the retrospective application, or prospective threat, of criminal investigation and prosecution of its soldiers or officials (Lietzau 2001, 126–7). This concern was not entirely misplaced, as the majority of states supporting a strong ICC clearly understood that an autonomous court could be used to shape the conduct of international affairs:

> Their goal was to limit the future discretion of individual states by obligating them to support prosecutions under specified circumstances, and by shifting decision-making authority from national government officials to judges and prosecutors independent of any state or particular group of states. More broadly, their goal was to shape what governments will in the future consider acceptable behaviour. (Wippman 2004, 160)

The United States remains the largest contributor to international humanitarian and peacekeeping operations. Critics therefore warned that an excessively ambitious jurisdictional regime that threatened US prerogatives would lead the only truly global power to decisively reject the Court and withdraw from other international interventions where its core security interests were not at stake. This, in turn, would greatly diminish the international community's ability to address grave human rights abuses (Bellinger 2008; Goldsmith 2003; Scheffer 1999a, 12, 18–19).

Observers have suggested that a willingness to concede to great power demands on matters of the exposure of non-party nationals, prosecutorial independence, and Security Council pre-eminence could have facilitated further great power engagement, and perhaps formal US membership (Schabas 2004). The United States delegation in particular complained that the final negotiation of 'the treaty text was subject to a mysterious, closed-door and exclusionary process of revision by a small number of delegates' in a rushed process that manipulated the diplomatic outcome and excluded the potential for gaining wider support for great-power favoured amendments (Scheffer 1999a, 20) Yet these same features were central to the Rome Statute's popularity among a broader array of participants such that their elimination would likely have significantly eroded enthusiasm among prominent backers, resulting in a weaker treaty and subsequent norm. Negotiations were thus emblematic of this study's animating concern with whether multilateral initiatives should prioritize breadth of membership or depth of obligations as the means of promoting strong international standards. This strategic calculation is at the heart of the judgement concerning the effectiveness of the ICC.

When taken together, the configuration of organizational structures and responsibilities enshrined in the Rome Statute constitutes a particular institutional solution to the problem of how to effectively punish the most heinous international crimes. At the same time, the Statute also articulates a vision of appropriate behaviour wherein states are obliged to investigate and prosecute grave violations of international humanitarian and human rights law via agreed international procedures. This is the basis for what I have termed the internationalized procedural justice norm, and serves as the reference point against which state change is measured in this study. Yet it is important not to lose sight of the fact that the decision to employ trials and penal sanction—as opposed to other potential responses including amnesties, asylum, or community-based remedies—under the explicit oversight of a supranational body represents a dramatic sea change in how states conceive of their domestic and international responsibilities. The very existence of a permanent international court with the ability to exercise legal authority over the nationals of all states 'represents a stunning change of course. Not only does the ICC promise more stringent enforcement of international crimes, it also takes away from sovereign states the discretion to decide when to initiate prosecutions—a right they have heretofore jealously guarded' (Simmons and Danner 2010, 226). This particular outcome was neither guaranteed at the outset, nor uncontroversial then or in hindsight, meaning that the extent of state adaptation and resistance must be systematically explained, rather than taken for granted.

CONCLUSION

This book seeks to provide as complete an assessment as possible of the impact of two non-great power treaties. In Chapters 4–7, I evaluate the MBT and Rome Statute of the ICC on the basis of the analytic framework developed above. To summarize: an effective treaty will substantiate new legal commitments and norms that shape state policy and hence the conduct of international politics. Following my conception of institutions as both regulative and constitutive, the evidence must address: (a) the empirical extent of *behavioural change* since treaty creation; and (b) the *perceived status* of legal norms among relevant actors. This research design therefore seeks to address the questions of *whether* and *why* states are (or are not) adhering to the treaties, and to relate the empirical findings to theorized roles that legal institutions play in shaping international political life.

While valuable in its own respect, such an endeavour can also contribute to the broader question of whether the strategic choice that typifies recent non-great power diplomacy provides a useful model to be replicated in other issue areas. As Wendt (2001, 1044) suggests, 'rather than explaining why we have chosen the road we have taken, which is only indirectly relevant to where we should go from here, the effectiveness problematique can tell us why some choices worked and some did not, which could directly affect the next ones we make.' That is, a fully satisfactory assessment of *these* treaties must compare outcomes and situate the evidence against a range of plausible alternative scenarios. I return to this challenge in the final section of the book.

4

Building a Community of Law

States Parties and the Mine Ban Treaty

The following four chapters (Chapters 4–7) transition from conceptual and theoretical concerns to a detailed exploration of the dynamics of legal implementation and norm development in two key cases. With respect to antipersonnel (AP) mines, this involves a reconceptualization of the weapons as a humanitarian scourge that are fundamentally incompatible with standards of international humanitarian law (IHL). To the extent that it takes hold, this marks a profound shift from the prior view of the weapons as 'force multipliers', 'sentinels', or 'deterrents', and thus legitimate tools of warfare (Beier 2002, 305). The key question, then, is whether this process is taking place in practice.

PATTERNS OF MEMBERSHIP IN THE MINE BAN TREATY

The vitality of a legal institution is partially judged in relation to its formal community of members. The Mine Ban Treaty (MBT) was initially signed by 122 states in December 1997, and became operational on 1 March 1999 in what is widely regarded as the most rapid entry into force for a major multilateral treaty (International Campaign to Ban Landmines 1999, 3).[1] There are currently 162 MBT States Parties and thirty-five non-parties (Figure 4.1).[2] The extent and pace of ratifications and accessions is important, since widespread and diverse membership is vital to the health of legal norms. As Kerry Brinkert (2008, 96) has argued, 'The large number of States Parties to

[1] The threshold of forty ratifications needed to trigger entry-into-force of the agreement was reached with Burkina Faso's deposit of its instrument of ratification on 16 September 1998.

[2] As of May 2016.

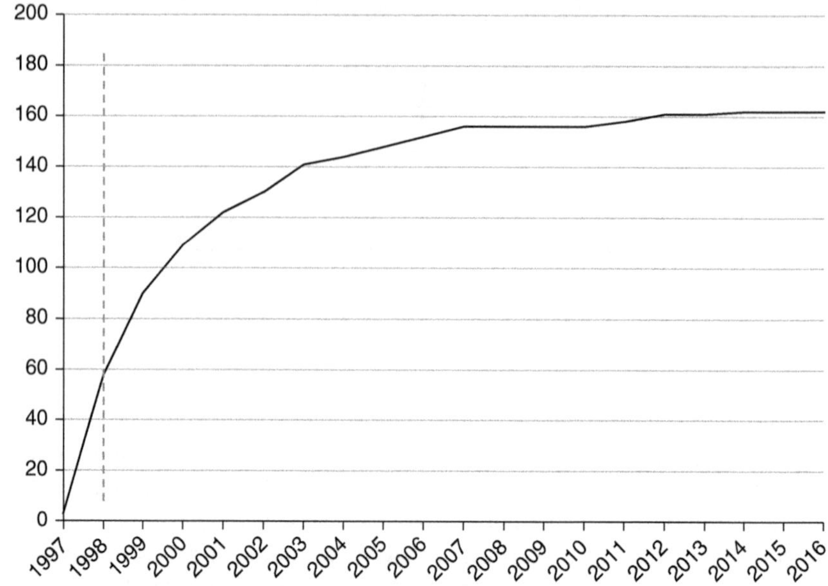

Figure 4.1. Mine Ban Treaty ratifications, 1997–2016

Note: Refers to the number of states that ratified or acceded to the MBT during a given calendar year. The broken line reflects the entry into force of the treaty. Data is derived from the United Nations Multilateral Treaties Deposited with the Secretary-General dataset, available at https://treaties.un.org/Pages/ParticipationStatus.aspx.

this demanding treaty has strongly countered conventional wisdom that suggests the more stringent a legal instrument, the more difficult it is to attract adherents.' In this respect, the MBT compares favourably against other relevant multilateral initiatives: most notably, Amended Protocol II (APII) to the Convention on Certain Conventional Weapons (CCW)—the primary alternative to the MBT whose creation gave impetus to the diplomatic push for a comprehensive AP mine ban—has 102 members.[3]

This does not, however, include many major military powers like China, Egypt, India, Israel, Iran, Pakistan, Russia, and the United States. This has led critics to charge that the treaty represents merely an unimportant commitment among states that would not have much use for AP mines in the first place, and excludes those actors that are most consequential to the conduct—and restraint—of military violence in the international system (Morgan 2002). Yet prominent non-parties do not in fact represent the only relevant constituency in judging the health of the mine ban norm. As Byers has noted, states that are 'specially affected' by a given legal innovation are generally understood to possess special importance in informing its development; this

[3] As of May 2016. See http://www.icrc.org/ihl.nsf/WebSign?ReadForm&id=575&ps=P.

determination need not strictly correspond to measures of material power, but would include all those states most directly impacted by the rule-making process (Byers 1999, 38). A more holistic conception would include not just those states that retain large arsenals or may wish to use AP mines, but also those states that are implicated in the humanitarian purpose of the mine ban norm. In this latter respect, the MBT does substantially capture the relevant constituency: all of the twelve most mine-affected states are treaty members (as are the majority of those states with mine contamination), as are forty-five of the seventy-two states considered mine-affected at the time of the treaty's negotiation (Department of State, United States of America 1998). This group also accounts for approximately half of all mines emplaced globally by 1998.[4] Finally, the MBT encompasses the majority of the largest former AP mine producers (International Campaign to Ban Landmines 2013a, 18; Vines 1998, 124). Moreover, as Chapter 5 makes clear, the extent of opposition from powerful MBT opponents may not be as uniform as their formal membership status suggests. Many prominent non-parties have undertaken policy changes to partially adapt to the mine ban norm, and recognize the desirability of a complete prohibition at some future point, both of which are modest yet politically consequential shifts from the previous status quo.

LOGICS OF MEMBERSHIP: HUMANITARIANISM AND THE DISCURSIVE LEGITIMACY OF THE MINE BAN

Hard Cases in the Adoption of the Mine Ban Treaty

The influence of new legal norms may be especially felt in instances where the mandated change presents significant implications for national security policy, since we would expect restrictive social standards to be least potent under such conditions. Support from actors involved in armed conflicts provides especially compelling examples of how the MBT has influenced the conception of state interests. Twenty-four states—including Colombia, Iraq, Liberia, the Philippines, and Uganda—joined the MBT during internal armed conflicts, or while engaged in foreign military campaigns.[5] A further fourteen states joined the treaty shortly after the end of hostilities and/or a significant transition of

[4] Afghanistan, Angola, Bosnia-Herzegovina, Cambodia, Croatia, Eritrea, Iraq (Kurdistan), Mozambique, Namibia, Nicaragua, Sudan, and Somalia. Somalia acceded to the MBT in April 2012. On the other hand, the ICBL notes that 'twenty-four (41%) of the 59 states believed to be affected by landmines are not party to the Mine Ban Treaty' (International Campaign to Ban Landmines 2013a, 22).

[5] Afghanistan, Algeria, Burundi, Central African Republic, Chad, Colombia, Côte d'Ivoire, Democratic Republic of Congo, Haiti, Iraq, Liberia, Namibia, Nigeria, the Philippines, Rwanda,

government, and where forms of domestic political instability and external tensions (such as border disputes) continued to generate insecurity.[6] In many of these examples AP mines had previously featured extensively in the conflicts. These developments challenge the expectation that states would avoid costly obligations that require they abandon a potentially useful weapon, or where they lack the capacity to make the necessary adaptations.

At the same time, the adoption of a comprehensive ban on a previously prominent weapon was also challenging for many states subsequently identified as primary MBT supporters. Members of the Core Group of pro-ban states such as Belgium, Canada, France, Germany, Italy, and the United Kingdom were all previously among the largest AP mine producers, and thus had substantial political, military, and industrial ties to the weapon (Vines 1998, 121 and 124). These states also have long experience operating as part of multinational military coalitions with the United States, both within the auspices of the NATO and in conflicts like the 1990–1 Gulf War. It was widely recognized at the time of the MBT's negotiation that the prohibition could have a significant impact on the future conduct of joint operations with the United States (Jacobs 2004; Vinson 1998). Governments in Canada, France, and the United Kingdom (among others) thus faced substantial resistance from military officials fearful that the elimination of AP mines from their arsenals would weaken operational defences, imperil alliance commitments, and endanger soldiers' lives (Lawson et al. 1998, 164–5; Tepe 2011, 93–6; Warmington and Tuttle 1998, 50). These states thus initially viewed a comprehensive ban on the weapons with great scepticism, and preferred to pursue any future regulation through the established Conference on Disarmament diplomatic process. Their subsequent enthusiastic support is therefore much more puzzling for sceptical theories than is often recognized, since the decision to abandon the weapons was both costly and contentious.

Explaining Membership

For a sizable number of states, therefore, engagement with the diplomatic processes surrounding the mine ban has helped recast what they regard as acceptable behaviour in the use of armed violence. Explaining these patterns is critical to understanding the role that international law can play in reshaping state identities and subsequent interests. In particular, the link to prior legal standards relating to military necessity, proportionality, and discrimination,

Senegal, Solomon Islands, Somalia, South Sudan, Sudan, Turkey, Uganda, Ukraine, and Zimbabwe.

[6] Angola, Bosnia and Herzegovina, Cambodia, Eritrea, Ethiopia, Guinea-Bissau, Indonesia, Mexico, Niger, Peru, Serbia and Montenegro, Sierra Leone, Tajikistan, and Timor-Leste.

and specific treaties like the Geneva Conventions and Additional Protocols, has provided important impetus in generating state support for the mine ban norm and legal instrument. This has involved, at heart, a substantial reversal of the terms of military utility by which the effectiveness of the weapons is now judged (Gard, Jr 1998, 137).

To that end, a large number of states with historical experience of mine use have endorsed the treaty by articulating a revised conception of national security in which AP mines no longer feature as an acceptable means of pursuing military objectives (Bosnia and Herzegovina 1997; Republic of Angola 1997; Republic of Croatia 2002; Republic of the Philippines 1997; Republic of Uganda 1997; States of Eritrea 2002). 'Sudan's signing of the Convention, despite limited resources and its security concerns which are well known to all, stems from its deep conviction and its strong belief that humanity should get rid of such dangerous weapons which threaten the lives of innocent populations' (Republic of Sudan 2004). In referring to his country's accession, a Turkish representative similarly noted that 'this was a bold decision. Turkey is situated in an extremely volatile region, with many of its neighbours outside the Convention. Moreover, Turkey was engaged in a struggle against terrorism. Nevertheless, sharing the vision and goals of the Convention Turkey took the leap for a better world' (Republic of Turkey 2007a).[7]

Hence the most fundamental effect of the MBT has been to serve as a symbolic demonstration of responsible statehood characterized by the introduction of a new role identity in which the elimination of AP mines is regarded as a potent indication of international good standing. In some cases endorsement of the mine ban has been explicitly understood to mark a break with the previous political order and signal induction into the international community (Serbia and Montenegro 2004). The MBT was thus the first treaty adopted by the newly created South Sudan:

> Since the declaration of our independence on 9 July 2011 . . . my country has promised the world it would honour all the principles of international law by playing an active role in peace and world security . . . Having seen the devastation including severe injury and environmental damage caused by landmines during the twenty-one years of fighting for freedom, the movement/army of liberation of the people of Sudan banned the use of landmines in all combat operations. We have defended the cause of the treaty before becoming a state.
>
> (Republic of South Sudan 2011; International Campaign to Ban Landmines 2011b)

[7] In interviews Turkish officials have reiterated the view that the decision to join the MBT was a 'very brave decision' due to the domestic and regional security environment that includes concerns over cross-border smuggling and ongoing military operations against Kurdish rebels. Nonetheless, joining the MBT was important because it constitutes 'one of the main dimensions of [Turkey's] security policy'. Interview with Dr Maike Selçuk Sancar, Counsellor, Permanent Mission of Turkey to the United Nations Office at Geneva. Geneva, 26 October 2009.

In another fascinating example, 'the [previous] use of landmines by the African National Congress (ANC) during its struggle against the apartheid regime in South Africa was specifically criticized by the Truth and Reconciliation Commission for being indiscriminate in its effects' (Maslen 2005, 1:11). Significantly, the incumbent ANC acknowledged its past actions, and suggested that it had abandoned the use of AP mines even before the formal advent of the MBT because the practice 'was, according to its own principled humanitarian norms, leading to an unacceptable loss of civilian lives'.[8] The adoption of this position was regarded, moreover, as a symbol of South Africa's reintroduction to the community of states during the transition from apartheid to democracy.

As the South African case demonstrates, the transformation in a core feature of national policy also occurred in states that came to be key supporters of the movement to ban AP mines—and hence allegedly easy cases for norm adoption. Looking back from the vantage point of today, the acceptability of a prohibition may seem over-determined. Yet before the advent of the mine ban movement, AP mines were not regarded as especially horrendous weapons worthy of particular opprobrium, even among subsequent diplomatic leaders like Canada (Tomlin 1998; Warmington and Tuttle 1998). In his seminal article, Price (1998) argued that exposure to the normative claims of the ban movement was instrumental in rapidly shifting elite opinion in a number of states to re-conceptualize military utility in light of new social expectation concerning humanitarian effects, via mechanisms of persuasion and emulation.[9] Italy, formerly one of the largest AP mine producers, therefore decided to join pro-ban constituency 'not because anti-personnel mines have in our view become militarily redundant or obsolete, but because we have accorded priority status to the disarmament and humanitarian aspects of the issue' (Italian Republic 2004). Similarly, 'the United Kingdom (UK) Ministry of Defence believe[d] that in renouncing anti-personnel mines it ha[d] lost an operational capability, but it ha[d] accepted to do so because of the humanitarian imperative' (Maslen 2005, 1:13).[10]

As this intersubjective process picked up pace, leaders of like-minded nations 'felt it intolerable to be left outside the club of responsible international citizens once they judged that the balance had tipped such that resistance

[8] Submission of the African National Congress to the Truth and Reconciliation Commission in Reply to the Section 30(2) of Act 34 of 1996 on the TRC 'Findings on the African National Congress', October 1998. Quoted in Maslen (2005, 1:11–12, n. 54).

[9] Detailed discussions of civil society movements in various key countries can be found in Cameron, Lawson, and Tomlin (1998).

[10] Diplomats familiar with the negotiations confirm this view, and acknowledge the difficult nature of the decision. Interview with Guy Pollard, Counsellor in the Nuclear and Conventional Weapons Section, United Kingdom Delegation to the Conference on Disarmament. Geneva, 8 December 2010. It is also widely believed that the death of Princess Diana, who had been intimately associated with the mine ban movement, added further pressure on the UK to join the ban.

signalled outlier status' (Price 1998, 635). Accordingly, Jody Williams and Stephen Goose report that the awarding of the Nobel Peace prize to the International Campaign to Ban Landmines (ICBL) was particularly instrumental in compelling Japan—long an ambivalent participant in the mine ban negotiations—to endorse the MBT as a centrepiece of Japanese policy (Williams and Goose 1998, 46). As Petrice Flowers points out, this constituted a radical departure even for an officially pacifist state, since the decision to join came in the face of extensive US pressure and cut against 'the entrenched idea that land mines were an essential tool necessary to defend Japan in case of land invasion' (Flowers 2009, 7; Japan 1997; Japan 2004). As with a number of other states, concerns for status and legitimacy ultimately provided the permissive conditions for formal membership, as Japan joined the mine ban in order to reinforce its identity as an advocate of humanitarianism and role model for the Asian region 'as part of Japan's international mission to pursue security through peace' (Flowers 2009, 139). The normative force of the treaty was thus instrumental in reshaping a basic expectation of state policy such that adherence to the prohibition of AP mines became the standard against which other competing interests—including the conduct of military operations and the territorial defence of the state—are assessed. This reflects both a constitutive redefinition of state identity in line with the humanitarian calculus of the ban norm, and the consequential acceptance of new behavioural standards reflecting this social role.

In other instances, recognition of new social expectations has created political space for the gradual transformation of state identities and interests even where immediate membership was regarded as unacceptable. A number of states have made a point of signalling their support for the humanitarian purpose of the MBT, even while asserting that domestic conditions—most notably armed conflicts, regional instability, or the lack of technical capacity to meet treaty obligations—precluded earlier membership (Federal Democratic Republic of Ethiopia 2001; Republic of Belarus 2000; Republic of Indonesia 1997; Republic of Indonesia 2004; Republic of Sudan 2001; Republic of Turkey 2007a; The Transitional Federal Government of Somalia 2004; Ukraine 2003). Here again, the adoption of pro-treaty discourse is not a mere diplomatic nicety, but can signal an important transition in the sensitivity of actors to relevant legal obligations and broader social expectations. Prior to joining the treaty as a full member, for example, Turkey implemented a formal moratorium on mine use that was explicitly justified in light of 'the changing defensive concept of border areas as well as the enhanced activities related to the prohibition of [AP mines] in the world' (Republic of Turkey 2003). These incremental changes also had political consequences, as the rhetorical endorsement of the mine ban norm narrowed the range of justifications for continued non-membership. Subsequent discussions consequently focused on these more specific criteria and the merits of the mine ban, and provided a rhetorical opening that was exploited by the ICBL and other states to push target governments to progressively close the gap between their stated aims and actual policies.

Finland and Poland, for example, were consistent principled supporters of the mine ban, even as both long insisted that their elimination of AP mines could only occur once alternative military systems were available to replace their operational functions in border security and the protection of military assets (Republic of Finland 2002; Republic of Poland 2007).[11] This discursive acceptance of an authoritative standard was not mere cynical rhetoric, designed to placate mine ban proponents without meaningful consequences, as sceptics would expect. Rather, the repeated profession of normative support drew both states into the diplomatic environment of the mine ban movement, and generated conditions in which domestic constituencies, civil society actors, and other states—most especially members of the European Union—could exert pressure on the respective governments to formalize their commitment via ratification. This played out via iterative engagements at MBT meetings and other diplomatic fora, involving the use of legal argumentation and broader forms of persuasion and social pressure.

The political desire to adhere to the mine ban, in turn, stimulated a dedicated search for alternative technologies to replace AP mines in the military doctrine of both states—an effort that interacted with a perceived improvement in their security situations.[12] Yet such assessments were not strictly rooted in a material judgement that mines are no longer useful, as a realist account would suggest, but rather relied to a substantial degree on shifting conceptions of appropriate behaviour occasioned by the MBT. The key here was the reciprocal interaction between an external social stigma and domestically derived perception of interests, in which relevant policy actors came to accept that national security goals could be achieved without AP

[11] The primary strategic concern for both nations has been perceived vulnerability to a Russian invasion on their eastern borders. In previous Polish military doctrine, AP mines were envisioned strictly as a means of protecting deployed anti-tank mine fields. Interview with Dr (Colonel) Marek Zadrożny, Counsellor and Military Adviser, Permanent Mission of Poland to the United Nations Office in Geneva. Geneva, 27 October 2009; and personal email correspondence, 16 June 2012.

[12] Interview with Elina Dakash, Attaché, Unit for Arms Control, Disarmament and Non-Proliferation, Ministry of Foreign Affairs of Finland. Geneva, 2 December 2010. Zadrożny interviews 2009 and 2010. Interview with Kasia Derlicka-Rosenbauer, Advocacy and Campaigning Officer, International Campaign to Ban Landmines. Geneva, 22 October 2009 and 7 December 2010. Interview with Kerry Brinkert, Director, Implementation Support Unit of the Antipersonnel Mine Ban Treaty. Geneva, 30 October 2009 and 8 December 2010. Given similar geographic and historical concerns relating to a perceived threat from the Russian Federation, it is interesting to compare the experiences of Finland and Poland with those of the Baltic states. Estonia, Latvia, and Lithuania all previously cited fragile security conditions as the reason for their ambivalence to the MBT. After being granted membership in the North Atlantic Treaty Organization, all three joined the MBT (Chamberlain and Long 2004, 87–8).

mines.[13] Ultimately, the legitimacy of the mine ban norm made it politically intolerable to remain outside of a community to which both states otherwise naturally align. Finland therefore ratified the MBT in January 2012 while Poland followed suit in December of the same year.

Among treaty members, therefore, the social legitimacy and legal authority of the AP mine ban is now well established. This discussion also draws attention to the competing considerations at play in the formulation of state policy, and suggest that national identities and interests are not immutable 'facts', but are instead subject to significant redefinition over time. Just as importantly, States Party discourse contains explicit reference to the treaty as the expression of a new international social standard: the legalized environment of the MBT is thus the reference point for the broader norm banning landmines.

CHANGING INTERNATIONAL BEHAVIOUR: COMPLIANCE WITH CORE PROHIBITIONS

Are States Parties modifying their practices in light of this new intersubjective expectation, and thus matching their statements of support with actions? After all, the experience from human rights treaties suggests that ratification often does not generate meaningful changes in policy, especially in vulnerable states (Hafner-Burton and Tsutsui 2007; Neumayer 2005). Yet in the present case, all of the most relevant metrics point to a rapidly declining reliance on AP mines over the past two decades.

The Use of Antipersonnel Mines

Since 1998 the deployment of AP mines has dropped dramatically across the international system. Fifteen state actors were confirmed to have used AP

[13] Derlicka interview 2010; Brinkert interview 2010; Dakash interview; and Zadrożny interviews 2009 and 2010 and email correspondence. Interestingly, this occurred within the uniformed armed forces prior to some members of the political elite. According to interview sources, a 2003–4 internal review by the Polish Armed Forces concluded that AP mines were no longer essential to their operational plans. This led to the 2004 announcement that Poland would ratify the Convention by 2006. Subsequent national elections resulted in a more nationalistic government in Poland that created favourable conditions for some defence experts and advisers to try to convince decision-makers that renunciation of AP mines would evidently be harmful to the Polish defence system. The new Minister of Defence (post-2006 election) was identified as the primary source of the decision to reverse the earlier commitment and delay ratification, initially until 2015. However, the Polish Ministry of Foreign Affairs had long been supportive of the MBT, and a compromise solution was reached for official ratification in 2012.

mines in 1998, when annual civil society reporting began; this figure has fallen precipitously in the years since, with a small uptick in 2011 and 2015 (Figure 4.2).[14] This trend line is notable because it is not matched by a similar decline in the frequency of violence in the international system: while the total number of armed conflicts has ebbed since the early 1990s, organized violence remains common. Moreover, intra-state conflicts—precisely those in which inexpensive and uncomplicated weapons predominate—continue in significant numbers.[15] Yet the use of AP mines has now become an aberration in international practice. Were it not for the effective stigmatization of the weapon initiated by the mine ban movement and treaty, we would expect AP mines to feature in a greater number of these conflicts, many of which had seen past use of the weapons. Moreover, as I show below, to the extent that violations of the norm persist, they are understood in qualitatively different terms than prior to the mine ban's emergence.

The MBT has been especially effective in consolidating behaviour among its members.[16] Virtually all confirmed cases of mine use since 1998 have involved non-parties to the MBT. However, credible evidence now suggests that Turkey (2009 and 2011) and Yemen (2011) engaged in new deployments of AP mines in contravention of their legal obligations (International Campaign to Ban Landmines 2013a, 3–7; United Press International 2010).[17] Violations by a States Party are especially damaging since they provide specific challenge to the absolute nature of the mine ban norm from within the legal community of treaty members. Angola, Ecuador, Ethiopia, Guinea-Bissau, and Senegal are known to have used AP mines as signatories to the MBT, but the actions in all cases ceased in advance of full membership.[18] Seven further states—Burundi, Cambodia, Rwanda, South Sudan, Sudan, Uganda, and Zimbabwe—are suspected of employing mines as signatories or full parties, though these allegations could not be decisively confirmed. These instances detract from the generally positive compliance picture concerning non-use.

[14] Myanmar is the only state that has used mines in every reporting year. Russia was a persistent user until 2009, but has apparently abandoned the practice since, though recent allegations of mine use in Crimea call this into question.

[15] Data on inter-state and intra-state conflicts is summarized in Human Security Report Project (2013).

[16] Mine use by non-party states and non-state armed groups is discussed further in Chapter 5.

[17] Detailed discussion of the empirical basis for the allegations can be found in the ICBL's Landmine Monitor updated Country Reports. http://www.the-monitor.org/index.php/cp/display/region_profiles/theme/3939 and http://www.the-monitor.org/index.php/cp/display/region_profiles/theme/4003.

[18] International law holds that signatories are bound not to act in contravention of the spirit of their legal commitments (*Vienna Convention on the Law of Treaties* 1969, Art. 18). Senegal deployed AP mines after ratification but before entry-into-force of the treaty.

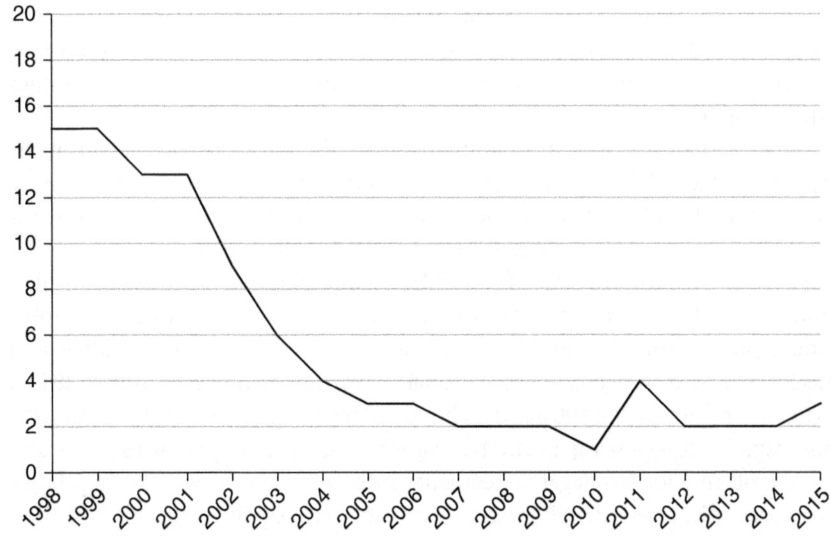

Figure 4.2. Confirmed antipersonnel mine use, 1999–2015

Note: Corresponding to the year of publication of Landmine Monitor. The annual report does not precisely overlap with the calendar year due to its usual publication in November. I checked all confirmed uses of AP mines to ensure that they were allocated to the correct year, and to guard against double-counting. The data for 1998 and 1999 years in the table are identical, since the first *Monitor* report (1999) covered December 1997–March 1999.

Production, Transfer, and Stockpiling of AP Mines

A very similar pattern can be discerned in respect to the production, transfer, and stockpiling of AP mines. These are critical to the efficacy of the treaty and ban norm because they constitute the enabling conditions for mine use. Here too the record strongly suggests a rapidly strengthening stigmatization. The ICBL has identified at least fifty states that produced AP mines in the decades preceding the ban; thirty-eight have now definitively ceased production:

> [These] include a majority of the big producers in the 1970s, 1980s, and early 1990s—those who bear much of the responsibility for the tens of millions of mines now in the ground. Eight of the twelve biggest producers and exporters over the past thirty years have signed the treaty and stopped production: Belgium, Bosnia, Bulgaria, Czech Republic, France, Hungary, Italy, and the United Kingdom. Other significant producers that have signed include Germany, Croatia, Chile, and Brazil.
> (International Campaign to Ban Landmines 1999, 5–6; Vines 1998, 120)

Only twelve states have not formally renounced the right to produce mines, and all are MBT non-parties.[19] Of that diminished group, the majority—

[19] China, Cuba, India, Iran, Myanmar, North Korea, Pakistan, Russia, Singapore, South Korea, the United States, and Vietnam.

including the United States, China, and Russia—have ceased active production; only India, Myanmar, Pakistan, and South Korea are thought to be currently producing mines (International Campaign to Ban Landmines 2015, 3 and 11).

The mine ban has also profoundly impacted the international market in the weapons: since 1997 there have been no confirmed cases in which mines have been sold or transferred from one state to another state or rebel group. This contrasts with an estimated thirty-four states that were regular exporters of AP mines prior to the advent of the MBT (International Campaign to Ban Landmines 1999, 7). To the extent that it endures at all, therefore, the 'global trade in antipersonnel mines has consisted solely of a low-level of illicit and unacknowledged transfers' (International Campaign to Ban Landmines 2013a, 1), further reflecting the substantial change concerning the weapon's legitimacy. This rapidly crystallizing norm has similarly generated pressures for states outside of the formal legal agreement, most commonly via the legislative moratoria, discussed in Chapter 5. Such acts are significant both for their practical effects—reducing the availability of the weapons—and for their symbolic reinforcement of the humanitarian principles at the heart of the MBT.

Progress in the destruction of national stockpiles is a further important measure of state adherence to the mine ban, since the physical elimination of AP mines is necessary to ensure they do not enter operational use at a later date. Here again compliance has been extensive: 154 states—including four non-parties[20]—are judged to have no remaining stockpiles, save for those permitted to be retained for training purposes.[21] In total, approximately 49 million mines have been destroyed by States Parties up to the end of 2013 (International Campaign to Ban Landmines 2015, 14). Moreover, in recent years major non-party states like China and the United States have destroyed millions of AP mines—one aspect of more general patterns of informal compliance discussed

[20] Palestine, Marshall Islands, Micronesia, and Tonga. The status of Palestinian statehood is hotly contested, and will not be addressed here. The ICBL regards Palestine as a political entity equivalent to a state for its reporting purposes. In the context of the ICC, see pages 124–5, this volume.

[21] Sixty-three States Parties never possessed AP mines, or destroyed their stocks prior to joining the treaty. In one respect this may be interpreted as a sign that the MBT did not impose significant new constraints on many members and thus provides only a weak independent influence on state policy. Yet the majority (87) of States Parties *did* possess AP mine stockpiles at the time of their ratification; the record of compliance on this score has been an important indicator of treaty health. Moreover, a few states completed destruction prior to joining the treaty, and with these obligations thus in mind. Article 3 of the MBT states that 'Notwithstanding the general obligations under Article 1, the retention or transfer of a number of anti-personnel mines for the development of and training in mine detection, mine clearance, or mine destruction techniques is permitted. The amount of such mines shall not exceed the minimum number absolutely necessary for the above-mentioned purposes.' However, the precise nature of this exception has been debated since the conclusion of the treaty and no precise agreement currently exists.

more fully in Chapter 5. The elimination of these weapons in the military arsenals of the overwhelming majority of states has reinforced the authority of the mine ban norm by placing AP mines beyond the realm of 'normal' military operations. To overcome the force of the injunction would therefore require the more substantial decision to reconstitute domestic production capacities or acquire mines from foreign sources. In this respect, the normative and material effect of the treaty has been to remove AP mines from the menu of options across a large portion of the international system.

On the other hand, the optimistic view of a strengthening norm is challenged by the fact that Belarus, Greece, Turkey, and Ukraine all failed to meet their stockpile destruction deadlines, placing them in serious breach of their legal obligations. It is also significant that the non-compliance has continued for a number of years: Turkey completed its destruction obligations in 2011 (Republic of Turkey 2011), yet the other three states still have nearly nine million AP mines remaining to be destroyed among them.[22] These violations have generally not been met with a forceful response from other States Parties. To the extent that non-compliance is not widely denounced as atypical and unacceptable, it risks eroding the taboo since it 'can be indicative of a lack of "congruence" between existing norms and international practice' (Brunnée and Toope 2010, 113). Yet the discourse of the non-compliant parties themselves suggests that contrary practice has not been normalized: as I show below, none of the implicated states has asserted a right to retain mines in contravention of the MBT, and each party has instead sought to characterize their violations as the product of specific technical challenges.

Clearance of Mined Areas

Article 5(1) of the MBT requires that all States Parties 'destroy or ensure the destruction of all anti-personnel mines in mined areas under its jurisdiction or control, as soon as possible but not later than ten years after the entry into force of this Convention for that States Party'. (Maslen 2005, 1:165–84) While accorded less attention in this study, mine clearance is an important feature of the broader prohibitionary effort as it reinforces the humanitarian purpose of the treaty. State progress in clearing mined areas has been much less dramatic than the destruction of mine stockpiles. By the time the MBT entered into force in 1999, 103 states had already declared themselves to be mine-free; this included

[22] In June 2011 Turkey announced that it had completed domestic destruction of its mine stockpiles, and had transferred the remaining 22,716 'ADAM'-type mines to Germany for immediate destruction, thus rendering itself compliant with Article 4 of the MBT. As of November 2015, mines were retained in the following quantities: Belarus (2,861,636), Greece (452,695), and Ukraine (5,767,600) (International Campaign to Ban Landmines 2015, 14).

forty-eight states that were by then full parties, thirty-three signatories, and twenty-two non-parties. This represents a baseline of unaffected states for which the obligations arising from Article 5 were largely irrelevant. Fifteen years later, only twenty-eight States Parties have subsequently declared their completion of their Article 5 commitments. In the overwhelming majority of cases, therefore, mine-free status occurred prior to, and thus independent of, ratification of the MBT. Sixty-one states are thought to be mine-affected including thirty-three States Parties that have continuing obligations to clear known mined areas (States Parties to the Antipersonnel Mine Ban Treaty 2014c, 17; International Campaign to Ban Landmines 2015, 17).

The relatively small increase in fully compliant states underscores the challenges inherent in addressing widespread AP mine contamination. Forty-one States Parties have sought—and received—extensions to their ten-year clearance deadlines, as permitted under the MBT (Gabelnick 2008).[23] While envisioned within treaty rules, the nature of many of these extensions suggests ambivalence toward the clearance obligation. On the one hand, many states receiving extensions exhibited limited effort during their initial compliance period. On the other hand, even severely affected states have frequently made only limited progress due to various impediments; indeed, only six states have subsequently completed their clearance obligations, and a number of states have now undertaken multiple extensions (International Campaign to Ban Landmines 2013a, 26). In particular, the ICBL has highlighted insufficient survey of suspected mined areas; poor planning, management, and reporting structures; and insufficient resource allocation (both domestically and from international donors) as fundamental impediments to greater progress in mine clearance (International Campaign to Ban Landmines 2009a). In most instances, these failings are indicative of a lack of political commitment. The ICBL has therefore expressed the view that persistent failure to demonstrate progress in clearance obligations should properly be regarded as a fundamental violation of the MBT.

Humanitarian Outcomes

While not the principal focus of this study, some brief attention must also be paid to the humanitarian impact occasioned by the behavioural patterns

[23] Afghanistan, Algeria, Angola, Argentina, Bosnia and Herzegovina, Cambodia, Chad, Chile, Colombia, Congo, Croatia, Cyprus, Democratic Republic of the Congo, Denmark, Ecuador, Eritrea, Ethiopia, Germany, Guinea-Bissau, Iraq, Jordan, Mauritania, Mozambique, Nicaragua, Niger, Oman, Peru, Senegal, Serbia, Somalia, South Sudan, Sudan, Tajikistan, Thailand, Turkey, Uganda, Ukraine, United Kingdom, Venezuela, Yemen, and Zimbabwe (International Campaign to Ban Landmines 2013a, 27). For documents pertaining to the extension requests, please see http://www.apminebanconvention.org/background-status-of-the-convention/clearing-mined-areas/article-5-extensions/states-parties-requests-for-extension-deadlines/.

described above. After all, the movement to ban AP mines was spurred and has been sustained most fundamentally by a profound moral commitment to rectifying the egregious consequences of the weapons for civilian populations. Here too the MBT has had important impact: most notably, there has been a substantial decrease in the number of new victims attributed to landmines (both AP and anti-vehicle) and explosive remnants of war (ERW) more generally, which would include any unexploded munitions including rockets, mortars, and artillery shells.[24] In 2014, there were 3,678 mine/ERW casualties reported globally, a figure that, while still morally objectionable, represents a dramatic decline—of approximately 60 per cent—from the 9,220 reported in 1999, the first year that the ICBL undertook annual monitoring.[25] Casualties were reported in fifty-eight states and other areas in, down from seventy-two in 1999 (International Campaign to Ban Landmines 2015, 25–6).

Interestingly, these changes occurred almost entirely among States Parties, with only limited decline in casualty rates in most non-party states (International Campaign to Ban Landmines 2014b, 3). This provides yet more evidence for the contention that engagement with the treaty is reshaping state behaviour; specifically, the observance of MBT commitments concerning non-use and mine clearance, combined with greater awareness for mine risk education, is leading to better humanitarian outcomes. While more difficult to capture succinctly, there has also been modest improvement in the provision of assistance for victims, whether taking the form of direct financial assistance; access to social programmes, rehabilitation, and physical infrastructure; and domestic legal changes (International Campaign to Ban Landmines 2013a, 43–57; States Parties to the Antipersonnel Mine Ban Treaty 2014c, 23–51). International funding for mine action (encompassing clearance, education, and victim assistance) has increased steadily over the past two decades. Over $400 million was donated to mine action programmes in fifty-two states in 2012, up from just over $300 million in 2002, but declining against previous years.[26] Whether these positive trends can be sustained—and further

[24] Given the challenges in determining the precise weapon responsible for an injury or death in many instances, the ICBL does not disaggregate their data by weapon type. However, the ICBL estimates that victim-activated weapons—such as factory-made AP mines and improvised explosive devices—accounted for 45% of casualties (International Campaign to Ban Landmines 2013a, 37, n. 4 and 41).

[25] Despite these important advances, civilians account for fully 80% of recorded victims, a figure that appears to be consistent across recent time. The ICBL also notes that 'due to incomplete data collection at the national level, the true casualty total is higher... It is estimated that there are approximately an additional 800–1,000 casualties each year that are not captured in its global mine/ERW casualty statistics, with most occurring in severely affected countries' (International Campaign to Ban Landmines 2013a, 40).

[26] In US dollars. Assistance is highly concentrated among a few key donors: while thirty-three states provided funding in 2014, three (the United States, Japan, and Norway) accounted for over half of all financial contributions. The European Union, Germany, the Netherlands, Australia, and the United Kingdom are also major contributors (International Campaign to Ban Landmines 2015, 38).

improved—in the future will depend largely on existing States Parties completing their obligations and the incorporation of current non-member states within the MBT legal community (States Parties to the Antipersonnel Mine Ban Treaty 2014b).

EXCEPTIONAL POLITICS: PUBLIC DISCOURSE AND THE STATUS OF THE MINE BAN NORM

The close temporal connection between the emergence of the MBT and the scale of behavioural change powerfully demonstrates the treaty's influence in altering state practice. Yet this provides only a partial window into the effectiveness of international institutions; what states *say* about legal developments—how they articulate conceptions of the nature and limit of obligations—is also indicative of the influence of international laws and norms.

In accordance with the expectations outlined in Chapters 2 and 3, the observed shift in social expectations has been largely reinforced in moments where the prohibition has come under threat from real or apparent violations. In assessing the impact of violations on the status of the mine ban norm, we are chiefly interested in how the given act is situated within the scope of possible behaviours—that is, whether it is understood as a genuine aberration, or a foreseeable (if regrettable) outcome that is to be expected. 'Important here is the intersubjective phenomenon that the transgressor feels compelled to justify (or deny) the violation because of mutually shared expectations that such behaviour is normally unacceptable and requires defence to reconfirm the status of the violator as a legitimate member of international society' (Price 2004a, 114). Discursive practices—both the initial claims and subsequent responses from states and other actors—have served to further reify the prohibition as the relevant community standard, thereby demonstrating additional ways that mine ban norm has altered the political space within which diplomatic engagements occur.

Public Denials

Reports of violations have, in the first instance, frequently been met with vigorous denials from the implicated actors. In addressing allegations that his country had deployed AP mines during operations in the Democratic Republic of the Congo, the Zimbabwean delegate to the Second Meeting of States Parties emphatically denounced the charges as 'wild and unsubstantiated':

> Such a falsehood only serves to destroy the spirit of the Convention. [The] ICBL's failure to provide evidence or concrete facts for the past two years to show that

> Zimbabwe is using anti-personnel mines in the Democratic Republic of Congo does not only invalidate these accusations but also smacks of a hidden agenda against my country... Zimbabwe will never be diverted or deterred from implementing the provisions of the Ottawa Convention because we have victims of landmines and we know the dangers of using landmines. In fact, Zimbabwe has assumed a leadership role in championing the ban on the use of landmines and their ultimate destruction. (Republic of Zimbabwe 2000)

This response is typical of a pattern that is apparent with other states including Burundi,[27] Cambodia,[28] Ethiopia,[29] Guinea-Bissau,[30] Rwanda,[31] Senegal,[32] Sudan,[33] and Uganda.[34] Such interventions offer important evidence of an expanding sense of obligation that can be traced directly to the MBT. Indeed, were it not for a strengthening international norm prohibiting the use of AP mines, such incidents would likely go unremarked upon, and there would be little reason for states to issue denials or otherwise obscure their behaviour. Even if the alleged acts did not in fact take place, and the state was merely correcting inaccurate information, it is significant that violations of the MBT are deemed sufficiently important as to be worthy of response at all.

The apparent need to refute accusations or otherwise conceal transgressions stems instead from a sensitivity to international standing in which the mine ban represents a core standard of appropriateness. This goes beyond a more generic concern for rule-following as a source of status: many treaties are violated and the infringements are often given little notice. It is only because AP mines have come to be so widely condemned that states should seek to specifically distance themselves from such behaviours so as to preserve their reputation as responsible actors. Importantly, the crux of each allegation and response focused not on a belief that general rules of war—such as deliberately targeting civilians or using disproportionate military force—had been transgressed, but on a more specific view that AP mines, as a class of weapons defined by the criteria of the MBT, were *particularly* illegitimate. Under such

27 International Campaign to Ban Landmines (2004, 234–7, esp. n. 17).

28 International Campaign to Ban Landmines (2013e); Kingdom of Cambodia (2008).

29 Fisseha Adugna, Chargé d'affaires, Embassy of Ethiopia, Washington, DC (1999). Ethiopia has also vigorously denied that it supplied landmines to Somalia in 2006 (International Campaign to Ban Landmines 2009b, 422, n. 6).

30 International Campaign to Ban Landmines (2000b).

31 International Campaign to Ban Landmines (2001b).

32 Senegal has categorically denied that it laid AP mines either on its own territory or in Guinea-Bissau (Republic of Senegal 1999).

33 Republic of Sudan (2000); Republic of Sudan (2001).

34 After allegations surfaced regarding the use of AP mines by Ugandan security forces during the violence in Kisangani, the government vigorously denied the charges and pledged a full investigation (Republic of Uganda 2001). The results of this internal process were never divulged. Uganda subsequently repeated this position, and also denied that they had resumed production of AP landmines (Republic of Uganda 2002; International Campaign to Ban Landmines 2009b, 758–9).

circumstances it is the the use of AP mines, rather than the failure to uphold binding legal commitments in the abstract, that provides the referent point for anticipated social sanctions constituting an unpalatable political cost. These developments only make sense in an international environment in which the prohibition concerning AP mines has expanded beyond a merely consensual commitment among sovereign units to become a prominent independent marker of legitimacy. De facto rhetorical support, even when detached from actual practice, can thus actually serve to reinforce rather than degrade the mine ban norm, as Chapter 3 contended.

Instrumentalizing Norms: Allegations as a Political Tool

Inversely, a number of conflicts involving parties to the MBT have featured accusations of mine use that had the apparent intention of discrediting the opposing side. This has been witnessed in conflicts between Ethiopia and Eritrea,[35] Cambodia and Thailand,[36] and most recently between Ukraine and the Russian Federation over control of the Crimean Peninsula.[37] In a number of other instances—including in the Philippines, South Sudan, Sudan, and Uganda—States Parties have publicly blamed rebel groups for mine use within their borders (International Campaign to Ban Landmines 2013b; International Campaign to Ban Landmines 2013c; Republic of the Philippines 2013; Republic of Uganda 2002). These engagements have served a dual function of simultaneously demonstrating restraint and good standing on the part of the accuser, and marking their opponents as irresponsible actors.

The deployment of allegations thus represents an attempt by actors to instrumentalize the mine ban in their political disputes either as a means of weakening their adversaries or deflecting blame from their own actions. Importantly, accusing states have invoked the mine ban as the relevant standard for assessing international status: 'Being a responsible State Party of the Ottawa Treaty, Ukraine remains adherent to its international obligations and is ready to undertake all necessary measures to destroy anti-personnel mines in mined areas under its jurisdiction. However, this could be done only after my country will regain control of the territory currently occupied by the aggressor' (Ukraine 2014c). Interestingly, such appeals have been directed both towards other States Parties—who possess legal obligations under the treaty—and those states like the Russian Federation or numerous non-state armed groups that do not. This,

[35] Fisseha Adugna, Chargé d'affaires, Embassy of Ethiopia, Washington, DC (1999); International Campaign to Ban Landmines (2000a).

[36] International Campaign to Ban Landmines (2009b, 243–4, 719–20); International Campaign to Ban Landmines (2013e); Kingdom of Cambodia (2008); Kingdom of Thailand (2008).

[37] Ukraine (2014c).

in turn, reflects the breadth and power of the stigma since states may seek to gain political advantage by associating their adversaries with the use of AP mines, even in instances where the alleged violators are outside the legal scope of the ban. In sum, successful strategic appeals must tap into collective standards that a relevant community of actors recognize as salient and worthy of respect. Yet this presupposes some potent collective expectation that interlocutors and relevant third parties can mutually understand and act on, further illustrating the utility of integrating instrumental/rationalist and normative/constructivist logics of international action (Bower 2015).

Claims of Exceptional Mitigation

In contrast, a few states have acknowledged violations, yet sought to portray their actions as fundamentally unique situations that did not invalidate their general respect for treaty obligations. Thus at the Second Meeting of States Parties in September 2000, the Angolan Ambassador specifically identified the ongoing civil war—and the existential threat faced by the current government—as necessitating the use of AP mines while signatories:

> We ask your understanding for the few antipersonnel mines that the…Armed Forces of Angola, have planted around strategic facilities, when the troops of Mr. Jonas Savimbi wanted to seize power by force, ignoring democratic institutions and bombing villages, communes and certain big cities of the country in an indiscriminate and blind manner. Allow us, Mr. President, to affirm here that mining or re-mining land has never been a right of the Angolan state…but rather…the unique way to survive for those that suffer from the injustice and murderous madness of the rebels. The mines that the Angolan army have used are marked and well located, they do not represent any danger for the population nor any difficulty to find them or destroy them. (International Campaign to Ban Landmines 2001a, n. 91)

Angola's statement is interesting both for its claim to exceptional justification, and for the fact that the acknowledged violations were framed as a limited and humane transgression within previously existing restraints of international law. More recently, Yemeni representatives have acknowledged the use of AP mines around a military base in 2011 during armed clashes with local tribes, on similar grounds of defending against the collapse of the state (Republic of Yemen 2014).

Discursive justifications of this kind present a challenge to the absolute prohibition of AP mines, as they suggest some—even highly circumscribed—conditions under which their use might be permitted. Stuart Maslen (Maslen 2005, 1:77) has argued, for example, that Angola's defence was based on a view 'that the Convention should implicitly allow an exception to the core obligations amid an ongoing armed conflict'. The net effect might therefore be to erode the authoritative absoluteness of the ban norm and degrade the central premise of the legal prohibition. While this concern is appropriate, the implications for the broader health of the MBT are more modest. First, the language of the interventions can be read as narrower and more dramatic anomalies—truly special cases in which the purported survival of the state is at stake. The particular severity of the situation was presented as a necessary exception to a more general support for the mine ban, and was not held to lead to a generalized right to use the weapons. In this sense, the exceptional circumstances actually serve to reinforce the authority of the prohibition under normal conditions, and in which the very criteria and scope of 'normal' has been greatly expanded. This again is a substantial change from the prevailing pattern before the mine ban movement, in which AP mines were regarded as thoroughly unproblematic weapons. Thus the threshold for violations remains exceedingly high, even if the absolute prohibition has been breached in some discrete cases.

Just as importantly, the justifications were not endorsed by other states as qualifying as legitimate exceptions to the prohibition. Without making reference to any instance in particular, delegates to the second Meeting of States Parties were clear in their condemnation of ongoing mine use: 'We implore those States that have declared their commitment to the object and purpose of the Convention and that continue to use anti-personnel mines to recognize that this is a clear violation of their solemn commitment. We call upon all States concerned to respect their commitments' (States Parties to the Antipersonnel Mine Ban Treaty 2000, para. 6). States Parties have issued repeated, if often cautious, statements reiterating the absolute prohibition since (e.g. States Parties to the Antipersonnel Mine Ban Treaty, 2014c, 72). In sum, a very few states have justified their use of AP mines under limited conditions, they have not deployed this claim as a means of systematically challenging the legitimacy of the MBT, and MBT States Parties have not recognized these cases as producing either de facto or *de jure* exceptions to the universal prohibition concerning AP mine use.

A number of States Parties have invoked claims of special circumstances in explaining other violations, however. For example, states like Iraq and Sudan have justified their slow progress in mine clearance in terms of ongoing armed conflict on their territories which has generated new mine contamination (from use by non-state groups) and led to a lack of sufficient resources for demining (Republic of Iraq 2014; Republic of Sudan 2014). More seriously, Belarus, Greece, Turkey, and Ukraine have each justified their non-compliance regarding stockpile destruction in terms of technical challenges. Both Belarus and Ukraine have noted the particular difficulties in destroying PFM-type mines containing volatile chemicals, and have repeatedly reiterated that they lack the independent capacities to meet their obligations.[38]

[38] These conditions are said to be exacerbated by the numerous national projects aimed at decommissioning Soviet-era weapons which collectively exact 'a heavy burden for the national

Interestingly, the failure has been blamed on the inability of the European Commission, as the contracting partner, to find suitable tenders for the destruction contracts (Republic of Belarus 2008; Ukraine 2014d). Greece has similarly blamed its non-compliance on contractual and technical challenges associated with the tendering process and the selection of two private companies to undertake destruction (Hellenic Republic of Greece 2010a; Hellenic Republic of Greece 2010b). Finally, before completing its obligations in 2011, Turkey has mounted perhaps the most systematic defence in asserting that its choice of destruction techniques—in particular its need to comply with European environmental standards regarding hazardous materials—had necessitated the delay (Republic of Turkey 2007b; Republic of Turkey 2008). Turkey's framing of the challenge is especially interesting, as it associated itself with purportedly superior operational standards in excusing its non-compliance, and thereby cultivated an image of a serious and responsible actor.

Yet claims of special mitigation have not been leveraged as a means of challenging the legitimacy of legal obligations or the authority of the mine ban more generally, but rather reflect the considerable power of the legal norm. Greek delegations for example have repeatedly evidenced sensitivity to legal obligations and the social consequences of their outlier status (Hellenic Republic of Greece 2010a; Hellenic Republic of Greece 2008). Civil society campaigners have suggested that Greek diplomats in Geneva are embarrassed by the lack of progress, and the resulting critiques from other states and the ICBL.[39] In that spirit, Greek delegates have repeatedly stated that 'the implementation hurdles in the destruction process of our remaining stockpiles should in no way be construed as a deliberate failure or lack of willingness to comply with the obligations stipulated by the Convention' (Hellenic Republic of Greece 2013). These states have therefore sought to regularly justify their non-conformance through public diplomacy—including updates concerning progress towards meeting commitments—as part of an iterative dialogue among other treaty parties and civil society observers (e.g. Republic of Belarus, 2010, 2014; Ukraine, 2010a, 2014b). These engagements appear to have reinforced the salience of collective expectations among mine ban community members, and generated greater sensitivity to the perceived social costs of non-conformance.

budget . . . and demand substantial engagement of human resources' (Ukraine 2010a). Both Belarus and Ukraine previously cited the lack of material capacity as the primary factor inhibiting them from joining the MBT at an earlier date (Republic of Belarus 1997; Ukraine 1997).

[39] Interview with Tamar Gabelnick, Treaty Implementation Director, International Campaign to Ban Landmines. Geneva, 19 October 2009.

The Discursive Structure of Accountability: Investigations and Social Status

Finally, these same dynamics are also apparent in instances where states have responded to non-compliance concerns with domestic policy action. The most serious recent allegations of mine use—in Cambodia, South Sudan, Turkey, Uganda, and Yemen—have all been met with promises of formal investigations and, where relevant, the punishment of responsible individuals (International Campaign to Ban Landmines 2004, 834–5; International Campaign to Ban Landmines 2013h; Kingdom of Cambodia 2008; Kingdom of Cambodia 2013; Republic of South Sudan 2013a; Republic of South Sudan 2013b; Republic of Turkey 2010b; Republic of Turkey 2013; Republic of Yemen 2013; Republic of Yemen 2014). In the most advanced case to date, Turkey announced in May 2013 that a Brigadier General had been sentenced to more than six years in prison by a Turkish Military Court Martial for 'causing death and injury by negligence' in relation to his ordering the use of AP mines in 2009 (Republic of Turkey 2013; International Campaign to Ban Landmines 2013d).

Sceptics might understandably question the sincerity of such initiatives. Indeed, the initiation of investigations may represent genuine attempts to address potential wrongdoing or strategic responses designed to deflect pressure. But regardless of the initial intentions, the fact that states must react at all reflects a recognition of the expectations of the wider treaty community. As argued already with respect to accusations of non-compliance, attempts to gain political advantage by association with legal rules and norms rely on the prior existence of a powerful shared standard of behaviour against which specific actions can be judged. In other words, strategic concerns for gaining status or reputation through compliance with legal institutions—as understood in many prominent rational choice models (Guzman 2008)—presuppose a normative environment in which a community of actors both shares a conception of rightful action and possesses the capacity to bestow or remove these social benefits. For this reason, it is significant that the states in question have used the announcement of investigations as opportunities to reinforce their fidelity to the treaty: 'We emphasize that Yemen is a state party of MBT and confirm its full commitment to the Convention articles and implementation of the obligations' (Republic of Yemen 2013). The very fact that states should seek to gain instrumental benefit from conformance with the MBT—regardless of the underlying motivations for their professed support—therefore only serves to reinforce the social power of the mine ban.

Given the intersubjective nature of international law, these engagements draw actors into a discursive environment in which their claims are interrogated by other states and civil society actors within the MBT community. The ICBL has therefore pushed target states to conduct thorough investigations and where necessary to enact suitable penal punishments, and to improve their transparency by providing more extensive details to fellow MBT members concerning the scope and pace of proceedings (International Campaign to Ban Landmines 2013h). The ICBL has been particularly critical of Turkey and Yemen for the lack of detail in their initial reports, and has additionally raised questions over the conviction of the Turkish General on terms that did not seem to specify the use of AP mines as a particular crime. As the next section makes clear, these reciprocal interactions grounded in information exchange and dialogue are vital to the development of the legal and normative community encompassing MBT members.

ENFORCING COMMUNITY EXPECTATIONS: RESPONSES TO VIOLATIONS AND THE IMPACT ON NORMS

As already suggested, discursive interventions by targeted states do not occur in a vacuum, but take place within a diplomatic context in which other state members and civil society actors frequently engage in forms of public and private diplomacy with the aim of reinforcing the legal authority of the treaty. Documentation from official MBT meetings reveals widespread participation on issues relating to the status and operation of the treaty, such as universalization of its membership and compliance challenges (States Parties to the Antipersonnel Mine Ban Treaty 2009; States Parties to the Antipersonnel Mine Ban Treaty 2014a; States Parties to the Antipersonnel Mine Ban Treaty 2014c).[40] As I argued in Chapter 2, these iterative engagements are crucial to building a collective sense of legal community and with it a commitment to the treaty as legitimate and obligatory. In this light, non-compliance is much more significant to the extent that contrary behaviours become a regular feature of international practice and discourse, since this would serve to erode the authority of norms. Price (1998, 117) has previously noted that 'violations provide the most opportune moments to define and discipline a particular practice as an aberration.' A key issue, then, is how relevant actors respond to acknowledged non-compliance—how routine, in effect, has deviance become?

The empirical record reflects States Parties and non-governmental campaigners seeking to forge a delicate balance between positive engagement and critique. The ICBL has long demanded unambiguous statements of

[40] See for example the extensive discussions of compliance issues at the Third Review Conference and recent annual Meetings of States Parties and Intersessional Meetings. Records of MBT meetings including official government statements are archived at http://www.apminebanconvention.org/.

support for the mine ban norm in the face of contrary behaviours, and has sought to stimulate broader discussion of non-compliance among treaty members. For example, the ICBL has publicly criticized States Parties that have violated core treaty obligations, along with the many states requiring extensions to their mine clearance deadlines (International Campaign to Ban Landmines 2009c; International Campaign to Ban Landmines 2011a; International Campaign to Ban Landmines 2012; International Campaign to Ban Landmines 2013h; International Campaign to Ban Landmines 2014a; International Campaign to Ban Landmines 2014d).[41] Some states have taken up the prompt from civil society and have expressed concern at the impact non-compliance may have on the health of the mine ban norm (States Parties to the Antipersonnel Mine Ban Treaty 2009, 2; Swiss Confederation 2014).

Yet public condemnation may come at a price, especially in the context of a legal community predicated on a spirit of 'cooperative compliance . . . that assumes goodwill on the part of all States Parties and emphasizes resolution of issues in a nonconfrontational manner and assistance to help States Parties to meet their obligations rather than criticism for failing to do so' (Goose 2008b, 106). Official critiques of other treaty members are politically unpopular, especially within the professional diplomatic community. In many instances, therefore, constructive engagement has been the preferred means of reinforcing treaty norms; this is the strategy utilized by the International Committee of the Red Cross (ICRC), for example, in light of its official neutrality (International Committee of the Red Cross 2014). Some diplomats involved in the MBT processes have suggested that naming-and-shaming tactics are likely to backfire and have negative implications for the health of political dialogue.[42] States Parties have therefore often sought to praise targeted states for their progress in addressing violations, while at the same time calling for increased efforts—including greater transparency—to meet treaty obligations (Kingdom of Norway 2013; Netherlands 2014; Swiss Confederation 2014).

As anticipated by my theoretical account, treaty proponents have utilized MBT meetings to engage in interventions in support of the treaty, and have relied on the status of the MBT to classify violations as particularly significant deviations from socially acceptable practice. In this respect the discourse reveals internal hierarchies concerning the assessment of non-compliance, in terms of both the types of violations and the assumed reasons behind them. Belarus and Ukraine are typically judged to be subject to significant constraints in their ability to independently complete stockpile destruction; these acknowledged technical challenges result in a generally permissive approach (Canada 2009; International Committee of the Red Cross 2010; States Parties

[41] Privately, campaigners have questioned the sincerity of official commitments, describing some notable violations as 'careless' and 'silly', Derlicka interview 2009.

[42] Pollard interview 2010; Brinkert interview 2010.

to the Antipersonnel Mine Ban Treaty 2014c, 12). And while Greece and Turkey have been subjected to greater critique especially from the ICBL, the general tendency has been to assume good faith and publicly emphasize the successful features of state policy (Italian Republic and Republic of Zambia 2009; International Campaign to Ban Landmines 2014d). Unsurprisingly, instances of mine use have been met with the most overt criticism, whether directed towards fellow States Parties or non-parties (Canada 2012; Canada 2013; European Union 2012; Islamic Republic of Afghanistan 2014; Kingdom of Norway 2012; Republic of Zambia 2013; Swiss Confederation 2014).

What might be the effects of these competing approaches on the health of the mine ban as a legal standard and norm? While salutary for the purposes of a positive environment, the current approach to compliance shifts the burden of norm enforcement onto a more limited number of state and civil society actors resulting in a highly decentralized and ad hoc process. In addition to decreased transparency and efficiency, ICBL campaigners worry that this approach generates a perceived divide between certain states and NGOs and the bulk of States Parties, leading to an 'us versus them' mentality.[43] By contrast, clear public condemnations are valuable in reinforcing the international stigma against norm-violating behaviours. Civil society actors have suggested that the absence of coordinated and persistent critique from treaty members has resulted in less social pressure on non-compliant states than might have been possible.[44] To the extent that violations are downplayed, responses can inadvertently suggest an endorsement of exceptions and compound the malign effect of the initial acts.

On balance, the mine ban regime has not witnessed such an erosion in its normative potency, for two reasons. First, despite notable gaps, the pattern of state discourse has not led to a normalization of mine use or other transgressions of treaty rules: the prohibition against AP mines remains rhetorically as well as behaviourally robust. Confronting proven or suspected violations—even when undertaken in less direct or confrontation terms—has therefore bolstered the norm since instances of deviance have been challenged rather than accepted as routine. Second, States Parties have of late demonstrated a renewed interest in proactively addressing compliance challenges, as indicated by the creation of a new committee on cooperative compliance (International Campaign to Ban Landmines 2014f). This process is ongoing, and future research should seek to extend the initial findings in the international relations

[43] Gabelnick interview 2010.

[44] In an interview, an ICRC representative expressed 'disappointment' at the limited response from States Parties concerning missed stockpile destruction deadlines. Interview with Camilla Waszink, Policy Adviser, Arms Unit, Legal Division, International Committee of the Red Cross. Geneva, 23 October 2009. This view has been reinforced in numerous discussions with ICBL representatives.

literature concerning the effects of public activism on the health of international norms (Hafner-Burton 2008; Price 2003, 585–6).

CONCLUSION: THE STATUS OF THE MINE BAN TREATY

In order for the MBT to be judged effective at changing state practice, we must be able to ascribe observed patterns of change to the influence of the treaty and its norm, rather than mere coincidence. Identifying ways in which behaviour and discourse converge and diverge provides an important window into legal influence. The present discussion strongly indicates the emergence of a powerful new social expectation prohibiting AP mines among the vast majority of states in the international system. Explicit public endorsements from States Parties suggest that much of this observed compliance is owing to a strong fidelity with the legal obligations enshrined in the MBT. Violations of core treaty rules are extremely rare, despite widespread contrary behaviour in the decades before the advent of the mine ban. At the same time, transgressors have reiterated their support for the spirit and purpose of the ban, and have done so by explicitly recognizing the specific content of *legal* obligations as defined by the treaty. And because deviance has not been normalized by either the violators or other actors, those relatively few cases of non-compliance have had the effect of reinforcing the legitimate authority and intersubjective status of the mine ban as both a legal obligation and social lodestar.

More specifically, the evidence supports a core theoretical claim that a legal institution can serve as the focal point for the consolidation of new collective expectations underpinning a community of actors. In this case, the MBT is the referent for a new role identity in which good international standing is signified by the elimination of AP mines and a parallel endorsement of a revised conception of the balance between military utility and humanitarian impact. The legal criteria provided by treaty rules have set the discursive conditions through which actors have both presented their claims—whether allegations, denials, or justifications—and responded to the assertions of others. The effects of this nested international social structure occur on two levels simultaneously, as the legitimate basis for the ban is explicitly framed in terms of existing international law norms, while subsequent behavioural questions are addressed within the context of the MBT's more particular legal structures. At the same time, the expectation that states will observe their legal commitments adds further potency to the social taboo governing AP mines. This further illustrates the extent to which the mine ban has gained impetus from its connection to the wider international legal system.

In this way, the relative precision and transparency provided by legal rules has shaped the public diplomacy in both defining compliance and disciplining deviation, as actors have had to frame their policies in terms of agreed commitments articulated by the treaty text. This observation in turn demonstrates the conditioning effect of legal processes, particularly by narrowing the range of socially legitimate behaviours. It is this fundamental shift that has driven adherence to treaty rules, rather than epiphenomenal factors like convenience or pre-existing policy symmetries. Rather, the fact of membership is itself significant, and the consequences are best explained in reference to the social account of legal influence developed in this study. This raises the question of how AP mines are conceived by states currently outside the MBT legal order, and how their practices might reflect upon the international authority of the mine ban norm. This is the subject of Chapter 5.

5

Informal Adaptation

Non-Parties and the Mine Ban Treaty

Chapter 4 demonstrated that States Parties to the Mine Ban Treaty (MBT) have largely succeeded in developing a powerful community of membership based around a collective conception of appropriate behaviour. On the other hand, continued resistance from a number of states presents a substantial challenge to the consolidation of the mine ban norm. Prominent global actors like China, Russia, and the United States have yet to join the treaty, as have other important regional actors including Egypt, India, Iran, Israel, Pakistan, and South Korea. Moreover, many of the remaining non-members are significant past and present users of antipersonnel (AP) mines, and possess the largest stockpiles of the weapons. These states would seem to be highly significant to the realization of an effective international treaty, and compelling global norm.

At the same time, the 'nested' theoretical account advanced in this book suggests that treaties may still have informal though nonetheless powerful effects on resistant states, principally due to their dense ties to prior legal and normative structures. In this light, it is important to highlight the significant extent to which many non-parties are already deeply implicated in the diplomatic processes of the mine ban. Non-parties regularly attend treaty meetings as observers and engage in discussions with other delegations, civil society representatives, and members of international organizations. These forms of interaction have drawn these actors into the environment of the MBT, consequently producing strong social pressures to more fully adapt to a new international standard. My goal in this chapter is to systematically explore the various ways that non-parties have (partially) endorsed the humanitarian objectives of the mine ban *and* maintained their opposition to the legal instrument, and to unpack the consequences of this tension. The empirical record reveals important ways in which the mine ban norm has already substantially altered the behaviour and discourse of resistant states—by changing national policies in direct contrast to the prior reliance on AP mines—while these actors have at the same time retained potentially potent forms of contestation.

DISCURSIVE ENGAGEMENT: NON-PARTIES AND NORMATIVE PULLS

Symbolic Politics: Humanitarianism and Partial Endorsement

Exposure to the mine ban has manifested itself first in the adoption of the humanitarian language of the treaty. Virtually every state still outside the MBT has identified AP mines as a significant threat to civilian populations, and accepted that legal restraints are the appropriate means of addressing these negative effects.[1] US President Clinton was the first world leader to call for the eventual elimination of AP mines (United States of America 1994b).[2] While continuing to assert their legitimacy under some contingencies, US delegations have repeatedly emphasized that 'the United States shares the humanitarian concern of parties to the Ottawa Convention and continues to demonstrate our commitment to addressing the potential humanitarian consequences caused by landmines' (United States of America 2012; United States of America 2013). For China:

> The Anti-Personnel Mine Ban Convention is an important achievement in the lofty cause of international humanitarianism. We are happy to witness the heartening progress achieved since the Convention came into effect 15 years ago, with production, use and transfer of anti-personnel mines (APL) considerably reduced, substantial progress made in global landmine action and stockpile destruction, and victim assistance and international cooperation significantly enhanced. (People's Republic of China 2014a)

These sentiments are shared widely among other prominent non-party states (Arab Republic of Egypt 2010; Islamic Republic of Iran 2012; People's Republic of China 2012b; Republic of India 2014a; Republic of Korea 2009).

In its broadest sense, therefore, the mine ban norm has generated a widespread shift in public discourse that accepts of the logic—if not the immediate political feasibility—of a prohibition. This type of general endorsement is surprising for sceptical readings of international law, since the states involved are not disinterested participants but rather, as current or recent mine users, are directly affected by the goal of a comprehensive legal ban (Democratic Socialist Republic of Sri Lanka 1999; Democratic Socialist Republic of Sri Lanka 2004; Federal Democratic Republic of Nepal 2007; Georgia 2006a; Kingdom of Morocco 2004; Republic of the Union of Myanmar 2011). Though one of the few recent users of mines, the Russian Federation has

[1] Uzbekistan appears to be the only non-party that has never made a public statement in support of the humanitarian objectives of the MBT.

[2] The US policy towards AP mines—and its evolution—is discussed in detail in the final section of this chapter, pages 116–20. For a review and critique of the US position concerning the mine ban negotiations, see Wareham (1998).

nonetheless previously advocated 'taking continuous efforts towards [the] goal [of a total ban on AP mines] ... Russia understands no less than anybody else the humanitarian component of the problem. We share the feelings of solidarity with innocent victims of anti-personnel mines' (Russian Federation 1996; Russian Federation 2002). Israel—a state that has been conspicuously absent from most mine-related discussions—has nevertheless indicated that it too 'supports a gradual process ... to reduce the indiscriminate use of landmines, toward the eventual goal of a total ban' (Israel 1999).

As anticipated in Chapter 2, the association with prior international legal developments has provided the basis for non-party recognition of the mine ban (Republic of India 2012; Republic of India 2014a; Islamic Republic of Pakistan 1999; People's Republic of China 1999; People's Republic of China 2014a; Republic of Korea 1997). China for example has pointedly associated the MBT with a long history of international legal efforts to ameliorate the effects of war:

> From *the St. Petersburg Declaration* and *the Geneva Conventions*, one can see the greatness of mankind and the progress it has made, testifying that humanitarianism, an important symbol and core element of our civilization, has become the common aspiration of all modern states. It is this common spirit of humanitarianism that we discern in *the Ottawa Convention* ... signifying a new and important effort to preserve human safety. It is for this reason that we applaud the objective in the Convention. (People's Republic of China 2003)

The linkage to existing standards of IHL is important, as it offers a point of reference in generating greater comfort with new obligations. Leading military powers including China, India, Israel, Russia, and the United States have consequently endorsed the goal of the global elimination of AP mines at some (as yet unspecified) future point (Second Review Conference of the States Parties to the CCW 2001, 11, para. 1). While incomplete, this itself is a significant development, as acceptance of the now-dominant social understanding that AP mines present distinctive humanitarian challenges that must be factored into any assessment of their utility can be clearly contrasted with the prior view of weapons as unexceptional features of military arsenals.

The discursive adoption of the MBT's humanitarian principles thus provides a reference point for assertions of responsible status even among non-parties. This is especially the case among states with histories of protracted conflict. For example, Myanmar has recently sought to portray its acceptance of international norms as a demonstration of its nascent civil-political transition; the new government has suggested that it may soon join the MBT as a component of these reforms, despite Myanmar's ongoing use of the weapons (Republic of the Union of Myanmar 2012). States like Libya (under the current Transitional Government), Nepal, Sri Lanka, and—perhaps most interestingly—Palestine have also utilized expressions of support for the mine ban as a means of demonstrating their re-entry into the international community (International Campaign to Ban Landmines 2014e) in much the same fashion as some States Parties discussed in Chapter 4.

Finally, a number of states have signalled that their current outlier status is the result of special circumstances—especially a lack of political or technical capacity—rather than opposition to ban norm itself. Latent armed conflicts resulting in ongoing border tensions (as with Armenia and Azerbaijan) or the lack of effective control over affected territory (as with Georgia) have been identified as key impediments to membership (Republic of Azerbaijan 2005; Georgia 2006b). States that lack extensive foreign and security policy institutions frequently find it difficult to stay on top of the myriad commitments present in modern international relations. For the Laos People's Democratic Republic, the state with the most severe concentration of unexploded ordinance on Earth, an inability to meet treaty obligations and a concern that these commitments will distract from more pressing tasks, is at the root of its failure to join the MBT (Lao People's Democratic Republic 2007). Though not facing these severe challenges, a number of small Pacific island states have justified their non-membership through a similar logic. Mongolia has further indicated that international assistance would be necessary to facilitate its accession and ensure it was able to meet its treaty obligations (Mongolia 2008). Claims of this kind are less detrimental to the legitimacy of the mine ban norm because the stated source of non-adherence is material incapacity, rather than principled opposition. It is worth remembering that a number of current MBT parties—notably Belarus, Finland, Poland, and Ukraine—previously tied their eventual entry to a resolution of technical challenges. Such impediments to ratification can therefore be overcome. Moreover, such examples further demonstrate how non-parties frequently engage with the implications of new treaties, suggesting yet again that legal developments not only bear on formal treaty members.

Military Utility and the Enduring Appeal of AP Mines

Despite this apparent convergence, many non-parties continue to envision a legitimate national security role for AP mines. The United States, for example, has long contended that it would 'not join the Ottawa Convention because its terms would have required us to give up a needed military capability' particularly with respect to its security commitments on the Korean peninsula (Department of State, United States of America 2004a; United States of America 1999; United States of America 2014c). Other prominent powers share the view that AP mines serve a vital function in defending borders and protecting forward-deployed military units (Arab Republic of Egypt 2010; Islamic Republic of Iran 2012; Islamic Republic of Pakistan 2013; Israel 1999;

People's Republic of China 2014a; Republic of India 2014a; Republic of Korea 2009; Russian Federation 1996).[3] This perspective is also reflected in the discourse of less materially powerful states[4] that frequently refer to the value of AP mines in providing an inexpensive defensive capacity. This belies any sceptical claims that the mine ban was an easy case for international governance since changing material conditions had already rendered the weapons obsolete.

Yet as noted already, these claims are set against a widespread recognition of the severe impacts AP mines present to civilian populations, which was itself the product of the initial genesis of the mine ban movement in the early 1990s. Non-parties have sought to address this noted tension by inverting the central causal claim of the mine ban—that AP mines by their design are inherently indiscriminate—and instead emphasizing the particular conditions of their use as the cause of unacceptable outcomes. 'Landmines, by this logic, are not illegitimate—only such practices as result in dire human consequences' (Beier 2002, 312; Maslen 2005, 1:18–22). In this view, restrictions on the use of AP mines, rather than an outright ban, are the most appropriate means of addressing the threat the weapons pose to civilians. In particular, 1996 Amended Protocol II (APII) to the Convention on Certain Conventional Weapons (CCW) has been widely endorsed by prominent opponents of the MBT as providing the appropriate balance of humanitarian protection while still recognizing the legitimate needs of military operations (Islamic Republic of Iran 2012; Islamic Republic of Pakistan 2007; People's Republic of China 1996; People's Republic of China 2013b; Republic of India 2008; Republic of India 2014a; Republic of Korea 2009; Russian Federation 1996; Russian Federation 2002).[5] Consequently, APII is held to enshrine best practices with respect to mine use, specifically concerning the employment of suitable fencing and signage, their prompt removal after the end of hostilities, and where possible the utilization of self-destruct and self-deactivation technologies.

The United States has, until very recently, been emblematic of this approach. In announcing a new US policy on AP mines in February 2004, the Bush administration explicitly identified the *persistence* of AP mines as the source of humanitarian threat, and asserted that a reliance on newer 'smart' mines would alleviate suffering caused by older technologies:

[3] For example, interview subjects have indicated that Russian officials remain sceptical of the MBT, and are unlikely to significantly revise their views in the foreseeable future. Brinkert interview 2010; Derlicka interview 2010. Interview with Peter Kolarov, Head of the Humanitarian Conventions Section, United Nations Office for Disarmament Affairs. Geneva, 21 October 2009.

[4] Such as Armenia, Azerbaijan, Cuba, Georgia, Lebanon, Libya, Mongolia, Morocco, Myanmar, Sri Lanka, Syria, Uzbekistan, and Vietnam.

[5] The key distinction here is that APII regulates—rather than bans altogether—the use, production, stockpiling, and transfer of AP landmines. For further discussion, see Chapter 3, pages 62–3.

> The evidence is clear that self-destruct and self-deactivate landmine munitions do not contribute to the grave risks of civilian injury that we find with persistent landmines that can and do, literally, wait for decades before claiming an innocent victim . . . In sum, the President's policy strikes an appropriate balance that accommodates two important national interests: It takes significant and comprehensive steps . . . toward surmounting the global problem caused by persistent landmines, while at the same time meeting the needs of our military for defensive capabilities that may save American and friendly forces' lives in combat.
>
> (Department of State, United States of America 2004b).

Hence the negative externalities from AP mines could be eliminated via technical changes and were not inherent in the class of weapons themselves.[6] This line of argumentation sought to portray a sub-set of AP mines as legitimate weapons that could be employed with due respect for the central IHL principles of discrimination and proportionality, and hence push back against the absolute prohibition demanded by mine ban proponents.

There are thus two separate legal institutions governing AP mines in contemporary international society. In the view of many practitioners, APII and the MBT are reinforcing and mutually compatible: despite considerable overlap in their subject matter, the treaties differ in terms of the range of the weapons they address (since the former also regulates anti-vehicle mines and improvised explosive devices), and the depth of the obligations they impose.[7] Many states that remain outside of the MBT are parties to APII, as are the majority of States Parties to the MBT.[8] From the perspective of this study, however, the enduring preference of some prominent states for the lower legal standard enshrined in APII holds direct implications for the prospective universalization of the mine ban norm. In short, supporters of the APII approach endorse the view that a properly designed and enforced regulatory regime can achieve the same humanitarian aim—to suitably reduce civilian casualties caused by AP mines—as a complete ban. On these normative terms, APII is thus best understood not as a parallel or subsidiary legal standard, but rather a different source of authority that undermines a prospective international consensus surrounding the prohibitionary AP mine norm. This repurposing of the humanitarian discourse thus suggests one way in which the nested effects discussed in Chapter 2 may actually provide grounds for *challenging* the extension of non-great power institutions, by providing a plausible alternative configuration of norms and rules to justify divergent policy choices.

[6] Indeed, some have gone so far as to argue that if the continued use of AP mines avoids employment of other, less discrete forms of violent force, they may result in a *more* humane outcome (Republic of Korea 1997; Beier 2002, 313).

[7] Kolarov interview.

[8] States that have yet to join the MBT are still subject to APII's regulatory regime governing anti-vehicle, AP, and various improvised weapons. For States Parties to the MBT, the MBT constitutes the binding—and more stringent—set of commitments with respect to AP mines.

Discursive Tensions and their Consequences

Non-parties therefore simultaneously acknowledge the humanitarian threat posed by AP mines while reaffirming their enduring necessity. In light of this disjuncture, pubic declarations of conditional support for an outright ban could be regarded as cynical efforts at evading international critique rather than a sincere engagement with new social expectations. Scholars have pointed out that states often appear to give facile support for norms without intending to follow these generic statements with actual policy change (Seymour 2014). At heart, then, sceptics would likely see little to suggest that ambivalent states have been influenced in any meaningful way by the mine ban norm, and would expect that non-party states—and especially predominantly powerful ones—can continue to ignore inconvenient institutional constraints.

Yet such a view underappreciates the political significance of the normative shift occasioned by the mine ban movement. Prominent non-parties have now accepted a partial reconception of responsible international behaviour that qualifies the value of AP mines with a more specific application of the principle of humanitarian protection (People's Republic of China 2014a). This rhetorical strategy of parsing the relationship between humanitarianism and national security is potentially problematic for non-parties, however. As Price (2004a, 112) has observed, non-parties 'that have sought legitimacy for their efforts to resist an emerging obligatory norm on AP landmines have been able to do so only by reinforcing the constitutive and customary norms of warfare and humanitarian law, and it is those very norms which lend support to an emerging customary norm against the use of AP landmines'. Here again the nested nature of international law provides crucial explanatory value, precisely because the discursive interventions are tied to the broader universe of norms and rules that structure the international community.

Even resistant states now accept that AP mines should be singled out for particular attention amongst the wealth of 'conventional' weapons in modern warfare. Seen in this light, even general endorsement of the MBT is not mere cheap talk as sceptics would suggest, since the employment of humanitarian discourse ultimately has the effect of drawing non-parties progressively further into the orbit of the MBT and its normative claims. These states feel it necessary to explicitly associate themselves with the core goals of the MBT, suggesting that they perceive social costs associated with more explicit defiance and, inversely, status benefits that may accrue through their (partial) endorsement. This in turn is consequential because IR scholars have already demonstrated that the instrumental use of discourse—agreeing with international norms without sincere internalization in order to achieve other political, economic, or social ends—can lead to a form of rhetorical entrapment that generates further socialization pressures over time (Bower 2015; Risse, Ropp, and Sikkink 1999; Risse, Ropp, and Sikkink 2013). J. Marshall

Beier perceptively noted over a decade ago that 'these developments have made it increasingly difficult for the holdouts to square their rhetoric with their actual conduct and, to the extent that they jockey to share in the new moral high ground associated with the prohibition . . . they are apt to find themselves bound by some measure of the obligations that accompany it' (Beier 2002, 308). While this study focuses primarily on the structural effects of norms at a global level, therefore, it is important to recognize that institutional developments generate the conditions for agency by other actors—including diplomats, civil society representatives, and international bureaucracies—in promoting new norms that can lead to the reconfiguration of national-level identities and interests. This has been the experience of recent MBT adopters, as discussed at length in Chapter 4.

One key effect of the mine ban norm has thus been to exclude previously acceptable forms of discourse, such that non-parties now express support for a legal institution to which they cannot fully adhere, and in which a reversal in favour of a broader claim to the 'normalcy' of AP mines would be recognized as a major deviation. This shift is incomplete, as the above section has demonstrated. However, it is important not to lose sight of the extent to which the reconception of a formerly central practice of war represents a genuinely transformative event in world politics. Yet the refusal to officially adopt the MBT leaves room at both political and military levels to envision the future use of AP mines. The balance of this chapter assesses the extent to which the broad pattern of discursive change has been reflected in subsequent state practice. Contrary to sceptical expectations, the empirical record clearly shows that non-party states have been largely in conformance with core treaty obligations. This convergence, moreover, cannot be accounted for by merely assuming that AP mines are no longer militarily relevant for these states; rather, as with States Parties in the previous chapter, the key to this behavioural transformation is found in a more fundamental change in the way in which AP mines are conceived of in global politics.

INFORMAL RESTRAINT: NON-PARTY ADAPTATION TO THE MINE BAN

Signalling Support: Voting on UN General Assembly Resolutions

As Chapters 2 and 3 maintained, multilateral treaties are fundamentally normative structures in that they aim to propagate collective standards of appropriate behaviour, and this influence may be felt beyond the discrete group of states that have signalled their formal acceptance of new legal rules.

Reciprocally, scholarship on customary international law has demonstrated that states shape the status of law—and more broadly, norms—via their actions and language, whether supportive or hostile. More specifically, the doctrine of 'persistent objection' recognizes that states should not be subject to new rules to which they maintain consistent opposition (Byers 1999, 180). States that have registered their formal disapproval of the MBT in various international fora might therefore be exempt from any broader international norm arising from the treaty. The most relevant setting is the annual United Nations General Assembly resolution on the MBT, since these resolutions explicitly promote universal membership (Byers 1999, 41–32, 58–60).[9] The ICBL has placed considerable emphasis on the resolution as a demonstration of international support for the aims of the mine ban.[10] Refusing to join the resolution may thus reasonably be interpreted as a form of sustained and public resistance to the treaty.

It is therefore significant that Cuba, Egypt, India, Iran, Israel, Myanmar, Pakistan, Republic of Korea, Russia, Syria, and the United States have consistently abstained from the annual resolution every year since its introduction in 1997, suggesting one means by which non-parties have succeeded in opposing the spread of the mine ban norm (International Campaign to Ban Landmines 2014c, 1). Yet there are two important caveats to this conclusion. The annual resolutions have received overwhelming support among the international community generally[11] as well as from a number of non-parties, most notably China since 2005, whose subsequent explanations regarding the votes have further reinforced the humanitarian legitimacy of the mine ban (People's Republic of China 2013b). This mirrors the experience of late-adopters such as Finland and Poland, who habitually endorsed the UNGA resolution in advance of official membership as a means of demonstrating their commitment to the mine ban. Such instances offer important examples of how such rhetorical support can be a meaningful presage to formal adoption at a later date.

[9] '*Emphasizing* the desirability of attracting the adherence of all States to the Convention, and determined to work strenuously towards the promotion of its universalization and norms' (United Nations General Assembly 2013b, para. preamble 9). Similar language can be found in operative Articles 1–3. The language of the resolution is essentially unchanged since 1997. Summaries of the annual UNGA sessions, including voting records and national statements, are available at http://www.un.org/en/ga/sessions/.

[10] Indeed, the ICBL frequently lobbies non-parties to vote in favour of the resolution, and suggests that this is a key way that such states may demonstrate progress towards accession. Derlicka interview 2010.

[11] Between 1997 and 2013, the annual UNGA resolution received an average of 154 votes in favour and 19 abstentions. Voting records are available at http://www.icbl.org/en-gb/the-treaty/treaty-meetings/un-first-committee.aspx.

Just as significantly, no states have voted *against* the resolution, but have uniformly chosen to abstain.[12] Such acts would seem to fall below the threshold of persistent and transparent resistance commonly understood as necessary in order to undermine an emerging customary rule in international law (Guldahl 2008, 53; D'Amato 2004, 3:22). In this sense, UNGA voting patterns may offer limited, contingent evidence of a widening collective expectation incorporating non-party states, suggesting that non-parties perceive social costs associated with public opposition.[13]

Compliance: Use, Production, Transfer, and Stockpiling

These processes of rhetorical adaptation are reflected in behavioural changes involving a rapidly declining reliance on the weapons. Most significantly, very few states continue to employ AP mines, as Chapter 4 outlined in some detail. This extends to the vast majority of states currently not party to the MBT, despite the fact that many remain engaged in various internal or international armed conflicts or have ongoing challenges in securing their frontiers in which mines have historical featured.[14] It is particularly notable that the United States has not used AP mines since the 1991 Gulf War, a period which includes intensive military operations in Afghanistan and Iraq (International Campaign to Ban Landmines 2013f; United States of America General Accountability Office 2002).[15] Indeed, many non-parties have explicitly stated

[12] The only state to have recorded a 'no' vote was Lebanon in 1999; after the vote, Lebanon informed the Chair that it had intended to abstain.

[13] Nevertheless, it would be wise not to read too much into such votes in isolation, as the relative cost of such demonstrations is low since the UNGA resolutions impose no specific legal obligations; in isolation, therefore, their contribution to the *extension* of the mine ban norm is limited (Byers 1999, 157). This view was reflected in some interviews conducted for this study. For example, one such opinion held that the annual UNGA vote constituted only a marginal part of state policy, and was thus not necessarily a valuable indicator of commitment to MBT norms. Brinkert interview 2010. Representatives of the ICBL do not share this view, as has already been noted.

[14] Like Armenia, Azerbaijan, China, Egypt, Georgia, India, Iran, Republic of Korea, Lebanon, Libya, Morocco, Pakistan, and the United States. Some of these states—notably China, India, Korea, Morocco, and Pakistan—do possess existing minefields from which they continue to presumably gain defensive benefits. However, these states have not sought to expand or replenish these existing minefields in recent years.

[15] In 2014, a review of US operations revealed that its forces deployed 'a single [AP] munition in Afghanistan in 2002' (Department of State, United States of America 2014). Human Rights Watch has previously reported that 'on October 10, the third night of the military action by the United States and United Kingdom against Taliban positions and facilities, B-52 and B-1 bombers reportedly dropped "area munitions," including CBU-89 Gators. The CBU-89 Gator is a mixed-mine system containing both antipersonnel and antivehicle mines' (Human Rights Watch 2001b, 4–5). If proven conclusively, this would represent a setback for the deepening authority of the non-use norm. However, the ambiguity here may actually buttress the prohibition enshrined in the MBT, as the fact that this allegation remains unverified speaks at least in

that they no longer actively rely on AP mines in their security operations, even as they reserve the right to do so (People's Republic of China 2014a; Republic of India 2012).

This pattern of widespread restraint cannot be explained by material factors alone, especially since the majority of these states continue to face similar security conditions as compared with the pre-MBT era. Rather, were it not for the effective stigmatization of the weapon initiated by the MBT and its parallel norm, we would expect AP mines to feature in the operations of a greater number of these actors. The resolution or moderation of some violent intra-state conflicts has also provided conditions for declining mine use. For example, the 2006 Comprehensive Peace Agreement (CPA) that officially ended hostilities between the Government of Nepal and the Maoist insurgency explicitly prohibited the use of AP mines and committed both sides to engage in the clearance of mined areas (Federal Democratic Republic of Nepal 2006, Articles 5.1.1(h), 5.1.2, and 5.1.4; International Campaign to Ban Landmines 2009b, 1041–2). A similar process appears to be at work in Sri Lanka. These examples mirror the processes through which AP mines were eliminated from military doctrine in a number of late adopters of the mine ban including Ethiopia and Eritrea, Greece and Turkey, and Sudan and South Sudan among many others. Yet as Chapter 4 insisted, such fundamental policy changes were not the result of unproblematic assessments of objective threats, but emerged as part of a reconceptualization of the nature of security and the appropriate means of ensuring the realization of national defence objectives in the context of a powerful new international social standard. This is a foundational way that norms influence the construction of state interests, with consequent impacts on decision-making and policy. It is possible, therefore, that initially limited domestic changes may provide openings for further engagement and adaptation.[16]

Despite their official ambivalence, therefore, many non-parties are in fact highly sensitive to international condemnation with respect to mine policy. In one interesting example, the ICBL has reported that Pakistan suspended plans to emplace new AP mines along its border with Afghanistan in 2006 and 2007

part to a desire among US officials to obscure any such actions. This in turn reflects a sensitivity to demands of an international norm, albeit one that the US does not officially endorse as legally binding. Interestingly, the 2014 report makes no mention of this alleged incident.

[16] Nepalese civil society practitioners have expressed the view that the CPA may serve as the catalyst for greater engagement with the MBT, potentially leading to formal accession. Interview with Purna Shova Chitrakar, Chairperson of the Nepalese Campaign to Ban Landmines. Geneva, 3 December 2010. However, government representatives have been careful to draw distinctions between the two initiatives, and suggest that the AP mine moratorium in the CPA does not commit Nepal to joining the MBT. Interview with Hari Odari, Second Secretary of the Permanent Mission of the Federal Democratic Republic of Nepal to the UN and other International Organizations and Embassy of the FDR of Nepal in Geneva. Geneva, 7 December 2010.

after substantial criticism. Though the minefields were regarded as vital to protecting against infiltration by militant and terrorist groups, the extent of mobilization against the plan both domestically—including by former security chiefs, parliamentarians, political parties, and civil society—and from international actors like the ICBL and states including Canada pressured the government to abandon the operation indefinitely (International Campaign to Ban Landmines 2007b; International Campaign to Ban Landmines 2008c). To the extent that the mine use persists, therefore, it is undertaken almost exclusively by states—such as Libya (under the Gaddafi regime), Myanmar, Syria, and the Russian Federation—regarded as among the most impervious to humanitarian and human rights norms and international advocacy.

Finally, while not the focus of this study, the MBT has also influenced the use of mines by non-state armed groups (NSAG) (Bower and Price 2013, 183–4; Geneva Call 2014; Moser-Puangsuwan 2008). NSAG are frequent participants in contemporary armed conflicts, and their adoption of the mine ban norm would be significant both for the improvement in real-world practice and humanitarian outcomes (capturing more of the behaviour the MBT seeks to prohibit) and widening the political scope of the norm. Civil society organizations—most especially the ICRC and Geneva Call[17]—have therefore sought to engage NSAG in the ban on AP mines. Yet such efforts are complicated by the fact that NSAG often emerge, merge, and disband in various combinations over time, making it difficult to maintain socialization efforts or indeed accurately measure the number of groups adhering to or violating international restraints on armed violence. NSAG may be regarded, moreover, as especially hard cases for the adoption of international norms for two reasons. On the one hand, such actors largely lack formal recognition in the international system: they are typically not entitled to legal status either in their own domestic society or under international law, complicating efforts at external engagement. On the other hand, the diffuse nature of many armed groups means that they may lack effective centralized command and control necessary to ensure compliance, while the asymmetric nature of many armed conflicts may incentivize NSAG towards using inexpensive low-tech weapons. Indeed, the vast majority of contemporary AP mine use does appear to come from non-state sources, with the ICBL recording instances of new AP mine deployments by NSAG on the territory of ten states in 2015, 'a significant increase of use by NSAGs from recent years, especially in States Parties' (International Campaign to Ban Landmines 2015, 5).[18]

[17] http://www.genevacall.org/what-we-do/landmine-ban/.

[18] According to the ICBL, NSAG used AP mines in the following number of territories: 7 (2014), 8 (2013), 6 (2012), 4 (2010), 6 (2009), 7 (2008), 9 (2007), 10 (2006), 13 (2005) (International Campaign to Ban Landmines 2008b, 5; International Campaign to Ban Landmines 2014g, 8).

At the same time, there is considerable evidence of norm adoption even in these challenging circumstances. At least sixty-four armed groups have endorsed the ban on AP mines—including forty-nine that have signed Geneva Call's *Deed of Commitment for Adherence to a Total Ban on Anti-Personnel Mines and for Cooperation in Mine Action*—and have undertaken a variety of operational activities to cease using the weapons, destroy their stockpiles, and assist in humanitarian demining and the treatment of victims (International Campaign to Ban Landmines 2014g, 6; Geneva Call 2013; Geneva Call 2014, 14–15). Anecdotal evidence suggests that NSAG frequently make these public declarations as a means of demonstrating their status as responsible actors—i.e. that they accept internationally agreed rules of behaviour in armed conflict, and possess the organizational capacity and authority to ensure compliance.[19] These processes can also generate parallel changes in states, by pressuring them to emulate the reputation-enhancing achievements of their non-state adversaries, signalling that the conditions of the conflict have changed and inviting reciprocity, or through the direct integration of former rebel groups into the political and military structures of the state. For example, the decision by the Sudan People's Liberation Movement/Army (SPLM/A) to sign the *Deed of Commitment*, and the subsequent conclusion of the Nuba Mountains Ceasefire agreement with the Government of Sudan in January 2002, helped pave the way for Sudan's ratification of the MBT. Similar experiences in places such as Nepal and Iraq further demonstrate the important role that NSAG play in the diffusion of international norms; further comparative study of this subject is therefore warranted.

The decline in mine use is mirrored in the introduction of moratoria on the production and transfer of the weapons by a number of major military powers (International Campaign to Ban Landmines 2013a, 18). China and the United States have informally halted the development and procurement of AP mines in recent years, while other formerly large-scale producers like Egypt and Israel and have followed suit in officially abandoning the practice. Interestingly, these latter two states appear to be clear instances where concerted civil society engagement produced significant political gains. Wareham reports that '[The ICBL] was largely responsible for obtaining formal public statements of policies renouncing production by four [non-party] states (Egypt, Finland, Israel, and Poland), by repeatedly requesting these governments to formalize their position in writing and make it public' (Wareham 2008, 59). As already noted, Finland and Poland's ultimate accession to the MBT was presaged by precisely these types of incremental policy adaptation. It is therefore

[19] Interview with Pascal Bongard, Program Director (Africa) and Policy Adviser, Geneva Call and Dr Ann-Kristin (Anki) Sjöberg, Strategy and Evaluation Officer, Geneva Call. Geneva, 2 November 2009. For a broader argument concerning status motivations and rebel group compliance with international humanitarian and human rights law, see Jo (2015).

additionally significant that the United States has not produced any form of AP mine since 1997 while recent policy changes—discussed further in the final section of this chapter—have confirmed a permanent abandonment of the practice. Most prominent non-parties have further enacted legislative prohibitions on the transfer of AP mines, including China, India, Israel, Korea, Pakistan, and the United States (People's Republic of China 2012b; Republic of India 2012; Republic of Korea 2009). These are yet further examples of how the interaction with international norms may foreclose policies that were unproblematic in a prior epoch, with important compounding effects over time as prior practices are removed from the menu of 'normal' policy options. The international stigmatization of AP mines has increased the political salience of the issue such that any future decision to resume mine production, transfer, or use would involve the most senior decision-makers, further de-emphasizing the role of AP mines in modern military arsenals (Price 2004a, 127).

By contrast, the retention of some fifty million AP mines by thirty-one non-party states undoubtedly weakens the stigma against the weapons even as the overwhelming majority are held by a few major military powers (International Campaign to Ban Landmines 2015, 10). Indeed, while China, Russia, and the United States have engaged in major destruction efforts in recent years, these processes are largely directed against mines that do not conform to the less stringent requirements of APII to the Convention on Certain Conventional Weapons.[20] The same is true of Indian and Russian moratoria on the production and export of AP mines that do not meet APII criteria (since 1997 and 1994, respectively), along with a variety of non-parties such as China, India, Pakistan, Republic of Korea, and Russia that have engaged in substantial domestic demining operations to remove and destroy mines on these same terms (International Campaign to Ban Landmines 2009b, 1068; Islamic Republic of Pakistan 2013; People's Republic of China 2014a; Republic of India 2014a; Republic of India 2014b; Republic of Korea 2009; Russian Federation 2002). While the changes in policy are still significant on the aggregate, the object is a *different* source of obligation, and one that imposes a lower standard than the absolute ban enshrined in the MBT.

THE RHETORICAL POLITICS OF MINES: NON-PARTY DISCOURSE AND THE SOCIAL STATUS OF THE BAN

As demonstrated already, non-party responses to the landmine issue are more varied than their formal membership status in the MBT alone would suggest.

[20] APII requires that Parties not employ AP mines that are undetectable (that is, lacking sufficient metallic content to be detectable by conventional means) or that are not self-destructing or self-deactivating.

Rendering a more holistic assessment of institutional impact thus requires attention to the various ways that the mine ban norm has shifted the social environment in which non-party states must operate. This can be evaluated in part through an examination of the way that such states frame their policy choices—in other words, the reasons they give for their actions, whether in support of or resistance to the obligations contained in the treaty.

Explaining Mine Use

Instances where states describe their use of AP mines as an unexceptional part of regular operational policy are most threatening to any prospective universalization of the ban norm. The Russian Federation, for example, has previously acknowledged using AP mines 'to protect facilities of high importance' and prevent the infiltration of terrorists and the transport of drugs and weapons in Chechnya, Dagestan, Tajikistan, and along the border with Georgia (International Campaign to Ban Landmines 2009b, 1071; York 2001). Russian officials have repeatedly stated that their use of mines by the armed forces, Interior Ministry troops, and border guards conforms to the standards of APII and is therefore permissible under international law (International Campaign to Ban Landmines 2007c). More recently, the governments of Libya (under the Gaddafi regime), Myanmar, and Syria have defended their use of mines as a normal part of military operations against internal enemies.

Yet even here there are important qualifications to be made. As with instances of violations by States Parties,[21] some non-parties have sought to justify their use of AP mines by invoking the language of special circumstances rather than via a generalized right. Azerbaijan and Sri Lanka have expressly claimed that their deployment of minefields was 'forced' or 'compelled' by the existential threat posed by armed attack from rival states or armed rebel groups. And mirroring Russian statements, these states have further indicated that the mine use conformed to the terms of APII and that they have not resorted to further use since (Democratic Socialist Republic of Sri Lanka 2004; Republic of Azerbaijan 2008). Some non-parties have gone as far as to explicitly recognize the authority of the MBT while they maintain policies directly at odds with the treaty. According to Nepal, which had employed mines the year before, 'it is an established fact that the use of antipersonnel mines is an act of severe criminal nature' (Federal Democratic Republic of Nepal 2007; Kingdom of Morocco 2004). These kinds of endorsements mark an important discursive shift in which states now rarely seek to defend AP mines as unproblematic weapons even during or soon after acknowledged transgressions.

[21] See Chapter 4, pages 91–5.

Silence, Denials, and Accusations

Yet more recently, a number of these same states have shifted from open acknowledgement to concealment, demonstrating further social pressures created by the strengthening global prohibition. When presented with plausible claims a range of non-parties including Georgia, Israel, Nepal, Pakistan, the Russian Federation, and Sri Lanka have sought to deny their use of AP mines (International Campaign to Ban Landmines 2007a; International Campaign to Ban Landmines 2008a; International Campaign to Ban Landmines 2008d; International Campaign to Ban Landmines 2013g; International Campaign to Ban Landmines 2014a; Russian Federation 2014a). These cases are particularly interesting because they have not come from treaty parties, which might be motivated by a fear of material or reputational sanction relating to the non-observance of binding commitments. Non-member states possess no legal obligations under the MBT according to a traditional consent-based reading of international law. The actors in question, moreover, have not used allegations —whether ultimately factual or not—as opportunities to openly challenge the mine ban and legitimize the use of AP mines.[22] This kind of deference to the norm can further reinforce its authority, since it suggests that non-parties recognize the salience of the social standard for a large constituency of international actors and consequently, that there exists a political cost associated with its overt violation.

Such processes are further evidenced in attempts to gain political advantage by attributing mine use to rival states or rebel groups. This has been undertaken by (among others) Georgia against both rebels in South Ossetia and Russian armed forces during the 2008 war, Russian counter-claims against Georgian forces, Sri Lanka against Tamil Tiger rebels, and recent Ukrainian allegations of mine use by Russian forces in the annexation of Crimea (Georgia 2006a; International Campaign to Ban Landmines 2008a; RIA Novosti 2008; International Campaign to Ban Landmines 2008d; International Campaign to Ban Landmines 2014a). The United States has also explicitly highlighted the use of AP mines by Syrian security forces as part of its widespread abuse of the civilian population (Department of State, United States of America 2012). Such claims follow an identical pattern to the one identified in Chapter 4, with the accusing states attempting to stigmatize an enemy through strategic appeal. They could, therefore, be regarded as cynical political manoeuvres that do not reflect any genuine normative development. Yet as I have already contended, the instrumental use of norms ultimately

[22] A similar dynamic is at play in the potential case of US mine use in Afghanistan noted above: while the claims were never decisively proven and may have been inaccurate, it is notable that US officials made no official comment and did not attempt to defend the deployment even as a hypothetical option.

hinges upon the recognition of claims by an external audience since the assessment of purported violations and any subsequent forms of material or social punishment can only be undertaken intersubjectively. Such efforts are only appealing because the ban norm has already become entrenched to such an extent that its observance is widely understood to constitute a basic condition of responsible statehood, with the use of AP mines regarded as *especially* indefensible.

Hence even resistant states may find benefit in selectively invoking the language and commitments of the AP mine ban. But again, such efforts are not cost-free, as they of necessity draw ostensibly ambivalent actors into the legal and normative environment of the mine ban, where they themselves may be held to the same standards. Price (Price 2004a, 119–20) has suggested the adoption of legalistic language is a key process through which states may progressively internalize the social expectations of legal obligations, resulting in potential changes in their fundamental identities and interests. This was precisely the process of socialization emphasized in Chapter 4. Even apparently strategic attempts to invoke legal or normative standards to deflect criticism can therefore have lasting consequences for the development of norms, by further reinforcing the social legitimacy of the particular institution as the arbiter of acceptable behaviour. Rather than ignoring inconvenient developments, therefore, non-party states are still part of an international social system in which shifting expectations have forced all constituent actors to acknowledge—if not fully accept—the mine ban as a feature of the international environment. This, in turn, has had a substantial impact on their policy choices and meaningfully shaped behavioural outcomes.

GULLIVER (INFORMALLY) BOUND: THE UNITED STATES AND THE MINE BAN

The United States provides a particularly vivid example of how the interaction with the mine ban has served to progressively transform national policies despite official opposition. As already noted, the United States was an active participant in early debates over international responses to the global landmine crisis, which initially culminated in President Clinton's call for the eventual elimination of AP mines (United States of America 1994b). Yet observers have also long highlighted a 'significant gap between rhetorical leadership and policy realities', as the United States attempted to balance its military objectives with a desire to be seen to be taking a leading role in addressing the humanitarian consequences of mine contamination (Wareham 1998, 212). Indeed, Clinton's 1994 speech explicitly stated that a global ban would only become practical 'as viable and humane alternatives are developed' (United States of America 1994a). The United States therefore sought support for a regulatory regime, to be negotiated via the Convention on Certain Conventional Weapons, in lieu of the immediate pursuit of a wholesale prohibition.

While far less than early ban proponents wanted, this diplomatic gambit did provide a rhetorical opening that could be exploited by pro-ban constituencies to push for further change. US policy on AP mines is therefore best understood as a case of gradually and reluctantly conceding to social pressures to more fully align its actual policy with its stated ambitions. Indeed, previous research has shown that the tentative involvement of the United States with the AP mine issue was determined not by a top-down process driven by the president or senior officials but rather by a coalition of domestic civil society under the banner of the nascent US Campaign to Ban Landmines and a limited number of political elites centred around Senator Patrick Leahy (Wareham 1998, 212–19). The linkage between these actors was instrumental in generating public notoriety that undermined opposition in policy circles: as Wareham (1998, 215) notes, 'Few uniformed military officials wanted to defend a weapon already seen as an indiscriminate killer of innocent civilians.' This led to the successful achievement of domestic moratoria on the export of AP mines (in 1992[23] and again for a three-year renewal in 1993) and, in 1995, 'on the use of AP mines, "except along internationally recognized borders or in demilitarized zones" in marked and guarded minefields' (Wareham 1998, 219). These initiatives were further extended by a 1998 Presidential Decision Directive that informally committed the United States to join the MBT 'by 2006 if efforts succeed to identify and field suitable alternatives to US anti-personnel landmines and mixed anti-tank systems by then' (Office of the President of the United States of America 1998).

Though limited, these initial steps were resisted within the senior military ranks and amongst the civilian defence bureaucracy, meaning that substantial internal divisions remained within US policy circles. The United States was therefore a unenthusiastic participant in the Ottawa Process, and largely joined the discussions in the hopes of limiting the outcome to a more modest set of restrictions that would accommodate existing US technologies and operational plans. As explained in Chapter 3, the United States was ultimately not able to steer the negotiations to an acceptable conclusion, and refused to support the resulting treaty (Cameron, Lawson, and Tomlin 1998; Rutherford 2009; United States of America 1999). The United States signed the treaty as a symbolic gesture in support of the humanitarian aims of the ban, but did not

[23] The initial moratorium is found in U.S. Congress (1992, sec. 1365).

seek ratification and largely withdrew from the mine ban regime.[24] Authors sceptical of the constraining potential of international law would thus find much to suggest that the United States has effectively avoided an international commitment it regards as injurious to its fundamental interests (Glennon 2001; Wohlforth 2012).

However, the US experience nicely illustrates the inability of holdout states to fully insulate themselves from the consequences of a rapid shift in international expectations occasioned by the successful conclusion of the MBT. The United States was subject to extensive pressure from middle power states (especially NATO allies like Canada, Norway, and the United Kingdom), civil society (especially the ICBL and its national affiliate the USCBL), sympathetic domestic political elites and public opinion that sought to exploit the deliberately vague statements of support for a mine ban in order to pressure for more specific changes. Initially, this saw the United States dramatically increase its contributions to humanitarian demining funding—to become the largest single donor globally—due to a belief among officials 'that the US had to be seen to be "doing something" on the landmine issue' (Wareham 1998, 239). Exposure to a new yet widely shared social standard thus provided conditions for the adoption of a range of unilateral policy decisions in line with the terms of the MBT, including extensions to the pre-MBT moratorium on AP mine export,[25] along with the de facto abandonment of the use and production of AP mines, as this chapter has already documented. Again, these forms of restraint are not well explained by simply assuming radically altered material conditions pertaining to the weapons, since non-parties continue to expressly assert their usefulness. And while potentially modest in isolation, forms of incremental adaptation take on greater significance when aggregated in number and over time, since they become embedded in regular procedures and practices, building momentum towards additional forms of accommodation and becoming more difficult to reverse.

One prominent effect of the mine ban norm, therefore, has been to stimulate a fundamental reconsideration of national policy goals and the means through which they should be pursed. In much the same fashion as late adopters like Finland and Poland, successive US administrations have responded to the growing international support for the mine ban with a wide-ranging search for alternative technologies that could replace AP mines in military doctrine (Committee on Alternative Technologies to Replace Antipersonnel Landmines 2001). In 2004 the Bush administration announced that it would eliminate all forms of 'persistent' mines (those without

[24] President Clinton signed the MBT on his final day in office, but advised his successor not to seek Senate ratification unless fundamental US concerns were addressed.

[25] The export moratorium has been extended on a number of occasions, most recently in the United States Congress (2007, sec. 634(j)).

self-destruct or deactivation features) from its arsenal, while retaining the right to develop and use so-called 'smart' mines that in its view addressed the indiscriminacy at the heart of objections to the weapons (Department of State, United States of America 2004a).

While initially regarded as a strategic concession to appease critics without fundamentally altering US capacity to deploy AP mines, the policy was consequential for two reasons. First, the elimination of persistent mines was itself a humanitarian achievement, since it removed a great number of the most problematic weapons from active inventories and reflected a further narrowing of conditions under which AP mines could be deployed.[26] Second, the employment of humanitarian discourse stimulated domestic political battles that led to further constraints on military procurement. The ICBL and US Campaign to Ban Landmines (USCBL) challenged the new policy on the grounds that it did not fully meet the standards of the MBT, since certain types of AP mines would still be permitted. After extensive lobbying by the USCBL and with prominent support from long-time ban advocate Senator Patrick Leahy, the United States Congress voted to withhold funding for Department of Defence research and development on prospective mine systems with victim-activated features (that would be prohibited under the MBT). This injunction specifically included new weapons that would otherwise be permitted under the 2004 directive. Subsequent weapons development has consequently focused solely on systems that conform to the legal criteria of the MBT (International Campaign to Ban Landmines 2009b, 1131–2; Malenic 2008). In this way AP mines have been further diminished as part of the normal menu of military tools.

US participation in the mine ban regime has deepened under President Obama, and has served as a deliberate symbol of a wider re-engagement with multilateral institutions and a generally more permissive view of international law. In 2009 the administration announced a comprehensive policy review to evaluate the continued necessity of AP mines in light of changing international conditions. This involved extensive engagement with domestic military, diplomatic, and political actors, other states, and representatives of civil society (International Campaign to Ban Landmines 2013f; United States of America 2011a). This process has recently culminated with two closely sequenced announcements. First, in June 2014 the US formalized its commitment not to 'produce or otherwise acquire any anti-personnel munitions that are not compliant with the Ottawa Convention in the future,' and to 'diligently pursu[e] other solutions that would be compliant with the Convention and that would ultimately allow us to accede to the Convention' (United States of

[26] As of January 2011, all persistent mines have been withdrawn and transferred for destruction (United States of America Permanent Mission to the United Nations and other International Organizations in Geneva 2012).

America 2014a). Most recently, in September 2014 the United States expanded its pledge to observe the obligations of the MBT—by abandoning the use of AP mines, refraining from assisting other states in acts that violate the treaty, and destroying mine stockpiles—in all circumstances *other* than with respect to the defence of South Korea (United States of America 2014c; United States of America 2014b).

Though still falling short of absolute adherence, this new position represents a substantial shift in the military policy of the pre-eminent global power, and one that would be inconceivable in the absence of the global stigma generated by the MBT. The United States has now accepted the application of the mine ban in all but the single most sensitive instance, reflecting a dramatic contraction in the terms under which it would contemplate—and seek to defend—the enduring necessity of AP mines. It is notable, for example, that the US policy makes no attempt to carve out a legitimate exception for ongoing or potential military operations elsewhere. Most fundamentally, the US experience confirms the core assumptions that animated the 'new diplomacy' of the mine ban movement: despite its preponderant material power the United States has been unable to effectively limit the impact of a major international diplomatic initiative in an area of national importance, and has instead been substantially 'captured' through its exposure to the strengthening international norm.

CONCLUSION: NON-PARTIES AND NORMATIVE PULLS

Despite an enduring commitment to the prospective utility of AP mines, recent practice demonstrates a marginalization of the weapons in the military doctrine of the United States and other powerful non-parties. Even in the absence of a formal legal commitment, therefore, these states bear the marks of the social expectations embodied in the MBT. Most generally, non-parties must now operate in an international system that has experienced a rapid change in a heretofore-stable expectation concerning the accepted use of military force. As a consequence, states like China, India, Russia, and the United States among others are unable to ignore the mine ban as a feature of international politics—as realists would expect (Glennon 2001; Wohlforth 2012)—but must engage with the prohibitionary norm as part of their diplomacy. In so doing, non-party states betray an accruing sensitivity to collective expectations they officially reject, first by largely conceding to the special status of AP mines amongst the range of conventional weapons. The adoption of this humanitarian framing—and the attendant notion that AP mines pose a distinctive threat to civilian populations—has in turn generated pressures towards greater adaptation in line with the core objectives of the mine ban. This is apparent both with respect to the rapid decline in the use, production, and transfer of the weapons, and in the ways in which non-parties justify their policy positions.

As anticipated in Chapter 2, the association with pre-existing international legal institutions has provided an entry point through which non-parties have gained comfort with the aims of the mine ban. First and foremost, engagement has had the effect of further drawing these states into the MBT's universe of legal and normative claims. This fact has forced the United States and other ambivalent states to publicly articulate, and in many cases defend, their policies on the terms of a new institution they officially reject. Even if undertaken for strategic reasons of avoiding international critique rather than the sincere endorsement of norms, the political consequences of such rhetorical shifts are significant, since they set a precedent for the assessment of future behaviour. By adopting this humanitarian discourse, therefore, non-parties have acknowledged the salience of the ban, and this fact has imposed new limits on the range of publicly defensible policy positions.

Many non-parties do retain specific objections to the MBT, however, and this fact belies any contemporary assessment that the mine ban norm has been effectively universalized. Resistant states have endorsed the *goals* of the MBT, while at the same time seeking to avoid its binding legal obligations through the promotion of APII as the solution to the humanitarian challenges posed by AP mines. The divergence between qualified, general recognition of MBT norms, and an enduring opposition under present circumstances is thus the primary cleavage for future diplomacy. Yet the strategic invocation of legal standards has not been cost-free, as I have attempted to show. Indeed, a principal effect of the wider mine ban norm has been to narrow the conditions under which AP mines may be permissibly employed, even among those states that adhere to the less stringent requirements of APII. This process, moreover, is interactive. It should be recalled that the negotiation of APII was itself a response to the early efforts of the nascent mine ban movement. The attempted avoidance of the ban through an alternative legal structure thus reflects the influence of the mine ban norm in shaping expectations concerning appropriate behaviour. This in turn has the effect of reaffirming the legal realm as the legitimate arbiter of state action and provides grounds for assessing policy outcomes on the basis of intersubjectively negotiated criteria. APII might therefore be properly understood, for some states at least, as an intermediary stage in full adoption of mine ban norm, in a similar way that many current MBT parties underwent a gradual but no less profound change in their identities and interests. Ostensibly adopting the principled framework advanced by ban advocates has thus left MBT opponents vulnerable to subsequent assessments on these grounds.

Evidence that observance of the restrictions embodied in APII has not stemmed the tide of new AP mine victims, for example, would likely generate further social pressure to formally adopt the full prohibition. Determining the relative humanitarian impact of the two treaties would thus go a long way to informing these political and legal debates, and is thus a valuable subject for future research. I briefly address this issue in Chapter 9.

Importantly for this analysis, the qualified endorsement from key non-parties arguably invalidates any legal claim as a 'persistent objector' to the parallel international norm (Benesch et al. 1999; Beier 2002, 308; Price 2004a, 121). And, in the same way that they have policed actions among formal members, States Parties have not recognized violations even by non-parties as constituting valid exceptions to the prohibition. For this reason, states that might otherwise serve as 'spoilers'—by undercutting the interpretation and application of new norms through their practices—have been unable to substantially weaken the treaty. These developments would have been inconceivable in the absence of the particular status enjoyed by the mine ban, and the social power accorded to international law more generally.

Scholars have rightly regarded the MBT as an archetypal example of how international legal institutions and norms may be created in the face of great power opposition. What has been much less apparent to this point is whether the initial diplomatic strategy has been borne out by subsequent experience. The preceding analysis demonstrates that, in large measure, it has: the MBT has proven effective at substantiating new legal commitments for the vast majority of states and has shaped state conduct even among non-parties. The available evidence thus strongly suggests that the mine ban, as both a legal and broader social phenomenon, has substantially shifted international practice concerning AP mines. Their stigmatization has shaped the ways that states across the international system conceive of their obligations and render judgements regarding appropriate conduct. The International Criminal Court presents different conclusions in many of these respects, as will be addressed in Chapters 6 and 7.

6

States Parties and the International Criminal Court

How should we evaluate the influence of the International Criminal Court (ICC), given its internal complexities and multifaceted roles? At its core, the Rome Statute seeks to establish a new international norm concerning the appropriate response to grave crimes. States are now obliged to investigate and, if necessary, criminally sanction individual human beings for acts of atrocity, via a set of internationally negotiated judicial standards. By joining the Rome Statute, states also accept a new supranational body with the authority to conduct its own investigations and trials, and to evaluate and potentially intervene in domestic legal proceedings. In this latter respect, the innovation of the Rome Statute concerns the willingness of states to turn over some measure of their sovereign right to prosecute their nationals to a permanent international body over which they cannot exercise complete control. Though an independent institution, however, the Court requires the active support of states to enact its requests for assistance and legal judgments, leading to an enforcement problem at the heart of the ICC regime.

The Court's dual roles—imposing obligations on states and operating as a stand-alone institution—makes the assessment of its impact a more complicated endeavour than with respect to a comparatively straightforward humanitarian disarmament agreement like the Mine Ban Treaty (MBT). Despite a rich and ever-growing literature, the *political* dimensions of the ICC's influence have received less attention. Evaluating the success of proceeding without the great powers implies a particular way of studying ICC implementation that focuses on the diffusion of core Rome Statute norms across the international system among both formal treaty members and non-party states. My approach therefore diverges from the bulk of writings on the Court that variously focus on its development as a legal body (Cassese, Gaeta, and Jones 2002; Human Rights Watch 2008; Stahn 2015; Zidar and Bekou 2014), experiences in discrete national settings (Clarke 2009; Nouwen 2013), or the relationship between justice and peace and the ICC's ability to actually deter large scale acts of violence (Mullins and Rothe 2010; Snyder and Vinjamuri 2004) to name but a few of the most prominent strands.

This shift in attention is justified by the need for a broader account of the dynamics in which the Court operates, and their consequences (Bosco 2014). Indeed, it was recognized early on that 'if the ICC is to become a successful global court that prosecutes persons for international crimes notwithstanding the international political context, the adoption of the statute must usher in a sea change in national attitudes' (Charney 1999, 460). As Chapter 3 made clear, the expectation of domestic prosecution conditioned by supranational oversight represents a new normative and institutional solution to the problem of how to address grave violations of human rights and the laws of war; yet the ICC seeks to transform international expectations against the express wishes of many of the most materially powerful states in the international system. Many sceptics remain unconvinced that the Court—as a key component of the international justice architecture—will alter the calculations of states, or indeed that it has become sufficiently entrenched in the international system to withstand even modest challenges to its authority. This chapter assesses the current status of the Court among its formal parties. I begin by exploring the patterns of membership in the treaty community. Despite important limitations, the ICC already includes a number of states that are significant to the determination of a robust international legal regime and norm. I then consider evidence of ICC influence on state behaviour in a variety of forms, and return to the question of discourse by evaluating how states articulate their policies with respect to the ICC. In brief, state adaptation and consequent compliance is more limited than with respect to the mine ban. This raises the prospect of a crisis of legitimacy facing the Court, particularly relating to the lack of state action on key matters of cooperation.

MEMBERSHIP IN THE ICC COMMUNITY

The Assembly of States Parties (ASP) (Assembly of States Parties 2006, 348) has noted that 'universality of the Rome Statute… is imperative if we are to end impunity for the perpetrators of the most serious crimes of international concern… and guarantee lasting respect for and enforcement of international justice'. Claims of a growing consensus around the rule of law in general, and the ICC in particular, would seem to find support in the development of ICC membership. The Rome Statute entered into force on 1 July 2002, after achieving sixty ratifications; this rapid transition from drafting to full legal personality is similar to that of the MBT. There are currently 124 States Parties to the Rome Statute (Figure 6.1),[1] comparable with other key human rights

[1] As of May 2016. This includes the recent accession by the State of Palestine on 2 January 2015. Palestine had previously accepted ICC jurisdiction for acts committed after 13 June 2014,

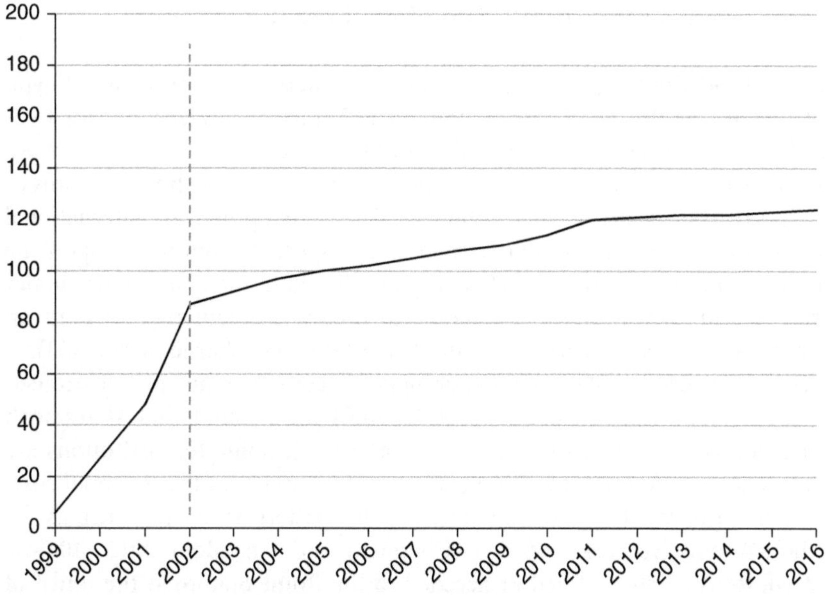

Figure 6.1. Rome Statute ratifications, 1999–2016

Note: Refers to the number of states that ratified or acceded to the Rome Statute during a given calendar year. The broken line reflects the entry into force of the Rome Statute. Data is derived from the United Nations Multilateral Treaties Deposited with the Secretary-General dataset, available at https://treaties.un.org/Pages/ParticipationStatus.aspx.

treaties including the 1966 International Covenant on Civil and Political Rights (ICCPR) and 1984 Convention against Torture (CAT), which have 168[2] and 156[3] parties respectively. This figure is particularly impressive when considering the pace of the expansion in membership: only sixty-six states ratified or acceded to the ICCPR during the first fifteen years of its existence, while 117 did so in the similar period for the CAT.[4] Consequently, Eve La Haye (2008, 165) has argued that these patterns of endorsement provide strong evidence of an emerging consensus among the society of states concerning the legitimacy of the Court and its underlying objective of combating impunity.

under Article 12(3) of the Rome Statute (State of Palestine 2014b). The ICC Office of the Prosecutor has determined that Palestine's status as a 'non-member observer State' (as conferred in UN General Assembly Resolution 67/19 of 29 November 2012) provides sufficient grounds for accession to the Rome Statute (Office of the Prosecutor, International Criminal Court 2015).

[2] International Covenant on Civil and Political Rights, New York, 16 December 1966. http://treaties.un.org/Pages/ViewDetails.aspx?src=TREATY&mtdsg_no=IV-4&chapter=4&lang=en.

[3] Convention against Torture and Other Cruel, Inhuman or Degrading Treatment or Punishment, New York, December 10, 1984. http://treaties.un.org/Pages/ViewDetails.aspx?src=TREATY&mtdsg_no=IV-9&chapter=4&lang=en.

[4] Twenty-four states have joined the ICCPR and thirty-two have joined the CAT since 2000, during the existence of the Rome Statute.

Hard Cases in the Adoption of the Rome Statute

Yet as David Bosco aptly highlights, non-members including China, Egypt, India, Iran, the Russian Federation, and the United States 'account for two-thirds of the world's population and almost three-quarters of its armed forces' (Bosco 2014, 5). This fact raises an important question regarding the status of the Court and its prospective influence. The development of international laws and norms is usually understood to be especially contingent upon the endorsement of those states particularly implicated in the types of acts under scrutiny, and for whom the new standards impose substantial constraints on current or potential future behaviour (Byers 1999, 38; Charney 1999, 463).

The risks posed to states by a supranational court are thus not distributed evenly. Chapman and Chaudoin (2013, 400) have found that states with higher levels of internal armed violence and weak domestic institutions are much less likely to ratify the Rome Statute, suggesting that the potential costs are well appreciated by governments. Yet this pattern is not uniform, as the authors themselves acknowledge (Chapman and Chaudoin 2013, 404–5). Indeed, twelve states ratified or acceded to the Rome Statute in the midst of internal armed conflicts,[5] while a further nine signed the Rome Statute during hostilities. A number of others—including Côte d'Ivoire,[6] Guinea, Liberia, Namibia, the Federal Republic of Yugoslavia, the Republic of Congo, Tajikistan, and Timor-Leste—joined the ICC soon after the end of civil conflicts and during fragile political transitions. In such cases, the potential for a renewal of hostilities and future exposure to ICC jurisdiction was a very real prospect. Since states engaged in various forms of organized violence are inherently more vulnerable to the types of crimes under the ICC's remit than those at peace, we might expect them to be more resistant to binding obligations that may disproportionately impact their own leaders and nationals. These cases therefore provide a partial rebuttal to the critical view that 'most countries that are engaged in or anticipate armed conflicts giving rise to war crimes have not joined the ICC regime' (Wippman 2006, 103).

The extent of ratification by conflict-prone states is, however, more modest than with the MBT.[7] Chapman and Chaudoin (2013, 400–3) have argued that states with established democratic institutions—most especially the rule of law and independent judiciaries—and an absence of internal violence will find adherence to ICC obligations to be much less costly. This pattern is indeed

[5] Afghanistan, Burundi, Central African Republic, Chad, Colombia, Democratic Republic of the Congo, Nigeria, the Philippines, Senegal, Sierra Leone, the States of Palestine, and Uganda.

[6] While not a full States Party until 2012, Côte d'Ivoire voluntarily accepted the jurisdiction of the Court for acts committed on its territory since 2003 (Republic of Côte d'Ivoire 2003; Republic of Côte d'Ivoire 2010).

[7] See Chapter 4, pages 75–6.

confirmed by the empirical record, as ninety-one States Parties were democracies in the year of ratification.[8] Inversely, Yvonne Dutton (2013, 36–7) has demonstrated that states with the worst domestic human rights records are considerably less likely to join the Rome Statute. Yet the argument that the ICC represents a case of self-selection into relatively low-risk institution is incomplete insofar as many internally peaceful and stable states—like Canada, France, and the United Kingdom—have prominent roles as members of military alliances. Since the 2002 entry into force of the Rome Statute, forty States Parties have participated in international armed conflicts, principally as part of the multinational coalitions in Afghanistan and Iraq.[9] Hence even states with little apparent risk still face potential exposure to ICC jurisdiction, as tentative preliminary investigations with respect to these two conflicts have demonstrated (Office of the Prosecutor, International Criminal Court 2014a, 11–13, 18–24; United Kingdom 2014). The Rome Statute also requires substantial alterations to national practices that have far-reaching domestic political and legal consequences for all members of the Court. Hence it would be incorrect to regard the ICC as an obviously low-cost commitment *ex ante*, because to do so assumes that the consequences of legal obligations were both minimally invasive and fully predictable from the outset.

Explaining Membership: The Discursive Power of the 'Rule of Law'

Official discourse concerning decisions to join the Court provides a further rejoinder to sceptical treatments, by highlighting the Rome Statute's constitutive function in reshaping conceptions of appropriate behaviour. While the Rome Statute emerges out of a much longer history of the progressive elaboration of international legal standards, the negotiation of the treaty was itself a moment in which state identities and interests were further reconfigured in favour of a robust and independent Court as a particular institutional solution

[8] Data is derived from the POLITY IV dataset, available at http://www.systemicpeace.org/inscrdata.html. Coding rules and discussion can be found in Marshall, Gurr, and Jaggers (2014). Seventy-one of these states were included in the POLITY dataset, while twenty were excluded as they did not meet the minimum population threshold of 500,000. Further coding by this author determined that the latter group should be included as democracies.

[9] The following States Parties to the Rome Statute contributed forces to Operation Enduring Freedom, the International Security Assistance Force, and/or the military occupation of Iraq: Albania, Australia, Austria, Belgium, Bosnia and Herzegovina, Bulgaria, Canada, Croatia, Czech Republic, Denmark, Dominican Republic, Estonia, Finland, France, Georgia, Germany, Greece, Honduras, Hungary, Iceland, Ireland, Italy, Japan, Korean Republic, Latvia, Lithuania, Luxembourg, Macedonia, Mongolia, Netherlands, New Zealand, Norway, Poland, Portugal, Romania, Slovakia, Slovenia, Spain, Sweden, and the United Kingdom. See http://www.isaf.nato.int/troop-numbers-and-contributions/index.php; and Marshall, Gurr, and Jaggers (2016).

to the problem of enforcing accountability for grave crimes (Chapter 3). States Parties frequently explain their decision to join the Court in reference to an affinity with its legal and normative purpose: 'The creation of the International Criminal Court is evidence of an emerging norm in international law in favour of ensuring that those accused of the most serious crimes are either prosecuted by competent national authorities or handed over for prosecution by a duly instituted international court' (Republic of South Africa 2003; Federal Republic of Nigeria 2004; Republic of Colombia 1998).

Importantly for the legitimacy of the Court, this view has been embraced by a number of the states most deeply implicated in the crimes under ICC jurisdiction. Simmons and Danner have suggested that ICC ratification can offer a means for states with a history of civil violence to provide credible commitments to domestic constituencies demonstrating a renewed fidelity to the rule of law (Simmons and Danner 2010, 227; Moravcsik 2000). These motivations are frequently reflected in official statements: 'Experiencing over three decades of war and being victim of war crimes, crimes against humanity and crime of aggression, we see the adoption of the Rome Statute, 15 years ago, as a historic achievement and a successful step forward toward bringing justice to victims of atrocities and heinous crimes. The Statute is an effective instrument for ending culture of impunity and a strong deterrence force to warn the criminals' (Islamic Republic of Afghanistan 2013).

In many cases—particularly in sub-Saharan Africa, the Balkans, and Latin America—adoption of the Rome Statute has been presented as a key feature of broader societal transformations as political communities seek to address past atrocities (Bosnia and Herzegovina 2002; Federal Republic of Yugoslavia 2002; Carrasco 2010; Sikkink 2011, 31–83). For the Democratic Republic of the Congo (DRC):

> The ratification of the Rome Statute was the culmination of a major mobilization of domestic public opinion and involvement in the process of creation of the ICC... The engine of this enthusiasm was unquestionably the serious injustices and damage caused by several years of war and grave breaches of human rights and international humanitarian law in the DRC and the conviction of the need to combat impunity as a close to dramatic cycles of violence and the desire to restore peace and reconciliation on the basis of sound justice. (Democratic Republic of the Congo 2008)

Of the forty-eight states that conducted at least one transitional human rights prosecution between 1979 and 2009, thirty-seven (77 per cent) are parties to the Rome Statute, while a further three are signatories (Sikkink 2011, 269). This phenomenon vividly illustrates the manner in which the ICC is embedded within larger domestic responses to past abuse.[10]

[10] The case of Argentina is especially instructive in this regard, as this state was at the forefront in developing domestic human rights trials for former high-ranking officials. Less

Much like the MBT discussed above, endorsement of the ICC has therefore served as a potent symbol of responsible statehood in the international system. The Rome Statute was the first international treaty that the new Tunisian government acceded to in the wake of the popular revolution that overthrew President Ben Ali:

> [A] decision which reflects the irreversible commitment of the new Tunisia to join the effort by the international community to end impunity for perpetrators of genocide, war crimes and crimes against humanity and provide justice to victims of such violations. It is a significant step and especially important for my country that has experienced profound democratic changes following the popular revolution of January 14, 2011 which put an end to decades of injustice, abuse and despotism. (Republic of Tunisia 2011; Republic of Tunisia 2013)

Civil society experts have suggested that the decision to join the Court and similar human rights agreements was explicitly intended by the new Tunisian regime to underscore the extent of the break with the former system.[11] For other states including Afghanistan,[12] Bangladesh,[13] Cambodia,[14] Congo,[15] Côte d'Ivoire,[16] DRC,[17] Kenya,[18] Mexico,[19] Palestine,[20] Peru,[21] the Philippines,[22] Serbia,[23] and South Africa,[24] adoption of the Rome Statute has similarly been presented as a marker of fidelity to international norms. While many states may join international institutions like the ICC to 'lock-in' new commitments to human rights and the rule of law, therefore, these actions are themselves situated within an international social context in which

than a decade later, Argentine diplomats were deeply involved in the negotiation of the Rome Statute, and a former prosecutor of the junta trials, Luis Moreno-Ocampo, became the first ICC Chief Prosecutor.

[11] Interview with members of the Coalition for the ICC Middle East and North Africa (MENA) section. New York, 15 December 2011.

[12] Islamic Republic of Afghanistan (2005).

[13] People's Republic of Bangladesh (2010; 2014); Dukalskis and Johansen (2013, 585).

[14] Statement by H.E. Ambassador Sun Suon, Deputy Permanent Representative of Cambodia to the United Nations, as quoted in Coalition for the International Criminal Court (2002, 5).

[15] Republic of Congo (2013). [16] Republic of Côte d'Ivoire (2013).

[17] Democratic Republic of the Congo (2008; 2013).

[18] Dutton (2013, 137–55). [19] Republic of Mexico (2005).

[20] State of Palestine (2014b; 2014a).

[21] Interview with Michelle Reyes Milk, Outreach Liaison for the Americas, Asia and the Pacific, Coalition for the International Criminal Court. New York, 19 December 2011.

[22] Republic of the Philippines (2011).

[23] Republic of Serbia (2007; 2013); Coalition for the International Criminal Court (2008, 16). In interviews and diplomatic meetings, officials from the Republic of Serbia and the International Criminal Tribunal for the Former Yugoslavia (ICTY) have specifically identified the importance of the political transition—notably the end of the Milosevic regime and emergence of a new government—as vital to generating greater engagement with international justice institutions, most specifically via political accommodation with the ICTY and the will to enact the requisite domestic changes.

[24] Republic of South Africa (2002, para. 2; 2013).

individual criminal accountability via regularized judicial processes has become the pre-eminent means of addressing past atrocity.

In more established liberal democracies, the nested nature of law has again played a vital role in facilitating the emergence of a collective identity—and attendant social pressure to conform—that regards adoption of the Rome Statute as a key indicator of good standing. For Western (and especially European) states, then, 'the ICC was an opportunity to confirm their liberal credentials, contribute to international peace and security, and, perhaps, to distinguish themselves from and even place a modest check on the unilateralist stance and actions of the United States' (Wippman 2004, 161). Yet this shift was not necessarily preordained or unproblematic, as the widespread acceptance of a genuinely independent ICC required the same shift in attitudes among ultimately supportive states as already documented with respect to the antipersonnel (AP) mine ban. Until very late in the negotiations, both France and the United Kingdom strongly resisted the prospect of a Court that challenged the prerogatives of the UN Security Council (UNSC). David Wippman (2004) has persuasively demonstrated the role of legal argumentation in negotiations over the Rome Statute, as engagement with human rights discourses and linkages to existing international humanitarian and criminal law norms was instrumental in framing the Court as an extension of international progress on human security and the domestic rule of law. This generated social pressure within the French and British governments (among others) to abandon their opposition and formally endorse the Like-Minded position (Wippman 2004, 167–8). The strategic use of legal claims thus led to the 'rhetorical entrapment' of many delegations wherein 'it became simply inappropriate to publicly oppose the ICC' (Deitelhoff 2009b, 57). For a number of other states, including later adopters like Japan, the close connection between the Rome Statute and already widely accepted treaties like the 1949 Geneva Conventions and 1977 Additional Protocols provided a vital opening in widening the window of possibility for ratification (Meierhenrich and Ko 2009, 255).

For a majority of states in the contemporary international system, therefore, the ICC has become a focal point for the elaboration of a new and potentially transformative international social standard. This reaffirms the point that treaties like the Rome Statute should not be regarded as low-cost agreements among already willing participants, but rather as a politically significant driver of changes in international identities. In many cases, it may appear that treaties merely serve to 'screen' supporters in that the content of the agreement reflects the existing preferences of a certain sub-set of states (Downs, Rocke, and Barsoom 1996; von Stein 2005; Simmons and Hopkins 2005). This view, however, misses the processes through which diplomatic interactions transform what states want and how they pursue these goals. This constitutive function is vital to the prospective power of the Court to re-shape international practice, and raises the question of whether states are living up to their professed commitments. After all, a sceptical view would suggest that states might cynically endorse the Rome Statute in order to distract from their own abuses or in order to subsequently employ judicial processes against domestic enemies (a prospect I consider in greater detail below). Yet this book has also maintained that there are potentially substantial costs associated with the instrumental use of norms, as it can open additional avenues of social pressure leading to greater unintended changes in state policy. A decision to join the ICC as easy 'cheap talk' thus holds the risk of backfiring, since the full scope and intent of the Court will only become apparent over time. The balance of the chapter assesses whether the general endorsements described above have translated into practical implementation of the Rome Statute's institutional demands.

IMPLEMENTATION AND COMPLIANCE: ACCOMMODATION WITH THE ROME STATUTE REGIME

While formal membership and general discursive endorsement suggest a widely accepted institution, this is not in itself sufficient evidence of the myriad ways that treaties may shape the conduct of international affairs. The act of ratification or accession does not guarantee that States Parties will respect their legal obligations, as previous scholarship has established (Hafner-Burton and Tsutsui 2005; Hathaway 2002). For this reason, it is necessary to examine the ways and extent to which ICC members have—and in some cases have not—adapted their behaviour in conformance with the Rome Statute's demands.

Domestic Legislation

As argued in Chapter 3, the particular structure of the ICC regime necessitates extensive changes to domestic legal orders to ensure that states possess sufficient capacity to investigate and (where necessary) prosecute crimes falling under the Court's remit. This provides the institutional basis for relieving the ICC of the burden of adjudicating potential cases and avoiding challenges under the principle of complementarity. At the same time, national legislation in needed to ensure that States Parties have the legal, judicial, and bureaucratic mechanisms in place to respond to requests for assistance from the Court (via the Office of the Prosecutor (OTP), defence council, or Registry) or other states. Legislative change is also a valuable indicator of national political will, since it requires that states take positive action to bring themselves in line with their legal obligations (International Centre for Criminal Law Reform and Criminal Justice Policy 2008, 12; Assembly of States Parties 2010a, para. 7). National adoption of Rome Statute standards is thus key to the process of norm dispersion, and provides a window into the internalization of international norms that is not captured by reference to formal institutional membership or other forms of compliance. For these reasons, domestic legal capacity is vital to the effective operation of the ICC, and has been identified by the International Bar Association (International Bar Association 2008, 1) as 'the missing link between the obligations within the Rome Statute and the implementation by States Parties'.

Thus far the empirical record is mixed, at best.[25] According to the most recent information, sixty-four States Parties (52 per cent) have enacted new laws, or amended existing ones, in order to specifically address some or all Rome Statute provisions; a further twenty-nine (24 per cent) have drafted, but have yet to formally adopt, similar legislation.[26] Implementation of core Rome Statute crimes has been modestly higher than for provisions relating to cooperation with Court activities. Yet these latter responsibilities, articulated in Part IX of the Rome Statute, are generally understood to impose specific legal obligations on treaty members; by contrast, the Statute does not require that states adopt legislation to incorporate ICC crimes.

Patterns of legislative adoption also provide important leverage concerning core theoretical claims in this study. As expected by previous scholarship, the adoption or amendment of laws is clustered among ostensibly 'pro-ICC' states. Forty-four States Parties with implementing legislation (69 per cent) were members of the Like-Minded Group of states that—along with civil society actors—stewarded the negotiations for an independent Court, and fully fifty-six (88 per cent) are democracies.[27] This supports the view that extensive incorporation of international legal obligations is most likely in states that are already deeply committed to the objectives of the treaty and possess a strongly institutionalized domestic rule of law. However, national implementation has also featured as part of broader societal transformations

[25] Unless otherwise noted, discussion in this section is based on data from Coalition for the International Criminal Court (2012). A detailed and comparative evaluation of the contents of national legislation is beyond the scope of this chapter and book. Recent discussions can be found in Bekou (2011; 2014).

[26] Interestingly, eleven non-parties to the Rome Statute have also adopted some form of legislation addressing either cooperation with the ICC or, more usually, crimes falling under its jurisdiction.

[27] With POLITY IV scores of 6 or greater in the year of legislative adoption. The exceptions are Bangladesh (5), Bosnia and Herzegovina (under external stewardship), Burkina Faso (2), Cambodia (2), Central African Republic (–1), Georgia (5), Niger (5), and Uganda (–1).

in a number of states such as Argentina, Colombia, and South Africa.[28] In some cases, the experience of internal armed conflict has led to greater engagement with the Court and an increased sensitivity to the legal standards contained in the Rome Statute. For example, Uganda's 2010 International Criminal Court Bill is explicitly modelled on the Statute and integrates many provisions directly from the treaty text (Parliament of Uganda 2006). Anecdotal evidence suggests that Ugandan officials modified the ICC Bill in specific ways to conform to the Statute (*New Vision* 2010). Hence challenging circumstances do not necessarily undermine state implementation, but may in fact provide the impetus for legal change.

Despite some evidence of adaptation, the transmission of ICC legal standards is occurring slowly even among those states that have formally endorsed the treaty. There are thus important limits in the extent to which the constituent Rome Statute norms and rules are gaining traction in domestic law. This finding is not limited to the ICC legal regime (Cryer 2005, 117–19), but is nonetheless problematic for two general reasons alluded to above. First, the absence of widespread and comprehensive domestic legislation weakens the normative power of the Statute and its model of supranational accountability. Second, gaps in domestic legal capacity reduce the practical ability of states to investigate and prosecute these crimes, and leave open the possibility that they will prove unable or unwilling to aid the Court in the pursuit of justice. These observations reinforce the call from many quarters to make national implementing legislation a priority (Assembly of States Parties 2011).

Changing Domestic Practice? The Application of Substantive ICC Law in National Systems

The process of legal implementation has also generated further institutionalization in a number of ICC member states, as with the creation of a dedicated Priority Crimes Litigation Unit in South Africa (Stone 2011, 307). Subjects of preliminary examinations or formal ICC investigations including Central African Republic (CAR),[29] Colombia,[30] DRC,[31] Georgia,[32] Guinea,[33]

[28] See for example contributions to *International Criminal Law Review* 10(4) (2010) and Stone (2011).

[29] Darehshori and Evenson (2010, 21–2).

[30] Republic of Colombia (2010); Ambos (2011); Office of the Prosecutor, International Criminal Court (2014a, 25–32).

[31] Avocats Sans Frontières (2009); Glasius (2011, 1213–16).

[32] Office of the Prosecutor, International Criminal Court (2014a, 33–7).

[33] International Criminal Court (2013b, 10; 2014c, 3); Office of the Prosecutor, International Criminal Court (2014a, 38–41).

Kenya,[34] Nigeria,[35] and Uganda[36] have created or modified judicial institutions and undertaken criminal investigations and (in some cases) trials in order to address alleged crimes at the national level. In doing so, these states bear the marks of international norms and rules on domestic legal practice. For example, since 2006 the military courts of the DRC have invoked aspects of the Rome Statute in some of their judgements (Avocats Sans Frontières 2009, 4). The conviction of Mai Mai commander Gédéon Kyungu Mutanga and twenty other combatants in March 2009 was particularly notable for the fact that the judges applied the criteria of crimes against humanity found in the Rome Statute (Human Rights Watch 2009). Similar trials in Uganda and have also drawn on substantive and procedural aspects of the Statute (Anyoli 2010).

One significant impact of the Rome Statute and its internationalized procedural justice norm, therefore, has been to generate pressures toward the—partial and still incomplete—harmonization of state responses to alleged acts of grave criminality. In some instances, as with Colombia, Georgia, and Kenya, domestic judicial processes have clearly been intended to demonstrate national political will and legal capacity, and thereby avoid a transfer of authority to the ICC via a complementarity challenge. Yet observers frequently suggest that domestic legal systems are often deeply corrupt and lacking the necessary capacity to effectively address past and ongoing crimes. Many have been further hampered by political instability and various bureaucratic obstructions (Office of the Prosecutor, International Criminal Court 2014a, 35 and 39). These processes are not without their detractors, therefore, and allegations persist that judicial processes have shielded senior officials from legal scrutiny (Alai and Mue 2011; Glasius 2011; Human Rights Watch 2009; Klein 2010, 676–80; Lyons and Reed-Hurtado 2010, 2–4; Murithi 2010).

Yet as with state responses to the mine ban, incomplete compliance can have important unintended long-term effects. First, the use of legal processes can serve to reinforce an expectation that these procedures should be followed, thereby locking in this response for future scenarios. For example, the Kenyan Commission of Inquiry into Post-Election Violence recommended 'the creation of a special tribunal with the mandate to prosecute crimes committed as a result of post-election violence [in 2007–8]' (Republic of Kenya 2008, ix). However, the final report also proposed that in the event that no tribunal could be agreed:

[34] Republic of Kenya (2013a, 10–11; 2013b). As Hobbs (2015, 79) notes, however, 'The International Crimes Act 2008, which incorporated the Rome Statute into Kenyan domestic law, only applies to international crimes committed after 1 January 2009; it could not therefore be applied retrospectively to the 2007–2008 events.' I return to the subject of Kenya's cooperation with ICC investigations below.

[35] Office of the Prosecutor, International Criminal Court (2014a, 42–5).

[36] British Broadcasting Corporation (2008); Human Rights Watch (2012a); Nouwen (2011).

> A list containing names of and relevant information on those suspected to bear the greatest responsibility for crimes falling within the jurisdiction of the proposed Special Tribunal shall be forwarded to the Prosecutor of the International Criminal Court. The Prosecutor shall be requested to analyze the seriousness of the information received with a view to proceeding with an investigation and prosecuting such suspected persons. (Republic of Kenya 2008, 473)

When the unity government failed to establish a tribunal, this sealed list was duly passed to the ICC OTP (Alai and Mue 2011, 1225–7). The key point here is that the Kenyan government has been obliged to engage with the Court both as a States Party with legal obligations to the institution, and on the basis of its prior acceptance of a political agreement that specifically envisioned a potential reliance on the Court. While resisting the indictments, Kenya has nonetheless sought to frame its challenge in terms of the legal criteria of the Rome Statute, as evident in the government's appeals to the Pre-Trial Chamber to vacate the cases (Republic of Kenya 2011a). A similar pattern can be witnessed in other cases, whereby the relevant states have sought to assert their sovereignty by upholding the norms of individual criminal accountability and the ICC's particular model of complementarity (Central African Republic 2010; Georgia 2010; Republic of Colombia 2010). The very fact that states often respond to actual or potential ICC investigations with their own domestic processes powerfully demonstrates how international norms and legal structures may change how states pursue their interests, by providing new benchmarks for appropriate action. These developments, moreover, may be politically consequential even when they emerge from apparently cynical efforts to strategically avoid international commitments; this is explored at greater length below.

Second, the existence of new legal standards can provide valuable tools for domestic actors to bypass powerful veto players. The Colombian case illustrates this well:

> For the Supreme Court, the ICC has been an important source of support and validation for its efforts to pursue accountability in a hostile political climate. In a recent case, the Criminal Cassation Chamber described its responsibility as 'avoiding at all cost impunity for the crimes allegedly committed and thereby to show the international community that intervention by the international criminal justice system is not necessary because Colombia is able to try those responsible for such crimes and to impose the punitive consequences established under national criminal law'. (Lyons and Reed-Hurtado 2010, 4)

These interactions reaffirm the ICC's procedural justice norm of domestic legal responsibility overseen by a supranational authority as the appropriate means of addressing alleged violations of international humanitarian and human rights law. More broadly, the reliance on the procedural and substantive criteria of the Rome Statute to pursue domestic goals further reinforces the legalistic basis of membership in the ICC treaty community.

The impact of the Rome Statute on domestic legal practice can also be seen in instances that fall outside of the strict scope of the ICC itself. As an exemplar of this phenomenon, Canada has used its *Crimes Against Humanity and War Crimes Act* (CAHWCA)—a centrepiece of its legislation implementing the Rome Statute in Canadian law—to prosecute Rwandan nationals Désiré Munyaneza and Jacques Mungwarere for acts of genocide committed during the 1994 violence (Ministry of Justice, Canada 2000; Canadian Centre for International Justice 2016; Lafontaine 2010). While the criminal acts in these cases pre-date the entry-into-force of the Rome Statute (and hence fall outside its jurisdiction), they are closely associated with the international and domestic responses to atrocity traced above. Indeed, the genesis of the CAHWCA was itself a response both to noted gaps in prior Canadian legislation that impeded war crimes prosecutions, and the more particular need to meet obligations deriving from Canada's ratification of the Rome Statute.[37] Other states including France and Germany have faced similar calls to pursue cases through the legal authority obtained in their ratification of the Rome Statute and other international legal agreements (Keaten 2010; Amnesty International 2008). Hence one notable impact of the ICC membership has been to increase pressure on states not currently implicated in crimes under ICC jurisdiction to address related legal issues by virtue of their endorsement of norms and practices associated with the grave crimes regime in general and the Rome Statute in particular.

Patterns of Compliance: Cooperation with ICC Operations

Since its inception, stakeholders have recognized the vital importance of state cooperation to facilitate Court operations (Assembly of States Parties 2007b; International Criminal Court 2013a). The record of compliance with ICC judicial activities provides additional evidence for the impact of the treaty, but the available metrics are highly imperfect. As a relatively new institution, there have only been a limited number of investigations and indictments that have generated the bulk of demands for state compliance. Moreover, the vast majority of these requests are not made public meaning it is difficult to determine when, and to what extent, states are actually fulfilling ICC requests (International Criminal Court 2007, 11). Yet keeping these caveats in mind, some broad patterns of state engagement can be discerned.

Since 2007, the OTP has made over 1,350 requests for assistance to individual states, inter-governmental organizations (principally UN bodies) and

[37] The CAHWCA (Articles 3 and 4) incorporates verbatim the crimes enumerated in Articles 6–8 of the Rome Statute. For critiques concerning the relatively limited number of criminal processes undertaken thus far, see Duggal (2012); Friscolanti (2011).

non-governmental organizations in respect of ongoing investigations and prosecutions.[38] These requests have predominantly concerned three main issues: investigations on national territory (including requests for assistance, transmission of information, and interviews); lifting of confidentiality; and access to financial assets (Assembly of States Parties 2009, 11).[39] The OTP reports that cooperation has been 'generally forthcoming' (International Criminal Court 2011, 1), with an initial 85 per cent 'execution rate' on its requests during 2007–9 which has dropped to approximately 70 per cent between 2009 and 2011 (Assembly of States Parties 2009, 11; International Criminal Court 2011, 3). No explanation is given for this decline, and more recent reports do not provide similar statistics.

A more fine-grained analysis of the available evidence suggests that certain types of requests have been particularly problematic. For example, between 2009 and 2011 only 30 per cent of requests to identify, freeze, or seize personal assets transmitted by the Registry were 'fully executed' (International Criminal Court 2011, 6). Most crucially, the Court has long noted that limited assistance in matters of arresting and surrendering ICC suspects remains a critical gap that adversely affects its capacity to deliver justice (Assembly of States Parties 2007a, 10). States Parties are legally obliged to execute warrants issued by the Court, yet of the thirty-six arrest warrants that have been issued thus far, thirteen remain outstanding, with three of these active since 2005 (International Criminal Court 2014b, 2).[40] As such, ICC reports acknowledge the need for more support for the Court's work, as well as greater coordination and political and legal commitment among states and other bodies.

The most glaring example concerns the ongoing failure to arrest Sudanese President Omar al-Bashir during his various international visits, including to ICC States Parties Chad, DRC, Djibouti, Kenya, Malawi, Nigeria, South Africa, and Uganda.[41] The Court has made a number of direct interventions in highlighting Bashir's prospective plans and requesting his immediate detention and transfer to The Hague (International Criminal Court 2013b, 3; International Criminal Court 2014c, 6–7).[42] When it failed to receive sufficient action, the Court has taken the further extraordinary step—as permitted by Article 87(7) of the Rome Statute—of publicly informing the Assembly of

[38] Various annual reports from Court organs are complied at http://www.icc-cpi.int/en_menus/icc/reports%20on%20activities/Pages/reports%20on%20activities.aspx.

[39] These figures exclude requests from the Registry relating to non-judicial cooperation with respect to matters of defence, victims and witnesses, and detention.

[40] Since the issuance of this report, Dominic Ongwen (a LRA commander) was transferred to ICC custody.

[41] Non-party states that have hosted President Bashir since his indictment include China, Egypt, Eritrea, Ethiopia, Libya, Iran, Iraq, Malaysia, Qatar, Saudi Arabia, South Sudan, and Zimbabwe, as discussed in Chapter 7 (Bosco 2014, 158).

[42] Court documents related to the Bashir case can be found at https://www.icc-cpi.int/darfur/albashir.

States Parties (ASP) of what it regards as deliberate non-compliance and, with respect to Chad, Djibouti, DRC, Malawi, South Africa, and Uganda, referring the violations to the UNSC for further consideration (ICC Pre-Trial Chamber I 2011a, 21; ICC Pre-Trial Chamber II 2013, 10–11; ICC Pre-Trial Chamber II 2014, 15–18; ICC Pre-Trial Chamber II 2016a; ICC Pre-Trial Chamber II 2016b).

The diplomacy surrounding these cases provides useful insight concerning the current status of the Rome Statute among its members, and the ability of the Court and other entities to enforce its obligations. In their official submissions on the matter, the CAR, Chad, the DRC, and Malawi have defended their inaction by invoking alternative legal principles. First, they contended that Heads of State retain some forms of immunity under international law irrespective of the ICC's legal authority in the particular case at hand. Second and relatedly, they claimed to be bound to uphold the African Union's (AU) position challenging ICC jurisdiction over President Bashir, and were therefore unable to act in contravention of the obligations as AU member states (ICC Pre-Trial Chamber I 2011a, 7–8; ICC Pre-Trial Chamber I 2011b, 5; ICC Registrar 2014; Assembly of States Parties 2014a, 6). All four states sought at the same time to reinforce their commitment to the ICC and international criminal justice more generally, albeit under a set of specific conditions. These interventions all share an explicit invocation of legal claims as the justification for contesting the Court's jurisdiction, a point to which I return at length later.

Court bodies have extensively disputed these claims and reiterated the legal basis of their actions under the Rome Statute and applicable international law (ICC Pre-Trial Chamber II 2014). The Pre-Trial Chamber found the respective states to be in non-compliance with ICC rulings and referred their actions to the Security Council and ASP for further action (ICC Pre-Trial Chamber I 2011a, 21; ICC Pre-Trial Chamber I 2011b, 8; ICC Pre-Trial Chamber II 2013; ICC Pre-Trial Chamber II 2014, 17). Yet the response from other states and organizations has been relatively muted. ICC States Parties have drawn attention to the apparently wilful non-compliance, and have called on the relevant states to meet their obligations to arrest and transfer ICC suspects (Assembly of States Parties 2013a; Assembly of States Parties 2014a; Assembly of States Parties 2014b), but there has been little effort to deploy more substantial material or social resources to induce cooperation. While the ASP has served as a forum for disseminating information and making general appeals in favour of compliance, therefore, there is scant evidence of specific socialization processes in these instances. In this respect, the ICC case deviates from that of the MBT presented in Chapter 4. The absence of political will, reinforced by gaps in domestic legal capacity, are the key reasons why states have yet to meet these core commitments concerning arrest and surrender of ICC suspects.

DEFERRING TO THE COURT? INSTRUMENTALIZING THE LEGAL PROCESS AND ITS CONSEQUENCES

Self-Referrals

At the same time, the early years of the Court featured a series of positive, and potentially surprising, instances of cooperation. For example, Uganda, DRC, the CAR,[43] and Mali formally requested that the Court investigate alleged crimes committed during their civil armed conflicts through so-called 'self-referrals' (Akhavan 2011; Clark 2011; Jones 2014). These were largely unanticipated developments, and ones that call into question the political motivations underlying these decisions. Indeed, the decisions are puzzling insofar as we might wonder why actors would willingly cede sovereign authority over such politically significant functions to an external body. For its part, the Court encouraged these referrals as a means of jump-starting the legal process in areas affected by conflict and without sufficient domestic capacity to provide accountability (Office of the Prosecutor, International Criminal Court 2003). Côte d'Ivoire, Palestine, and Ukraine also voluntarily accepted ICC jurisdiction while non-member states—in all three cases in the midst of various forms of armed conflict (Republic of Côte d'Ivoire 2003; Republic of Côte d'Ivoire 2010; States of Palestine 2014b; Ukraine 2014b; Ukraine 2015). Both Côte d'Ivoire and Palestine subsequently formally joined the Rome Statute.

The ICC Prosecutor has repeatedly suggested that the referrals are clear evidence of political commitment to addressing atrocities. Yet self-referrals are potentially problematic insofar as they appear designed to target some actors while sparing others from similar scrutiny. A variety of observers have voiced concerns that these initiatives were undertaken on the part of sitting governments to undermine their enemies (either the leadership of rebel movements or political opponents) without an expectation that they themselves might be implicated in the same criminal inquiries (Branch 2007; Rastan 2009, 173–6; Schiff 2008, 194–226 and 242–7; Tiemessen 2014).[44] The empirical record would seem to confirm this suspicion. To this point, the Court has not issued indictments for any current members of the government or security services in any of the self-referring states. Moreover, it appears that the governments in question have deliberately shaped their cooperation to impede any prospective investigations of their own behaviour, principally by only turning over

[43] The government of the CAR recently submitted a second referral for crimes allegedly committed since 2012 (Central African Republic 2014; Office of the Prosecutor, International Criminal Court 2014a, 46–51).

[44] Civil society actors have voiced similar scepticism regarding the political motivations of self-referrals. Interview with Francis Dako, Africa Coordinator for the Coalition for the International Criminal Court. New York, 15 December 2011.

evidence that implicates enemies while withdrawing assistance on matters that question their own actions.

On the one hand, apparently cynical attempts to deploy norms for self-interested gain provide a valuable window into the relationship between strategic and normative logics of action, as Chapter 2 suggested. At their core, self-referrals involve an attempt to characterize legitimate and illegitimate actors on the basis of their rejection of international norms. Nouwen and Werner (2010, 941) argue, for example, that the Ugandan government has 'used the ICC's intervention to brand opponents as *hostis humani generis*, or enemies of mankind, and to present themselves as friends of the ICC, and thus friends of the international community'. The government of the DRC has similarly invoked arrest warrants to label rebel actors—most notably Bosco Ntaganda—as illegitimate 'criminals' and 'terrorists' (Democratic Republic of the Congo 2013). These discursive practices have also featured in more recent episodes. In the wake of the overthrow of Ukrainian President Victor Yanukovych, the new Ukrainian regime used its ICC declaration to specifically accuse Mr Yanukovych and senior members of his government of committing crimes against humanity during the attempted repression of protests, and has subsequently alleged similar crimes on the part of separatist rebels in the ongoing conflict (Ukraine 2014a; Cullinane 2015). The Palestinian referral and accession has been widely regarded as much a political as legal manoeuvre, with the dual aim of delegitimizing Israeli actions in Gaza and the West Bank, and using an international institution to constrain Israeli state policy (States of Palestine 2014a).

But employing institutions in this way is only effective to the extent that such efforts tap into salient intersubjective beliefs held by a relevant audience—in this case, the international community writ large—by invoking discourses of international law (Bower 2015). While much of this rhetoric betrays an instrumental view of the ICC, it simultaneously reaffirms the relevance of the Rome Statute as the appropriate metric for assessing state commitment to ending impunity for grave crimes. Hence:

> The Government of Uganda (GoU) decided to refer the case to the ICC not because the Government was unable or unwilling to try the [Lord's Resistance Army] itself but because the ICC was established specifically to deal with crimes of this magnitude and the GoU was unable to access the LRA who were operating outside its territory. We thought that the ICC would galvanize international cooperation and compel those countries harbouring the LRA to act appropriately.
> (Republic of Uganda 2006)

Darehshori and Evenson (2010, 21) similarly report that the CAR's decision to refer alleged crimes committed in 2002–3 to the ICC came about 'after CAR's Court of Appeal recognized the inability of domestic courts to investigate and prosecute war criminals effectively'. The governments in question have sought to portray the referrals as a demonstration of their fidelity to the Court despite an inability to meet the conditions of legal accountability themselves. While not encompassing the totality of motivations, therefore, official statements demonstrate the impact of norms in shaping state policy by informing the calculation of prospective costs and benefits; such efforts only make sense in the context of a social setting in which the ICC has already achieved considerable social standing.

On the other hand, my of account international law's social basis and effects suggests that the deployment of legal discourse can have unintended consequences, insofar as it exposes claim-makers to subsequent examination on the same grounds. Despite the apparent intention to use international legal sanction as a means of generating coercive pressure for the settlement of a conflict on the government's terms, the ICC retains jurisdiction over the 'situations' in the country and not just specific cases, meaning that it may choose to widen the scope of its inquiry at a future date.[45] All parties to the conflicts are subject to the legal authority of the Court, and so the initiating governments remain potential targets of an ICC investigation. Early cooperation from authorities in affected countries has also reinforced expected ways of behaving that narrows future policy choices. Conforming to the expectations of the treaty community sets a precedent that *other* actors including fellow governments and civil society groups can exploit to hold states to account if they fail to continue to meet the standards they purportedly endorse.

For example, efforts by the Government of Uganda to revoke the ICC indictments in exchange for LRA demobilization during the failed peace process faced criticism precisely because of the government's prior public support for the ICC process. The government has repeatedly found it necessary to defend Ugandan proposals against responses from the Court and other states that explicitly invoke the legal criteria of the Rome Statute as the basis of Uganda's ongoing obligation. Consequently, the indictments have remained in force, and Ugandan statements regarding the withdrawal of ICC arrest warrants have notably receded in recent years. This has proven relevant again with the capture of LRA indictee Dominic Ongwen to the ICC: while Ugandan officials including President Museveni insisted that domestic courts were capable of conducting a fair trial, they were unable to prevent Mr Ongwen's transfer to the Hague (British Broadcasting Corporation 2015).

[45] It is notable that the Government of Uganda's initial referral was directed towards the LRA specifically, though the Prosecutor extended this to all crimes allegedly committed in Northern Uganda (Office of the Prosecutor, International Criminal Court 2004a). Notwithstanding the original focus on LRA atrocities, the OTP continues to gather and analyse information relating to alleged abuses by state forces in Uganda (International Criminal Court 2014c, 11). The referrals for CAR, DRC, and Mali referenced potential crimes committed anywhere on the territories of the subject states (Office of the Prosecutor, International Criminal Court 2004b; 2005; Republic of Mali, Ministry of Justice 2012).

Hence there are potential costs associated with the strategic use of the ICC legal process, even if one reads the motivations as largely self-interested. So far, however, there is only limited evidence that this has occurred among subject states. William Schabas has written that in the Ugandan case the ICC Prosecutor has in practice only focused on the LRA, 'effectively ignoring the allegations of criminal behaviour by the government forces' (Schabas 2011, 160 and 162–3). To this point, therefore, self-referring states have proven quite successful at insulating themselves from serious legal inquiry. As will be shown further below, moreover, other ICC members have generally been unwilling to actively voice concerns about state cooperation—or lack thereof—with ongoing ICC legal processes.

Kenya: *Proprio Motu* and the Challenge of ICC Jurisdiction

In many respects, the Kenyan case provides the most problematic example to date of the potential limits of the ICC's socializing power (Alai and Mue 2011). It is also a key test case for the legal and political authority of the Court since it involves the sitting Head of State of a Rome Statute member: both the current President and Deputy President of Kenya have faced indictment by the Court over their alleged role in violence that followed the disputed 2007–8 election.[46] The ICC involvement in Kenya therefore presents a second instance in which the core ICC norm of non-immunity from prosecution comes into contact with political prerogatives of states (the other, concerning Sudanese President Omar al-Bashir, will be discussed in Chapter 7). The Kenyan situation is controversial for the additional reason that it represented the first use of the ICC Prosecutor's *proprio motu* powers to independently commence a formal investigation (ICC Pre-Trial Chamber II 2010). By this act, the ICC took jurisdiction over alleged crimes, meaning that its own legal processes take precedence over national ones. Indeed, as the basis for its authorization of an investigation, the Court found that there had been a lack of substantive judicial proceedings in relation to the specific crimes under ICC jurisdiction (ICC Pre-Trial Chamber II 2010, 69–73).

The Kenyan case provides an important example of a state party seeking to advance its interests within the structures of a legal institution, and in ways that may directly conflict with the objectives of the institution itself. The initial response to the ICC investigation was largely one of accommodation: the Government of Kenya signed a Memorandum of Understanding with the Court and indicated its willingness to cooperate with ICC processes. Following

[46] *Prosecutor* v. *Uhruru Muigai Kenyatta*, ICC-01/09-02/11 (Trial Chamber) and *Prosecutor* v. *William Samoei Ruto and Joshua Arap Sang*, ICC-01/09-01/11 (Trial Chamber); charges were confirmed for both Mr Kenyatta and Mr Ruto on 23 January 2012.

summonses to appear issued on 8 March 2011, six suspects, including Uhuru Kenyatta (President) and William Ruto (Deputy President), voluntarily appeared in The Hague. The government has continued to insist that it is fully compliant with Court requests (Republic of Kenya 2013a, 4 and 8), but in parallel has sought to employ ICC legal procedures to bypass investigations from The Hague. First, Kenya claimed that its own domestic reforms and ongoing investigations met the conditions of ability and willingness enshrined in the complementarity principle, and therefore superseded the ICC process (Republic of Kenya 2011a; Republic of Kenya 2013b). Kenya further submitted a request for the Court to turn over all relevant evidence to facilitate national investigations (Republic of Kenya 2011b). The Court rejected both these requests (Appeals Chamber, International Criminal Court 2011), leading to a series of filings and counter-filings by the Kenyan government and Court in which the former sought to contest the ICC findings concerning its lack of legal capacity and political will (Hobbs 2015).[47]

With the broader complementarity challenge in limbo, Kenya engaged in a range of additional efforts aimed more specifically at exempting Kenyatta and Ruto from ICC prosecution. Irrespective of its prior acceptance of the Statute, the Kenyan government has long asserted that 'as the Rome Statute is a treaty like any other it must be read within the framework of international law that confers immunity to sitting Heads of States and Governments' (Republic of Kenya 2013a, 11). It first lobbied the AU to seek, via a UNSC resolution, the suspension of both leaders' trials until they concluded their terms of office (Assembly of the African Union 2011a, para. 6; Assembly of the African Union 2013, paras. 10(ii, ix–xi)). This initiative was not successful, as the UNSC voted against a proposed resolution that would have suspended legal proceedings for one year as permitted by Article 16 of the Rome Statute (United Nations Security Council 2013b).[48] Second, the Kenyan government returned to the ICC in an attempt to have Kenyatta and Ruto excused from constant attendance at trial, in order to allow them to conduct their official duties (Hobbs 2015, 88–95). Here there was a particular invocation of the demands of national security, especially in the wake of the Westgate Mall terrorist attacks. In parallel to this development, the ASP revised the ICC Rules of Procedure and Evidence to permit the excusal of defendants 'mandated to fulfill extraordinary public duties at the highest national level' for a period of their trial (Assembly of States Parties 2013b). These latter efforts constitute more narrow challenges to ICC jurisdiction in that they rely upon

[47] Official public Court records are available at http://www.icc-cpi.int/en_menus/icc/situations%20and%20cases/situations/situation%20icc%200109/court%20records/Pages/index.aspx.

[48] Azerbaijan, China, Morocco, Pakistan, Russia, Rwanda, and Togo voted in favour of the proposed resolution, while Argentina, Australia, France, Guatemala, Luxembourg, the Republic of Korea, the United Kingdom, and the United States abstained.

an interpretation and arguably, extension, of Rome Statute rules. The engagement by Kenya, moreover, evidences iterative legal argumentation, a key vector through which my theoretical account expects that States Parties will be socialized into the obligations of the treaty community.

However, more recent state practice calls this optimistic reading into question, as Kenya has responded to its failed complementarity claim by adopting a policy of open obstruction. This has involved, most dramatically, a vote by the Kenyan Parliament in September 2013 to withdraw from the Rome Statute, but has also featured the suspension of various forms of cooperation relating to witnesses and the provision of evidence. This position has been supported by the AU in its recent high-level meetings (Assembly of the African Union 2013). In December 2014 the Court found, inter alia, that 'it is apparent that the Kenyan Government has taken no meaningful steps to compel production of the requested materials' (ICC Trial Chamber V(B), 2014, 37). This more belligerent strategy appears to have paid off. The ICC Prosecutor announced on 5 December 2014 that she was withdrawing charges against President Kenyatta, citing the absence of sufficient evidence to support the likelihood of a successful prosecution (Office of the Prosecutor, International Criminal Court 2014b).[49] This outcome has more recently been repeated with the decision of ICC Trial Chamber V(A) to vacate the charges against Deputy President Ruto on similar grounds (ICC Trial Chamber V(A) 2016).

Recent developments with respect to the Kenyan situation thus provide a challenge to the theoretical expectations of this study. Most specifically, the legal proceedings against President Kenyatta and Deputy President Ruto are instances where the use of legal procedures by a States Party does not result in greater sensitivity to treaty rules and norms, or in compliance with legally binding obligations. Rather, the adoption of legalistic discourse and practices has been used to challenge the jurisdictional claims of the ICC, resulting in its diminished institutional efficacy. This is further evidenced in the recent decision by the Kenyan Court of Appeal to suspend an ICC arrest warrant for a further suspect, Walter Osapiri Barasa, while his legal challenge to the warrant is heard in domestic courts (Maliti 2014). The instrumental invocation of certain Rome Statute provisions, and the hostility more generally, are problematic not only because they have undermined ongoing ICC judicial processes but equally because they have opened up new fissures in the status of the non-immunity norm. This latter development has involved a shift into an even more fundamental form of critique and is arguably of greater importance to the *political* future of the Court, as explored in the proceeding section.

[49] On 13 March 2015, Trial Chamber V(B) announced that it had terminated the proceedings against Mr Kenyatta and vacated its prior summons to appear (International Criminal Court 2015).

CONTESTING THE COURT: DEBATES OVER THE JURISDICTION AND STATUS OF THE ICC

As Chapter 3 made clear, a central feature of the ICC's normative architecture is the principle, expressed in Article 27(1) of the Rome Statute, that its legal authority 'shall apply equally to all persons without any distinction based on official capacity'. There remain, however, important disagreements concerning how the non-immunity norm should be operationalized as a matter of law and practice, as the discussion of the Kenyan situation has revealed. Recent States Party discourse reveals two principal points of contention, concerning the application of legal sanction to sitting Heads of State, and the consequences this may hold for wider efforts to resolve domestic conflicts and establish lasting conditions for peace. The international debate over the status of Kenyan leaders under ICC jurisdiction is also an archetypal example of the permeation of the language of law in international diplomacy, and for this reason I employ it here as a window into these wider debates.

Privileging Politics: Discourses of Sovereignty, Justice, and Peace in Subject States

The question of whether current political leaders should be subject to ICC jurisdiction has emerged as a key battleground in contemporary debates over the Court, first in the context of the indictment of Sudanese President Omar al-Bashir—addressed in Chapter 7—and subsequently with respect to the legal proceedings against President Kenyatta and Deputy President Ruto. The AU has emerged as an especially vocal opponent of the arrest warrants for African leaders, and has invoked both the specific terms of the Rome Statute and broader principles of international law in seeking to block the application of ICC jurisdiction in these cases (African Union 2012). The AU is composed of both a great number of ICC members as well as many non-parties, and therefore reflects a complex balance of external legal commitments within a regional body.

Most fundamentally, the AU disputes the legitimacy of Rome Statute Article 27, which in its view conflicts with established customary norms of international law concerning the legal immunity of senior officials during their tenure in office (Assembly of the African Union 2011a; Assembly of the African Union 2013; Federal Republic of Nigeria 2013; Kingdom of Lesotho 2014). Relatedly, the AU has raised the spectre of ICC investigations and trials imperilling the fragile domestic reconciliation undertaken by the Kenyan state and threatening regional security. In particular, it is contended that external legal processes impede the ability of senior officials to dispense the official duties of their office. On the one hand, this is said to constitute an interference in national-level efforts to ensure accountability and societal peace (Republic of Kenya 2013b; Republic of Kenya 2014). Various actors have specifically referenced the 2013 elections that brought Kenyatta and Ruto to office as evidence of the will of the Kenyan people, and have argued that democratically elected leaders (unlike dictators) 'should be allowed to discharge their mandate and address the developmental challenges of their countries without the distractions... until the end of their tenure' (Federal Republic of Nigeria 2013). The AU has therefore expressed its 'strong conviction that the search for justice should be pursued in a way that does not impede or jeopardize efforts aimed at promoting lasting peace' (Assembly of the African Union 2013, para. 3). This mirrors calls to suspend ICC processes in order to facilitate peace agreements in other subjects states such as Uganda and the CAR.

On other hand, in the wake of the terrorist attack against the Westgate Mall in Nairobi, AU members have frequently referred to Kenya's position as 'a frontline state in the fight against terrorism at regional, continental and international levels' and voiced concern that the ICC indictments against the senior political leaders 'will distract and prevent them from fulfilling their constitutional responsibilities, including national and regional security affairs' (Assembly of the African Union 2013, para. 6; Republic of Uganda 2013). Kenyan officials have repeatedly complained that the ICC indictments constitute unnecessary and counterproductive developments in light of the substantial domestic reforms, and amount to a violation of the principle of complementarity (Republic of Kenya 2013a, 4, 9–11). This has led to public accusations of an 'unaccountable ICC prosecutor—with a political axe to grind' and the spectre of a 'politicized prosecution' (Republic of Kenya 2013a, 1–2; Assembly of the African Union 2013, para. 4).

The Politics of Accountability among ICC Member States

Despite these provocative challenges to ICC authority, AU member states including Kenya regularly express their commitment to general international norms of justice, ending impunity for grave crimes, and promoting the rule of law, along with support for 'an effective, impartial International Criminal Court (ICC), operating in line with the aspirations advanced in the Rome Statute' (Republic of Kenya 2013a, 1; Assembly of the African Union 2013; Republic of Uganda 2013; Kingdom of Lesotho 2014). Rather than dismiss the Court outright, therefore, contestation has taken place on the specific terms of the Rome Statute—in relation to broader legal principles—and has been characterized by iterative argumentation between African states, other States Parties, civil society actors, and the Court itself. This is most apparent in the ultimately unsuccessful effort on the part of African states to secure a UNSC sponsored deferral of the Kenyatta and Ruto proceedings in November 2013.[50]

The core of the AU objection—echoed in the individual interventions of many African ICC members such as Ethiopia and Kenya, and non-members like Rwanda—is that the Court has unfairly targeted African leaders and, along with the wider international community, is not sufficiently respectful of local or regional approaches to these conflicts (Kingdom of Lesotho 2014; United Republic of Tanzania 2013). While this is ultimately a political contention, the public discourse concerning the Court's legitimate role revolved around legal interpretation. In particular, African states and their supporters sought to employ Article 16 of the Statute which permits the UNSC, acting under its Chapter VII authority (concerning threats to international peace and security) to defer ongoing ICC investigations for one year. More broadly, this process again implicated the principle of complementarity and its purported intention in giving states the benefit of the doubt in disputes over the development and application of domestic legal procedures. Most crucial here was the view, previously articulated in AU resolutions, that the offices of President and Deputy President were protected by existing international legal immunities, and were moreover critical to ongoing efforts and ensuring domestic reconciliation.[51] For this reason, a variety of African ICC member states asserted that the proposed deferral was perfectly compatible with their continued commitment to the Court since it relied upon the existing institutional rules and thereby sought to find the appropriate balance between legal obligation, peace, and justice (Republic of South Africa 2013; Republic of Uganda 2013).

Opponents of the proposed deferral—including Argentina, Australia, France, Luxembourg, and the United Kingdom—also articulated their policy preferences in reference to the legal criteria of the Rome Statute. Most specifically, Security Council members employed an alternative interpretation of Article 16 and asserted that the Kenyan situation did not meet the standard of a threat to international peace and security necessary to warrant the invocation of Chapter VII of the UN Charter (United Kingdom 2013). These same states additionally contended that the Court (via the Trial Chambers and Appeals Chambers) could accommodate the needs of both defendants by staggering their trial proceedings and exempting their attendance in exceptional circumstances. Indeed, these states inverted the linkage between peace and justice advanced by African states and their allies, maintaining that the two should not be sequenced but were rather necessarily complements and mutual enablers (Federal Republic of Germany 2013). In this respect it is

[50] Unless otherwise noted, references in this section are derived from national statements in the UNSC meeting on 15 November 2013 (United Nations Security Council 2013a).

[51] This latter claim was supported in the UNSC debate by non-parties Azerbaijan, China, Ethiopia, Pakistan, Russia, and Rwanda.

especially interesting that the United States explicitly adopted this framing in the UNSC debate: 'We believe that justice for the victims of that violence is critical to the country's long-term peace and security. It is incumbent on us all to support accountability for those responsible for crimes against humanity.' This phenomenon of non-party states invoking the terms of the Rome Statute to advance policy goals is a central theme of the next chapter. Finally, resistant states complained that the AU initiative was unnecessarily provocative: since the sponsors knew ahead of time that the draft resolution had no prospect of success, their insistence on bringing it to a vote, in the words of the Guatemalan delegate 'erect[ed] a barrier of distrust between the two bodies [UNSC and ICC] that is harmful to both and to the community of nations in general'. Any deferral in this case would have set a negative precedent of impunity for future situations; the opposition from within the UNSC was therefore based on a principled reading of the Rome Statute and its relationship to the UN Charter, and was not born of any antipathy to Africa.[52]

The failure to secure a majority vote in support of the deferral was regarded by African states as a betrayal of the Rome Statute: in practical and legal terms, the ongoing regional instability stemming from terrorism seemed to perfectly constitute a threat to international peace and security necessary for the UNSC to act under its Chapter VII powers, as Kenya, Rwanda, and Uganda all explicitly noted. More darkly, a number of delegations saw the outcome as further demonstration of the inherent double standards and power politics associated with international diplomacy. For Rwanda:

> Article 16 was never meant to be used by an African States or any of the developing countries. It seems to have been conceived as an additional tool for the big Powers to protect themselves and protect their own... Today's disappointing vote undermines the principle of the sovereign equality of States enshrined in the Charter of the United Nations, and confirms our long-held view that international mechanisms are subject to political manipulation and are used only in situations that suit the interests of some countries.

In light of these critiques, African states have continued to contend that the Statute as presently constituted is, in the words of Kenya, 'clearly deeply flawed, inoperable and inapplicable in the context of the [UN Security] Council' and thus requires immediate reconsideration (Assembly of the African Union 2014, para. 6–7; Republic of South Africa 2013; United Republic of Tanzania 2013).

As a result of this fundamental disagreement, action over Head of State legal exposure has since shifted to efforts at institutional renegotiation. The AU has encouraged its members to pursue amendments to the Rome Statute—especially

[52] These views were echoed by Argentina, Australia, France, Guatemala, the Republic of Korea, and the United Kingdom.

Articles 16 and 27—to address the perceived problems encountered in the Kenyan and Sudanese situations (Assembly of the African Union 2014, para. 10(i); Federal Republic of Nigeria 2013; Kingdom of Lesotho 2014; Republic of Kenya 2013b; Republic of Uganda 2013). One proposal that has emerged in the wake of the Kenyatta and Ruto affair is to alter the Rome Statute so as to enshrine legal immunity while in office for leaders elected through recognized democratic processes—in effect fulfilling the contention that ICC proceedings should not impede the popular will of a democratic state nor the sovereign right of a government to pursue national reconciliation alongside peace and security (Federal Republic of Nigeria 2013). In these ways, the AU and its constituent members have sought to embed the issue of Head of States immunity in future Assembly of States Party discussions (Assembly of the African Union 2014, para. 10). At the same time, the AU has also sought to expand the jurisdictional scope of the African Court on Human and Peoples' Rights as an institutional alternative to the ICC (Assembly of the African Union 2013, paras. 10(iv–v); Human Rights Watch 2012b; Human Rights Watch 2014a). More provocatively, the AU has further pressured its members to 'comply with African Union Decisions on ICC' and 'adhere and articulate commonly agreed positions in line with their obligations under the Constitutive Act of the African Union' (Assembly of the African Union 2014, paras. 10(i–ii))—a demand that implies openly defiance of Court requests. This confrontational approach is addressed further in Chapter 7 in the context of the Bashir case.

The Kenyan government and other African states have therefore used legal arguments in an attempt to advance distinctive political goals, and in this way the nested structure of international law has offered an avenue for contesting rather than adopting an international standard. Yet by the same token, a consequence of this engagement is that is has drawn these states into an iterative process of argumentation on a specific set of legal criteria, and provided the resources through which other actors—both states and transnational civil society—were able to resist the proposed deferral. Thus far, the majority of ICC members have maintained a narrow reading of exceptions to the more general accountability norm, insofar as the Kenyan situation was not judged to meet the standards of Article 16 and did not warrant a fundamental change to the anti-immunity norm articulated in Article 27.

Yet in the context of the core concerns of this study, the Kenyan case also reveals important uncertainty in the contemporary legal and normative status of the Court. This is apparent in a couple of respects. First, the actions of the Kenyan government and its allies in Africa and elsewhere have clearly impeded the work of the Court, leading most spectacularly to the recent abandonment of the cases against President Kenyatta and Deputy President Ruto. It is important to recognize that, irrespective of the potential merits (or lack thereof) of the case, the proceeding was dropped due to a lack of cooperation from the Kenyan state and not, as the government has alleged, as the result of an affirmative absence of incriminating evidence. This effort to delegitimize the Court has succeeded, in part, because the Court itself and other ICC parties have been generally unwilling to deploy social or material punishments in response to Kenyan non-cooperation. Despite mounting concerns, the Trial Chamber declined to refer Kenya to the ASP for further sanction, and ASP members have refrained from concerted public condemnation. Civil society groups have regularly called for greater State Party efforts in upholding Rome Statute standards through their official discourse and in pursuing stronger enforcement procedures in instances of non-compliance (Amnesty International 2012; Human Rights Watch 2014c; Human Rights Watch 2014b; Kenyans for Peace with Truth and Justice 2014). These calls have received only limited response thus far.

This is consequential for a third reason, since it suggests that the content and limits of core ICC standards are substantially unsettled. In this case at least, there is only limited evidence by which to affirm the recent EU assertion that 'the irrelevance of the official capacity of the person concerned with regard to his or her personal criminal responsibility, in proceedings before the ICC, has been an essential achievement in international criminal justice' (Italian Republic 2014). Moreover, there is no current agreement among ICC member states—and indeed the wider international community—concerning when Article 16 should be employed, and what criteria would meet the threshold for a deferral. This is doubly relevant in light of US efforts to employ the same rule for their own ends, as discussed in Chapter 7. While current state practice has not led to a serious erosion of the ICC's internationalized procedural justice norm—yet—core features of the ICC legal regime clearly remain in considerable flux.

CONCLUSION: THE ICC AND ITS MEMBERSHIP

Antonio Franceschet (2006, 244) has argued that 'the apparently strong endorsement of the ICC by a wide variety of states suggests that a reasonably wide consensus is now available on the "rule of law" globally.' The above analysis suggests that this hopeful view is only partially justified. Though more difficult to measure, the available evidence does reflect a more varied and challenging picture of behavioural adaptation than in the case of the AP mine ban. Most notably, there is a greater degree of non-compliance among ICC member states, relating to the incorporation of Rome Statute crimes and procedures in national legal systems, the pursuit of domestic judicial accountability, and cooperation with ongoing ICC legal processes. Official discourse also reveals substantial contestation on the meaning and limits of these fundamental concerns. Other States Parties have been reluctant to draw public attention to apparent violations or deploy various punishments as witnessed in the MBT case (Chapter 4). These gaps in implementation have clearly impacted the Court's operations, resulting in a less effective institution. In other words, a core expectation of this study—that the formal adoption of legal instruments and inclusion in a treaty community will generate social pressures towards compliance and deeper internalization of norms—has only been partially realized in the ICC case. The reasons for the apparently different trajectories between the two core treaty cases will be explored at greater length in Chapter 8, in light of the assessment of non-party interaction with the Court.

In keeping with my theoretical account, however, legal discourses do offer a key vector through which member states pursue political efforts aimed at promoting or challenging the ICC. Debates over the legitimacy of the ICC thus still play out on the terms of the Rome Statute and its relationship to wider international norms. In some circumstances, the nested structure of international law has provided a means of undermining the institution, as has been demonstrated above. A more optimistic take would suggest that contestation on the terms of the institution is still preferable, as it largely restricts challenges to matters of legal interpretation within a defined set of parameters. Chapter 2 has suggested that this distinction between *legal* and *political* practice matters for the prospect of norm development in world politics. More specifically, the engagement with ICC norms and rules offers the prospect for reconciliation, as states are further drawn into legal argumentation in ways that are defined by the Rome Statute. This expectation can be further examined in the context of states that remain outside of the formal ambit of ICC membership, both in terms of their own policies—whether of accommodation or resistance—and the response from current States Parties to these strategies. Chapter 7 takes up this subject.

7

Non-Parties and the International Criminal Court

The view of an expanding—if uneven and still problematic—community of International Criminal Court (ICC) members discussed in Chapter 6 is challenged by the fact that a number of other prominent states remain deeply opposed to the institution.[1] These include most prominently the United States, China, India, and Russia, along with regional powers like Egypt, Iran, Israel, Pakistan, and Turkey. These states possess a substantial proportion of the material assets—including global military capacity, economic output, and population—typically associated with power in International Relations scholarship.

Yet this study has contended that the formal membership is not the final or best determinant of whether a treaty can exert influence over actors. The case of the ICC is particularly illuminating with respect to this dynamic, as close attention to the development of the ICC reveals a variety of ways in which the behaviour and discourse of non-parties have been transformed through their interaction with the Court and its constitutive text the Rome Statute. Powerful opponents have not fully withdrawn from engagement with the new institution, as sceptics might have expected, but have instead been deeply involved in its development through formal negotiations (at the Preparatory Commission and annual Assembly of States Parties meetings) and various informal modes of cooperation. At the same time, the ICC has emerged as a major subject of contestation both among its membership, as Chapter 6 detailed, and for non-party states that are the subject of this chapter. This process is bi-directional,

[1] Thirty-one states are currently signatories to the Rome Statute. As noted already, while the act of signature does not constitute full acceptance of treaty obligations, common practice as enshrined in Article 18 of the Vienna Convention on the Law of Treaties dictates that signatories are 'obliged to refrain from acts which would defeat the object and purpose of a treaty'. In this sense, signatories can be held to have signalled their endorsement of the spirit and principles of the agreement. Both the United States and Israel have subsequently notified the United Nations Secretary-General that they do not intend to ratify the Rome Statute and consequently possess no legal obligations emanating from their signature. Both states have therefore requested that they be removed from the official list of signatories (Bolton 2002). The prospect of 'unsigning' a multilateral treaty is a fraught and complex subject, and one I do not examine here.

as the ICC has shaped non-party policies while these actors have themselves influenced the conduct and efficacy of the ICC as a judicial body. David Bosco has thus recently argued that the current practice of the ICC reflects a 'mutual accommodation' between the Court and its powerful opponents. Court officials—especially the Office of the Prosecutor (OTP)—have largely directed their investigations away from actors and conflicts that might directly implicate core national interests of powerful non-parties, thereby reducing the perceived threat from the institution and further embedding it within the contemporary international political arena (Bosco 2014, 20–1). These states, in turn, have come to regard the Court as a useful tool, in some circumstances, for pursuing objectives that include, but are not limited to, ensuring criminal accountability and the promotion of human rights in fragile states.

This chapter seeks to extend these insights, by focusing on the legal and normative dynamics of non-party interaction with the Court. In doing so, I show the two sides of the engagement coin: how the efforts of non-party states have impacted on the global status of the Court, but equally how the instrumental deployment of ICC norms and institutional procedures has had substantial unanticipated consequences in limiting their own political room for manoeuvre. Following the theoretical account developed in Chapter 2, I contend that the nested structure of international law has provided opportunities for pro-norm adaptation—as ambivalent states become progressively more comfortable with the institution and its demands—but also offers a vital source of alternative claims through which states have challenged the legitimacy and application of the Court. The type of legal argument is especially important to this process. Non-parties have been most effective at challenging the Court through reference to more foundational legal principles and institutions (such as the UN Charter and Security Council), in conjunction with overt applications of power politics. This contestation has proven much more substantial and enduring than with respect to the Mine Ban Treaty (MBT), and is therefore ultimately more consequential.

However, in many instances non-parties have sought to further their claims by invoking specific ICC rules, and this has in turn drawn them into more particular legal discourses that, through iterative argumentation, have generated increased social pressure towards greater cooperation. In this respect, the effectiveness of non-party diplomatic efforts has declined to the extent that they shift on to the terrain of the Rome Statute itself. This finding is fully consonant with the theoretical account adopted in this study. While moderating the most provocative and damaging forms of resistance, therefore, accommodation has not as yet produced deep acceptance of core institutional commitments. In other words, engagement with the Court has generated some meaningful adaptation, but not internalization of many ICC norms.

THE PRINCIPLE OF INTERNATIONALIZED JUSTICE IN NON-PARTY DISCOURSE

No state publicly argues that grave violations of international humanitarian and human rights law should go unpunished. In this respect the ICC is one component of a relatively recent push for accountability at national, regional, and global levels—what Kathryn Sikkink has termed a 'justice cascade' in world politics (Sikkink 2011; Bass 2001). More interesting for present purposes is the extent to which the idea of a permanent international court as the appropriate mechanism for addressing certain forms of grave criminality has become embedded in international discourse.

While pointedly rejecting the Court in its current configuration, the vast majority of non-member states have nonetheless expressed support for the ICC's mission of ending impunity. For example:

> Although China is not a party to the Rome Statute, it always supports the purposes and objectives for which the ICC was established and is in favor of setting up an independent, impartial, effective and universal international criminal tribunal, as a supplement to national judicial systems to punish the gravest international crimes and to promote world peace and realize judicial justice.
> (People's Republic of China 2009; People's Republic of China 2002; People's Republic of China 2013a)

For the Russian Federation:

> The strength of the Court consists not only in its ability to punish but also in the fact that its only existence can influence drastically both the world political climate and national legislation of States. It is a kind of a sword of Damocles for those who admit a possibility of achieving political goals by committing mass murders, extermination and violating international law. Therefore, already today at the initial stage of the ICC existence we can affirm that the Court has fulfilled itself and found its own place in the world. (Russian Federation 2010)

These sentiments are widely shared in official statements.[2] Many of these same states—including those most hostile to the Court—have made frequent reference to their long-term involvement in its negotiation and subsequent development (Islamic Republic of Iran 1998; People's Republic of China 2010; Russian Federation 2010; United States of America 2010a; Scheffer 1999a, 12–17). In this respect, at least, there is near-uniform acceptance of a general obligation to punish acts of atrocity, including with respect to the characterization of the core crimes of genocide, crimes against humanity, and war crimes

[2] Algeria, Angola, Cameroon, Cuba, Egypt, Guatemala, Indonesia, Iran, Israel, Kuwait, Laos, Malaysia, Pakistan, Qatar, Russia, Sudan, Syria, Thailand, Turkey, Ukraine, the United States, and Vietnam have all made public statements of support for the ICC's foundational mission of ending impunity.

(though not, notably, the crime of aggression, which is discussed separately below). Moreover, the recognition of the legitimate need for *some form* of permanent global judicial body opens up space for further accommodation in the future. This kind of broad endorsement, while not constituting full recognition of the particular institution, can nevertheless provide a pathway for the extension of treaty norms to encompass ambivalent states within the social and, potentially, legal community defined by the Rome Statute. In this light, it is noteworthy that many current non-parties participate in Assembly of States Parties (ASP) meetings, while some—including Indonesia and Turkey—have previously indicated that they are actively considering ratification or accession (Republic of Indonesia 2010; Republic of Turkey 2010a).

Even below that threshold, however, the strength of the internationalized procedural justice norm is such that even resistant states now concede that the ICC has a role in the enforcement of criminal accountability at the international level. The annual United Nations General Assembly (UNGA) resolution on the ICC is the most relevant source for such speech acts, particularly as the resolution is explicitly understood as providing a political endorsement for the ICC. It is therefore significant that each resolution has been adopted by consensus without a vote.[3] The fact that so few states are willing to publicly voice opposition to the Court in this venue suggests at minimum that the ICC has gained a degree of legitimacy such that overt dissent is politically unpalatable. Nevertheless, the relative cost of such demonstrations is low since the UNGA resolutions impose no specific legal obligations; in this respect, their contribution to the *extension* of international norms is limited (Byers 1999, 157).

LOGICS OF RESISTANCE: CONTESTATION OVER THE COURT

While many states previously supported the idea of international justice for grave crimes, these general ambitions were given a specific reference point with the advent of the Rome Statute. Future debates over the proper response to domestic and international violations of human rights and the laws of war must now engage with the Court as *the* central global institution for addressing atrocities. Expressing general—if equivocal—support for a legal development while continuing to resist the full weight of its obligations is therefore

[3] Annual resolutions relating to the ICC can be found at http://www.un.org/en/ga/documents/index.shtml. There was no resolution in 2011.

not without consequences, as Chapter 2 detailed at some length. For example, the fact that so many non-parties have acknowledged the emergence of the ICC as a positive development can lead to charges of hypocrisy if these same states do not narrow the gap between their stated general support and actual policy toward the Court.

Yet this endorsement includes within it more particular disagreements concerning how a general norm of individual criminal accountability should be operationalized, and whether the ICC as currently constituted represents the proper institution to pursue this goal. This can be explained in part as a consequence of the diplomatic strategy adopted at the Rome Conference, wherein states were forced to vote on the entire draft Statute as a single document, rather than in sections as some delegations wished. Moreover, as reservations to the text are not permitted, states cannot exempt themselves from portions of the institution they do not endorse.[4] This is particularly significant since the negotiation of the Rome Statute revealed vastly different preferences concerning 'the powers, jurisdiction, and role of the new court' (Struett 2008, 24–5). In the interests of clarity and analytical leverage I focus here on a limited selection of the most important debates, measured both in terms of the volume of discourse and the way in which these rhetorical engagements have impacted upon the contemporary status of the Court.

State Sovereignty and the Legal Exposure of Non-Party Nationals

Benjamin Schiff has noted that 'the conflict between the universal nature of the Statute's normative claims and the particularistic nature of national sovereignty is at the root of opposition to the Court' (Schiff 2008, 166). This has played out frequently in the context of objections to the Court's ability to exercise jurisdiction over the citizens of non-party states, as provided for in Article 12.1(a) of the Rome Statute. In the view of great powers in particular, this arrangement violates the foundational tenet of international law that states cannot be bound by rules to which they do not consent. As David Scheffer, US Ambassador-at-Large for War Crimes Issues under President Clinton explained:

[4] There are two exceptions to this general rule. Article 124 of the Rome Stature permits new States Parties to exempt themselves from ICC jurisdiction over war crimes for a period of seven years (from the date of the Statute's entry into force for that state). This provision was included as the result of a demand from the French delegation during the Rome negotiations, but was recently removed by a vote of the ASP (Assembly of States Parties 2015b). The amendment incorporating the crime of aggression into the Statute also permits ICC members to 'opt-out' of the jurisdiction for this crime.

> Fundamental principles of treaty law still matter and we are loath to ignore them with respect to any state's obligations vis-à-vis a treaty regime. While certain conduct is prohibited under customary international law and might be the object of universal jurisdiction by a national court, the establishment of, and a state's participation in, an international criminal court are not derived from custom but, rather, from the requirements of treaty law. (Scheffer 1999b)

This objection was also a centrepiece of US opposition to the Court during the administration of George W. Bush (Grossman 2002), and is at the core of Chinese, Indian, and Russian concerns as well (People's Republic of China 1995; Republic of India 1998; Russian Federation 2003). ICC non-parties, and especially leading powers, have thus persistently sought to restrict the legal scope of the Rome Statute and Court—despite the fact that the ICC's jurisdictional claim does not substantially diverge from established international practice concerning the legal exposure of third-party nationals.

Head of State Immunity in International Affairs

Relatedly, the legal exposure of senior state officials has emerged as a key point of contestation over the ICC, as was already demonstrated with respect to the Kenyan situation and is further apparent in the international debate over ICC legal processes in Sudan and Libya, discussed later in this chapter. Sceptical states regard Head of States immunity as an active principle of customary and statutory international law that cannot be obviated by new legal institutions without the consent of the affected state(s). Here too the debate centres crucially on questions of sovereign equality and the permissible limits on external interference in the domestic affairs of the state. Official statements suggest, for example, that the necessity of removing Head of State immunity currently presents a barrier to ICC membership in a number of smaller states.[5] Interestingly, this specific constitutional objection is rarely raised by the great powers or other prominent ICC opponents such as Egypt, India, and Iran to justify their own non-ratification or accession.

Institutional Autonomy and the Place of the ICC in the System of States

Debates over the ICC ultimately return to the question of how the Court should operate with respect to other, prior institutions and thus, in effect, its proper place in the international system of states. These objections have

[5] Azerbaijan, Belarus, Malaysia, Monaco, Morocco, Sudan, Thailand, and Uzbekistan.

tended to centre on the Prosecutor's ability to launch an investigation *proprio motu*—that is, on his or her own authority without prior agreement of the state(s) whose nationals are implicated or the approval of the UN Security Council (UNSC). For China, Russia, and the United States this legal structure is particularly problematic as it does not respect the Security Council's pre-eminent responsibility for maintaining international peace and security or the particular prerogatives given to its permanent members in the form of the veto—both of which are at the heart of the post-World War II international order (Schabas 2004). As such, these states regard an independent ICC as incompatible with constitutive norms of the international system entrenched in the UN Charter that are both temporally prior and superior as sources of international obligation (People's Republic of China 2010; Jia 2006, 91).

This concern has been most evident in the long-running debate over how (or indeed whether) to include the crime of aggression under ICC jurisdiction, a subject I address at greater length later in this chapter as a key example of non-party influence over the development of the Court. For now it is simply worth noting that prominent ICC non-members contend that determinations concerning the illegal use of force are the sole prerogative of the UNSC (People's Republic of China 2012a; Russian Federation 2014b). Any claim by the Court to render judgements on the existence of a breach of inter-state peace would therefore fail to respect a core feature of the UN Charter. Moreover, by unsettling the existing processes for assessing the legality of the resort to armed force, the incorporation of the crime of aggression in the Rome Statute could undermine international interventions aimed at protecting vulnerable populations (People's Republic of China 2009; United States of America 2014d).

The Court's relationship to the United Nations thus implicates the proper distribution of rights and duties in the international system. The three permanent Security Council members that have not joined the Rome Statute demand that the Court respect the current international structure and the special responsibilities bestowed upon materially powerful states. This privileging of great power politics seeks to subordinate the ICC to other international structures and is thus a fundamental challenge to the Court's independence. The logical corollary of this position is seen in the selective efforts by the great powers to employ the Court—via Security Council referral—in certain discrete instances to serve their interests. This assertion of pre-eminent status has been vigorously opposed by *other* ICC non-parties, who have rejected the legitimacy of using UNSC resolutions to bind other non-member states while enjoying exemptions for themselves via the veto power (Republic of India 1998), as seen in the referrals of Sudan (Darfur) and Libya.

Ultimately, such assertions are not directed towards legal principles in the abstract, but are animated by very practical considerations. David Wippman has argued that US objections do not primarily focus on the prospect of individual prosecutions of American personnel for grave crimes, since the US already accepts the legal validity of these crimes, and authorities would likely be willing to undertake similar judicial processes.[6] Rather, if 'the Court will pursue cases arising from the implementation of military doctrine... the US fears that the Court will serve as a vehicle to constrain the exercise of US military power' (Wippman 2006, 127–8). In this view, the United States possesses special responsibilities for the maintenance of international order by virtue of its status as the only genuinely global hegemon, and hence far greater exposure to politically motivated uses of international legal process intended at undermining the projection of American military power (Scheffer 1999a). This concern has been at the heart of US contestation since the outset, and has remained a largely consistent feature across administrations.

INSTRUMENTALIZING THE COURT: THE POLITICS OF SECURITY COUNCIL REFERRALS

A central theme of this study concerns the complex ways in which international legal institutions contribute to evolving conceptions of appropriate behaviour that in turn shape the strategic pursuit of state interests. In this respect, the ICC provides rich evidence for how the Rome Statute has become a prominent referent point in the conduct of international diplomacy, even among non-parties. To illustrate these dynamics, I focus my attention on the political and legal interplay between the UNSC and the Court in the context of the Darfur and Libya referrals, as key exemplars of the broader phenomenon.

UNSC Resolutions 1593 and 1970

The decision of the UNSC to refer the cases in Sudan (Darfur) and Libya to the ICC Prosecutor appear to be particularly prominent moments in the expansion of the Court's global legitimacy, especially since they occurred with the acquiescence of the three veto-holding permanent members that are not parties to the Rome Statute. On 31 March 2005, in response to a widely documented humanitarian crisis attributed to the actions of the Sudanese government and allied militias, the Security Council passed Resolution 1593 in which it 'refer[red] the situation in Darfur since 1 July 2002 to the Prosecutor of the International Criminal Court' (United Nations Security

[6] Of course, the recent experience with torture under the administration of President George W. Bush, and the subsequent unwillingness to pursue criminal prosecutions of senior officials, call this commitment into question (McKeown 2009; Brunnée and Toope 2010, 220–70).

Council 2005, para. 1). The resolution passed with eleven affirmative votes, with Algeria, Brazil, China, and the United States abstaining.[7] Six years later, just weeks before the initiation of a NATO-led intervention, the UNSC again used its referral powers to give the ICC jurisdiction over alleged crimes committed in Libya (United Nations Security Council 2011). Significantly in this instance, Resolution 1970 was approved by consensus, with both China and the United States—along with India, another persistent ICC opponent—voting in favour.

These were remarkable developments since they reversed the prior position of detachment among the great powers towards ICC operations. Some scepticism is warranted with respect to the Security Council processes, however. It has been suggested that the Darfur and Libya cases were comparatively easy instances for action, since the great powers had no specific and overriding interest in protecting the regimes. Instead, the resolutions could be regarded as a cost-effective way to further isolate unpopular political figures as part of wider political and military campaigns at little direct cost to the initiators. Indeed, both resolutions explicitly exempted the nationals of non-party states from ICC jurisdiction, with the exception of the targeted states of Sudan and Libya (United Nations Security Council 2005, para. 6; United Nations Security Council 2011, para. 6). But equally, they provided no mechanism for enforcing cooperation, nor any UN funds to support the ICC investigations stemming from the referrals, substantially restricting the Court's prospective efficacy. In these ways, the great powers' use of international rules embedded a form of unequal and non-reciprocal legal status, a theme I return to later. Indeed, by directing the ICC Prosecutor towards time-consuming and expensive investigations in 'safe' circumstances, the strategic use of referrals could actually serve as a way of deflecting prospective Court attention away from more sensitive investigations of powerful states or their allies—rendering the ICC yet another tool for the enactment of power politics, rather than a genuine instrument of justice (Bosco 2014, 21).

Such an instrumental use of legal process thus raises important questions concerning the prospective expansion of ICC norms among prominent non-parties. Yet the referrals remain significant, as they provide specific evidence for the ways in which value-based considerations may inform the content of state interests. The explanations associated with the UNSC votes clearly demonstrate how the Court has come to be associated with the cause of ending impunity for international crimes. Thus for the Russian Federation, Resolution 1593 'reaffirmed that the struggle against impunity is one of the most important elements of a long-term political settlement in Darfur and the Sudan as a whole' (Russian Federation 2005). While more measured in its

[7] The minutes of the UNSC debate can be found at http://www.un.org/en/ga/search/view_doc.asp?symbol=S/PV.5158.

endorsement, the United States also plainly recognized the Court's place as a consequential international institution for pursuing justice:

> By adopting this resolution, the international community has established an accountability mechanism for the perpetrators of crimes and atrocities in Darfur... While the United States believes that the better mechanism would have been a hybrid tribunal in Africa, it is important that the international community speak with one voice in order to help promote effective accountability... We decided not to oppose the resolution because of the need for the international community to work together in order to end the climate of impunity in the Sudan and because the resolution provides protection from investigation or prosecution for United States' nationals and members of the armed forces of non-State parties. (United States of America 2005)

It is particularly significant that the Bush administration's decision not to block the Darfur referral was informed by its interpretation of existing legal obligations under the Genocide Convention, and a determination that the conflict met the standards of genocide (Department of State, United States of America 2004d). With determined advocacy by French and British diplomats, a view crystallized among senior American officials that US opposition to the referral would amount to impunity for Sudanese leaders responsible for horrific atrocities, and would be regarded as deeply hypocritical by the international community (Bosco 2014, 112 and 179).

This conditional support, which was shared by China, came with the important caveat of substantial objections to the structure and purpose of the Court. Non-parties have thus sought to strike a delicate balance between ongoing principled rejection of the ICC on the one hand, and recognition of its potentially valuable role in achieving politically desirable ends, on the other. This calculus was again apparent with respect to the Libyan referral, as frequent reference was made to the particularly desperate humanitarian conditions and a belief that an ICC legal process 'would have the effect of an immediate cessation of violence and the restoration of calm and stability' (Republic of India 2011).[8] These views did not emerge by chance, but were the result of ongoing efforts by ICC member states and civil society campaigners to rhetorically link the Court with a political commitment to accountability. In light of these pressures, 'it appears that the perceived diplomatic and image cost of opposing a referral was deemed too high' (Bosco 2014, 180). It is through such diplomatic initiatives that a utility-based assessment of the Court's likely contribution to conflict de-escalation—in pressuring the Sudanese and Libyan governments to change their behaviour and marginalizing key perpetrators of the violence—interacted with fundamental norms

[8] Similar sentiments were expressed by the representatives of China, the Russian Federation, and the United States at the same meeting.

concerning humanitarian protection and the rule of law to provide the political space necessary for UNSC action.[9]

Despite non-party intentions to the contrary, the instrumental use of the ICC can have the effect of further legitimizing the institution over time, principally by associating the Court with the purposive actions of the international community and by indicating some measure of public acceptance of its underlying norms. Using indictments to stigmatize political actors like Omar al-Bashir and Muammar Gaddafi reinforces the social expectation that the Court is the appropriate institution for addressing grave international crimes when domestic remedies fall short. Hence one way that public diplomacy can prove consequential to the development of legal institutions and their associated norms is by further locking states into an iterative dialogue on these new terms. More specifically, the use of the ICC in particular circumstances leaves non-parties vulnerable to charges of hypocrisy if they seek to deviate from the nascent behavioural pattern—if the Court is good enough to deal with the leaders of Libya or Sudan, why should great powers not also subject themselves to its legal authority? This potential was recognized in the Darfur referral, wherein both the Chinese and US delegates explicitly sought to disconnect their country's abstention on Resolution 1593 from any change in the respective government's positions vis-à-vis the Court (People's Republic of China 2005; United States of America 2005).[10] Yet for the same reason, it is significant to note that subsequent statements concerning the Libyan referral excluded any reference to these objections. Scholarship on customary international law and constructivist IR accounts have made clear that the extension of international norms can occur through acquiescence to a given legal development as much as through affirmative acceptance. In this light, the more ambiguous diplomacy from the US and China appears relevant to the status of the ICC and its norm of internationalized procedural justice, especially if one adopts a longer view.

Global Responses

Given the intersubjective way in which state policies are assessed and given meaning in an international social system, the response to the UNSC referrals is of as much significance to the health of ICC and its associated norm as the acts themselves. This is brought into sharp relief by the extensive debate over the subsequent indictment of Sudanese President Omar al-Bashir for crimes

[9] Interview with John Washburn, Convenor, American Non-Governmental Organizations Coalition for the International Criminal Court. New York, 20 December 2011.

[10] This effort was also recognized, grudgingly, by civil society proponents of the Court. Washburn interview; CICC MENA interview.

against humanity, war crimes, and genocide (ICC Pre-Trial Chamber I 2009; ICC Pre-Trial Chamber I 2010). The Sudanese government responded to the issuance of an arrest warrant by openly rejecting the Court and applying extensive diplomatic pressure on other regional actors to refrain from cooperating in his arrest. As part of this campaign, President Bashir visited at least eighteen countries—including China, Egypt, and Iran, and a number of ICC States Parties, as detailed in Chapter 6—in defiance of the arrest warrant (Bosco 2014, 158). This is significant since Sudan (along with all other states) is under a legal obligation to comply with the Court as a result of the Security Council referral in Resolution 1593.

Opposition to the Bashir indictment has taken two main forms. First, a number of states—principally from Africa and the Middle East—have challenged the indictment on the grounds that it constitutes an unacceptable interference in the sovereign affairs of the state, especially one that has not joined the Court (Republic of Sudan 2008). The African Union (AU) has repeatedly endorsed this view and invoked Article 98 of the Rome Statute, arguing that this provision recognizes 'that the Statute is not capable of removing an immunity which international law grants to the officials of States that are not parties to the Rome Statute' (Assembly of the African Union 2012, para. 6). The AU has maintained, therefore, that its members do not possess a legal obligation to arrest and surrender President Bashir (African Union 2012). A second, more explicitly political objection holds that the ICC process has had a negative effect on the prospects for resolving the conflicts in Darfur and Libya (African Union 2008; Assembly of the African Union 2009; Assembly of the African Union 2011b, para. 6; Republic of Sudan 2008). These concerns—relating both to the legal protection for Heads of State and the more specific implications for peace and security—were echoed by a number of states both within the region and elsewhere.

These cases thus provide further examples of iterative legal argumentation that mirrors the Kenyan situation discussed in Chapter 6. It is in light of these concerns the AU, at the urging of the Sudanese and Libyan governments (the latter under the then leadership of Gaddafi), has repeatedly requested that the UNSC Security Council defer the ICC investigation in Darfur, as permitted in Article 16 of the Rome Statute (African Union Peace and Security Council 2008; Assembly of the African Union 2011b, para. 6; Jalloh, Akande, and Plessis 2011). Yet the AU has equally sought to reiterate that its policy does not imply an endorsement of impunity, but rather reflects 'the best possible sequencing so that the most immediate matters of saving lives and easing the suffering of the people of Darfur are dealt with first' (African Union 2008). The initial AU request was supported by some, principally non-Western members of the Security Council, on the grounds that the pursuit of a ICC trial against President Bashir would unsettle the nascent peace process in Darfur and could lead in turn to an escalation in violence; China and the Russian Federation were the most prominent proponents of this position.[11]

Despite considerable backing, the Security Council refused to endorse the AU deferral requests. As in other instances of contestation, the justifications are vital to the overall assessment of the status of the ICC and its norm of internationalized procedural justice. At the initial 31 July 2008 UNSC meeting where a prospective Article 16 deferral was indirectly considered, a number of states—most notably France, the United Kingdom, and United States, but also Belgium, Costa Rica, Croatia, Italy, and Panama—indicated their opposition to the proposed suspension with frequent reference to principled concerns for accountability.[12] At the same time, a host of states called on all members of the international community to meet their obligations to cooperate with Court activities relating to Darfur, thereby implicitly rejecting the AU's position.[13]

The United States was notable among non-member delegations for its refusal to support a deferral on the grounds that 'ending impunity for crimes against humanity, including crimes on the staggering scale of those committed in Darfur, ranks high among our commitments' (United States of America 2009b). While the United States has clearly regarded the ICC as a useful tool in stigmatizing the Sudanese regime, it has also upheld its position despite counter-veiling pressures that have at times regarded the Bashir arrest warrant as a barrier to diplomatic efforts at promoting peaceful resolution of the Darfur conflict and succession of South Sudan. The evidence suggests that this calculation was shaped by the interaction of moral and instrumental considerations, as the Bush (and later Obama) administration came to increasingly regard the ICC process as a key demonstration of the international community's commitment to justice and accountability in the region (Bosco 2014, 158–81). For the United States, the need to be seen to

[11] See statements by China, the Russian Federation, Burkina Faso, Libya, and Vietnam at the United Nations Security Council, 63rd year, 5947th meeting, Agenda Item: Reports of the Secretary-General on the Sudan, New York, 31 July 2008 (S/PV.5947). http://www.un.org/en/ga/search/view_doc.asp?symbol=S/PV.5947.

[12] The Security Council never entertained formal discussions of a draft resolution concerning a deferral of the Bashir or Gaddafi cases, but did address the issue indirectly in a series of meetings on the subject of Sudan. The two most relevant discussions since the issuance of the Bashir arrest warrant are 4 December 2009 (S/PV.6230) and 5 June 2012 (S/PV.6778). The United Kingdom, United States, Mexico, France, Japan, Costa Rica, Austria, Turkey, and Croatia made positive statements in the December 2009 meeting. The United Kingdom, United States, France, Portugal, Colombia, Guatemala, Togo, Russia, and Germany did so in the 2012 meeting. In each instance, only two states opposed the indictments (Libya and Burkina Faso, and Morocco and India, respectively) while four others made statements that did not assert a clear position.

[13] Statements by Belgium, Burkina Faso, France, Italy, South Africa, and Vietnam to the United Nations Security Council, 63rd year, 6028th meeting, Agenda Item: Reports of the Secretary-General on the Sudan, New York, 3 December 2008 (S/PV.6028); and Statements by the United Kingdom, United States of America, Mexico, Japan, Costa Rica, Croatia, and Uganda to the UNSC, 4 December 2009.

be upholding its rhetorical support for justice has provided the necessary political conditions in which successive administrations could support specific ICC initiatives despite their ongoing discomfort with the Court. For other ICC opponents like China and Russia, the international political climate and the particular opprobrium attached to the Sudanese and Libyan regimes restricted their perceived freedom of action, and led both permanent Security Council members to refrain from public statements of opposition to the indictments.

The UNSC demurral contributed to complaints among many African leaders to the effect that 'the ICC is a hegemonic tool of western powers' and that 'the ICC is an institution which is targeting or discriminating against Africa' (du Plessis 2010, 13). In response, the AU sought to institutionalize its ambivalence, first by proposing an amendment to the Rome Statute permitting the General Assembly to authorize a deferral in the face of UNSC inaction, and by empowering African Court on Human and Peoples' Rights to expand its jurisdiction to ICC crimes (Assembly of the African Union 2009, para. 5; Jalloh, Akande, and Plessis 2011, 26–37). Most problematically, the AU Heads of State—ironically at the initiative of Libyan leader Muammar Gaddafi—made it official policy that 'AU Member States shall not cooperate pursuant to the provisions of Article 98 of the Rome Statute of the ICC relating to immunities, for the arrest and surrender of President Omar El Bashir of The Sudan' (Assembly of the African Union 2009, para. 10), a position replicated with respect to the subsequent Libyan referral (Assembly of the African Union 2011b, para. 6).[14] This latter initiative poses a substantial challenge to the authority of the Court, since it creates a situation in which a regional organization demands that its members violate an international legal obligation they collectively share in order to prioritize an alternative commitment to a political body. Recall that all states are obliged to cooperate with the ICC in respect of the Darfur situation by virtue of its origins in a Security Council referral. This, of course, is in addition to the fact that many AU members are also States Parties to the Rome Statute.

States responses within and outside Africa are not monolithic, however. There is some—albeit limited—evidence that discursive support for the Court has provided opportunities for civil society actors to pressure states into withdrawing support for President Bashir. This is seen primarily in decisions to rescind prior invitations to major multilateral meetings—as occurred with Denmark, France, Nigeria, Malawi, and Turkey—and instances where President Bashir has cancelled or shortened his foreign visits in order to avoid threatened arrest (Coalition for the International Criminal Court 2010, 1 and 3; Coalition for the International Criminal Court 2015, 9; Mills 2012, 433 and 438).

[14] This position has been reiterated subsequently. See for example Assembly of the African Union (2016, para. 4).

Yet the prevailing pattern of state discourse with respect to the Bashir indictment suggests that the international criminal accountability norm is not deeply entrenched within Africa and among prominent non-parties, since a core feature of the norm is its application in all circumstances including for Heads of State. Moreover, states such as Kenya and South Africa that had previously made public commitments to arrest Bashir have more recently reversed their position, highlighting a potential further means by which the norm may be eroding. Bashir's recent visit to South Africa is emblematic of this tension (BBC News 2015). The welcoming of an ICC indictee by a prominent member state (and formerly key ICC proponent) undoubtedly further challenges the Court's legitimacy, especially because the ANC government explicitly argued that Bashir had immunity as he was travelling as Head of State to an official AU event. Yet the controversy may also lead to a renewed commitment to the individual criminal accountability norm. It is notable that the South African incident generated a great deal of media attention which local and transnational civil society were keen to exploit. Interestingly, the Supreme Court of South Africa also took a very dim view of the visit, and sought to compel the government to hold Bashir pending its ultimate determination that he was indeed subject to arrest and surrender under ICC jurisdiction. This is an important example of domestic judicial actors seeking to bypass political obstruction to apply an international legal standard and though it ultimately failed in this instance, the legal process is ongoing and will generate further interpretive judgements concerning the status of international legal rules and customary norms. Some states and the Court itself have also criticized South Africa's inaction, and thereby sought to reinforce the underlying accountability norm (Kirby 2015; Assembly of States Parties 2015a; ICC Pre-Trial Chamber II 2015b). Time will tell if this more optimistic reading is borne out with respect to the institution more broadly.

Despite professed commitments to the ICC's role in Sudan/Darfur from many states, however, the Sudanese government has proven very adept at defying the Court. On 9 March 2015, the Court formally issued a finding of non-compliance against the Government of Sudan, and transmitted this finding to the Security Council for prospective punishment (ICC Pre-Trial Chamber II 2015a). Before and since this intervention, however, the international community appears to have little interest in enforcing the ICC arrest warrant. As David Bosco points out, pro-ICC states have made general statements of support, but were unwilling to deploy more direct coercion—such as the denial of aid or imposition of sanctions—in order to force the issue (Bosco 2014, 157–8). The Court has had little success in generating support at the UNSC or ASP for specific responses to such non-compliance.[15] This has recently led the ICC Prosecutor, in an act that mimics the experience in Kenya, to suspend

[15] Documents relating to the Bashir case, including concerning alleged non-compliance by ICC non-party states, can be found at https://www.icc-cpi.int/darfur/albashir.

investigations in Darfur due to inaction—and arguably active interference—by Security Council members, most especially China (BBC News 2014b).

Commitment to Justice? Security Council Referrals and the Pursuit of Accountability

The ICC's involvement in Sudan and Libya has raised important questions concerning the role of powerful non-party states in the operation of the Court and, by extension, the future prospects for the institution. The indictment of senior political leaders in both states generated a great deal of political controversy, and has exposed enduring disputes concerning the status of legal immunities under international law. A number of ICC opponents, with the Russian Federation and China chief among them, have used these cases (along with the Kenyan situation discussed previously) as a wedge for reasserting their view that Heads of State continue to enjoy protection from international criminal tribunals (Russian Federation 2014b; People's Republic of China 2014b).

The more recent Libyan situation has arguably further unsettled the international commitment to pursuing criminal accountability for senior state officials. The death of Muammar Gaddafi at the hands of rebels removed the prospect of a second sitting Head of State facing an ICC trial. Yet before his demise, a number NATO allies had mooted the prospect of asylum for Gaddafi as a condition of ending the conflict (Sanger and Schmitt 2011; Watt and Norton-Taylor 2011). The AU reiterated its earlier position regarding Head of State immunity and the view that the indictment of Gaddafi 'seriously complicates the efforts aimed at finding a negotiated political solution to the crisis in Libya', and again called on its members not to cooperate with the ICC arrest warrant (Assembly of the African Union 2011b, para. 6). The ongoing dispute over the proper venue for prosecuting his son and de facto Prime Minister, Saif Al-Islam Gaddafi, has only further exacerbated tensions in the implementation of the ICC's jurisdiction by reviving competing visions of what justice should entail (International Criminal Court 2014a). While the initial referral and subsequent ICC indictments proved valuable in isolating the Gaddafi regime, the international community has again shown scant interest in ensuring that fugitives are delivered to ICC custody. Indeed, some Western states in particular have appeared willing, if not eager, to see local judicial processes supplant the ICC arrest warrant for Saif Gaddafi, as has already been the case with respect to the third original Libyan indictee, Abdullah Al-Senussi (Kersten 2014; Bosco 2014, 171).[16] As with Sudan

[16] On 27 July 2014 the ICC Appeals Chamber upheld the previous Pre-Trial Chamber I ruling that the case against Mr Al-Senussi was inadmissible before the ICC due to an ongoing domestic legal proceeding in Libya meeting the conditions of complementarity.

and Kenya, the Libyan government has proven unwilling to cooperate with the Court in the case of Saif Gaddafi. This has led the ICC to issue another finding of non-compliance, and refer the matter to the UNSC for further consideration and prospective sanction (ICC Pre-Trial Chamber I 2014). Given the current international climate, such action appears unlikely.

While the Security Council referrals represent a watershed moment in terms of great power engagement with the Court, therefore, they have not in and of themselves generated deeper internalization of ICC norms or indeed greatly increased the prospects of formal membership among these states. There has been meaningful accommodation, to be sure, and the cooperation from non-party states—and the United States most of all—would have been inconceivable in the early years of the Court. Yet there are also clear limits to this change, and the particular conditions of the Sudanese and Libyan referrals are of critical importance in explaining great power policy. In the view of prominent ICC opponents, the Court should not have legal authority over non-parties, unless the general legal norm of consent is overridden by another equally foundational principle of international order, manifest in the pre-eminence of the UNSC. Hence the referrals of Darfur and Libya to the ICC, and the subsequent legal exposure of non-party nationals of these states, were acceptable precisely because—and *only* because—the initiative came from the Security Council. The limits of this potential has been starkly revealed by the May 2014 veto by China and Russia of a UNSC draft resolution that aimed to refer the crimes committed in the Syrian civil war to the ICC (BBC News 2014a). Iterative legal dialogue has led to some important changes in non-party behaviour that would be hard to envision in the absence of the Rome Statute and its associated institutions and norms. Thus far, however, there is little to suggest that these particular engagements have stimulated a more far-reaching reappraisal of the legitimacy of the Court.

SHAPING FUTURE ICC JURISDICTION: NEGOTIATIONS OVER THE CRIME OF AGGRESSION

The decision to wage war is among the most fundamental capacities accorded to the state. Negotiations over whether and how to institutionalize international legal oversight of this policy domain have proven especially controversial because they intrude upon core aspects of sovereignty and the constitutional structure of the contemporary international system. Yet in June 2010, delegates to the ICC Review Conference in Kampala, Uganda concluded an amendment that, sometime after 2017, will give the Court jurisdiction over 'the planning, preparation, initiation and execution of the most serious forms of the illegal inter-State use of force' (McDougall 2013, 1; Assembly of States Parties 2010b). A detailed review of the decades-long negotiating history and its incorporation in the Rome Statute is beyond the scope of this chapter; interested readers would be well advised to consult recent specialist studies (Barriga and Kress 2011; McDougall 2013).[17] Instead, I focus on the political dynamics of this process. Indeed, while the resolution was ultimately a matter that could only be decided by ICC member states, the negotiation of the crime of aggression is a key example of the influence wielded by powerful non-party states, most especially China, Russia, and, above all, the United States.[18] Their efforts were supported at various points by the other permanent members of the Security Council (and ICC States Parties) France and the United Kingdom. These states were instrumental in determining the content and operationalization of the resolution amending the Rome Statute, and in this way had a meaningful impact in further shaping the Court's prospective future conduct. For this reason, I have chosen to address the subject in this chapter rather than the previous one.

Great power views concerning the nascent crime of aggression focused on four inter-related issues. First, they (and especially the US) argued for a narrow definition of the crime, so as to encompass only egregious examples of waging aggressive war and thereby excluding legitimate—but often contentious—instances of humanitarian and other military interventions (United States of America 2010b; McDougall 2013, 25). Second, echoing the long-standing critique discussed above, these states insisted that the UNSC be vested with exclusive domain for determining an act of aggression, in recognition of 'the specific role and responsibilities entrusted to the Security Council by the UN Charter in responding to aggression or its threat' (United States of America 2009a; Russian Federation 2014b). Third, given the political sensitivities at play, the incorporation of the crime of aggression must be founded on a strict respect for state consent, and exclude the prospect of nationals from non-member states facing ICC jurisdiction (as was the case with the other core crimes). Finally, any amendment to the Rome Statute on a matter of this gravity and potential impact needed to come about through consensus on core matters of content and jurisdiction—but sceptical states argued repeatedly that no such agreement existed (United States of America 2010b; United States of America 2010a). In the lead up to the Kampala negotiations, the US representative at the ASP

[17] A list of further academic articles is compiled on the following website: http://crimeofaggression.info/resourcessearch/academic-articles/. A collection of ICC documents concerning the negotiation of the crime of aggression can be found at https://asp.icc-cpi.int/en_menus/asp/crime%20of%20aggression/Pages/default.aspx.

[18] The United States brought thirty accredited representatives and advisers to the Kampala Review Conference, a clear demonstration of the importance it attached to the negotiations. By contrast, China had five officials, while the Russian Federation had seven (International Criminal Court 2010, 43, 49–50, 52–4).

meeting warned that these demands would need to be respected and that negotiations handled 'with extreme care' so that the Court avoided 'being drawn into a political thicket that could threaten its perceived impartiality' (United States of America 2009a).

In keeping with the theoretical account advanced in this study, the delegations repeatedly invoked legalistic discourse—framed in terms of both their interpretation of statutory law including the Rome Statute, and principles of customary international law—in an attempt to limit the scope of the proposed aggression amendment. This effort produced some highly significant successes, as will be shown; but the legalistic mode of engagement also restricted the opportunities for argumentation and bargaining in two important ways. On the one hand, discussions oriented around the prior draft texts produced by the Special Working Group on the Crime of Aggression, meaning that some key aspects were regarded as largely settled. On the other hand, the emphasis on legal claim-making displaced other, more explicitly political assertions as justifiable reasons. What is notable, then, is the near total absence of official reference to power politics, even as the demands of the great powers lingered very obviously in the background.

The final amendment reflects great power influence on all four of the key issues noted above. First, the vast majority of states had long favoured an expansive definition of an 'act of aggression' modelled on UN General Assembly Resolution 3314 of 14 December 1974. At Kampala, US negotiators sought to further narrow the definition to the most serious breaches of interstate peace only. In this respect the United States was only partially successful. The definition had been widely agreed during previous negotiations—most of which the United States did not attend, in contrast to both China and Russia who were active participants—and as a workable compromise was adopted in the final resolution essentially unchanged (McDougall 2013, 25; Wiesbord 2013, 111).[19] However, the United States did succeed, with the support of France and the United Kingdom among others, of inserting a series of understandings to the amendment that had the effect of confining prospective ICC jurisdiction to only 'the most serious and dangerous form of the illegal use of force' (Assembly of States Parties 2010b, 22).

Second, all five permanent Security Council members agreed that the UNSC should retain an exclusive capacity to determine whether certain state conduct amounted to an act of aggression, and thereby to refer potential cases to the ICC Prosecutor. These states shared the view that such a restrictive jurisdictional trigger mechanism was vital for maintaining the UNSC's pre-eminence in the existing international system, particularly its singular authority in

[19] For example, the Russian Federation (Russian Federation 2014b) has expressed its support for the final definition, 'since that definition is based on the resolution of the UN General Assembly of 1974'.

addressing violations of international peace and security. Importantly, this was framed not as an issue of power politics per se, but rather as a legal matter involving the constitutional role of the UN Charter. This demand was in stark contrast to the position of most states and civil society actors who wanted the Court (via the Pre-Trial Chamber and OTP) to retain an independent ability to launch investigations, as with the other core crimes under the Statute. In this respect the pressure from powerful states failed, as the final amendment includes the potential for the initiation of an investigation via States Party referral and *proprio motu* absent a determinative Security Council finding (Assembly of States Parties 2010b, 19). It is especially notable that a prior proposal for a 'green-light' process requiring that the UNSC first pre-determine that an act of aggression had occurred (before the ICC could act) was abandoned in the face of widespread resistance. However, the resolution does include the same Article 16 deferral process as for existing crimes, and adds a new mechanism whereby States Parties can explicitly opt out of ICC jurisdiction over the specific crime of aggression. This latter innovation was especially unpopular among the majority of participants, but was grudgingly accepted as a necessary condition of retaining British and French support.

On the third key issue, the most obvious victory for non-parties concerns the complete exclusion from ICC jurisdiction for the nationals of non-party states with respect to the crime of aggression (Assembly of States Parties 2010b, 19). This again was strongly resisted by most ICC member states and their civil society allies, but proved to be a matter that was simply too politically sensitive to address otherwise—particularly in light of the solidarity shown by a number of US allies such as Canada, France, Germany, Japan, and the United Kingdom. Fourth and finally, the great powers succeeded in delaying the entry into force of the aggression amendment to a period after 2017, in a formula that will require an additional vote (with the support of 2/3 of all ICC members) at a future ASP meeting. A number of the protagonists insisted that this window would, in the words of the US delegate, 'permit examination of the practical implications of the... operationalization of this crime', potentially leading to further revisions to its substance (United States of America 2010c). This final manoeuvre, which was again deeply unpopular amongst the majority, was regarded as a necessary compromise to ensure that France and the United Kingdom did not seek to block adoption of the resolution due to their objections concerning the non-exclusive role of the UNSC.

The agreement of the Kampala amendment on the crime of aggression was undoubtedly a watershed moment in the history of international criminal law, as it marked the first time that the waging of aggressive war had been outlawed in a permanent criminal court with legal powers over the highest ranking officials of the state (McDougall 2013, 31). The process also reveals two key points with respect to this study's interest in non-great power norm-building generally, and the efficacy of the ICC in particular. On the one hand, the negotiations in Kampala provide an especially potent example of the ways in which non-member states can involve themselves in the operation of a legal institution they formally reject, and employ legal processes to advance their own political goals. Prominent ICC opponents had a tremendous impact on the final outcome: shortly afterwards, the leaders of the US delegation declared that while they would have preferred no amendment at all, 'the outcome protected our vital interests' (Department of State, United States of America 2010). Despite this, the structure of legal argumentation in Kampala, and the extensive work undertaken in advance of this, did limit the scope of non-party contestation in meaningful ways. On the other hand, the 'Kampala compromise' is also an example of prominent ICC members—especially France, Japan, and the United Kingdom—using their political power to advance policies in common with non-members, and against the majority view of States Parties. This was achieved through careful diplomacy, but ultimately with the threat of withdrawing their support and thus undermining consensus at the last moment (McDougall 2013, 29). The amendment is far from irrelevant, as it provides a functional benchmark in the gradual development of a norm prohibiting the use of aggressive force; this matters despite the inherent imperfections of compromise. But the legal outcome was also weakened by political considerations in important ways: 'the P5 (joined by several other major powers) used their political weight to protect themselves and to limit the court's ability to pursue these cases. That outcome will help direct the court away from investigations that most threaten major-power freedom of action' (Bosco 2014, 183). This clearly will hold implications for the future operation of the Court when it ultimately takes up jurisdiction over the crime.

ACCOMMODATION AMID RESISTANCE: THE UNITED STATES AND THE ICC

As is the case with the ban on antipersonnel (AP) mines, the role of the United States looms largest amongst non-party states. US objections to the ICC have been well articulated elsewhere, both by virtue of its own vocal opposition to the Court, and the voluminous academic literature that has grown up in response (Birdsall 2010; Lietzau 2001; Ralph 2007; Schabas 2004; Scheffer 1999a; Sewall and Kaysen 2000; Wedgwood 1999). Yet it is also important to remember that the United States made major contributions to the drafting of the Rome Statute—including winning significant concessions that limited the scope of the final text (Scheffer 1999b)—and even at its most defiant, never disappeared from debates over the Court's development. Here I briefly chart three periods in the arc of US policy, which demonstrate a growing comfort with the Court despite significant lingering concerns. This amounts to a pattern of selective engagement featuring adaptation but with important limits to this change. Most fundamentally, the US experience illustrates both the potential and perils of using the law to advance policy goals: the invocation of ICC rules was initially successful in generating exemptions from Court jurisdiction, yet these efforts also drew US representatives into iterative legal argumentation and provided resources of counter-mobilization for pro-ICC actors, increasing the political costs of open resistance. Gradual US accommodation can therefore be regarded as strategic, but these policy choices have been powerfully shaped by an international social context underpinned by law.

Hesitant Engagement after Rome (1998–2000)

In the wake of its failure to secure adequate concessions during the Rome Conference, the United States did not fully withdraw as had been feared, but instead sought out ways of remaining involved in the ensuing diplomacy that would transition the nascent ICC from legal document to institutional reality. The Clinton administration had not abandoned its substantive concerns about the Rome Statute, but regarded engagement as the most effective means of influencing the subsequent evolution of the Court and mitigating what it perceived to be its worst features. In particular, US representatives participated actively in the subsequent Preparatory Commission (PrepCom) negotiations that were entrusted with finalizing key features of the new Court including the elements of crimes, rules of procedure and evidence, and relationship agreements with various international bodies. At the time, the lead US negotiator voiced his view that the PrepCom offered a venue at which 'the problems in the treaty which prevent us from signing it can be solved' (Scheffer 1999b). Core US proposals concerning additional safeguards in the Court's complementarity regime and exemptions for non-party nationals involved in 'official acts' were ultimately not adopted (Ralph 2007, 123–5). However, US negotiators continued to view participation in the PrepCom process as the best opportunity for gradually re-shaping the emerging Rome regime onto more favourable grounds.

From 2001 onwards, however, PrepCom sessions would be restricted to ICC members and signatories.[20] In light of this deadline, President Clinton signed the Rome Statute on 31 December 2000, the final possible day. The

[20] As per Article 125 of the Rome Statute, the treaty was open for signature between 17 July 1998 and 31 December 2000. After this date, states could only accede to the treaty, becoming full legal members.

instrumental value of this action was clearly a motivating factor, as the president himself acknowledged: 'Signature will enhance our ability to further protect US officials from unfounded charges and to achieve the human rights and accountability objectives of the ICC' (United States of America 2000). US signature was also regarded as a symbolic demonstration of an enduring commitment to countering impunity and in this way, provides an early example of how the Court has come to be associated with good behaviour in the international system. This effort, however, came with a clear caveat that the incoming administration should not seek to ratify the Rome Statute and formally join the Court 'until our fundamental concerns are satisfied' (United States of America 2000). Core views had not changed, but key US officials continued to see the benefits of working with the new institution as a means of securing US interests.

Open Defiance (2001–5)

The advent of the new administration of George W. Bush led to a marked shift in US attitudes toward international institutions in general and the ICC in particular. Despite initially running on a platform of modest foreign policy, the first Bush administration was notable for the prominent positions held by ideological sceptics of international law and multilateralism. In the first year of the new administration the Court received only limited, if uncomplimentary, attention. However, the rapid pace of ratifications and imminent entry into force of the Rome Statute on 1 July 2002 caught both ICC supporters and opponents by surprise. In response, the US government launched an aggressive campaign aimed at further insulating US nationals from prospective ICC jurisdiction and more broadly undermining the Court's future operations.

First, under the initiative of Under-Secretary of State John Bolton, the United States deposited a letter with the UN Secretary General notifying him that the United States would not become a party to the Rome Statute, and thus no longer regarded its prior signature as operative (Bolton 2002). This so-called 'unsigning' of the Rome Statute was of limited importance as a matter of law,[21] but was of great symbolic value as an expression of US discontent with the new ICC. In parallel with this development, the US Congress passed the American Service-Members Protection Act (ASPA).[22] The controversial law prohibited, inter alia: federal, state, and local governments and agencies from cooperating

[21] See page 152, this volume.

[22] United States Congress (2002). The ASPA was passed the House of Representatives on 24 May 2002, the Senate on 7 June 2002, and was signed into law by President Bush on 2 August 2002. For a collection of international reaction to APSA, see http://www.amicc.org/usicc/legislation.

with the ICC (including in surrendering suspects, transferring intelligence or other sensitive information to Court officials, or permitting ICC investigations on US territory); US forces from participating in UN peacekeeping operations without explicitly-agreed immunities; and US military assistance to ICC member states (excluding NATO and major non-NATO allies or in cases of 'important national interest'). Most provocatively of all, the ASPA authorized the president to 'use all means necessary and appropriate to bring about the release of any person . . . who is being detained or imprisoned by, on behalf of, or at the request of the International Criminal Court' (United States Congress 2002, Sec. 2008(a)).

Third, the US Department of States pressured states around the world to adopt bilateral immunity agreements (BIAs) in which they committed never to surrender US citizens to ICC custody (Akande 2003, 640–6; Scheffer 2005; United States of America 2002a). These arrangements—which were ostensibly modelled on Article 98 of the Rome Statute[23]—were imposed by coercion, as states that refused to enter into an agreement faced the credible threat of sanction in the form of a withdrawal of military and development aid (Kelley 2007; Nooruddin and Payton 2010). Finally, the United States sought to further entrench blanket immunities for its nationals by inserting clauses into Security Council resolutions (re-)authorizing peacekeeping forces in Bosnia and Liberia, and referring the Darfur and Libyan cases to the ICC (United Nations Security Council 2002; United Nations Security Council 2003a; United Nations Security Council 2003b; United Nations Security Council 2005; United Nations Security Council 2011). US officials made clear that the exemption was a precondition for gaining their support; without it, the United States would withdraw its forces from the UN missions and would not support the UNSC referrals, critically imperilling prospects of the various initiatives.[24]

Notably, US diplomacy featured a combination of power politics and legalistic argumentation. Indeed, US officials went to great lengths to frame their proposals in terms of the Rome Statute itself, in conjunction with broader principles of international law (Bower 2015). During the debate over the

[23] Article 98(2) reads: 'The Court may not proceed with a request for surrender which would require the requested State to act inconsistently with its obligations under international agreements pursuant to which the consent of a sending State is required to surrender a person of that State to the Court, unless the Court can first obtain the cooperation of the sending State for the giving of consent for the surrender.'

[24] The threat of US punishment clearly hung over the diplomatic proceedings. One month before Resolution 1422 was introduced, US officials had attempted to get a similar immunity provision included in a Security Council resolution authorizing the peacekeeping mission in East Timor. When this effort failed, the United States withdrew its three military observers and seventy-five civilian police from the operation.

renewal of the peacekeeping mission, the US delegate contended that the plain language of the treaty explicitly permitted the envisioned exemption:

> Our latest proposal uses article 16 of the Rome Statute—as we were urged to do by other Council members—to address our concerns about the implications of the Rome Statute for nations that are not parties to it, but which want to continue to contribute peacekeepers to United Nations missions... We believe that [our approach] is consistent both with the terms of article 16 and with the primary responsibility of the Security Council for maintaining international peace and security. (United States of America 2002b)

The intervention also made reference to the United States' unique role in upholding the international system via overseas military deployments including peacekeeping. From the US perspective, therefore, 'the demand... that no individual be above international humanitarian or human rights law and that states cooperate with the ICC on that basis, was deemed to be in conflict with the "smooth working" of international society' (Ralph 2007, 166).

The global debate surrounding BIAs also relied extensively on a legalized discourse, as US officials contended that their initiative simply followed the intention of Article 98(2) in respecting legal obligations concerning non-surrender between states (Department of State, United States of America 2002; Scheffer 2005).[25] Despite its instrumental intentions, the US approach again provides interesting insight into the impact the Statute has had in shaping global responses even among the most powerful states. After all, the Bush administration could have ignored the Court completely, and relied on its preponderant material advantages unadorned with legalistic justification to pursue its goals, as anticipated by realist accounts (Goldsmith 2003). Yet the administration instead sought legitimacy for its policy through reference to the Rome Statute, which in turn influenced the manner in which the world's pre-eminent military power articulated its interests in a key area of national security policy.

As these instances demonstrate, resistant states may exploit the connections between specific institutions and prior international norms and rules to counteract unwelcome legal developments. In this regard the US effort to undermine the Court's jurisdiction was initially a success. A total of 102 states—including forty-eight ICC States Parties—signed BIAs in the period 2002–6 (American Non-Governmental Organizations Coalition for the International Criminal Court 2015a; Coalition for the International Criminal Court 2006e). The UNSC also authorized sequential one-year exemptions from ICC jurisdiction to peacekeepers from non-ICC member states in Bosnia (Resolutions 1422 and 1487) well as permanent immunities for forces engaged in operations

[25] A collection of statements by US officials concerning the BIA campaign can be found at http://www.amicc.org/usicc/biastatements.

in Liberia, Darfur, or Libya (Resolutions 1497, 1593, and 1977). There is thus ample evidence of states acquiescing in efforts to contest the basic legal and operational premises of the Court, highlighting potential limitations of nested effects in generating support for non-great power treaties.

Importantly, however, the official record reveals that the overwhelming majority of states accepted the US demands not on substantive grounds, but rather as the result of an overriding need to retain US cooperation with international stabilization efforts. Similarly, discourse from states signing BIAs makes clear that in the majority of cases, these decisions were motivated by a desire 'to avoid a sanction or to appease the United States' rather than an endorsement of the US position concerning the legal validity of the agreements (Kelley 2007, 583; Coalition for the International Criminal Court 2006a). The notable absence of principled support for the US position is significant for the present analysis since it suggests an important qualification to the US claim for establishing precedent. The acquiescence by ICC proponents did, however, contribute to a partial recognition of non-party immunities in international practice that could become increasingly settled if it continues.

While initially gaining grudging support, the US initiatives also had unintended consequences that substantially impacted upon the subsequent development of US policy. In short, the adoption of legal reasoning opened discursive space for other actors to interrogate US claims on their merits, within a shared context of legal reasoning. This, in turn, provided pro-ICC actors with resources with which to confront the various immunity efforts through a rhetorical strategy that invoked alternative interpretations of Rome Statute rules and their relationship to wider international norms. The vast majority of states speaking at the Security Council meetings raised both practical and principled objections to the US Article 16 initiative.[26] Court supporters first argued that the Rome Statute already contained sufficient procedural checks and balances to effectively eliminate US-stated concerns for politically motivated prosecutions.[27] More fundamentally, they objected on the grounds that, quite to the contrary of US assertions, the proposal for granting immunity prior to a specific incident and in perpetuity expressly

[26] Unless otherwise noted, statements refer to the UNSC meetings of 10 July 2002 (S/PV.4568 and Resumption 1) and 12 June 2003 (S/PV.4772). Only China, India, and Russia supported the US position in the Council discussions before voting was held on the 2002 draft resolution. This is contrasted with twenty-eight states—including two speaking on behalf of the European Union and Rio Group—that voiced explicit concerns over the US proposal. Seven other states made interventions that could not be clearly identified as fundamentally supportive or resistant. A similar pattern emerged in 2003, with only Pakistan explicitly endorsing the US view and Angola, Bulgaria, China, and the Russian Federation making more ambiguous statements of understanding.

[27] See inter alia statements by Canada, France, Jordan, Ireland, Brazil, and Switzerland to the United Nations at the 2002 UNSC meeting.

violated the terms of the Rome Statute.[28] Especially relevant here were discourses of legal equality and fairness, and respect for norms regulating the modification of international legal instruments (Canada 2002). Numerous countries argued that the US demand would set a precedent for the Security Council to unilaterally re-interpret existing multilateral agreements without the approval of the treaty parties—a power that was not granted by the UN Charter.[29] This was widely understood to constitute an extra-legal interference in the treaty-making process, undercutting the sovereign right of states to undertake and observe legal commitments, and an unwarranted over-reach of UNSC authority 'that would destabilize and undermine the international legal regime' (Syrian Arab Republic 2002). Delegations thus voiced concern that a blanket immunization as envisioned in Resolutions 1422 and 1487 'attempted to elevate an entire category of people to a point above the law—a concern exacerbated still further when thought is given to the revolting nature of the crimes covered by the Court's jurisdiction' (Hashemite Kingdom of Jordan 2003). Other delegations described this outcome as 'an unconscionable double standard' (New Zealand 2002) that would weaken the ICC and 'reverse the positive gains and historic milestones of the Rome Diplomatic Conference' (Republic of Malawi 2003).

Principled arguments were also at the heart of global responses to the Article 98 BIA campaign. As Kelley (2007, 574–5) points out, the sheer aggressiveness of the Bush administration's global strategy meant that virtually all states faced with a dilemma of whether to persist with their prior commitment to the Court and face substantial costs, or concede to US demands. Nearly half of all states, including fifty-seven ICC members, did not sign BIAs, often resulting in the loss of significant economic and military assistance (Coalition for the International Criminal Court 2006d; Ribando 2006). Contemporary statements reveal that resistance for many was driven by affinity with the ICC as an embodiment of international justice while for others was motivated by a more generalized belief that international commitments must be observed (American Non-Governmental Organizations Coalition for the International Criminal Court 2015b; Coalition for the International Criminal Court 2006b; Kelley 2007). Expressions of normative commitment were thus anything but 'cheap talk' as some scholars might expect.

Rather, norm-based concerns for upholding the ICC system often interacted with strategic considerations in shaping policy responses. This is particularly

[28] See for example statements by Canada, Costa Rica, Brazil, Switzerland, Mexico, New Zealand, and Liechtenstein at the 2002 meeting; and those by Canada, New Zealand, Jordan, Switzerland, the Netherlands, and Liechtenstein to the United Nations Security Council, 58th year, 4772nd meeting, Agenda Item: United Nations Peacekeeping, New York, 12 June 2003 S/PV.4772. This objection was also reiterated by the UN Secretary-General at the 2003 meeting.

[29] Statements by Canada, Colombia, Costa Rica, Germany, Iran, Jordan, Liechtenstein, Mexico, New Zealand, and South Africa (2002).

notable with respect to the linkage between EU membership and endorsement of the EU's common position in support of the Court (Council of the European Union 2001). For example, it appears that a number of Eastern European governments—including Bulgaria and Serbia and Montenegro—decided against signing BIAs as a consequence of concerns over their future membership in the European Union.[30] Yet instrumental logics that associate rejection of a BIA with countervailing benefits are incomplete for two important reasons. First, in contrast to the US approach, the EU did not impose explicit economic or diplomatic sanctions for signing a BIA (Kelley 2007, 575). Second, even self-seeking behaviour that sought to weigh the relative benefits of cooperating with US versus EU demands still relied on a prior social agreement concerning the normative value of the Court. Indeed, the use of EU membership as political leverage is only significant here because the EU had already adopted an official policy in support of the ICC and against US efforts to undermine the institution. Hence for many states, commitment to international norms—whether concerning the content of the Rome Statute or broader principles of international justice —was sufficient to outweigh direct material costs, an outcome that runs contrary to realist and institutionalist expectations.

Rather than fully achieving its intended aims, therefore, the use of legal argumentation had important unintended consequences in limiting the success of US diplomacy. With respect to the Security Council immunities effort, the invocation of legal justifications provided the crucial rhetorical opening for pro-ICC states to narrow the scope of the successive UNSC resolutions. The United States initially proposed language to amend the reauthorization of the UN mission that would have absolved US forces *in perpetuity* for acts committed as part of operations in Bosnia (Coalition for the International Criminal Court 2004). ICC proponents countered with language that specifically included Rome Statute Article 16 for the first time, limiting prospective deferrals of ICC investigations or prosecutions 'on a case by case basis'. The opposition faced within the Security Council compelled the United States delegation to hew more closely to the wording of Article 16, limiting the impact of the exemption contained in Resolution 1422. And, while Security Council members submitted to US demands in the short run, few states were willing to recognize the request as anything other than a temporary concession, as demonstrated by the successful Canadian insertion of a clause ensuring annual UNSC oversight via a renewal.[31] These were significant modifications since they placed the US position under regular scrutiny, ensuring

[30] This calculus was captured in the comment by then-European Commission President Romano Prodi that 'if Bulgaria bows to US pressure and signs an agreement granting ICC immunity for US citizens, it may [as] well forget about EU membership' (Coalition for the International Criminal Court 2006b).

[31] See for example statements by Canada, France, Guinea, Spain, and the United Kingdom at the 12 June 2003 UNSC meeting.

that representatives would have to continue to engage in public justifications on the terms of the Rome Statute. Despite the re-authorization in Resolution 1487, reference to exceptional circumstances meant that immunity was not normalized even as the international system's highest political body temporarily conceded to US pressure.

These limits proved highly consequential as the Security Council deliberated a further renewal of the UN mission in Bosnia in 2004. Yet in the intervening period, a series of revelations concerning US policies in the War on Terror—especially the release of photographs documenting serious abuses at Abu Ghraib Prison in Iraq—drew widespread condemnation, and further increased scrutiny on US efforts at the Security Council. In light of this, the United States announced that it would not seek another immunity provision as a precondition for an extension of UN operations. In doing so, US representatives indicated that they had not changed their views regarding the ICC, but recognized that members of the Council were no longer willing to support their demands (Department of State, United States of America 2004c). The longer-term impact of the US effort, moreover, has been modest: since 2002 there have been more than 200 UNSC resolutions authorizing or renewing peacekeeping operations; of that substantial list, only the five mentioned above contain provisions exempting non-party nationals, or UN personnel more broadly, from ICC jurisdiction. The attempt to establish a blanket immunity for non-party nationals was resisted, therefore, as was the attempt to give the Security Council greater authority over an independent organization. When considered in this light, the short-term concessions from pro-ICC states resemble isolated tactical accommodations rather than a genuine shift in the international status quo.

In a similar vein, the widespread opposition to BIAs imposed specific costs on US foreign policy in the form of military and intelligence failings:

> In testimony to a congressional panel in 2005, US Army General Bantz Craddock said enforcement of [the American Service Members' Protection Act] had made it impossible for him to fulfill his duties as head of the Southern Command, in charge of US forces in Latin America. He stated that several countries in Latin America had refused to sign [bilateral immunity agreements] and as a result, certain foreign aid for these countries has been held up. These statements were ultimately reflected in Secretary of State Condoleezza Rice's conclusion that the [BIA] policy had been 'sort of the same as shooting ourselves in the foot'. (Glick 2009, 6)

The subsequent suspension of the BIA programme and termination of domestic legislation punishing states that refused to sign agreements were both the direct result of these challenges (Coalition for the International Criminal Court 2006c; DiCicco 2009).[32] Thus even a dominant military power like the

[32] While existing Article 98 agreements remain in force, no new agreements have been sought since 2007. Various legislation that penalized states that refused to sign BIAs was either

United States can face material consequences when its behaviour is widely judged to contradict community standards that it does not fully share. While the United States proved able to get states to acquiesce to its demands in the short term, it had much less success in convincing them of the legitimacy or legal validity of its claim to an expansive exemption of non-party nationals. Instead, the iterative argumentation on the terms of the Rome Statute generated countervailing pressures that made US resistance increasingly costly, leading to a public reversal of its policy. This outcome is particularly significant given the high importance that senior members of the Bush administration attached to the immunities efforts.

Cautious Re-engagement (2005–15)

The pronounced failure of the US policy of directly confronting the ICC led to a shift during the second Bush term, characterized by an increasing openness to the Court and recognition that in some discrete circumstances, US interests could intersect with, and be advanced by, those of the ICC. At a very practical level, this process was spurred by a revival in direct contact between US actors (such as judges and government officials but also private actors like lawyers) and the Court, the consequence of years of both institutional and civil society outreach. In particular, discourses of human rights and accountability—both within and outside the administration—convinced key officials that the Court could serve as a selective tool for advancing international justice causes. It is understood, for example, that widespread outrage within the US government and public concerning human rights abuses in Darfur was at the heart of the US decision not to oppose the Security Council referral (addressed more fully above).[33] In parallel with this increasingly proactive position the United States also amended its domestic legislation to soften its most provocative challenges to the Court and enable a much wider array of cooperation with international justice efforts (United States Congress 2008).

These processes have been reinforced during the Obama administration, which has signalled a more open approach to the Court since taking office. Recent US experience further highlights the interaction of instrumental and normative influences on policy development, and the subtle yet powerful way that norms may still stimulate a partial re-conception of state interests under conditions of formal ambivalence. ICC observers have suggested that increasing familiarity with the Court has removed some of the ideological opposition to the ICC,

abandoned or substantially amended during the final years of the Bush Administration, and was officially repealed by the Obama administration in 2009. Detailed discussion of US legislation can be found at http://www.amicc.org/usicc/legislation.

[33] Washburn interview. This episode is also recounted in Bosco (2014).

allowing the Bush (in its second term) and Obama administrations to make decisions on the basis of cost–benefit considerations that would have been foreclosed formerly.[34] The decision to begin attending ASP meetings in 2009 for example—the first such US engagement since the PrepCom negotiations—was motivated by a desire to retain influence over the impending discussion of the crime of aggression at the ASP and Kampala Review Conference (United States of America 2009a). Yet this was only possible because the United States had come to accept the ICC as a feature of the international system. The increasingly deep and sustained interaction with the Court has also clearly influenced the way in which the US government pursues foreign policy goals relating to the promotion of human rights and the rule of law. The Obama administration has given greater attention and institutional support to these concerns, including through the creation of an Atrocities Prevention Board that appears to explicitly envision cooperation with the ICC (Office of the President of the United States of America 2012). The decision to deploy military advisers to Uganda to aide in the capture of Lord's Resistance Army suspects is a further demonstration of this shift (Office of the President of the United States of America 2011; United States of America 2011b). It is particularly notable that President Obama described this latter initiative—as one example of a wider commitment to preventing mass atrocities—as in 'the national security and foreign policy interests of the United States' (Office of the President of the United States of America 2011).

These brief examples demonstrate how a new international norm may influence strategic decision-making on important matters of national policy by constituting a new role identity that invites or even explicitly requires internationalized responses to grave crimes. This is best appreciated in a wider context of great power politics and the ICC's presumed role in international affairs. While incomplete, the US position, and the more muted responses from other non-parties, nonetheless contributes to the legitimacy of the Court by reinforcing the perception that the ICC is one—and increasingly *the*—appropriate mechanism for addressing large-scale atrocities. These outcomes are particularly surprising from a sceptical perspective that assumes, first, that powerful states can largely bypass inconvenient legal constraints and second, that an institution such as the ICC would be critically weakened in the face of sustained US pressure.

CONCLUSION

The emergence of a permanent global court, in conjunction with a series of ad hoc tribunals, has led some observers to conclude that 'while incomplete and

[34] Washburn interview.

with significant shortcomings', we are witnessing 'the increasing criminalization of international and even domestic violent conflict and repression' (Lee and Price, 2004: 123; also Sikkink, 2011; Sikkink and Kim, 2013). As with the AP MBT, non-member states' interaction with the ICC provides an important window into the institution's contemporary efficacy. This chapter has charted a complex relationship, characterized by concessions from both supporters of an independent ICC and powerful non-party states. It is clear that the latter group have come to regard the Court, in certain circumstances, as a useful tool in pursuing their policy goals, and have often succeeded in shaping Court operations to meet their demands. This dynamic is especially notable with respect to the Sudan and Libya referrals, but is also evidenced in a variety of other actions discussed above. The result has been an ICC that at important moments appears to have been reduced to 'an instrument in the toolkit of major powers responding to instability and violence in weaker states' (Bosco 2014, 187), with attendant concerns for double-standards and power politics dominating an impartial pursuit of justice.

Yet there have been consequences from this selective engagement, and non-parties have clearly been influenced by the norms embodied in the Rome Statute and the ICC's own institutional development. Most importantly, these states frequently rely on the legal criteria of the Statute in justifying their policy responses. In order to appear as good international actors, states must increasingly accord—or at least appear to accord—with the procedural and normative commitments embodied in the Rome Statute. These kinds of changes reflect a closing-off of certain rhetorical possibilities in response to the social expectations fostered by the treaty. This intersubjective environment has thus imposed important constraints on the actions that powerful states pursue and are willing to openly defend, and has provided a set of diplomatic resources by which less powerful actors can challenge great power policies.

In other words, the contemporary ICC features pushes and pulls in two directions, or what Bosco (2014) terms 'mutual accommodation' between sceptical powers and Court supporters. ICC members—which, of course, constitute the majority of states—have made allowances in the face of often aggressive campaigns from great powers. The inclusion of limited immunities for non-party nationals in UNSC resolutions, or the more expansive exemption in the context of the nascent crime of aggression, are important instances in which the independence and impartiality of the ICC have been weakened. In these ways, engagement by non-parties—as opposed to a form of nihilistic isolationism of which they are often accused—has succeeded in establishing modes of informal control over an institution they officially reject. By the same token, however, pro-ICC states have not as a general rule been willing to renegotiate the core competencies of the Court, but rather to temporarily limit them in the pursuit of specific forms of great power participation. Indeed, amid the concessions there has also been extensive push-back against efforts to narrow the scope of ICC jurisdiction, as was demonstrated in the case of US efforts to secure immunities for their citizens. Here again the resort to the language of international law matters, since it has served as the dominant mode of diplomatic transaction. As a consequence, the Court and parallel norm of internationalized procedural justice have proven more resilient than many would have anticipated. The fact that this process is uneven and substantially incomplete should not detract from its significance as a matter of international politics and law.

8

Lessons from the Cases

The animating question of the present study is whether the decision to proceed with multilateral treaties in the face of great power resistance was worth it given the presumed costs of excluding key states from the legal community. Assessing the wisdom of the 'new diplomacy' that generated the Mine Ban Treaty (MBT) and the International Criminal Court (ICC) can only be accomplished by detailing the actual performance of the treaties that did emerge, and contrasting these outcomes with the prospective consequences of other potential institutions. This chapter engages in the first half of this broader evaluative exercise through three key tasks. I first present a comparative review of the operation of the MBT and ICC, focusing on five key themes developed in the preceding analysis. I then attempt to account for this observed variance with reference to some hypothesized factors drawn from the IR literature. Finally, the chapter assesses the actually existing MBT and ICC against a counterfactual consideration of how the principal institutional alternatives—conceding to great power demands in the negotiations or abandoning multilateral efforts altogether—might have addressed the policy challenges that motivated the treaty-making in the first place. Would such approaches have generated stronger norms and greater state change? I believe the most reasonable answer is no: either would have resulted in less, rather than more international governance capacity. This provides the basis for the concluding chapter's reflections on the status of non-great power multilateralism in its other current manifestations and future opportunities.

COMPARING THE MBT AND ICC

Compliance: Changing State Practice

First, it is clear that both treaties have substantially—though unevenly—influenced the conduct of international politics as compared with the era before their creation. Certainly it is easier to make this case with respect to the MBT: the pattern presented in Chapters 4 and 5 is one of widespread restraint in relation to the most consequential obligations aimed at eradicating antipersonnel (AP) mines. The weapons have thus been largely marginalized as tools of contemporary warfare, despite the continued prevalence of armed violence globally. The mine ban appears robust even in moments where its authority is challenged by violations, as these are typically denied outright or defended as the product of special circumstances rather than unproblematic acts. These discursive practices further illustrate the disciplinary effect legal institutions may have in international society. Indeed, were it not for the existence of a strong international prohibition, the political costs of public non-conformance would be considerably lower. For this reason, exceptions to date have tended to reinforce rather than degrade the status of the mine ban norm as a legal and social obligation. The normative force of the MBT has therefore shifted AP mines into the realm of 'exceptional' politics and away from the previous view of the weapons as uncontroversial features of military arsenals. This outcome is all the more significant given the prior prevalence of AP mines in a great many states' military doctrine and the fact that many might still find benefit in their use.

The ICC presents a more varied picture, not least because the institution itself, and the demands it makes of states, is considerably more complex and multifaceted than with respect to the MBT. At the broadest level of analysis, there is now undoubtedly widespread acceptance that the most serious international crimes must be addressed via judicial processes in which individuals are the subjects of criminal punishment. The scale of ratifications of the Rome Statute, along with other important forms of state change, suggests that the ICC is increasingly entrenched as a feature of the international political landscape. Yet as Chapters 6 and 7 demonstrated at length, this has not translated into comprehensive respect for core ICC commitments: incorporation of the Rome Statute in domestic law is currently modest at best and, more problematically still, there are substantial barriers to cooperation with Court proceedings among States Parties and non-member states alike. This suggests that, despite a significant shift in social conditions (discussed in the next section), behavioural changes are less deeply entrenched and more conditional than for the MBT. These experiences point to a worrying malaise, as ICC parties fail to observe their obligations and denounce non-compliance by others. At the same time, non-parties have been able to assert greater influence over the development of the Court, by selectively engaging with the ICC while remaining more aloof from its compliance pull than with the mine ban norm. The net result has been an uneven and 'ad hoc rather than routinized system of state cooperation with and support for the court' (Bosco 2014, 136) that has generated important gaps in ICC capacity, as witnessed most dramatically in the recent collapse of the cases against the leaders of Kenya and Sudan.

Socialization: Redefining Identities and Interests

Constructivists have convincingly argued that material conditions are not inherent, but are given meaning through processes of social interaction that inform the content of actor identities and subsequent interests (e.g. Wendt 1992; Wendt 1999). Hence a primary way that treaties—and international norms and law more generally—'matter' is in changing the context in which actors conceptualize what they want, and the means by which they seek to achieve their goals. This, in turn, justifies this study's attention to the interaction of behavioural and discursive measures of actor change, which it has been claimed—and I believe demonstrated—provides a richer and more nuanced view of institutional impact.

This instantiation of appropriate conduct has clearly occurred in both the MBT and ICC cases, but there are notable differences in the depth and breadth of change. Increasingly, being a responsible state is synonymous with the elimination of AP mines. This is seen most clearly in the numerous 'hard' cases of membership—among conflict-prone states, members of military coalitions, and late adopters like Finland, Japan, Poland, and Turkey—but is also apparent in various informal adaptations by prominent non-party states. Stimulating a redefinition of 'standard military practice' is a prominent way that international norms may exert influence in the international system (Price 2004a, 125). The experience of the MBT suggests that while concerns for military necessity can impede the full acceptance of treaty obligations, such fundamental national goals may also be reshaped through engagement with an external social standard. In other words, how states understand their security—and the acceptable means for pursuing it—is powerfully informed by dominant conceptions of what behaviours are permissible and, inversely, what actions are to be excluded irrespective of their potential efficacy. The realist expectation that bans will follow, rather than precede, judgement of a weapon's declining utility therefore fails to capture the totality of the processes at work in this case. Instead, the advent of the mine ban movement has produced a constitutive change in international society in which states—including many of those that resist the legal expression of the norm—have adopted a new role identity that dramatically modifies the previous conception of a weapon formerly in frequent use.

For the vast majority of states, therefore, the MBT has become the unambiguous standard for articulating responsibilities with respect to the weapons. Non-parties frequently invoke Amended Protocol II (APII) of the Convention on Certain Conventional Weapons (CCW) as an alternative marker of legality and legitimate authority, and in this respect the MBT cannot be claimed as the sole reference point in the international system. Yet even here, the social power of the mine ban is such that even openly resistant states routinely refer to the treaty in their diplomacy. And despite some concerted efforts, powerful MBT sceptics have had little traction in situating APII as a genuinely alternative social standard for the global response to the humanitarian crisis posed by AP mines.

By contrast, foundational elements of the ICC legal regime remain in greater flux. At a general level, the pattern appears broadly similar to the mine ban case. For a majority of the international community, the Rome Statute—as a legal text and parallel norm of internationalized procedural justice—has come to embody the appropriate institutional solution for pursuing individual criminal accountability for grave international crimes. Among States Parties, therefore, support for the ICC has become a prominent marker of social status, serving more specifically as a symbol of commitment to human rights and, for many fragile societies, respect for the rule of law and democratic governance. Attention to this constitutive function of law deepens and contextualizes the instrumental account of membership. For example, Simmons and Danner's (2010) conception of the ICC as a means of making credible commitments for restraint does not account for why the particular institutional structure embodied in the Rome Statute has come to be regarded by the majority of states as the socially acceptable means of punishing acts of atrocity. Deploying the Court as a signalling device thus presupposes its intersubjectively agreed symbolic value and in this way, constructivist attention to social content of strategic decision-making complements and extends rationalist insights regarding the deliberate development of institutions (Fehl 2004; Deitelhoff 2009b; Fearon and Wendt 2002). Discursive support for the fight against impunity is also widely apparent among states not party to the ICC, to the extent that many have identified the Court as a principal resource in this effort. The use of ICC processes for political gain further illustrates this social function, such that declared adherence to its precepts is de facto evidence of good international standing. This particular phenomenon is often missed in discussions of the ICC's contemporary status.

While the creation of the Rome Statute has by no means done away with sovereignty as conventionally understood, it has generated a competing—and as yet incompletely solidified—international social expectation that conditions national obligations to punish grave crimes with significant international oversight. The experience post-Rome can be contrasted with the prior era in which, with a few notable exceptions, a generalized expectation of impunity governed relations within and between states. By establishing the Court as an element of the international system, therefore, member states have accepted a revised relationship between national and international authority. This task, however, is substantially incomplete, as evidenced by important gaps in state compliance with Rome Statute commitments and more specific Court requests. More deeply, Chapters 6 and 7 revealed fundamental disagreements regarding the nature and limits of the ICC's jurisdictional claim, most especially in the context of the removal of immunity for senior state officials and the Court's relationship to the United Nations Security Council (UNSC).

Adaptation and Contestation: Nested Social Structures and the Normative Pull of Treaties

A central claim of my theoretical account is that institutional linkages are vital for the prospective development and consolidation of a new multilateral treaty and norm. The embedded nature of contemporary international law and politics, and the dense reciprocal connections that develop between particular treaties and the wider universe of principles, norms, and rules, provide the structural conditions and intellectual resources that underpin this form of social power. At the same time, however, these connections also offer pathways for challenging new treaties: international law's nested nature is a potential source of contestation as much as convergence. The two treaty cases provide much evidence for these bi-directional forces.

The stigmatization of AP mines has clearly benefitted from an association with foundational international humanitarian law (IHL) principles. Yet this process also involved the application of existing rules and norms to new circumstances that helped to reconstruct the meaning of these prior standards in a new social setting. These processes are interactive, further illustrating the dynamic social environment in which international law resides. Discursive interventions over actual and alleged non-compliance frequently refer to the MBT as the standard against which actions are to be assessed: this is apparent both in the justification of policies, and the response received from other state and civil society actors. This is a significant way that the MBT can be said to have altered the international social environment.

A similar narrative, in its broad strokes at least, can be told about the ICC. A norm of individual criminal accountability for atrocities—described eloquently by Bass (2001) and Sikkink (2011), among others—has clearly gained prominence in the international community, and can be understood as both a precipitating factor in the creation of the Court, and a chief source of its legitimacy. Equally, the broad international agreement concerning the special gravity of the crimes under ICC jurisdiction (if not their specific operationalization in all cases), along with many modalities of international criminal jurisdiction and procedure, provided a reservoir of shared expectations that greatly facilitated the Court's emergence and subsequent development. And by the same token, engagements over the practice and limits of ICC authority—discussed in a moment—take place on the terms of the Rome Statute and its relationship to more general conceptions of rights and duties under international law, and largely exclude public reference to realpolitik considerations alone. In this respect, a key impact of the ICC as both a legal institution and norm has been to frame the articulation of state interests on a key matter of national concern, and thereby inform responses to particular real-world scenarios. The fact that many ICC non-parties already accept temporally prior international norms and rules embodied in the Rome Statute should offer an important vector for bringing these states into closer accord with the particular legal innovation. It would seem significant, therefore, that a number of current non-parties have expressed an interest in the Court and kept open the prospect of future membership.

While neither the MBT nor ICC are universally observed as legally binding institutions, therefore, they provide foundational reference points for a diverse set of debates over the meaning and extent of obligations in the international system. In the case of the MBT, this has served to substantially limit the effects of contestation. As Chapter 5 showed, MBT non-parties have sought to challenge the mine ban via an alternative set of linkages to existing IHL standards, in effect arguing that the regulation of AP mines is both in keeping with IHL requirements and better respects the balance between military necessity and humanitarian protection. For reasons discussed already, this effort has proven largely ineffective, most fundamentally because the counter-grafting efforts of prominent ban opponents like China, India, Russia, and (especially) the United States did not succeed in reversing the ascendant intersubjective stigma against the weapons. In other words, the alternative institutional solution and norm embodied in CCW APII has not displaced the MBT as the dominant global standard, despite the concerted efforts of great powers.

By contrast, while the association with prior international law has clearly been central to the broad endorsement the ICC has enjoyed, the more revolutionary features of the Rome Statute have faced far greater hostility. A number of states—including States Parties—have challenged the Statute's assertion of authority over senior political leaders on the grounds that it expressly violates long-established statutory and customary rules of immunity for such officials and thus represents a serious infringement of constitutive norms of state sovereignty and non-interference. This critique has been met with considerable sympathy among non-Western states, particularly in Africa and Asia, calling into question the robustness of the anti-immunity provision as both a legal rule and broader social standard. Similarly, China, Russia, and the United States have attacked the institutional autonomy enjoyed by the Court as contrary to the established international order based on the political prerogatives of great powers reinforced by norms of sovereignty and voluntary consent. Yet unlike the ambivalence concerning immunities, which has diffused rather more widely, the great powers themselves have had only limited success in generating support for subsuming the Court under UNSC dominion. As Chapter 7 showed, the vast majority of states—including ICC non-members—have rejected the idea that the Security

Council should have exclusive authority in determining the jurisdiction of the ICC, particularly as this would give five states (three of which are not members of the Court) the power to protect themselves from ICC jurisdiction with their veto at the expense of other, weaker actors.

In isolation, these kinds of disputes do not necessarily prohibit the emergence of widely accepted norms. Treaties often face interpretive challenges as actors seek to apply complex and frequently ambiguous legal standards to changing circumstances or, more instrumentally, to meet their particular needs. Discursive challenges are therefore more damaging to the extent that they are widely endorsed and replicated. For this reason, the ongoing contestation concerning immunities would appear to be the most potent barrier to the ICC's further entrenchment. Shifts in the discursive acceptance of the Court as a legitimate tool for punishing some acts of international criminality and the reliance on the Court in discrete circumstances are significant, but must be assessed in this wider context.

'Using' the Law: Instrumentalization and its Consequences

A penultimate theme concerns the utility and perils of invoking legal rules and norms for self-interested ends. Both the MBT and ICC provide ample evidence of actors attempting to delegitimize adversaries through accusations that the latter have violated core treaty rules. Interestingly, this is not confined merely to formal members but frequently involves non-parties as both the initiators and targets of such claims, suggesting that the respective treaties have transcended their legal status to become more broadly relevant markers of socially acceptable behaviour.

In a narrow sense, the instrumental employment of norms does not provide proof of deep internalization by the accusing party: the action could be entirely cynical and aimed only at causing damage to an opponent and thereby gaining some political benefit. But I have insisted that self-interested actions of this kind provide crucial evidence of the social power of international law and norms because they inherently rely for their potency on a community defined by common expectations. Attempts to undermine an adversary through challenges to their status or prestige are only possible—and certainly only effective—to the extent that they invoke widely shared standards. References to supposed violations of specific treaties, whether sincerely proffered or not, thus cannot help but reinforce the intersubjective legitimacy of the underlying rules and norms and their suitability in adjudicating other actual and potential scenarios. This, I have argued extensively already, has implications for future behaviour, as non-parties can be challenged to further adapt their policies to accord with their conditional support for the institutions. The instrumental invocation of treaties, and the attendant shift to legalized argumentation, has therefore narrowed the scope for state claims and consequently imposed unanticipated constraints on their decision-making.

This returns us to the question of whether the resistance by non-parties and especially the great powers of China, Russia, and the United States has succeeded in inhibiting the development of the mine ban and ICC. This is central to the present analysis, since the original purpose of the majority of states and civil society actors was to create institutions that were insulated from dominance by powerful states. The most general conclusion to be drawn in this regard is that great powers have shaped the institutions, but much less substantially than sceptical observers predicted. Powerful non-parties found that they were unable to achieve their goals through isolation; attempts at modifying the treaties and protecting themselves from their jurisdiction have almost exclusively transpired via sustained engagement with the legal regimes. This finding runs contrary to the expectations of realist IR and legal scholars, who would anticipate a far greater ability for powerful states to ignore or otherwise marginalize legal developments they do not formally endorse (Glennon 2001; Goldsmith and Posner 2005; Mearsheimer 1994). At the same time, however, these states have succeeded in limiting the scope of the treaties in important ways. This is most notable—and most significant for the institution itself—in the case of the ICC, as Chapter 7 made clear.

The United States and Non-Great Power Norms

Finally, this study has paid particular attention to the relationship between the United States and the respective treaties, both because the United States is the remaining global superpower with the greatest prospective influence over international cooperation and governance, and because it has been the most prominent opponent of the MBT and ICC. For these reasons, the United States has also been the subject of voluminous scholarly attention, much of it sceptical that global institutions could survive without active US support. The balance of this work, moreover, has assumed that any reconciliation would involve far greater concessions from the institutions themselves than from the American hegemon. It is therefore worth briefly reflecting on the changes witnessed in US policy that amount to quite substantial accommodation, since these developments might seem surprising to contemporary observers. Two points are worth emphasizing. On the one hand, US recognition that it could (partially) advance its goals by engaging with the treaty regimes was the result of its own embeddedness in an international social system. This fact, in turn, has provided the conditions to empower external actors—both fellow states and, importantly, transnational civil society (TCS) groups associated with the International Campaign to Ban Landmines (ICBL) and Coalition for the International Criminal Court—to deploy social pressure towards greater adaptation. On the other hand, this increased engagement has led to reciprocal socialization, as successive US administrations have become increasingly comfortable with the institutions. Despite the lack of any foreseeable prospect for ratification, the United States has substantially adjusted its policies in accordance with core institutional demands. As with many other aspects described above, this process is more pronounced with respect to the MBT, though the ICC also features modest, but still important, forms of accommodation.

The MBT and ICC have come to be identified as constituent elements of international society such that non-conformance has implications even for non-member states. Non-parties—including powerful treaty opponents such as the United States—have consequently found themselves partially constrained by laws that they do not recognize as binding on themselves. This finding, as with the others presented already, has varied across actors and especially between the two treaty cases at the heart of this study. Understanding why this might be so is the subject of the next section.

EXPLAINING VARIATION IN NON-GREAT POWER NORMS

This book is ultimately about the social power of law to remake international politics. Yet this influence is clearly uneven with respect to both the breadth and depth of change. These observations require some attention to the potential causes of discrepancies in the efficacy of the AP mine ban and ICC, as a window into the broader question of whether multilateralism without the great powers can or should be replicated in other issue areas. This subject has received some initial attention already (Brem 2009; Goose and Williams 2008). I do not seek to resolve this issue here, but instead present three general hypotheses derived from the existing IR literature as a way of suggesting some comparative lessons from the implementation of the two cases, and a path forward.

Hypothesis 1: Issue Area

First, it is widely hypothesized that characteristics of the particular governance challenge shape the prospects for generating strong institutions (Hafner-Burton, Victor, and Lupu 2012, 60–9). Keck and Sikkink (1998, 204), for example, famously suggested that 'issues involving bodily harm to vulnerable individuals, and legal equality of opportunity' are most likely to lead to successful development of new norms and (potentially) legal rules (similarly

Price 2003, 598). These assumptions can also be applied to the implementation of treaties that is the focus of this study.

The AP mine ban and ICC both clearly share this broad motivation, animated as they are by a goal of protecting vulnerable populations by eradicating the humanitarian consequences of AP mine use and punishing grave atrocity crimes. Yet the more particular characteristics of the respective subjects—and their relative complexity—may help account for differences in the extent of observed compliance. One potential, and quite compelling, explanation for the noted challenges in ICC implementation is that the Rome Statute imposes more substantial and wide-ranging obligations that in turn demand extensive changes to national practices. Fully complying with the Court requires that states modify their domestic legislation (including in some instances constitutional provisions), ensure additional bureaucratic capacities to meet Court requests for assistance (including by providing access to intelligence and witnesses, turning over relevant evidence, permitting Court officials to operate on their territory, and arresting and surrendering suspects), and actually act on such requests even in circumstances that concern their own senior officials or those of their allies. Effective policy change also implicates a greater range of domestic institutions and actors—including political and military leaders, officials in justice and foreign ministries, and judges—than would be concerned with the ban on AP mines. This, in turn, increases the number of potential veto players that may seek to limit compliance—though the degree to which this occurs will naturally vary considerably by domestic regime type (Hafner-Burton, Victor, and Lupu 2012, 69–71). The potential for obstructionism is clearly apparent in the most contentious ICC cases, notably the failed proceedings against President Kenyatta of Kenya and President Bashir of Sudan. Yet the ability and willingness of state actors to selectively cooperate with Court investigations is also more widespread, as demonstrated at length already.

This is not to suggest that the mine ban was or is unproblematic. The decision to permanently abandon the use of a previously ubiquitous weapon—and equally to cease research and development, production, and export, and to make the positive actions to destroy stockpiles and clear mine-infested territory—were no small matters, but imposed substantial contemporary and future costs. These commitments moreover necessitate positive changes in military doctrine and training, procurement, and operational planning ranging across both defence and foreign policy. The claim that states have adopted and adhered to the MBT because they no longer 'needed' AP mines only begs the question of how this rather substantial transformation came about, which is itself a vital part of the explanation for why the MBT has proven so effective. This is also true of the ICC. Hence issue complexity is clearly not a satisfactory explanation on its own: indeed, recognition that cooperative problems are not fixed properties but are substantially 'created'—that is, identified, interpreted, promoted, and contested—through intersubjective processes is a core feature of constructivist IR scholarship. Yet it does seem plausible that the MBT, as a prohibition of a discrete weapon, imposes more modest demands that are easier for actors to both comprehend and implement.

Hypothesis 2: Sovereignty Costs

A second and closely related factor concerns the sovereignty costs associated with an institution. We might expect cooperation and compliance to be both harder and more tentative when rules substantially infringe on core interests and prerogatives of the state such as the conduct of war and peace, maintenance of order, and responsibilities (including the administration of justice and protection of livelihoods) for citizens. From this perspective, the greater contestation surrounding the ICC stems from the fact that the Court represents a more fundamental challenge to foundational tenets of statehood than the comparatively more limited intrusion of the AP mine ban. This is most apparent in the Rome Statute's extension of jurisdiction over non-party nationals and attempt to eliminate legal immunities for senior state officials. This explanation is anticipated by the notion of nested or embedded legal and social structures advanced in Chapter 2: since treaties gain much of their legitimacy from their association with prior norms and rules, it is unsurprising that those elements that most sharply diverge from past experience should face the greatest challenge. Though the Rome Statute is not wholly innovative on core matters of international law, questions of international legal jurisdiction over citizens of third (and especially non-party) states and Heads of States remain hotly contested both within the ICC regime and more broadly. The MBT can by contrast be understood as a more straightforward—albeit still controversial—application of prior IHL norms to a particular weapon system. An enforcement mechanism for the punishment of grave international crimes, however, is potentially much broader in its range and impact and could well infringe on state interests in awkward and unpredictable ways.

Hypothesis 3: The Enforcement Scenario

Given these challenges, a further explanation for the divergent successes of the MBT and ICC involves the differing nature of public goods and their provision. Scholarship in economics and political science has long recognized that subjects of international collective action face varying degrees of free-rider problems and incentives towards defection (Sandler 2004; Hafner-Burton,

Victor, and Lupu 2012, 62–9). Yet in an anarchic international system without world government, efforts to address non-conformance—whether unilateral, bilateral, or collective—are inherently decentralized. This in turn shapes whether a specific governance challenge can be addressed through largely voluntary cooperative enforcement among actors, or requires the unique coercive capabilities of great powers (Tams 2007; Thompson 2013). Rationalist approaches would generally expect that cooperation is most tenuous in areas that most directly infringe on core competencies of the state, and it is here that concerted enforcement from leading states is most crucial. Inversely, proponents of the 'managerial' school have suggested that states possess a generic normative commitment to obey the law, and enter into agreements with the belief that compliance will be the dominant pattern. Violations are generally not the product of attempts to flout commitments on the basis of self-interested calculations, but rather stem from a lack of state capacity or information and coordination problems within the regime itself (Chayes and Chayes 1993).

The MBT and Rome Statute do not contain robust verification and enforcement measures, but are instead predicated on mutual monitoring by states and civil society. In the case of the mine ban, this has not proven especially problematic largely because, as defensive weapons, AP mines would seem to be less governed by concerns for reciprocity and deterrence that often shape patterns of use and restraint with offensive systems such as weapons of mass destruction or aerial bombing (Hafner-Burton, Victor, and Lupu 2012, 63; Morrow 2007).[1] The MBT entrenches forms of unofficial monitoring, but has limited enforcement provisions—and these have never been employed. International involvement has instead typically emphasized 'cooperative compliance' focusing on diplomatic initiatives by states and civil society—involving private engagements as well as public persuasion and naming and shaming most often by the ICBL and its affiliates—and material support in the form of financial assistance and technical training (Brinkert 2008; Goose 2008b). The consolidation of a critical mass of states, backed by civil society actors, has been sufficient to establish a potent social stigma against the weapons that has been generally reinforced during moments of apparent crisis in the regime. Consequently, there has been much less need for powerful states—alone or in concert—to deploy coercive threats or force to uphold global observance of rules. This is especially true of the wider humanitarian objectives of the treaty,

[1] The use of AP mines by an adversary could complicate military operations and further endanger soldiers and civilians in the battle space. However, such a development would not substantially shift the balance of capabilities so as to threaten the prospect of a military victory or, more seriously, the survival of the state in the way that the introduction of some other weapons might.

which are addressed through voluntary contributions coordinated by the MBT Implementation Support Unit and affiliated organizations. The United States is the leading donor to international mine action causes (encompassing mine clearance and victim assistance programmes), but a number of other states—most of them MBT States Parties like Germany, Japan, Norway, the Netherlands, and the United Kingdom—also make substantial contributions and are leading providers of technical assistance in areas such as humanitarian demining and stockpile destruction (International Campaign to Ban Landmines 2014g, 45–6). In other words, there is a much-reduced demand for special responsibilities undertaken by great powers since these roles are more broadly shared within the international community.

Much of the administration of the ICC is organized on similar principles; yet core ICC functions concerning the conduct of investigations and the arrest and surrender of suspects are reliant on the resources of states. Great power engagement is thus more critical for two related reasons. On the one hand, there are only a limited number of states that possess the intelligence-gathering, logistical, and operational capabilities to aide in ICC criminal investigations and enforce arrest warrants. Arguably, only the United States enjoys the global military and diplomatic presence suitable to the task; its selective participation in ongoing Court proceedings has naturally substantially influenced the efficacy of these initiatives. On the other hand, great powers are also especially relevant for responses to actual or apparent noncompliance both for their own coercive capacities and their role as permanent members of the UNSC, which may sanction states for failing to cooperate with Court requests. The general unwillingness on the part of China, Russia, and the United States—but also ICC parties like France and the UK—to utilize these dual powers has clearly impacted upon the ICC's enforcement capacity, with serious implications for its effectiveness.

The flipside of this concern with enforcement is the expectation that a great power is more likely to resist, and ultimately succeed in obstructing, legal initiatives in areas that directly impinge on its security, economic, or diplomatic interests. The case studies do confirm this intuition—to a point. Major military powers like China, Egypt, India, Iran, Israel, Pakistan, Russia, and the United States have all opposed the AP mine ban and ICC. Yet their subsequent influence over the development of the institutions is mixed. The three permanent Security Council members that are not parties to these treaties have succeeded in partially shaping their operation, with the most obvious forms of control applied to the ICC. This influence is far from absolute, however, and is arguably much more limited than sceptical observers would have anticipated at the time of the treaties' creation. Just as significantly, great powers and other powerful states have themselves experienced considerable pressure towards conformance, as the previous chapters have documented.

SHARED CONDITIONS OF POSSIBILITY

Finally, it is worth noting those factors that *do not* vary between the two treaty cases. Most obviously, both share broadly similar conditions of emergence. As Chapter 1 detailed, the creation of the MBT and Rome Statute was characterized by close coordination between sympathetic middle power states and transnational civil society groups. The latter were particularly important as epistemic communities of experts in framing the respective problems and proposing technical solutions incorporated in the treaty texts. The negotiations were conducted in ad hoc diplomatic forums with rules that were explicitly designed to provide greater equality among participants, as a means of limiting the influence of resistant powers. This shift away from traditional diplomatic settings dominated by consensus decision-making and power politics arguably created conditions that more closely approximated the idealized shared lifeworld that communicative action theorists suggest is necessary for genuinely rational argumentation (Deitelhoff 2009b; Risse 2000).

These features have proven equally important to subsequent efforts aimed at securing widespread adoption of the core treaty commitments. The role of transnational civil society actors as norm entrepreneurs has been widely noted in the IR literature (e.g. Keck and Sikkink 1998; Price 2003), and the MBT and ICC provide ample evidence for how these actors matter (Bernstein 2008; Schroeder and Tiemessen 2014; Wareham 2008). Treaty proponents have used diplomatic fora as venues for the promotion of compliance and the stigmatization of non-conformance, principally by invoking the legal criteria of the treaties and drawing reference to associated external norms and rules. Here again the strategy of grafting—and thus the nested social structure of international law and politics—provides a crucial resource for implementation. However, evidence of substantial contestation raises the question of whether the previously more-or-less cohesive coalitions among middle power states and civil society have broken down. This could provide a further angle in explaining the divergent experiences between the two treaty cases.

ALTERNATIVE INSTITUTIONAL WORLDS: COUNTERFACTUALS AND THE IMPACT OF THE MBT AND ICC

The strategy of non-great power norm-building via law should be assessed not only through an account of how institutions have fared in the actually existing world, but also an appreciation for what the outcomes could have been had negotiators made different strategic choices in Ottawa and Rome. As Price has observed, 'critics of just war norms importantly underscore that these norms suffer from inadequacies in restraining the character of contemporary large-scale violence—but, one must ask compared to what?' (Price 2008, 208). Two chief alternatives are of greatest interest. On the one hand, negotiators may have chosen to bow to the demands of powerful states, likely resulting in a weaker set of rules. On the other hand, states and their civil society allies could have abandoned the goal of a multilateral treaty, relying instead on informal arrangements or 'mini-lateral' agreements among select states, or forsaking cooperation altogether in the given domain. What, in other words, would have been the extent of norm adoption with a *different* treaty, or the *absence* of a formal treaty altogether?

This assessment, in turn, relies on the use of counterfactual analysis to adjudicate amongst an array of possibilities that cannot be observed directly (Fearon 1991; Sikkink 2008; Grynaviski 2013). This is particularly essential in small-*n* studies with a limited pool of actual cases (Biersteker 1993; Sylvan and Majeski 1998). In establishing these scenarios, however, attention must be paid to selecting theoretically and logically coherent possibilities: the more closely proposed counterfactuals follow the actual flow of events, the greater their analytical leverage. This can be achieved by identifying 'critical branching points' from which alternative historical pathways could plausibly have emerged (Biersteker 1993, 331). In both cases, reference to the negotiating histories reveals a set of issues that, had they been addressed differently, would have satisfied the demands of key non-parties potentially leading to their formal inclusion. In addition, it is possible to contrast the observed impact of the MBT and ICC against actually existing institutions that have been promoted by some states as alternatives to the particular institutions under examination here.

The Ban on Antipersonnel Mines

While the United States participated extensively in the negotiations that led to the MBT, it did not join the final agreement. US opposition centred on two unmet demands: that negotiators include an exemption for US landmines deployed for the defence of South Korea, and that the treaty be re-worded to exclude AP mines used as 'anti-handling' devices attached to anti-vehicle mine systems. President Clinton later claimed that had these red lines been achieved, the United States would have signed and sought to ratify the resulting treaty (Clinton 1997). It is thus conceivable that the modification of the draft MBT to incorporate these demands would have resulted in the inclusion of the United States as a full treaty party.

What can be said about the likely consequences of this development in terms of the stigmatization of AP mines? It is important to recognize in the first place that the proposed US amendments would have resulted in a substantively weaker treaty and international norm by eliminating the unqualified prohibition on the weapons. This is significant since the animating view of the mine ban movement was that the humanitarian consequences of AP mines could only be adequately addressed via a complete ban that gained its legal and moral force from its absoluteness. The ICBL opposed the US proposals on precisely these grounds (Williams and Goose 1998). This proposed trade-off gets to the essence of the breadth-versus-depth dilemma identified in Chapter 1. Yet even if the United States could have been brought into the formal legal community on these terms, its inclusion—especially when weighed against the costs—may not have contributed to the further development of an international norm against the weapons. The United States does not appear to have used AP mines since the advent of the MBT, and has similarly ceased their production and transfer; US policy has thus been heavily influenced by the mine ban norm even as it remains outside the legal agreement. The same is broadly true of many other major military powers, as Chapter 5 documented.

A broader 'demonstration effect' from early American membership above and beyond these informal effects is also questionable. It is not obvious, for example, that China, India, or the Russian Federation would have abandoned their objections had US demands been met. All three (and other resistant states besides) recognize a broader scope for AP mines than that envisioned in the initial US negotiating position, and have resisted subsequent US efforts to redefine 'legitimate' landmines with technological solutions for autonomous deactivation and self-destruction. Hence even a more modest treaty that permitted some types of AP mines would still have excluded many key states that insisted on the right to use all kinds of AP mines. It is equally uncertain that US endorsement of a limited mine ban would have substantially impacted the policies of remaining AP mine-users like Myanmar and Syria, who are among the most impervious to external social pressure. In other words, to the extent that we can observe policy change in those remaining non-parties, the influence appears to stem from the global norm against AP mines itself, rather than US or other great power endorsement of it.

On the other hand, a US exemption during negotiations would surely have led other states to seek additional concessions that, if successful, would have further eroded the treaty text and prohibitionary norm, with predictable consequences in terms of greater mine use and higher casualty rates. In light of this, an arguably more appropriate subject for counterfactual evaluation exists in the form of Amended Protocol II (APII) to the Convention on Certain Conventional Weapons (CCW). APII was negotiated in April and May 1996, and thus is the immediate precursor to the MBT. APII is especially relevant since the negotiations were conducted via consensus decision-making rules that allowed powerful states to limit the scope of the resulting agreement to terms they found acceptable. The key distinction here is that APII regulates—rather than bans altogether—the use, production, stockpiling, and transfer of AP mines.[2] In particular, Article 5(2) of the treaty permits the use of AP mines that contain self-destruct or self-deactivation mechanisms, or in instances where the minefields are fenced and actively patrolled. It was this perceived failure to produce sufficiently restrictive obligations that stimulated the separate Ottawa Process and the full prohibition of AP mines in the MBT. APII can thus be read as the primary institutional alternative to the MBT as it articulates a divergent view of the appropriate legal restraints for addressing the humanitarian effects of AP mines.

The available evidence suggests that APII alone would not generate a more effective stigma against AP mines—since that is not the aim of the treaty—or produce better humanitarian outcomes. Currently 102 states are parties to APII; this contrasts with the 162 MBT parties.[3] Only ten states are members of APII but *not* the MBT.[4] While this list does include the most prominent opponents of the mine ban prohibition, the vast majority of APII members are subject to the more rigorous standards of the MBT. Indeed, APII does not appear to have exerted much influence at all on the use of AP mines. Six of the ten states that are members of APII but not the MBT (Georgia, India, Israel, Pakistan, Russia, and Sri Lanka) have used AP mines in some instances under conditions that would violate Article 5(2) of APII. Moreover, twenty-five non-parties to the MBT—over two-thirds of the remaining non-members—have also failed to join the less ambitious APII, leaving them outside of both sets of legal restraints.[5] This latter list includes a number of regional powers including Egypt, Iran, and Saudi Arabia, as well as recent mine-users Libya, Myanmar, Nepal, and Syria which appear to have deployed mines that would violate the terms of APII. APII also excludes states locked in protracted conflicts such as Armenia, Azerbaijan, the Democratic People's Republic of Korea, and Lebanon that might be most in need of restraints on future behaviour.

By contrast, the substantial decline in annual mine victims (briefly discussed in Chapter 4) can be clearly credited to the advent of the MBT. Indeed, while the past nearly twenty years have seen major improvements in humanitarian outcomes around the world, the largest gains (in terms of reducing casualties and increasing land clearance and assistance to victims) have been

[2] APII also deals with anti-vehicle mines and booby-traps, but discussion here is limited to its implications for AP mines.

[3] As of May 2016.

[4] China, Georgia, India, Israel, Korea, Morocco, Pakistan, the Russian Federation, Sri Lanka, and the United States.

[5] Armenia, Azerbaijan, Bahrain, Cuba, the Democratic People's Republic of Korea, Egypt, Iran, Kazakhstan, Kyrgyzstan, Laos People's Democratic Republic, Lebanon, Libya, Marshall Islands, Micronesia, Mongolia, Myanmar, Nepal, Palestine, Saudi Arabia, Singapore, Syria, Tonga, United Arab Emirates, Uzbekistan, and Vietnam.

achieved in MBT member states (International Campaign to Ban Landmines 2014g, 2–3, 21–43). It is also important to point out that many non-parties—especially military powers like China and the United States—have been informally following the higher standards of the MBT. In sum, it is highly unlikely that APII, in isolation as the sole international instrument regulating AP mines, would have provided a superior—or even comparable—degree of restraint over the weapons or mitigation of the adverse humanitarian outcomes associated with their use. Rather, the widespread and largely successful stigmatization of AP mines is attributable to the MBT, despite the noted costs associated with its creation.

The International Criminal Court

Assessing the alternatives to the ICC is more difficult, as there is no single existing institution that would credibly replace the Court. Nevertheless, it is possible to make some initial judgements regarding the likely outcomes of an alternative arrangement versus current ICC operations. Various critiques of the ICC ultimately concern the independence of the Court from established modes of political power in the international system. It is therefore plausible that a Rome Statute that entrenched Security Council dominance, most centrally concerning an exclusive right to refer situations to the Court (with the possible addition of self-referrals) and defer active investigations, would have significantly increased the chances that one or more of the great powers would have joined (United States of America 2000; Scheffer 1999b; Schabas 2004, 701). What are the most likely implications of this scenario for the influence of the Court and the extension of its norm of internationalized procedural justice?

To begin, the case selection of the Court would clearly have been affected by UNSC dominance. Most notably, the Kenyan, Ivorian, and recent Georgian[6] situations came under ICC jurisdiction via the Prosecutor's independent *proprio motu* authority, and would therefore have been impossible had this jurisdictional filter been removed in the Rome negotiations. The Security Council would of course retained the capacity to refer these cases itself; but in the years preceding the ICC Prosecutor's initiation of proceedings there was little indication of any particular interest in this possibility among the Council's permanent members. The subsequent ambivalence concerning the trials of Mr Kenyatta and Mr Ruto further underlines the unlikelihood of concerted

[6] On 27 January 2016 the ICC Pre-Trial Chamber formally authorized the Chief Prosecutor to open an investigation into alleged crimes committed on Georgian territory during the 2008 war between Georgia and the Russian Federation (ICC Pre-Trial Chamber I 2016).

international action to grant the ICC authority in these instances. Questions of organizational capacity and the specific justification of these cases aside, it seems impractical to assume that the loss of these legal processes would represent a net gain for the cause of international justice.

An emphasis on UNSC referral would likely not have impacted present ICC activities in the other six situation countries, however. While the self-referrals by Uganda, the Democratic Republic of Congo, the Central African Republic, and Mali fall outside of Security Council control, this modality was not explicitly rejected by the United States and others during the Rome negotiations, principally because it was not anticipated to prove especially relevant to early Court activities (Kress 2004, 944). At the same time, the Darfur and Libyan situations would have been unaffected since it was a Security Council referral that activated these investigations. And there is little reason to believe that the permanent Security Council members—three of whom are ICC non-parties—would have used their exclusive authority to refer additional situations to the Court, since there is nothing stopping them from doing so now. Outside of the (significant) examples of Kenya and Côte d'Ivoire and impending developments with respect to Georgia, therefore, the present caseload of the ICC may not have been substantially different under a scenario in which the Court did not possess an independent authority to launch investigations.

There are, of course, other important potential consequences of increased great power participation, principally relating to the scope of the ICC legal community, and practical considerations for cooperation with Court proceedings. It has been suggested that early endorsement by the United States and others would have further increased the legitimacy of the institution, while at the same time improving its capacity to collect evidence and arrest suspects. US support in particular could have generated additional ratifications and accessions through its example. Previous research in IR has suggested that leading powers can have an important influence on the adoption of international norms by smaller states, many of whom have already joined the MBT independently but remain outside the ICC (Ikenberry and Kupchan 1990; Fordham and Asal 2007). Formal US membership would also have removed the substantial challenge presented by Article 98 agreements and parallel domestic law withdrawing funds from states that did not sign these bilateral non-surrender agreements. This would have had the significant effect in not bringing over a hundred states into overt conflict with the Court.

Yet this demonstration effect must be set against the fact that a large number of states—especially members of the Like-Minded Group—and most civil society actors strongly opposed any effort to limit referral authority to the Security Council. Nicole Deitelhoff has demonstrated that the 1998 Rome negotiations generated a profound shift in state attitudes in which the overwhelming majority of states (some 80 per cent of those speaking) came to strongly support the Like-Minded Group's demands for an independent Court including *proprio motu* capacity and limits on UNSC powers to defer ongoing investigations or trials (Deitelhoff 2009b, 50–1; Schabas 2004, 714–17). This finding is reinforced by subsequent discourse, as demonstrated in Chapters 6 and 7. Acceding to great-power demands during negotiations would have at minimum substantially undercut the enthusiasm for the new institution among its most dedicated proponents, and could plausibly have unravelled the existing support for a Court at the Rome negotiations, leading to a weaker treaty or no treaty at all.

This is additionally significant since it is by no means certain that the concession on UNSC control would have translated into rapid ratifications by the likes of China, Russia, and the United States. Schabas (2004) is persuasive in arguing that the issue of Security Council authority—and the Court's place in the prevailing international order—was and remains the central US objection to the ICC. However, I am not convinced that any amount of acquiescence to US demands would have led to American ratification by this point, principally due to the long time frames frequently required in receiving the 'advice and consent' of the Senate. It is notable, for example, that it took forty years for the United States to ratify the Genocide Convention; the United States also has yet to accede to the International Convention on the Suppression and Punishment of the Crime of Apartheid, nearly thirty years after its creation. Hence even legal efforts that have broad public and political support can fall short of formal US adoption. This is especially relevant since in the wake of the 2000 presidential election that brought George W. Bush to power, the United States entered a period of profound hostility towards a number of multilateral institutions. Members of the new administration, led most publicly by Under Secretary of State John Bolton, asserted a host of additional objections to the ICC involving judicial practice and constitutional law that had not occupied US diplomats during the 1994–8 negotiations (Bolton 2002). Under these circumstances, it seems unlikely that President Bush would have actively sought ratification of an international instrument that was portrayed by many conservative Republicans as infringing on traditional notions of sovereignty for reasons that went beyond Security Council control. The much more multilaterally inclined Obama administration has faced similar constraints in securing Senate support for a variety of major domestic and foreign policy initiatives, as experiences over the past eight years have repeatedly demonstrated.

On the other hand, a Court that was more broadly deferential to US interests, even if still unacceptable when applied to American nationals, could conceivably have faced a more muted response from the Bush administration. This would most plausibly have entailed a strategy in which the United States did not actively seek to undermine the Court via Article 98 agreements and the withdrawal of foreign aid, and expanded US assistance to the Court much earlier on by providing access to satellite imagery and other intelligence as evidence in ICC investigations or through the training and capacity-building of local security forces to enable more timely arrest and surrender of suspects (as was later approved by President Obama with respect to Uganda). However, nothing in the diplomatic record suggests that a less hostile United States would have actively contributed to the arrest of fugitives like Omar al-Bashir. The same goes for other prominent non-parties, all of whom possess much more limited capacities for overseas operations than the United States. I also see little support for the idea that a UNSC-dominated ICC would have contributed more strongly to the larger goal of preventing atrocities. Such a court would have a narrower jurisdictional scope, and would therefore be able to threaten judicial punishment under a more limited set of scenarios. Given the historical intransigence of Security Council politics, many combatants might then quite reasonably assume that their crimes would escape the reach of the ICC.

Finally, it is worth briefly considering whether the absence of an ICC altogether—certainly a possible outcome in the face of great-power demands during the Rome negotiations—would have led to a more potent international response to grave crimes and a stronger norm of individual criminal accountability. Would an international criminal regime constituted solely by ad hoc tribunals and domestic trials have fared better in promoting international justice? In short, I can see no reason to believe so. This is principally because it was the perceived limitations of the alternatives that spurred the creation of the ICC in the first place. Ad hoc tribunals are costly to establish and maintain and are circumscribed in their scope in both geographic and temporal terms. Given these constraints, there is hardly any guarantee they would be established in all relevant cases. Temporary institutions are also cumbersome by their nature, since they must be created in response to outbreaks of widespread and systematic violence; building sufficient political will in the international community takes time, as historical examples demonstrate. Ad hoc tribunals are necessarily focused on particular conflicts, and thus have little bearing on prospective crimes in other places, unless combatants assume another tribunal will be established for their own situation. And while the rise in criminal trials in the 'justice cascade' (Sikkink 2011) were a precipitating factor in the creation of the ICC, domestic and international prosecutions of genocide, crimes against humanity, and war crimes have clearly not met the scale of these acts. A great hope for the ICC is that it would encourage greater accountability both through its own legal processes and by stimulating necessary improvements in national responses to grave crimes. This process is substantially incomplete, as I have already shown, but a network of impermanent tribunals is unlikely to have stimulated better incorporation of criminal and human rights norms than the existing ICC.

Reservations and Treaty Influence

A final counterfactual concerns an alternative means of accommodating great-power demands during negotiations: simply permitting states to lodge reservations or declarations that exempt themselves from particular aspects of the treaty they find unacceptable. This returns us to the question of diplomatic strategy at the core of my interest in the MBT and Rome Statute. Among the innovations that have defined the 'new diplomacy' is the decision to prohibit all reservations to the treaties—a reversal of the common practice for most multilateral legal instruments (Maslen 2005, 314–18; Schabas 2010, 1166–73).[7] 'It is often argued that a degree of tolerance of reservations encourages ratifications, by providing States with a mechanism by which small difficulties with a treaty text can be made inapplicable to them' (Schabas 2010, 1166). Yet recent experience has suggested that reservations are often employed as a means of avoiding the most consequential aspects of a legal agreement, thus undermining the very benefits presumed to accrue from more states endorsing treaty norms as legal obligations.

Paradoxically, while international politics has become increasingly legalized, the removal of reservations as a tool for accommodating state concerns has shifted such discussions largely out of the realm of legal interpretation and back into that of politics. In other words, the strategic approach favoured in MBT and ICC cases has had the effect of *de-legalizing* particular commitments over which states might genuinely object, making treaty membership an all-or-nothing enterprise that does not allow for variation in the scope of obligation.[8] The dilemma of this approach is that in seeking a treaty in which all members share the same full complement of legal commitments, the agreement may well exclude some potentially highly consequential states that would otherwise join were they allowed to moderate the scope of their obligations. For the sake of argument, I assume two things for this counterfactual. First, the decision to permit reservations would have led to an increased number of ambivalent states joining the respective agreements, especially (and most importantly for our purposes) among the hostile great powers. This is plausible since the United States in particular pushed for the inclusion of reservations in order to facilitate its own participation (Maslen 2005, 315; Schabas 2010, 1166). Second, in doing so, these states would have exempted themselves from significant aspects of the treaty, largely following the same core objections discussed already.

[7] This distinction is not absolute, as both the MBT and Rome Statute permit states to lodge declarations that in some circumstances could amount to de facto reservations. The scope for such exemptions, however, is far more circumscribed than in other analogous treaties.

[8] I thank Richard Price for suggesting this framing.

The key question is how much more rule-following could be expected if current non-parties were full members of the respective treaties under such conditions, and whether this would be likely to lead to better outcomes in terms of basic treaty goals. Without rehashing the discussion of other scenarios above, I see many parallels with previous counterfactuals that suggest that the impact of reservations would have been limited. First, states making use of reservations are no more likely—at least initially—to comply with the full spectrum of treaty obligations, since the express purpose of reservations is to avoid commitments that a given state finds objectionable. It is certainly possible that once established as members of the treaty community, additional socialization pressures would lead these states to observe the full range of treaty rules, either by withdrawing or ignoring their reservations. But this is at best a plausible long-term outcome that would depend heavily on the contingencies of particular experience. Second, states that met a lesser standard defined by their reservations might not ultimately have behaved much differently, if one assumes (as I do) that the reservations would largely mirror the objections raised during treaty negotiations. Thus the difference between compliance under the current situation and that of a treaty with broad discretion for exceptions is likely to be marginal.

As with other hypothetical concessions discussed above, the prospective gains from including reservations must be set against the potential damage to the spirit and efficacy of the legal agreement both during negotiations and since. Proposals to include reservations were strongly resisted by the core groups of state supporters at both Ottawa and Rome (Maslen 2005, 315; Schabas 2010, 1167). Thus the allowance for reservations might have threatened the cohesion and momentum of the 'pro-treaty' groupings in much the same way that specific concessions to US demands were hypothesized to. Again, the net effect would have been basically the same as simply conceding to great power demands to alter the treaty text at the outset. For some actors, reservations may have been preferable to a weaker treaty, since they would allow states to selectively recognize constituent rules, rather than excluding these features entirely. But once the practice was rendered permissible, many additional states might have taken advantage of the opportunity to carve out exceptions for themselves as well. One of the great strengths of the Ottawa and Rome processes is the comprehensive way in which the final negotiations were handled. Breaching the commitment to the adage of 'no exceptions, no reservations, no loopholes'[9] would have undermined the legitimacy of the treaties in the eyes of their most ardent supporters, and could therefore have substantially weakened their socializing power.

[9] This phrase was coined by Mines Action Canada.

The preceding sections, when considered in light of the theoretical claims and empirical evidence presented in the previous chapters, do provide important reasons to regard the MBT and ICC as at least as efficacious as their most likely alternatives. This is an important contention, since many observers have argued that modesty may be the better virtue in seeking long-term and sustainable international change. Brunnée and Toope (2010, 76) have therefore suggested that when social expectations widely diverge on a given governance issue, 'It may be preferable to settle for a less ambitious project, and to patiently build up the legality elements that may enable a community of practice gradually to expand its stock of shared understandings.' This caution was echoed in sceptical responses to the mine ban and ICC movements cited elsewhere. In my view, however—and in these cases at least—the benefits of absolutism outweigh the presumed advantages of having additional but only partially committed states inside the formal treaty community.

CONCLUSION

The decision to proceed without the great powers has not, on balance, been detrimental to the causes of eliminating AP mines or providing criminal accountability for grave violations of international atrocity law. Both the MBT and Rome Statute have generated substantial change in state behaviour across the international system, though with differences noted above and in previous chapters. Most fundamentally, the treaties have served as touchstones for a re-conception of state identities as appropriate means of restraining violence and ordering international affairs. While these new norms are as yet incompletely and unevenly adopted, they have nonetheless served to dramatically re-shape the articulation and subsequent pursuit of state interests in their image. Sceptics of these non-great power initiatives must therefore explain how their prospective or retrospective concerns square with empirical reality in a highly imperfect world. What reasonable alternatives would have produced better outcomes, and why? Yet this discussion has also revealed important variation in institutional efficacy that should provide impetus for considering the wisdom of treaty-making without the great powers more generally. This subject is addressed in the next, and final, chapter, Chapter 9.

9

Conclusion

Towards a Research Agenda on Non-Great Power Institutions

This final chapter returns to the original motivation for this study: understanding whether, and when, multilateral legal instruments can serve as an effective means of generating changes in the international system under conditions of great power ambivalence or hostility. This involves, most fundamentally, a consideration of the main strategic options facing actors in a prospective negotiating scenario in light of the prevailing opportunities and constraints. International Relations (IR) scholars and diplomatic practitioners have, for at least two decades now, recognized that many areas of prospective global cooperation contain an inherent trade-off between the demands of a majority of (comparatively weaker) states and civil society actors for rigorous international commitments, and the requirements of a powerful few who condition their participation on the inclusion of special exemptions and generally more limited rules. Understanding when to privilege one over the other in the pursuit of strong norms and effective governance is thus at the heart of contemporary multilateralism, rife as it is with complex global challenges that leading states often seem little inclined to address.

Despite a wealth of excellent scholarship tracing these various diplomatic processes, we still have relatively little systematic understanding of whether the strategic calculation to proceed without the great powers has paid off. This study constitutes a modest contribution to rectifying this gap. The assessment of two cases—albeit important ones—is however necessarily limited in its explanatory scope. Here I broaden my consideration further still, to begin a conversation about the future of multilateralism without the great powers. The main aim is to bring to bear the factors that explain variance in the implementation of the Mine Ban Treaty (MBT) and the International Criminal Court (ICC) (Chapter 8) to develop some tentative ideas concerning when differing diplomatic choices may lead to successful or unsuccessful norm development in *other* issue areas. The chapter, and book, concludes by briefly outlining an agenda for future research on non-great power governance.

NON-GREAT POWER TREATIES IN WIDER CONTEXT

A comprehensive assessment of non-great power multilateralism should seek to gain an appreciation for the full range of cases, by situating the Mine Ban Treaty and Rome Statute within the experiences of other actually existing institutions *and* the alternative choices of concessions or the abandonment of binding commitments (Brem and Stiles 2009; Fehl 2012). This requires first a comparative examination of the relative efficacy of other recent non-great power treaties, most notably the Kyoto Protocol and Convention on Cluster Munitions (CCM).

The 1997 Kyoto Protocol to the United Nations Framework Convention on Climate Change (KP) is a less clear-cut example of this phenomenon, as the initial negotiations were conducted via consensus decision-making and with the participation of key states like China, India, Russia, and the United States. However, the follow-up implementation measure agreed at Bonn in 2001 did follow the broad model of the mine ban and ICC negotiations, with middle power (especially European) states pushing ahead with a binding agreement even once it was clear that the United States and other major emitters would not accept the outcome. This shift was characteristic of the strategic calculation animating other non-great power processes:

> While accommodating the US in the original [1997] negotiations came at a high environmental cost, it would have been more detrimental to lose the largest emitter of greenhouse gases. After the US withdrawal [in 2001], however, non-hegemonic cooperation was more beneficial than the alternative of abandoning the protocol, particularly because European negotiators hoped for an eventual US return to the Kyoto framework. (Fehl 2012, 112)

This approach was regarded as possible—though by no means ideal—because the European bloc was thought to be of sufficient size and cohesiveness to sustain necessary economic and industrial changes during the initial shift towards a low-carbon economy in the absence of key states. As we will see later, this has not been the case in other instances, such as the recent Arms Trade Treaty (ATT).

The KP entered into force in 2005 but is widely regarded as a failure. Despite positive steps by EU states in particular, there has been limited progress in the enactment of voluntary and mandatory commitments by states and some substantial reversals, such as the withdrawal of Canada in December

2012 (Secretariat of the UNFCCC 2013; *The Guardian* 2011). Moreover, informal adaptation among prominent non-party states is much more modest than with the MBT and ICC, where such actions have clearly contributed to those treaties' comparative efficacy. Indeed, large emitters like China, India, and, until very recently, the United States appear to have been far more successful in ignoring the institution and limiting its development. Most critically of all, global greenhouse emissions continue to grow, albeit at a slower rate than previously, due to the absence of buy-in from these and other key states.[1]

Each of the hypothesized factors from Chapter 8 can help to explain the substantive weakness of the Kyoto regime. First, addressing the causes of global climate change might fairly be regarded as 'the most difficult collective action problem in the world' (Busby 2009, 87) since high-carbon energy sources are central to the modern world economy, with no ready substitutes.[2] For this reason, committing to major reductions in greenhouse gas emissions implies substantial burdens for industry and governments that are both technically challenging and extremely costly. Such obligations also implicate national sovereignty concerns insofar as protection of industries and promotion of economic growth are widely regarded as core duties of the state. To these political constraints are added ideological opposition that interacts with material concerns in prominent opponents like the United States (Brunnée 2004) and Canada under the recent Harper government. An additional aspect that did not feature in the MBT and ICC cases, therefore, is the role of major industry as impediments to strong international cooperation. The most obvious caveat to this is Europe, where the depth of integration renders it a relatively coherent economic bloc with considerable market power. Internal measures such as emission trading schemes may be sustainable under such circumstances, but are unlikely to influence third state (and especially major emitter) policies, at least in the near term (Fehl 2012, 128–31).

The third proposed hypothesis—the enforcement scenario—is also crucially important here in two respects. On the one hand, any successful effort to regulate carbon-intensive industries would have to substantially capture the relevant actors (Carin and Mehlenbacher 2010). Yet under the current arrangement all of the largest emitting nations (with the exception of the EU considered as a bloc) are excluded from binding reduction targets. On the other hand, the KP seeks to substantially reduce greenhouse gas emissions in a

[1] According to some recent figures from the Netherlands Environmental Assessment Agency, 'in 2012 and 2013, emissions increased by 2%, about 50% slower than in the ten years before, when the annual increase was 3.8% on average', http://infographics.pbl.nl/website/globalco2-2014/.

[2] By contrast, chlorofluorocarbonin presented a considerably easier target for regulation since other compounds were available to replace its use, and the vast majority of production was centred in one company, Dupont (Busby 2009, 88).

context in which concerns for cheating and free-riding abound, and present substantial threats to market competitiveness. Research in IR has long held that cooperation under such conditions is only viable when it is backed by monitoring and sanctioning capacities (Hafner-Burton, Victor, and Lupu 2012, 63–4). Yet the KP and its follow-on instruments enshrine weak enforcement provisions, meaning that any attempts to facilitate compliance will be undertaken outside of formal regime procedures. This, in turn, necessitates the inclusion of the great powers of China, Russia, the United States, and—in this issue area at least—India for the demonstration effect of their commitment and coercive economic potential. Their importance as both participants and prospective enforcers has given these states tremendous leverage in global climate diplomacy, while their substantive absence has gravely weakened the prospects for multilateral governance.

The 2008 CCM[3] presents a further archetypal example of non-great power multilateralism, as its emergence closely followed the pattern of the Ottawa Process a decade earlier (Borrie 2009; Goose 2008a). Indeed, the Oslo Process that led to a ban on cluster munitions (CM) consciously borrowed not only intellectual precedents from the mine ban movement in seeking a global prohibition on a class of weapons based on their humanitarian impact, but equally its diplomatic structure and human capital in the form of diplomats in pro-ban states and civil society advocates (Nystuen and Casey-Maslen 2010). In this respect the CCM offers another example of the power of grafting and the nested structure of international law. By the same token, the CCM also provides evidence for how these linkages can work against the creation of rigorous rules. Prominent participants in the cluster munitions negotiations, informed by their experiences in the Ottawa Process, appear to have been more careful to guard against the development of inconvenient or excessively restrictive rules. This is seen, most notably, in the Convention's definition of 'cluster munitions'—which excludes from the ban particular types of munitions not judged to pose unacceptable harm to civilian populations—and the inclusion of a more expansive allowance for joint operations with non-CCM states, including involving the actual or potential use of the weapons (Diplomatic Conference for the Adoption of a Convention on Cluster Munitions 2008, Art. 2.2 and 21). The ability to conduct joint operations with allies outside the CCM was a primary concern for NATO allies like Canada, France, Germany, Italy, and the UK, who indicated that such an allowance was a 'line in the sand' with respect to their own support for the treaty. Without a guarantee that joint operations would not expose States Parties to charges of violating the treaty, many middle powers involved in the negotiations—and arguably critical to the Convention's future success—would have failed to join.

[3] http://www.clusterconvention.org/the-convention/convention-text/.

As a much more recent development, the extent of norm adoption in the CM case is harder to assess, especially when compared against the MBT which has enjoyed an additional decade in existence. However, a few broad trends are apparent. Like the MBT and ICC, the CCM experienced a rapid negotiation and transition to legal status: the final treaty text was adopted in May 2008 and opened for signature in December of the same year, and entered into force on 1 August 2010. Currently there are 100 States Parties and a further nineteen signatories[4] though as with the mine ban, these figures exclude major military powers China, Egypt, India, Israel, Pakistan, Russia, South Korea, and the United States. Unlike antipersonnel (AP) mines, however, CM have featured in comparatively fewer conflicts, and with considerably less volume; the ban was therefore motivated more by the prospective harm to be caused by future use, rather than an existing humanitarian crisis as with the MBT (United Nations Institute for Disarmament Research 2008). There have been no confirmed violations by CCM States Parties since the adoption of the treaty, though CM have been used in seven non-party states since 2010 (Cluster Munition Coalition 2015, 1).[5] According to a US government report, the United States has not employed CM since 2003, despite some conflicting allegations; US-made and supplied CM have been used by forces in the Saudi-led military intervention in Yemen, however (Cluster Munition Coalition 2014d; Cluster Munition Coalition 2015, 16–17). The CCM has also faced criticism from civil society advocates who have questioned the commitment of states to rigorously uphold the ban in practice. For example, there are already concerns relating to the interpretation and implementation of treaty obligations among prominent middle powers like Australia and Canada (Cluster Munition Coalition 2014b; Cluster Munition Coalition 2014c).

The hypothesized factors from Chapter 8 again provide useful traction in explaining current trends and anticipating future challenges for the CM ban. Achieving an effective global ban on CM may be more challenging than in the case of AP mines for two key reasons. First, many states continue to regard CM as highly useful weapons, which increase the sovereignty costs in joining the treaty. This is underscored by the fact that both current and prospective members have recognized the weapons' value in conventional military operations—against massed infantry and military vehicles and, more controversially, as 'area denial' weapons—and where alternative technologies have yet to demonstrate they can adequately replace these functions. These constraints are true of the mine ban as well, of course, and a key thrust of this study has been to suggest that ostensibly materially derived conceptions of

[4] As of May 2016.

[5] Interestingly, 'due to the relative sophistication of cluster munitions and their delivery systems, very few non-state armed groups (NSAGs) have used these weapons and none have done so since 2006' (Cluster Munition Coalition 2014a, 15).

interest are themselves deeply informed by evolving social standards. So these issues are by no means immutable barriers to legal and normative development. However, it is conceivable that more concerted resistance from the United States and others could substantially impede the development of a global norm against the weapons.

As a weapon with more obviously offensive characteristics, moreover, CM might engender greater concerns for reciprocity. In other words, the retention and use of CM by an adversary could arguably more directly impact the conduct of an operation and hence the prospects for military victory or defeat. Under these circumstances we might expect greater emphasis on traditional disarmament provisions for monitoring and verification. Yet the CCM, like the MBT, contains no formal enforcement mechanisms. Having the United States and other military powers inside the treaty regime would therefore be useful both for their demonstration effect and in providing potential sources of coercive power to bolster compliance. This prospect, however, seems extremely unlikely in the foreseeable future. Time will tell whether this institutional choice will slow the pace of ratifications and accessions among sceptical states.

The KP and CCM are the two most prominent recent examples of non-great power treaty-making but as Chapter 1 suggested, there are at least a dozen or so other instances that meet the basic conditions described here.[6] Future research should therefore evaluate the MBT, ICC, KP, and CCM directly against these treaties to uncover broader patterns of institutional efficacy across time and space. Have certain issue areas—for example restraints pertaining to weapons and the laws of war, human rights, or environmental protection—proven more or less susceptible to effective legal institutions? Relatedly, it would be important to explore whether the strategies of great powers vary noticeably by issue area: are certain subjects likely to face more active resistance while in other areas informal accommodation is more common, and why might this be?

ALTERNATIVE CHOICES: MULTILATERALISM (OR NOT) WITH THE GREAT POWERS

A fully formed account of the prospects for non-great power multilateralism would also have to compare existing institutions against negative cases drawn from two alternative governance scenarios where the international community (a) includes concessions to great powers in order to secure their inclusion in a formal treaty; or (b) abandons binding agreements in the face of opposition and

[6] See Table 1.1, this volume.

pursues informal arrangements or none at all. Over a decade ago, Richard Price (2003, 584–5) noted that 'there has long been an implicit debate about the value of producing treaties of international law that initially are very weak... but we do not really know how often and to what extent such tactics work, particularly in other areas.' The global initiative to regulate small arms and light weapons (SALW) is a notable example of this phenomenon. The effort—enshrined first in the 2001 UN Programme of Action (PoA) and recently in the 2013 Arms Trade Treaty—emerges from the same human security agenda as the MBT, ICC, and CCM, among others (Krause 2002; Wisotzki 2009; Erickson 2015). Indeed, 'the UN identified in the early 1990s the uncontrolled dispersal of small arms and light weapons as a major challenge for achieving peace and security in zones of conflict' (Wisotzki 2009, 26).

Despite the acknowledged scale of the problem, the SALW issue is also a key instance where the international community determined that the necessity of including key powers exceeded the desire for strong rules. Consequently, both agreements instantiate principles of best practice and norms aimed at eradicating the illicit trade in arms, but with only modest legally binding restraints (United Nations General Assembly 2013a; Geneva Academy of International Humanitarian Law and Human Rights 2013). Most importantly, the ATT prohibits states from transferring conventional weapons in violation of UN arms embargoes or in situations where they have reasonable grounds to believe that the weapons would be used in the commission of genocide, crimes against humanity, and war crimes. Yet the standards are intentionally vague and beyond mandatory annual reporting there is little scope for external monitoring or enforcement. This can be explained by the fact that the final ATT was negotiated in traditional UN fora and by consensus, which, by giving powerful states an effective veto over the outcome, decisively limited the extent of what could be achieved. The ATT entered into force a little over a year and half after its negotiation, representing a similarly rapid process to that of the MBT, ICC, and CCM. There are currently eighty-five States Parties, including five out of the top ten arms-exporting nations (France, Germany, Italy, Spain, and the United Kingdom), and a further forty-eight signatories (including Israel, Republic of Korea, and the United States).[7]

While it is too soon to render any clear verdicts on the efficacy of this agreement—either in terms of its influence over the flow of SALW or its role in advancing global norms relating to the arms trade—the hypothesized factors do help explain the strategic decision to grant concessions to major arms-exporting states to secure their endorsement.[8] To begin,

[7] As of May 2016.

[8] The United States voted in favour of UNGA draft resolution A/67/L.58 of 2 April 2013 (Resolution 67/234 B) that adopted the ATT, but China and the Russian Federation abstained.

a comprehensive regime for regulating the global trade in such politically sensitive commodities would be extremely challenging under any circumstances, not least due to the complexity involved in monitoring the great range of weapons under consideration in an industrial sector where states and companies have traditionally demonstrated little interest in transparency. For this reason, the SALW issue directly implicates core matters of national sovereignty in ways that are arguably more pronounced than in other, broadly analogous, areas such as the AP mine ban. Jennifer Erickson (2015) has demonstrated how leading arms exporting democracies have proven willing to accept some restrictions on their security and economic policies with respect to arms exports, including by adopting potentially invasive reporting requirements. However, even here there were important limits to what would be contemplated. Most fundamentally, the United States, along with some allies such as Canada, opposed more rigorous constraints due to concerns that international efforts may impede civilian ownership of guns and the legitimate trade in conventional arms as a matter of national interest (Geneva Academy of International Humanitarian Law and Human Rights 2013, 12; Wisotzki 2009, 29–31).

The advocacy agenda has been further curtailed by the fact that, unlike the Ottawa, Rome, and Oslo processes, negotiations over the PoA and ATT could not rely on a similarly coherent alliance between middle power states and civil society dedicated to achieving stringent rules. On the one hand, there was no core constituency of implicated states that were willing to lead this cause in the absence of great powers like the United States. While key arms exporters like France, Germany, Italy, and the United Kingdom supported the ATT process (and in this respect resemble the leadership in the mine ban movement provided by former AP mine-producer states), these states were only willing to accept some comparatively limited constraints. In this respect there never emerged a serious political and economic counterweight to sceptical great powers, as did transpire in the various treaties discussed above. The prospect of more invasive rules has been further undercut by the considerably more decentralized structure of the primary civil society organization advocating in favour of a global regime on the arms trade (IANSA), and the existence of powerful non-governmental opponents of any international regulations (most prominently in the form of the National Rifle Association in the United States).

The decision to limit the scope of legal rules to what key arms-exporting nations would accept can be explained, in the final analysis, by the particular

154 states voted for the resolution, with three votes against and twenty-three abstentions. http://www.un.org/en/ga/search/view_doc.asp?symbol=A/67/PV.71.

cooperation scenario. Simply put, the global trade in conventional arms is so pervasive that any plausible scheme for addressing it, even a relatively modest arrangement, had to encompass these key actors. On the one hand, the majority of the arms trade is concentrated among a small group of advanced industrial states, and so capturing a sufficiently large portion of the global market could only be achieved through the formal participation of states like France, the United Kingdom, and the United States. Since major European arms exporters were also opposed to more stringent restrictions, accommodating US demands did not substantially weaken the agreement as compared with what would have been achieved in its absence (Fehl 2012, 140). In this way the ATT differs markedly from the core cases of this study. On the other hand, the cooperation dynamics will likely correspond to those of other economic products (such as fossil fuels), wherein cheating and free-riding can produce market advantages and disadvantages. This is of course above and beyond any security threats that may emerge from other states illicitly transferring weapons to governments or non-state actors. For these reasons, the ATT would again seem to require the enforcement capacity of leading powers, both for their normative demonstration effects, and for their material coercive power. Hence as Fehl (2012, 158–9) observes, the primary NGO proponents of SALW regulation never argued for a legal regime that excluded key arms-exporting nations.

The ATT is yet the most recent example of the international community undertaking specific efforts to accommodate the United States in multilateral negotiations by weakening proposed rules. Other instances include, but are not limited to, concessions incorporated into the 2002 Optional Protocols to the Convention on the Rights of the Child (Heckel 2009, 57) and the renegotiation of Part XI of the United Nations Convention on the Law of the Sea—a treaty to which the United States is notably not a member (Klein 2003, 266). This approach has largely been premised on an assumption that initially weak norms can provide a framework for generating stronger commitments in the future—a strategy that has been frequently employed in the environmental sphere (Miles, Andresen, Carlin, Skjaerseth, and Underdal 2002, xiii). Gaining a wider appreciation for whether these efforts have aided in the gradual expansion of international norms—and with them, meaningful behavioural change that addressed global governance challenges—would further advance our appreciation of the merits of non-great power multilateralism. As Price has fairly noted, 'to be validated, however,' findings regarding this strategy 'would have to be balanced by case studies of initially weak efforts to establish new norms that were stillborn, languished, and/or faded away' (Price 2003, 585).

Engaging non-cases offers a third dimension for evaluating multilateralism in times of great power ambivalence. There are a variety of examples where the international community has abandoned efforts at concluding new binding legal rules in the face of concerted resistance from the United States and other powerful states. Such a list would include the failed conclusion of a verification regime for the Biological and Toxin Weapons Convention (BTWC) and the regulation of private military and security companies (Fehl 2012, 163–88; Percy 2012), but could also encompass other cases from the fields of arms control and disarmament, human rights, and trade, to name but a few. Radoslav Dimitrov and his colleagues have pointed out that instances of 'non-regimes'—that is, policy areas with little or no institutional development and policy coordination—are especially puzzling in areas where external conditions raise the need for cooperation and states stand to mutually benefit from their interactions (Dimitrov et al. 2007).

Yet the cases mentioned here seem to adhere to the hypothesized factors already discussed at length above. In the case of the BTWC, the Bush administration determined in 2001 that the proposed verification protocol did not meet the national security interests of the United States because it was at once too invasive (threatening US defence research and private intellectual property) and too weak in its oversight capacities. In turn, the absence of the United States was judged to be sufficiently costly as to render any institution unworkable from the outset. It was widely understood that US participation in the verification of the BTWC was absolutely essential, first because of the political value for other states (such as China and Russia); second due to the need to include the US superpower within any prospective restraints; and third because the United States was one of the few states with the military, diplomatic, and scientific capacities to effectively monitor and enforce compliance with an agreement.

While failed negotiations are relatively easy to identify, prospective diplomatic processes that failed to get off the ground to any significant extent introduce a much more amorphous and potentially unbounded set of possibilities, making the attempt to arrive at some overall assessment of the ratio of success among the universe of possible cases necessarily elusive. These considerations call for further comparative case analysis, drawn from all three potential diplomatic strategies and modelled on the approach adopted in this study. Incorporating instances where the United States and others powers did successfully limit the scope of new institutions will provide greater analytic leverage in evaluating the prospects and costs of governance in their absence—the more particular focus of this study. Yet as I have also suggested, any such assessments must be further refined through a consideration of the most likely outcomes had negotiators made a different strategic choice in a given governance scenario. Is some form of binding multilateral agreement (with or without great powers) always preferable, or might in some circumstances it ultimately prove better to pursue more modest goals (such as non-binding statements of principle) or do nothing at all? Systematic research can suggest whether certain issue areas are more or less susceptible to the type of multilateralism discussed here, and when alternative legal and non-legal approaches may be more appropriate.

FUTURE GOVERNANCE WITHOUT THE GREAT POWERS: CONSIDERING ACTORS AND AGENCY

The nature of a governance challenge clearly matters to the prospects for legal and normative development. At the same time, however, another central contention of this study is that issues are not innately susceptible or hostile to regulation, but are rather shaped by wider social processes of creating meaning in the international system. Indeed, the core of my theory holds that the embedded structure of the international environment provides empowering resources by which a range of actors can use international law to promote new norms. This is the essence of the social power of international law.

The Future Prospects of Coalitional Politics

Thinking of particular institutions as part of a nested international legal and social system offers important additional leverage in explaining the divergent outcomes noted above. Actors promoting new legal institutions are not creating the world anew, but are rather tapping into a highly resonant shared legal heritage within an international community that already privileges law as a particularly legitimate mode of claim-making. Framing is therefore crucial: emergent subjects that can be persuasively connected to existing norms are much more likely to become widely respected international standards since they can be presented as important yet not entirely novel developments. Inversely, institutions that sharply diverge from past experience should be expected to face the greatest challenge at both the negotiation and implementation phases. Humanitarian concerns were at heart of the creation of the MBT and ICC, and have featured extensively in their implementation, as this study has demonstrated. Similar logics propelled the development of the CCM and—in a broader sense of harm to the natural environment and human populations made vulnerable by climate change—the KP. By the same token, however, the greater degree of normative change may help to explain the subsequent implementation challenges facing especially the ICC and KP. While such discourses appear critical, therefore, they are not sufficient in isolation: the non-adoption of a comprehensive treaty banning child soldiers, for example, would also seem to fit the criteria of humanitarian impact that has pervaded successful cases.

These linkages are not automatic, therefore, but must be cultivated, which brings into focus the crucial role of norm entrepreneurs as well as the recipients of these efforts. A key lesson from the core case studies and alternatives is the need for a cohesive coalition of middle power states and transnational civil society to offset the loss of material and normative resources from great powers. The strategic choices that made non-great power treaties possible in the first place must therefore be maintained in the subsequent implementation phase (Goose, Wareham, and Williams 2008, 4–8; Goose and Williams 2008, 183–8). The above discussion has suggested that such coalitions may be more feasible for certain governance challenges, but further research also needs to explore the particular dynamics through which state and non-state actors engage with new international social standards.

Great Powers and International Institutions

As the pre-eminent global power, the US role in creating or impeding international governance has been extensively studied. However, for all this concern, much less has been said about the impact of new international norms on US policy, or the potential that US resistance has for the health of legal agreements. One important contribution of the present study, therefore, is to add further theoretical and empirical detail in assessing the functional limits of hegemony—a key debate in the contemporary literature (Byers and Nolte 2003; Clark 2011; Reich and Lebow 2014; Ikenberry, Mastanduno, and Wohlforth 2011b).

Yet I made clear from the outset that my concern encompassed more than just the United States in isolation, as a number of other current and emerging powers also have profound interest in the development of international institutions (Cai 2013; Hurrell 2006; Hurrell 2007). Future studies could seek to elaborate on the findings presented here in two respects. On the one hand, how have the likes of China, India, and Russia interacted with a range of other multilateral initiatives: have they been gradually influenced by the informal effects of legal norms (as with the MBT and—less so—ICC), and to what extent have these key states managed to shape the institutions towards their own ends (as was most apparent with respect to the ICC)? Alternatively, what role do emerging powers have in solidifying new social standards? This is particularly important since not all of these actors inherently reject new legal developments: Brazil, Nigeria, and South Africa, for example, are all supporters of the MBT and the ICC. Another interesting project could thus seek to trace the role of emerging global and regional powers on a variety of governance initiatives.

Studying Socialization within the State

As a global account of multilateralism, this study has focused on the macro-structural influence of legal institutions and norms in shaping state policy. It has therefore largely, though not entirely, avoided a sustained discussion of the micro-processes that lead to the adoption of norms *within* states. Socialization—which Checkel (2005, 804) defines as 'a process of inducting actors into the norms and rules of a given community'—provides the key frame of reference for conceptualizing this process. The AP mine ban and ICC offer rich opportunities for assessing previously theorized mechanisms of socialization—notably persuasion, social rewards and punishments, and emulation—as well as instrumental explanations that emphasize positive inducements or coercive threats to explain behavioural adaptation or the lack thereof (Goodman and Jinks 2013; Greenhill 2010; Johnston 2001; Johnston 2005; Johnstone 2011; Risse 2000; Goldsmith and Posner 2005; Guzman 2008; Schimmelfennig 2005).[9] Importantly, however, it is not 'the state' as an abstract political entity but its representatives that must be socialized. To be most persuasive, therefore, research on socialization must focus at the level of individuals (diplomats, military officials, and political elites) and their aggregation in policymaking groups. This emphasis is fully compatible with the approach to studying institutional impact employed herein, but takes the analysis to a greater level of granularity at the expense of the wide-angle view appropriate to the present research question. In particular, a future study should build on insights developed above concerning the connections between institutional environments and the processes of norm adoption. Organizational fora are inherently social environments, and 'can therefore be thought to catalyze the process of international norm diffusion by providing a site within which the ideas held by policymakers from one country can be effectively transmitted to the representatives of another' (Greenhill 2010, 129–30). This was a key claim advanced in Chapter 2 and illustrated—albeit broadly rather than via detailed sub-state case studies—in the empirical chapters.

Relatedly, the above discussion largely brackets detailed consideration of domestic political factors in favour of an account of norm adoption across the system of states. The IR literature has long been interested with how domestic characteristics like regime type and connections to the international system render states more or less susceptible to socialization (Hafner-Burton, Victor, and Lupu 2012, 69–72; Price 2003, 592–4). One key finding, for example, is that while authoritarian governments frequently join international agreements, this does not necessarily improve their subsequent performance on key indicators; democracies are far more observant of the commitments they undertake (Hafner-Burton and Tsutsui 2007; Neumayer 2005). Yet this may not always be the case. Indeed, the MBT and, to a lesser extent, ICC cases have

[9] These explanations rarely act in isolation, as norms and legal obligations frequently constitute the 'good' upon which instrumental choices are based and inversely, rational utility-regarding actors often promote new norms via deliberate entrepreneurship and strategic social construction—dual processes which have been illustrated at length in this study.

demonstrated that status considerations often loom large even for autocratic governments that are assumed to be much more insulated against international social pressures. Meaningful state change and compliance, especially with respect to the MBT, is therefore not limited to democratic states. Future research could thus seek to systematically explore variation in socialization and behavioural change on the basis of political type, across a range of institutions.

Expanding the Subjects of Law: Non-State Actors in World Politics

Finally, a broader account of multilateralism with and without the great powers must come to grips with the vital contributions of non-state actors to the development of international law and norms. A vibrant literature has detailed the various roles of transnational civil society in raising and promoting new norms across a range of issue areas (Price 2003; Spiro 2013). Comparatively less attention has been accorded, however, to their subsequent involvement in the implementation of institutions (Betts and Orchard 2014; Dai 2007; Risse, Ropp, and Sikkink 2013). This is true of the MBT and ICC cases, though there are some limited exceptions (Bernstein 2008; Haddad 2013; Schroeder and Tiemessen 2014; Wareham 2008). The emphasis of much of the constructivist IR literature on norm-building was entirely appropriate to the goal of demonstrating the salience and impact of norms, but necessarily leaves a gap in our understanding with respect to how TCS efforts may continue, and potentially shift in focus, over time. The valuable initial studies cited here can be supplemented with further detailed analysis of TCS strategic engagement—including via monitoring, providing technical assistance, and deploying social pressure to improve state adherence—and their consequences. This emphasis also speaks to a related question, addressed briefly in this study, concerning the most appropriate strategies for dealing with non-compliance. Is it best to publicize violations in the hopes of compelling changes in behaviour, or keeping such transgressions quiet and working with the offending actors to ameliorate their policies, and under what circumstances should one approach be preferred (Forsythe 2005; Kellenberger 2004)?

These dynamics are also important in thinking through the prospects for future non-great power governance, since any prospective initiative would have to be supported by transnational civil society. Charli Carpenter (2014) has persuasively showed that the distribution of decision-making authority within and among transnational advocacy networks has an important influence over what issues are adopted and promoted by these groups. I drew attention to the International Campaign to Ban Landmines and Coalition for the International Criminal Court, yet these organizations are themselves composed of myriad organizations and individuals spanning peace activists, religious and community groups, academics, former government officials, lawyers, and so on. In the future, particular attention should be paid to identifying the composition and structure of these domestic and transnational actors, specifying the various roles and degrees of access they enjoy, and demonstrating how these factors vary across particular political communities and governance issues. Such a research agenda would contribute additional empirical data to refine theoretical expectations concerning the place and impact of transnational civil society in world politics.

A richer account of normative change must also seek to account for the role of entities like multinational corporations and non-state armed groups (NSAG). These diverse actors are excluded from many formal multilateral agreements, but are substantively engaged in the practices of global governance (Avant, Finnemore, and Sell 2010). There are particular methodological challenges in studying socialization in such entities, since the former are typically not directly involved in relevant diplomatic settings and the latter often exist on the periphery of international recognition and may lack a stable composition and leadership structure. Yet such actors play an important role in the reception and spread of global norms, not least because they are frequently implicated in violations concerning armed violence, human rights, and environmental protection (among many issue areas). Recent research, moreover, has demonstrated that NSAG are sensitive to international standards, and may be motivated by both social (status and legitimacy) and instrumental (access to material goods) incentives (Jo 2015). Examining these processes systematically also offers an opportunity to compare how mechanisms for generating compliance operate in state and non-state contexts.

CONCLUSION

Investigating the possibility and potential limits of non-great power diplomacy adds an important dimension to our understanding of international politics, but this subject has not been adequately addressed thus far. The Antipersonnel Mine Ban Treaty and Rome Statute of the ICC are key test cases for this phenomenon, and it is for this reason that the two treaties have received such extensive attention here. Both demonstrate the potent role that legal institutions may play in altering international practice in the face of resistance from the most materially powerful states—though this influence is felt to differing degrees. The most fundamental finding of this study is thus that developing treaties without great power support can prove a successful approach to creating strong international norms, even in challenging contexts that implicate core matters of state security and sovereignty. In this way, the account presented here provides a partial rebuttal to the sceptical view of international institutions as low-cost tools that (usually preponderantly powerful) states use to pursue their prior interests. At the same time, the noted variance in outcomes provides a valuable frame for thinking about the suitability of a similar diplomatic approach for other governance challenges.

Ultimately, the MBT and ICC might be judged as exceptional outliers to the general trend of great power directed multilateralism (Brem 2009, 175). But equally, the preceding analysis has suggested a wider potential for international law to transcend dominant configurations of material power to instantiate new standards of appropriate behaviour that reshape aspects of international relations. In addition to the initiatives already discussed, there are nascent campaigns to address a range of issues in the field of international security—such as non-lethal military technologies (Fidler 2005), autonomous and robotic weaponry (Anthony and Holland 2014), explosive remnants of war, and a global ban on nuclear weapons (Acheson, Nash, and Moyes 2014)—where we can anticipate substantial resistance from great and rising powers, including perhaps actors like Brazil, France, Japan, and the United Kingdom that supported previous efforts. The larger question is: how would we know whether—or more appropriately, under what conditions—the sceptical or optimistic view is correct? This chapter has sought to suggest some avenues for taking this discussion forward. Much remains to be said about how the accumulation of material and social power, and its gradual realignment, will contribute to the expansion and contestation of international law and, more broadly, global order. The preceding study has validated the initial interest in non-great power multilateralism, and has offered impetus for further detailed research to help scholars and policymakers alike better understand the promise and perils of this strategy.

APPENDIX

List of Interviewees Cited in the Text

Professional titles listed here reflect the interviewee roles at the time of the interview.

1. **Pascal Bongard**—Program Director (Africa) and Policy Adviser, Geneva Call. Geneva, 2 November 2009.
2. **Kerry Brinkert**—Director, Implementation Support Unit of the Antipersonnel Mine Ban Treaty. Geneva, 30 October 2009 and 8 December 2010.
3. **Purna Shova Chitrakar**—Founder, Coordinator, and Chairperson, Ban Landmines Campaign Nepal. Geneva, 3 December 2010.
4. Members of the Coalition for the International Criminal Court Middle East and North Africa (MENA) Team. New York, 15 December 2011.
5. **Elina Dakash**—Attaché, Unit for Arms Control, Disarmament and Non-Proliferation, Ministry of Foreign Affairs of Finland. Geneva, 2 December 2010.
6. **Francis Dako**—Africa Coordinator, Coalition for the International Criminal Court. New York, 15 December 2011.
7. **Kasia Derlicka-Rosenbauer**—Advocacy and Campaigning Officer, International Campaign to Ban Landmines. Geneva, 22 October 2009 and 7 December 2010.
8. **Tamar Gabelnick**—Treaty Implementation Director, International Campaign to Ban Landmines. Geneva, 19 October 2009 and 7 December 2010.
9. **Peter Kolarov**—Head of the Humanitarian Conventions Section, United Nations Office for Disarmament Affairs. Geneva, 21 October 2009.
10. **Hari Odari**—Second Secretary, Permanent Mission of the Federal Democratic Republic of Nepal to the United Nations and other International Organizations and Embassy of the FDR of Nepal. Geneva, 7 December 2010.
11. **Guy Pollard**—Counsellor, Nuclear and Conventional Weapons Section, United Kingdom Delegation to the Conference on Disarmament. Geneva, 6 November 2009 and 8 December 2010.
12. **Michelle E. Reyes Milk**—Outreach Liaison for the Americas, Asia, and the Pacific, Coalition for the International Criminal Court. New York, 19 December 2011.
13. **Dr Malike Selçuk Sancar**—Counsellor, Permanent Mission of Turkey to the United Nations Office in Geneva. Geneva, 26 October 2009.
14. **Dr Ann-Kristin (Anki) Sjöberg**—Strategy and Evaluation Officer, Geneva Call. Geneva, 2 November 2009.
15. **John Washburn**—Convenor, American Non-Governmental Organizations Coalition for the International Criminal Court. New York, 20 December 2011.

16. **Camilla Waszink**—Policy Adviser, Arms Unit, Legal Division, International Committee of the Red Cross. Geneva, 23 October 2009.
17. **Dr Colonel (retired) Marek Zadrożny**—Counsellor and Military Adviser, Permanent Mission of Poland to the United Nations Office in Geneva. Geneva, 27 October 2009 and 3 December 2010.

Bibliography

Academic Sources

Abbott, Kenneth W., Robert O. Keohane, Andrew Moravcsik, Anne-Marie Slaughter, and Duncan Snidal. 2000. 'The Concept of Legalization'. *International Organization* 54 (3): 401–20.

Abbott, Kenneth W., and Duncan Snidal. 1998. 'Why States Act through Formal International Organizations'. *The Journal of Conflict Resolution* 42 (1): 3–32.

Abbott, Kenneth W., and Duncan Snidal. 2000. 'Hard and Soft Law in International Governance'. *International Organization* 54 (03): 421–56.

Abbott, Kenneth W., and Duncan Snidal. 2013. 'Law, Legalization, and Politics: An Agenda for the Next Generation of IL/IR Scholars.' In *Interdisciplinary Perspectives on International Law and International Relations: The State of the Art*, edited by Jeffrey L. Dunoff and Mark A. Pollack, 33–56. Cambridge: Cambridge University Press.

Acharya, Amitav. 2011. 'Norm Subsidiarity and Regional Orders: Sovereignty, Regionalism, and Rule-Making in the Third World'. *International Studies Quarterly* 55 (1): 95–123.

Adler, Emanuel, and Vincent Pouliot, eds. 2011. *International Practices*. Cambridge; New York: Cambridge University Press.

Akande, Dapo. 2003. 'The Jurisdiction of the International Criminal Court over Nationals of Non-Parties: Legal Basis and Limits'. *Journal of International Criminal Justice* 1 (3): 618–50.

Akande, Dapo. 2004. 'International Law Immunities and the International Criminal Court'. *The American Journal of International Law* 98 (3): 407–33.

Akhavan, Payam. 2011. 'International Criminal Justice in the Era of Failed States: The ICC and the Self-Referral Debate'. In *The International Criminal Court and Complementarity: From Theory to Practice*, edited by Carsten Stahn and Mohamed M. El Zeidy, 283–303. Cambridge; New York: Cambridge University Press.

Alai, Christine, and Njonjo Mue. 2011. 'Complementarity and the Impact of the Rome Statute and the International Criminal Court in Kenya'. In *The International Criminal Court and Complementarity: From Theory to Practice*, edited by Carsten Stahn and Mohamed M. El Zeidy, 1222–34. Cambridge; New York: Cambridge University Press.

Alter, Karen. 2014. *The New Terrain of International Law: Courts, Politics, Rights*. Princeton, NJ: Princeton University Press.

Ambos, Kai. 2011. 'The Colombian Peace Process (Law 975 of 2005) and the ICC's Principle of Complementarity'. In *The International Criminal Court and Complementarity: From Theory to Practice*, edited by Carsten Stahn and Mohamed M. El Zeidy, 1071–96. Cambridge; New York: Cambridge University Press.

Anghie, Antony. 2007. *Imperialism, Sovereignty and the Making of International Law*. Cambridge: Cambridge University Press.

Atkinson, Carol. 2006. 'Constructivist Implications of Material Power: Military Engagement and the Socialization of States, 1972–2000'. *International Studies Quarterly* 50 (3): 509–37.

Avant, Deborah D., Martha Finnemore, and Susan K. Sell, eds. 2010. *Who Governs the Globe?* Cambridge; New York: Cambridge University Press.

Axworthy, Lloyd. 1998. 'Towards a New Multilateralism'. In *To Walk without Fear: The Global Movement to Ban Landmines*, edited by Maxwell A. Cameron, Robert J. Lawson, and Brian W. Tomlin, 448–69. Toronto: Oxford University Press.

Bailey, Sheree, and Tun Channareth. 2008. 'Beyond Rhetoric: The Mine Ban Treaty and Victim Assistance'. In *Banning Landmines: Disarmament, Citizen Diplomacy, and Human Security*, edited by Jody Wiliams, Stephen D. Goose, and Mary Wareham, 143–62. Lanham, MD: Rowman & Littlefield Publishers.

Barnett, Michael, and Raymond Duvall. 2005. 'Power in International Politics'. *International Organization* 59 (1): 39–75.

Barriga, Stefan, and Claus Kress, eds. 2011. *The Travaux Préparatoires of the Crime of Aggression*. Cambridge; New York: Cambridge University Press.

Bass, Gary Jonathan. 2001. *Stay the Hand of Vengeance: The Politics of War Crimes Tribunals*. Princeton, NJ: Princeton University Press.

Behringer, Ronald M. 2005. 'Middle Power Leadership on the Human Security Agenda'. *Cooperation and Conflict* 40 (3): 305–42.

Beier, J. Marshall. 2002. 'Siting Indiscriminacy: India and the Global Movement to Ban Landmines'. *Global Governance* 8 (3): 305–21.

Bekou, Olympia. 2011. 'In the Hands of the State: Implementing Legislation and Complementarity'. In *The International Criminal Court and Complementarity: From Theory to Practice*, edited by Carsten Stahn and Mohamed M. El Zeidy. Cambridge; New York: Cambridge University Press.

Bekou, Olympia. 2014. 'National Approaches to the ICC Statute Crimes'. In *Contemporary Challenges for the International Criminal Court*, edited by Andraz Zidar and Olympia Bekou, 19–34. London: British Institute of International and Comparative Law.

Benedetti, Fanny, Karine Bonneau, and John Washburn. 2013. *Negotiating the International Criminal Court: New York to Rome, 1994–1998*. Leiden: Martinus Nijhoff Publishers.

Benedetti, Fanny, and John L. Washburn. 1999. 'Drafting the International Criminal Court Treaty: Two Years to Rome and an Afterword on the Rome Diplomatic Conference'. *Global Governance* 5 (1): 1–37.

Benesch, Susan, Glenn McGrory, Cristina Rodriguez, and Robert Sloane. 1999. 'International Customary Law and Antipersonnel Landmines: Emergence of a New Customary Norm'. International Campaign to Ban Landmines. http://www.the-monitor.org/index.php/publications/display?url=lm/1999/appendices/custom_law.html.

Bernstein, Elizabeth. 2008. 'Still Alive and Kicking: The International Campaign to Ban Landmines'. In *Banning Landmines: Disarmament, Citizen Diplomacy, and Human Security*, 31–48. Lanham, MD: Rowman & Littlefield Publishers.

Betts, Alexander, and Phil Orchard, eds. 2014. *Implementation and World Politics: How International Norms Change Practice*. Oxford; New York: Oxford University Press.

Biersteker, Thomas J. 1993. 'Constructing Historical Counterfactuals to Assess the Consequences of International Regimes: The Global Debt Regime and the Course of the Debt Crisis of the 1980s'. In *Regime Theory and International Relations*, edited by Volker Rittberger and Peter Mayer, 315–38. New York: Clarendon Press.

Birdsall, Andrea. 2010. 'The "Monster That We Need to Slay"? Global Governance, the United States, and the International Criminal Court'. *Global Governance* 16 (4): 451–69.

Bolton, Matthew, and Thomas Nash. 2010. 'The Role of Middle Power–NGO Coalitions in Global Policy: The Case of the Cluster Munitions Ban'. *Global Policy* 1 (2): 172–84.

Borgen, Christopher. 2009. 'The Language of Law and the Practice of Politics: Great Powers and the Rhetoric of Self-Determination in the Cases of Kosovo and South Ossetia'. *Chicago Journal of International Law* 10 (1): 1–33.

Borrie, John. 2009. *Unacceptable Harm: A History of How the Treaty to Ban Cluster Munitions Was Won*. Geneva: United Nations Institute for Disarmament Research.

Bosco, David. 2014. *Rough Justice: The International Criminal Court's Battle to Fix the World, One Prosecution at a Time*. Oxford; New York: Oxford University Press.

Bourgon, Stephane. 2002. 'Jurisdiction Ratione Loci'. In *The Rome Statute of the International Criminal Court: A Commentary*, edited by Antonio Cassese, Paola Gaeta, and John R. W. D. Jones, 1:559–69. Oxford: Oxford University Press.

Bower, Adam. 2015. 'Arguing with Law: Strategic Legal Argumentation, US Diplomacy, and Debates over the International Criminal Court'. *Review of International Studies* 41 (2): 337–60.

Bower, Adam, and Richard Price. 2013. 'Moral Mission Accomplished? Assessing the Landmine Ban'. In *Justice, Sustainability, and Security: Global Ethics for the 21st Century*, edited by Eric A. Heinze, 131–69. New York: Palgrave Macmillan.

Branch, Adam. 2007. 'Uganda's Civil War and the Politics of ICC Intervention'. *Ethics & International Affairs* 21 (2): 179–98.

Brem, Stefan. 2009. 'Is There a Future for Non-Hegemonic Cooperation? Explaining Success and Failure of Alternative Regime Creation'. In *Cooperating without America: Theories and Case Studies of Non-Hegemonic Regimes*, edited by Stefan Brem and Kendall Stiles, 173–85. London: Routledge.

Brem, Stefan, and Kendall W. Stiles. 2009. *Co-Operating without America: Theories and Case Studies of Non-Hegemonic Regimes*. London: Routledge.

Brinkert, Kerry. 2006. 'Understanding the Ottawa Convention's Obligations to Landmine Victims'. *Journal of Mine Action* 10 (1).

Brinkert, Kerry. 2008. 'An Emphasis on Action: The Mine Ban Treaty's Implementation Mechanism'. In *Banning Landmines: Disarmament, Citizen Diplomacy, and Human Security*, edited by Jody Williams, Stephen D. Goose, and Mary Wareham, 87–104. Lanham, MD: Rowman & Littlefield Publishers.

Brooks, Stephen G., and William C. Wohlforth. 2008. *World out of Balance: International Relations and the Challenge of American Primacy*. Princeton, NJ: Princeton University Press.

Brown, Michael E., Owen R. Cote Jr., Sean M. Lynn-Jones, and Steven E. Miller, eds. 2009. *Primacy and Its Discontents: American Power and International Stability*. Cambridge, MA: MIT Press.

Brunnée, Jutta. 2004. 'The United States and International Environmental Law: Living with an Elephant'. *European Journal of International Law* 15 (4): 617–49.

Brunnée, Jutta, and Stephen J. Toope. 2010. *Legitimacy and Legality in International Law: An Interactional Account*. Cambridge; New York: Cambridge University Press.

Bukovansky, Mlada, Ian Clark, Robyn Eckersley, Richard Price, Christian Reus-Smit, and Nicholas J. Wheeler. 2012. *Special Responsibilities: Global Problems and American Power*. New York: Cambridge University Press.

Bull, Hedley. 2012. *The Anarchical Society*. 4th ed. New York: Palgrave Macmillan/ Columbia University Press.

Busby, Josh. 2009. 'The Hardest Problem in the World: Leadership in the Climate Regime'. In *Cooperating without America: Theories and Case Studies of Non-Hegemonic Regimes*, 73–104. New York: Routledge.

Byers, Michael. 1999. *Custom, Power and the Power of Rules: International Relations and Customary International Law*. Cambridge: Cambridge University Press.

Byers, Michael. 2008. 'International Law'. In *The Oxford Handbook of International Relations*, edited by Christian Reus-Smit and Duncan Snidal, 612–34. Oxford; New York: Oxford University Press.

Byers, Michael, and Georg Nolte, eds. 2003. *United States Hegemony and the Foundations of International Law*. Cambridge; New York: Cambridge University Press.

Cai, Congyan. 2013. 'New Great Powers and International Law in the 21st Century'. *European Journal of International Law* 24 (3): 755–95.

Cameron, Maxwell A. 1999. 'Global Civil Society and the Ottawa Process: Lessons from the Movement to Ban Anti-personnel Mines'. *Canadian Foreign Policy Journal* 7 (1): 85–102.

Cameron, Maxwell A., Robert J. Lawson, and Brian W. Tomlin, eds. 1998. *To Walk without Fear: The Global Movement to Ban Landmines*. Toronto: Oxford University Press.

Carin, Barry, and Alan Mehlenbacher. 2010. 'Constituting Global Leadership: Which Countries Need to Be around the Summit Table for Climate Change and Energy Security?' *Global Governance* 16 (1): 21–37.

Carpenter, Charli. 2014. *'Lost' Causes: Agenda Vetting in Global Issue Networks and the Shaping of Human Security*. Ithaca, NY: Cornell University Press.

Carrasco, Herencia. 2010. 'Implementation of War Crimes in Latin America: An Assessment of the Impact of the Rome Statute of the International Criminal Court'. *International Criminal Law Review* 10 (4): 461–72.

Cassese, Antonio, Paola Gaeta, and John R. W. D. Jones, eds. 2002. *The Rome Statute of the International Criminal Court: A Commentary*. 2 vols. Oxford: Oxford University Press.

Chamberlain, Paul, and David Long. 2004. 'Europe and the Ottawa Treaty: Compliance with Exceptions and Loopholes'. In *Landmines and Human Security: International Politics and War's Hidden Legacy*, edited by Richard A. Matthew, Bryan McDonald, and Kenneth Rutherford, 81–96. Albany, NY: State University of New York Press.

Chapman, Terrence L., and Stephen Chaudoin. 2013. 'Ratification Patterns and the International Criminal Court'. *International Studies Quarterly* 57 (2): 400–9.

Charney, Jonathan I. 1999. 'Progress in International Criminal Law?' *American Journal of International Law* 93 (2): 452–64.

Chayes, Abram, and Antonia Handler Chayes. 1993. 'On Compliance'. *International Organization* 47 (02): 175–205.

Checkel, Jeffrey T. 2001. 'Why Comply? Social Learning and European Identity Change'. *International Organization* 55 (03): 553–88.

Checkel, Jeffrey T. 2005. 'International Institutions and Socialization in Europe: Introduction and Framework'. *International Organization* 59 (4): 801–26.

Ciampi, Annalisa. 2002. 'Other Forms of Cooperation'. In *The Rome Statute of the International Criminal Court: A Commentary*, edited by Antonio Cassese, Paola Gaeta, and John R. W. D. Jones, II:1705–47. Oxford: Oxford University Press.

Clark, Ian. 2011. *Hegemony in International Society*. Oxford: Oxford University Press.

Clark, Phil. 2011. 'Chasing Cases: The ICC and the Politics of State Referral in the Democratic Republic of the Congo and Uganda'. In *The International Criminal Court and Complementarity: From Theory to Practice*, edited by Carsten Stahn and Mohamed M. El Zeidy, 1180–203. Cambridge; New York: Cambridge University Press.

Clarke, Kamari Maxine. 2009. *Fictions of Justice: The ICC and the Challenge of Legal Pluralism in Sub-Saharan Africa*. Cambridge: Cambridge University Press.

Coleman, Katharina P. 2013. 'Locating Norm Diplomacy: Venue Change in International Norm Negotiations'. *European Journal of International Relations* 19 (1): 163–86.

Cooper, Andrew, John English, and Ramesh Thakur, eds. 2003. *Enhancing Global Governance: Towards a New Diplomacy?* Tokyo: United Nations University Press.

Cortell, Andrew P., and James W. Davis. 1996. 'How Do International Institutions Matter? The Domestic Impact of International Rules and Norms'. *International Studies Quarterly* 40 (4): 451–78.

Crawford, Neta C. 2002. *Argument and Change in World Politics: Ethics, Decolonization, and Humanitarian Intervention*. Cambridge; New York: Cambridge University Press.

Cryer, Robert. 2005. *Prosecuting International Crimes: Selectivity and the International Criminal Law Regime*. Cambridge; New York: Cambridge University Press.

D'Amato, Anthony. 1988. 'Custom and Treaty: A Response to Professor Weisburd'. *Vanderbilt Journal of Transnational Law* 21 (3): 459–72.

D'Amato, Anthony A. 1971. *The Concept of Custom in International Law*. Ithaca, NY: Cornell University Press.

D'Amato, Anthony A. 2004. *International Law Sources: Collected Papers*. Vol. 3. Leiden; Boston: Martinus Nijhoff.

Dai, Xinyuan. 2007. *International Institutions and National Policies*. Cambridge; New York: Cambridge University Press.

Darehshori, Sara, and Elizabeth Evenson. 2010. 'Peace, Justice, and the International Criminal Court'. Oxford Transitional Justice Research—Research Article 1. Oxford. http://otjr.crim.ox.ac.uk/materials/papers/38/DarehshoriandEvenson2010.pdf.

Davenport, David. 2002. 'The New Diplomacy'. *Policy Review*, 116: 17–30.

de Nevers, Renee. 2007. 'Imposing International Norms: Great Powers and Norm Enforcement'. *International Studies Review* 9 (1): 53–80.

Deitelhoff, Nicole. 2009a. 'Isolated Hegemon: The Creation of the International Criminal Court (ICC)'. In *Cooperating without America: Theories and Case Studies of Non-Hegemonic Regimes*, edited by Stefan Brem and Kendal Stiles, 147–72. New York: Routledge.

Deitelhoff, Nicole. 2009b. 'The Discursive Process of Legalization: Charting Islands of Persuasion in the ICC Case'. *International Organization* 63 (1): 33–65.

Destradi, Sandra. 2010. 'Regional Powers and their Strategies: Empire, Hegemony, and Leadership'. *Review of International Studies* 36 (4): 903–30.

Dimitrov, Radoslav S., Detlef F. Sprinz, Gerald M. DiGiusto, and Alexander Kelle. 2007. 'International Nonregimes: A Research Agenda'. *International Studies Review* 9 (2): 230–58.

Dinstein, Yoram. 1997. 'Comments on Protocol I.' *International Review of the Red Cross* 320 (October): 515–19.

Dolan, Michael, and Chris Hunt. 1998. 'Negotiating in the Ottawa Process: The New Multilateralism'. In *To Walk without Fear: The Global Movement to Ban Landmines*, edited by Maxwell A. Cameron, Robert J. Lawson, and Brian W. Tomlin, 392–423. Toronto: Oxford University Press.

Downs, George W., David M. Rocke, and Peter N. Barsoom. 1996. 'Is the Good News about Compliance Good News about Cooperation?' *International Organization* 50 (3): 379–406.

Drumbl, Mark A. 2007. *Atrocity, Punishment, and International Law*. Cambridge; New York: Cambridge University Press.

du Plessis, Max. 2010. *The International Criminal Court That Africa Wants*. ISS Monograph No. 172. Pretoria, South Africa: Institute for Security Studies. http://www.issafrica.org/anicj/uploads/Du_Plessis_The_ICC_that_Africa_wants.pdf.

Dukalskis, Alexander, and Robert C. Johansen. 2013. 'Measuring Acceptance of International Enforcement of Human Rights: The United States, Asia, and the International Criminal Court'. *Human Rights Quarterly* 35 (3): 569–97.

Dunoff, Jeffrey L., and Mark A. Pollack, eds. 2013. *Interdisciplinary Perspectives on International Law and International Relations: The State of the Art*. Cambridge: Cambridge University Press.

Dupuy, Pierre-Marie. 2002. 'International Criminal Responsibility of the Individual and International Responsibility of the State'. In *The Rome Statute of the International Criminal Court: A Commentary*, edited by Antonio Cassese, Paola Gaeta, and John R. W. D. Jones, 2:1085–99. Oxford: Oxford University Press.

Dutton, Yvonne. 2013. *Rules, Politics, and the International Criminal Court: Committing to the Court*. Abingdon: Routledge.

Eaton, Robert. 2008. 'An Indispensible Tool: The Mine Ban Treaty and Mine Action'. In *Banning Landmines: Disarmament, Citizen Diplomacy, and Human Security*, edited by Jody Williams, Stephen D. Goose, and Mary Wareham, 127–42. Lanham, MD: Rowman & Littlefield Publishers.

Elder-Vass, Dave. 2010. *The Causal Power of Social Structures: Emergence, Structure and Agency*. Cambridge; New York: Cambridge University Press.

Epstein, Charlotte. 2008. *The Power of Words in International Relations: Birth of an Anti-Whaling Discourse*. Cambridge, MA: MIT Press.

Erickson, Jennifer. 2015. *Dangerous Trade: Arms Exports, Human Rights, and International Reputation*. New York: Columbia University Press.

Fearon, James D. 1991. 'Counterfactuals and Hypothesis Testing in Political Science'. *World Politics* 43 (2): 169–95.

Fearon, James D., and Alexander Wendt. 2002. 'Rationalism v. Constructivism: A Skeptical View'. In *Handbook of International Relations*, edited by Walter Carlsneas, Thomas Risse, and Beth A. Simmons, 52–72. London: SAGE Publications.

Fehl, Caroline. 2004. 'Explaining the International Criminal Court: A "Practice Test" for Rationalist and Constructivist Approaches'. *European Journal of International Relations* 10 (3): 357–94.

Fehl, Caroline. 2012. *Living with a Reluctant Hegemon: Explaining European Responses to US Unilateralism*. Oxford: Oxford University Press.

Feith, Douglas J. 1985. 'Protocol I: Moving Humanitarian Law Backwards'. *Akron Law Review* 19 (4): 531–5.

Ferguson, Niall. 2005. *Colossus: The Rise and Fall of the American Empire*. Reprint edition. New York: Penguin Books.

Fidler, David P. 2005. 'The Meaning of Moscow: "Non-Lethal" Weapons and International Law in the Early 21st Century'. *International Review of the Red Cross* 87 (859): 525–52.

Finnemore, Martha. 1996. *National Interests in International Society*. Ithaca, NY: Cornell University Press.

Finnemore, Martha. 2000. 'Are Legal Norms Distinctive'. *New York University Journal of International Law and Politics* 32 (3): 699–705.

Finnemore, Martha, and Kathryn Sikkink. 1998. 'International Norm Dynamics and Political Change'. *International Organization* 52 (4): 887–917.

Finnemore, Martha J., and Stephen Toope. 2001. 'Alternatives to Legalization: Richer Views of Law and Politics'. *International Organization* 55 (3): 743–58.

Flowers, Petrice. 2009. *Refugees, Women, and Weapons: International Norm Adoption and Compliance in Japan*. Stanford: Stanford University Press.

Foot, Rosemary, S. Neil MacFarlane, and Michael Mastanduno, eds. 2003. *US Hegemony and International Organizations: The United States and Multilateral Institutions*. Oxford: Oxford University Press.

Fordham, Benjamin O., and Victor Asal. 2007. 'Billiard Balls or Snowflakes? Major Power Prestige and the International Diffusion of Institutions and Practices'. *International Studies Quarterly* 51 (1): 31–52.

Forsythe, David. 2005. 'Naming and Shaming: The Ethics of ICRC Discretion'. *Millennium* 34 (2): 461–74.

Franceschet, Antonio. 2006. '"Global(izing) Justice": The International Criminal Court'. In *Bringing Power to Justice? The Prospects of the International Criminal Court*, edited by Joanna Harrington, Michael Milde, and Richard Vernon, 244–65. Montreal and Kingston: McGill-Queen's University Press.

Franck, Thomas M. 1990. *The Power of Legitimacy Among Nations*. New York: Oxford University Press.

Gabelnick, Tamar. 2008. 'The Article 5 Extension Request Process'. *The Journal of ERW and Mine Action* 12 (2). http://www.jmu.edu/cisr/journal/12.2/sp/gabelnick/gabelnick.shtml.

Gaeta, Paola. 2002. 'Official Capacity and Immunities'. In *The Rome Statute of the International Criminal Court: A Commentary*, edited by Antonio Cassese, Paola Gaeta, and John R. W. D. Jones, 1:975–1002. Oxford: Oxford University Press.

Gard, Jr., Robert G. 1998. 'The Military Utility of Anti-Personnel Landmines'. In *To Walk without Fear: The Global Movement to Ban Landmines*, edited by Maxwell A. Cameron, Robert J. Lawson, and Brian W. Tomlin, 136–57. Toronto: Oxford University Press.

George, Alexander L, and Andrew Bennett. 2005. *Case Studies and Theory Development in the Social Sciences*. Cambridge, MA: MIT Press.

Glasius, Marlies. 2005. *The International Criminal Court: A Global Civil Society Achievement*. London; New York: Routledge.

Glasius, Marlies. 2011. 'A Problem, Not a Solution: Complementarity in the Central African Republic and Democratic Republic of the Congo'. In *The International Criminal Court and Complementarity: From Theory to Practice*, edited by Carsten Stahn and Mohamed M. El Zeidy, 1204–21. Cambridge; New York: Cambridge University Press.

Glennon, Michael J. 2001. *Limits of Law, Prerogatives of Power: Interventionism after Kosovo*. New York: Palgrave.

Glennon, Michael J. 2005. 'How International Rules Die'. *Georgetown Law Journal* 93: 939–91.

Goldsmith, Jack L. 2003. 'The Self-Defeating International Criminal Court'. *University of Chicago Law Review* 70 (1): 89–104.

Goldsmith, Jack L., and Eric A. Posner. 2005. *The Limits of International Law*. New York: Oxford University Press.

Goodman, Ryan, and Derek Jinks. 2013. *Socializing States: Promoting Human Rights through International Law*. New York: Oxford University Press.

Goose, Stephen D. 2008a. 'Cluster Munitions in the Crosshairs: In Pursuit of a Prohibition'. In *Banning Landmines: Disarmament, Citizen Diplomacy, and Human Security*, edited by Jody Williams, Stephen D. Goose, and Mary Wareham, 217–39. Lanham, MD: Rowman & Littlefield Publishers.

Goose, Stephen D. 2008b. 'Goodwill Yields Good Results: Cooperative Compliance and the Mine Ban Treaty'. In *Banning Landmines: Disarmament, Citizen Diplomacy, and Human Security*, edited by Jody Williams, Stephen D. Goose, and Mary Wareham, 105–26. Lanham, MD: Rowman & Littlefield Publishers.

Goose, Stephen D., Mary Wareham, and Jody Williams. 2008. 'Banning Landmines and Beyond.' In *Banning Landmines: Disarmament, Citizen Diplomacy, and Human Security*, edited by Jody Williams, Stephen D. Goose, and Mary Wareham, 1–14. Lanham, MD: Rowman & Littlefield Publishers.

Goose, Stephen D., and Jody Williams. 2008. 'Citizen Diplomacy and the Ottawa Process: A Lasting Model?' In *Banning Landmines: Disarmament, Citizen Diplomacy, and Human Security*, edited by Jody Williams, Stephen D. Goose, and Mary Wareham, 181–98. Lanham, MD: Rowman & Littlefield Publishers.

Greenhill, Brian. 2010. 'The Company You Keep: International Socialization and the Diffusion of Human Rights Norms'. *International Studies Quarterly* 54 (1): 127–45.

Grynaviski, Eric. 2013. 'Contrasts, Counterfactuals, and Causes'. *European Journal of International Relations* 19 (4): 823–46.

Guldahl, Camilla G. 2008. 'The Role of Persistent Objection in International Humanitarian Law'. *Nordic Journal of International Law* 77 (1): 51–86.

Guzman, Andrew T. 2008. *How International Law Works: A Rational Choice Theory*. Oxford; New York: Oxford University Press.

Haddad, Heidi Nichols. 2013. 'After the Norm Cascade: NGO Mission Expansion and the Coalition for the International Criminal Court'. *Global Governance* 19 (2): 187–206.

Hafner-Burton, Emilie M. 2008. 'Sticks and Stones: Naming and Shaming the Human Rights Enforcement Problem'. *International Organization* 62 (04): 689–716.

Hafner-Burton, Emilie M., and Kiyoteru Tsutsui. 2005. 'Human Rights in a Globalizing World: The Paradox of Empty Promises'. *American Journal of Sociology* 110 (5): 1373–411.

Hafner-Burton, Emilie M., and Kiyoteru Tsutsui. 2007. 'Justice Lost! The Failure of International Human Rights Law to Matter Where Needed Most'. *Journal of Peace Research* 44 (4): 407–25.

Hafner-Burton, Emilie M., David G. Victor, and Yonatan Lupu. 2012. 'Political Science Research on International Law: The State of the Field'. *The American Journal of International Law* 106 (1): 47–97.

Hart, H. L. A. 1994. *The Concept of Law*. 2nd ed. Oxford: Oxford University Press.

Hathaway, Oona A. 2002. 'Do Human Rights Treaties Make a Difference?' *Yale Law Journal* 111 (8): 1935–2042.

Heckel, Heather. 2009. 'The Campaign to End the Use of Child Soldiers'. In *Cooperating without America: Theories and Case Studies of Non-Hegemonic Regimes*, 44–72. New York: Routledge.

Helm, Carsten, and Detlef Sprinz. 2000. 'Measuring the Effectiveness of International Environmental Regimes'. *Journal of Conflict Resolution* 44 (5): 630–52.

Henckaerts, Jean-Marie. 2005. 'Study on Customary International Humanitarian Law: A Contribution to the Understanding and Respect for the Rule of Law in Armed Conflict'. *International Review of the Red Cross* 87 (857): 175–212.

Herby, Peter, and Kathleen Lawand. 2008. 'Unacceptable Behavior: How Norms Are Established'. In *Banning Landmines: Disarmament, Citizen Diplomacy, and Human Security*, edited by Jody Williams, Stephen D. Goose, and Mary Wareham, 199–216. Lanham, MD: Rowman & Littlefield Publishers.

Higgins, Rosalyn. 1994. *Problems and Process: International Law and How We Use It*. Oxford: Oxford University Press.

Hobbs, Patricia. 2015. 'Contemporary Challenges in Relation to the Prosecution of Senior State Officials before the International Criminal Court'. *International Criminal Law Review* 15: 76–100.

Hopf, Ted. 2013. 'Common-Sense Constructivism and Hegemony in World Politics'. *International Organization* 67 (2): 317–54.

Hovi, Jon, Detlef F. Sprinz, and Arild Underdal. 2003. 'The Oslo-Potsdam Solution to Measuring Regime Effectiveness: Critique, Response, and the Road Ahead'. *Global Environmental Politics* 3 (3): 74–96.

Hurd, Ian. 1999. 'Legitimacy and Authority in International Politics'. *International Organization* 53 (2): 379–408.

Hurrell, Andrew. 2005. 'Power, Institutions, and the Production of Inequality'. In *Power in Global Governance*, edited by Michael Barnett and Raymond Duvall, 33–58. Cambridge: Cambridge University Press.

Hurrell, Andrew. 2006. 'Hegemony, Liberalism and Global Order: What Space for Would-Be Great Powers?' *International Affairs* 82 (1): 1–19.

Hurrell, Andrew. 2007. *On Global Order: Power, Values, and the Constitution of International Society*. Oxford; New York: Oxford University Press.

Ikenberry, G. John. 2001. *After Victory: Institutions, Strategic Restraint, and the Rebuilding of Order after Major Wars*. Princeton, NJ: Princeton University Press.

Ikenberry, G. John, ed. 2002. *America Unrivaled: The Future of the Balance of Power*. Ithaca, NY: Cornell University Press.

Ikenberry, G. John, 2011. *Liberal Leviathan: The Origins, Crisis, and Transformation of the American World Order*. Princeton, NJ: Princeton University Press.

Ikenberry, G. John, and Charles A. Kupchan. 1990. 'Socialization and Hegemonic Power'. *International Organization* 44 (3): 283–315.

Ikenberry, G. John, Michael Mastanduno, and William C. Wohlforth. 2011a. 'Introduction: Unipolarity, State Behavior, and Systemic Consequences'. In *International Relations Theory and the Consequences of Unipolarity*, edited by G. John Ikenberry, Michael Mastanduno, and William C. Wohlforth, 1–32. Cambridge: Cambridge University Press.

Ikenberry, G. John, Michael Mastanduno, and William Curti Wohlforth, eds. 2011b. *International Relations Theory and the Consequences of Unipolarity*. New York: Cambridge University Press.

Jacobs, Christopher W. 2004. 'Taking the Next Step: An Analysis of the Effects the Ottawa Convention May Have on the Interoperability of United States Forces with the Armed Forces of Australia, Great Britain, and Canada'. *Military Law Review* 180: 49–114.

Jalloh, Charles C., Dapo Akande, and Max du Plessis. 2011. 'Assessing the African Union Concerns about Article 16 of the Rome Statute of the International Criminal Court'. *African Journal of Legal Studies* 4 (1): 5–50.

Jia, Bing Bing. 2006. 'China and the International Criminal Court: The Current Situation'. *Singapore Year Book of International Law* 10: 87–97.

Jo, Hyeran. 2015. *Compliant Rebels: Rebel Groups and International Law in World Politics*. Cambridge; New York: Cambridge University Press.

Johnston, Alastair Iain. 2001. 'Treating International Institutions as Social Environments'. *International Studies Quarterly* 45 (4): 487–515.

Johnston, Alastair Iain. 2005. 'Conclusions and Extensions: Toward Mid-Range Theorizing and Beyond Europe'. *International Organization* 59 (04): 1013–44.

Johnstone, Ian. 2011. *The Power of Deliberation: International Law, Politics, and Organizations*. New York: Oxford University Press.

Jones, Annika. 2014. 'State Referrals at the International Criminal Court: From Vision to Practice'. In *Contemporary Challenges for the International Criminal Court*, 73–91. London: British Institute of International and Comparative Law.

Keck, Margaret E., and Kathryn Sikkink. 1998. *Activists beyond Borders: Advocacy Networks in International Politics*. Ithaca, NY: Cornell University Press.

Kellenberger, Jakob. 2004. 'Speaking Out or Remaining Silent in Humanitarian Work'. *International Review of the Red Cross* 86 (855): 593–609.

Kelley, Judith. 2007. 'Who Keeps International Commitments and Why? The International Criminal Court and Bilateral Nonsurrender Agreements'. *The American Political Science Review* 101 (3): 573–89.

Kennedy, Paul M. 1989. *The Rise and Fall of the Great Powers: Economic Change and Military Conflict from 1500 to 2000*. New York: Vintage Books.

Keohane, Robert O. 1984. *After Hegemony: Cooperation and Discord in the World Political Economy*. Princeton, NJ: Princeton University Press.

Keohane, Robert O. 1993. 'The Analysis of International Regimes: Towards a European-American Research Programme'. In *Regime Theory and International Relations*, edited by Volker Rittberger and Peter Mayer, 23–45. New York: Clarendon Press.

Kern, Holger Lutz. 2004. 'Strategies of Legal Change: Great Britain, International Law, and the Abolition of the Transatlantic Slave Trade'. *Journal of the History of International Law* 6 (2): 233–58.

Kersten, Mark. 2014. 'Justice after the War: The International Criminal Court and Post-Gaddafi Libya'. In *Transitional Justice and the Arab Spring*, edited by Kirsten J. Fisher and Robert Stewart, 188–207. Abingdon: Routledge.

Kirgis, Frederic L. 1987. 'Custom on a Sliding Scale'. *The American Journal of International Law* 81 (1): 146–51.

Kirsch, Philippe, and John T. Holmes. 1999. 'The Rome Conference on an International Criminal Court: The Negotiating Process'. *The American Journal of International Law* 93 (1): 2–12.

Klabbers, Jan. 2006. 'The Meaning of Rules'. *International Relations* 20 (3): 295–301.

Klein, Pierre. 2003. 'The Effects of US Predominance on the Elaboration of Treaty Regimes and on the Evolution of the Law of Treaties'. In *United States Hegemony and the Foundations of International Law*, 363–91. Cambridge: Cambridge University Press.

Klein, Sabine. 2010. 'Uganda and the International Criminal Court Review Conference: Some Observations of the Conference's Impact in the "Situation Country" Uganda'. *Goettingen Journal of International Law* 2 (2): 669–88.

Klotz, Audie. 1993. 'Norms Reconstituting Interests: Global Racial Equality and U.S. Sanctions against South Africa'. *International Organization* 49 (3): 451–78.

Klotz, Audie. 2009. 'Case Selection'. In *Qualitative Methods in International Relations: A Pluralist Guide*, edited by Audie Klotz and Deepa Prakash. Basingstoke: Palgrave Macmillan.

Koremenos, Barbara. 2013a. 'Institutionalism and International Law'. In *Interdisciplinary Perspectives on International Law and International Relations: The State of the Art*, edited by Jeffrey L. Dunoff and Mark A. Pollack, 59–82. Cambridge: Cambridge University Press.

Koremenos, Barbara. 2013b. 'The Continent of International Law'. *Journal of Conflict Resolution* 57 (4): 653–81.

Koremenos, Barbara, Charles Lipson, and Duncan Snidal. 2001. 'The Rational Design of International Institutions'. *International Organization* 55 (4): 761–99.

Koskenniemi, Martti. 2002. *The Gentle Civilizer of Nations: The Rise and Fall of International Law 1870–1960*. Cambridge: Cambridge University Press.

Krasner, Stephen D. 1999. *Sovereignty: Organized Hypocrisy*. Princeton, NJ: Princeton University Press.

Kratochwil, Friedrich. 2000. 'How Do Norms Matter?' In *The Role of Law in International Politics: Essays in International Relations and International Law*, edited by Michael Byers, 35–68. Oxford; New York: Oxford University Press.

Kratochwil, Friedrich. 2014. *The Status of Law in World Society: Meditations on the Role and Rule of Law*. Cambridge; New York: Cambridge University Press.

Kratochwil, Friedrich, and John Gerard Ruggie. 1986. 'International Organization: A State of the Art on an Art of the State'. *International Organization* 40 (4): 753–75.

Krause, Keith. 2002. 'Multilateral Diplomacy, Norm Building, and UN Conferences: The Case of Small Arms and Light Weapons'. *Global Governance* 8 (2): 247–63.

Krebs, Ronald R., and Patrick Thaddeus Jackson. 2007. 'Twisting Tongues and Twisting Arms: The Power of Political Rhetoric'. *European Journal of International Relations* 13 (1): 35–66.

Kress, Claus. 2004. '"Self-Referrals" and "Waivers of Complementarity" Some Considerations in Law and Policy'. *Journal of International Criminal Justice* 2 (4): 944–8.

Krisch, Nico. 2003. 'More Equal than the Rest? Hierarchy, Equality and US Predominance in International Law'. In *United States Hegemony and the Foundations of International Law*, edited by Michael Byers and Georg Nolte, 135–75. Cambridge: Cambridge University Press.

Krisch, Nico. 2005. 'International Law in Times of Hegemony: Unequal Power and the Shaping of the International Legal Order'. *European Journal of International Law* 16 (3): 369–408.

Kurki, Milja. 2006. 'Causes of a Divided Discipline: Rethinking the Concept of Cause in International Relations Theory'. *Review of International Studies* 32 (02): 189–216.

La Haye, Eve. 2008. *War Crimes in Internal Armed Conflicts*. Cambridge; New York: Cambridge University Press.

Lafontaine, Fannie. 2010. 'Canada's Crimes against Humanity and War Crimes Act on Trial: An Analysis of the Munyaneza Case'. *Journal of International Criminal Justice* 8 (1): 269–88.

Lawson, Robert J., Mark Gwozdecky, Jill Sinclair, and Ralph Lysyshyn. 1998. 'The Ottawa Process and the International Movement to Ban Anti-Personnel Mines'. In *To Walk without Fear: The Global Movement to Ban Landmines*, edited by Maxwell A. Cameron, Robert J. Lawson, and Brian J. Tomlin, 160–84. Toronto: Oxford University Press.

Lee, Joanne, and Richard Price. 2004. 'International Tribunals and the Criminalization of International Violence'. In *The United Nations and Global Security*, edited by Richard Price and Mark Zacher, 123–38. New York: Palgrave.

Lietzau, William. 2001. 'International Criminal Law after Rome: Concerns from a U.S. Military Perspective'. *Law and Contemporary Problems* 64 (1): 119–40.

Lupovici, Amir. 2009. 'Constructivist Methods: A Plea and Manifesto for Pluralism'. *Review of International Studies* 35 (1): 195–218.

Malanczuk, Peter. 2000. 'The International Criminal Court and Landmines: What Are the Consequences of Leaving the US Behind?' *European Journal of International Law* 11 (1): 77–90.

Malone, David, and Yuen Foong Khong, eds. 2003. *Unilateralism and U.S. Foreign Policy: International Perspectives*. Boulder, CO: Lynne Rienner Publishers.

Mandelbaum, Michael. 2005. *The Case for Goliath: How America Acts as the World's Government in the 21st Century*. New York: Public Affairs.

Marshall, Monty G., Ted Robert Gurr, and Keith Jaggers. 2016. 'POLITY IV Project, Political Regime Characteristics and Transitions, 1800–2015: Dataset Users' Manual'. Center for Systemic Peace. http://www.systemicpeace.org/inscr/p4manualv2015.pdf.

Martin, Lisa L. 2013. 'Against Compliance'. In *Interdisciplinary Perspectives on International Law and International Relations: The State of the Art*, 591–610. Cambridge: Cambridge University Press.

Maslen, Stuart. 2005. *Commentaries on Arms Control Treaties: The Convention on the Prohibition of the Use, Stockpiling, Production, and Transfer of Anti-Personnel Mines and on their Destruction*. 2nd ed. Vol. 1. Oxford: Oxford University Press.

Maslen, Stuart, and Peter Herby. 1998. 'An International Ban on Anti-Personnel Mines: History and Negotiation of the "Ottawa Treaty"'. *International Review of the Red Cross*, 325 (December): 693–713.

McDougall, Carrie. 2013. *The Crime of Aggression under the Rome Statute of the International Criminal Court*. Cambridge; New York: Cambridge University Press.

McKeown, Ryder. 2009. 'Norm Regress: US Revisionism and the Slow Death of the Torture Norm'. *International Relations* 23 (1): 5–25.

Mearsheimer, John J. 1994. 'The False Promise of International Institutions'. *International Security* 19 (3): 5–49.

Mégret, Frédéric. 2011. 'Too Much of a Good Thing? Implementation and the Uses of Complementarity'. In *The International Criminal Court and Complementarity: From Theory to Practice*, edited by Carsten Stahn and Mohamed M. El Zeidy, 361–90. Cambridge; New York: Cambridge University Press.

Meierhenrich, Jens, and Keiko Ko. 2009. 'How Do States Join the International Criminal Court? The Implementation of the Rome Statute in Japan'. *Journal of International Criminal Justice* 7 (2): 233–56.

Meron, Theodor. 1994. 'The Time Has Come for the United States to Ratify Geneva Protocol I'. *American Journal of International Law* 88 (4): 678–86.

Miles, Edward L., Steinar Andresen, Elaine M. Carlin, Jon Birger Skjaerseth, and Arild Underdal. 2002. *Environmental Regime Effectiveness: Confronting Theory with Evidence*. Cambridge, MA: MIT Press.

Miles, Edward L., Steinar Andresen, Elaine M. Carlin, Jon Birger Skjaerseth, Arild Underdal, and Jorgen Wettestad. 2002. 'Preface'. In *Environmental Regime Effectiveness: Confronting Theory with Evidence*, xi–xix. Cambridge, MA: MIT Press.

Mills, Kurt. 2012. '"Bashir Is Dividing Us": Africa and the International Criminal Court'. *Human Rights Quarterly* 34 (2): 404–47.

Moravcsik, Andrew. 2000. 'The Origins of Human Rights Regimes: Democratic Delegation in Postwar Europe'. *International Organization* 54 (2): 217–52.

Morgan, Matthew J. 2002. 'A New Kellogg-Briand Mentality? The Anti-Personnel Landmine Ban'. *Small Wars and Insurgencies* 13 (3): 97–110.

Morgenthau, Hans J. 1940. 'Positivism, Functionalism, and International Law'. *The American Journal of International Law* 34 (2): 260–84.

Morrow, James D. 2007. 'When Do States Follow the Laws of War?' *American Political Science Review* 101 (3): 559–72.

Moser-Puangsuwan, Yeshua. 2008. 'Outside the Treaty Not the Norm: Nonstate Armed Groups and the Landmine Ban'. In *Banning Landmines: Disarmament, Citizen Diplomacy, and Human Security*, edited by Jody Williams, Stephen D. Goose, and Mary Wareham, 163–78. Lanham, MD: Rowman & Littlefield Publishers.

Mullins, Christopher W., and Dawn L. Rothe. 2010. 'The Ability of the International Criminal Court to Deter Violations of International Criminal Law: A Theoretical Assessment'. *International Criminal Law Review* 10 (5): 771–86.

Murithi, Tim. 2010. 'The Spectre of Impunity and the Politics of the Special Tribunal in Kenya'. In *Debating International Justice in Africa: OTJR Collected Essays, 2008–2010*, 97–8. Oxford: The Centre for Socio-Legal Studies, University of Oxford.

Neumayer, Eric. 2005. 'Do International Human Rights Treaties Improve Respect for Human Rights?' *Journal of Conflict Resolution* 49 (6): 925–53.

Nooruddin, Irfan, and Autumn Lockwood Payton. 2010. 'Dynamics of Influence in International Politics: The ICC, BIAs, and Economic Sanctions'. *Journal of Peace Research* 47 (6): 711–21.

Norrlof, Carla. 2010. *America's Global Advantage: US Hegemony and International Cooperation*. Cambridge; New York: Cambridge University Press.

Nouwen, Sarah. 2011. 'Complementarity in Uganda: Domestic Diversity or International Imposition?' In *The International Criminal Court and Complementarity: From Theory to Practice*, edited by Carsten Stahn and Mohamed M. El Zeidy, 1120–54. Cambridge; New York: Cambridge University Press.

Nouwen, Sarah M. H. 2013. *Complementarity in the Line of Fire: The Catalysing Effect of the International Criminal Court in Uganda and Sudan*. Cambridge: Cambridge University Press.

Nouwen, Sarah M. H., and Wouter G. Werner. 2010. 'Doing Justice to the Political: The International Criminal Court in Uganda and Sudan'. *European Journal of International Law* 21 (4): 941–65.

Nystuen, Gro, and Stuart Casey-Maslen, eds. 2010. *The Convention on Cluster Munitions: A Commentary*. Oxford: Oxford University Press.

O'Connell, Mary Ellen. 2008. *The Power and Purpose of International Law: Insights from the Theory and Practice of Enforcement*. Oxford; New York: Oxford University Press.

Percy, Sarah. 2007a. 'Mercenaries: Strong Norm, Weak Law'. *International Organization* 61 (2): 367–97.

Percy, Sarah. 2007b. *Mercenaries: The History of a Norm in International Relations*. Oxford: Oxford University Press.

Percy, Sarah. 2012. 'Regulating the Private Security Industry: A Story of Regulating the Last War'. *International Review of the Red Cross* 94 (887): 941–60.

Pouliot, Vincent. 2007. '"Sobjectivism": Toward a Constructivist Methodology'. *International Studies Quarterly* 51 (2): 359–84.

Price, Richard. 1998. 'Reversing the Gun Sights: Transnational Civil Society Targets Land Mines'. *International Organization* 52 (3): 613–44.

Price, Richard. 2003. 'Transnational Civil Society and Advocacy in World Politics'. *World Politics* 55 (4): 579–606.

Price, Richard. 2004a. 'Emerging Customary Norms and Anti-Personnel Landmines'. In *The Politics of International Law*, edited by Christian Reus-Smit, 106–30. Cambridge: Cambridge University Press.

Price, Richard. 2004b. 'Hegemony and Multilateralism'. *International Journal* 60 (1): 129–50.

Price, Richard. 2006. 'Detecting Ideas and Their Effects'. In *The Oxford Handbook of Contextual Political Analysis*, edited by Robert E. Goodwin and Charles Tilly, 252–65. Oxford; New York: Oxford University Press.

Price, Richard. 2008. 'Moral Limit and Possibility in World Politics'. *International Organization* 62 (2): 191–220.

Price, Richard, and Nina Tannenwald. 1996. 'Norms and Deterrence: The Nuclear and Chemical Weapons Taboos'. In *The Culture of National Security*, edited by Peter J. Katzenstein, 114–52. New York: Columbia University Press.

Ralph, Jason. 2007. *Defending the Society of States: Why America Opposes the International Criminal Court and its Vision of World Society*. Oxford: Oxford University Press.

Rastan, Rod. 2009. 'The Responsibility to Enforce—Connecting Justice With Unity'. In *The Emerging Practice of the International Criminal Court*, edited by Carsten Stahn and Goran Sluiter, 163–82. Leiden: Martinus Nijhoff Publishers.

Ratner, Steven R. 2013. 'Persuading to Comply: On the Development and Avoidance of Legal Argumentation'. In *Interdisciplinary Perspectives on International Law and International Relations: The State of the Art*, edited by Jeffrey L. Dunoff and Mark A. Pollack, 568–90. Cambridge: Cambridge University Press.

Raustiala, Kal, and Anne-Marie Slaughter. 2002. 'International Law, International Relations and Compliance'. In *Handbook of International Relations*, edited by Walter Carlsneas, Thomas Risse, and Beth A. Simmons, 538–58. London: SAGE Publications.

Ray, James Lee. 1989. 'The Abolition of Slavery and the End of International War'. *International Organization* 43 (3): 405–39.

Reich, Simon, and Richard Ned Lebow. 2014. *Good-Bye Hegemony!: Power and Influence in the Global System*. Princeton, NJ: Princeton University Press.

Reus-Smit, Christian. 1997. 'The Constitutional Structure of International Society and the Nature of Fundamental Institutions'. *International Organization* 51 (4): 555–89.

Reus-Smit, Christian. 1999. *The Moral Purpose of the State: Culture, Social Identity, and Institutional Rationality in International Relations*. Princeton, NJ: Princeton University Press.

Reus-Smit, Christian. 2003. 'Politics and International Legal Obligation'. *European Journal of International Relations* 9 (4): 591–625.

Reus-Smit, Christian. 2004a. 'Introduction'. In *The Politics of International Law*, edited by Christian Reus-Smit, 1–13. Cambridge: Cambridge University Press.

Reus-Smit, Christian, ed. 2004b. *The Politics of International Law*. Cambridge: Cambridge University Press.

Reus-Smit, Christian, ed. 2004c. *The Politics of International Law*. Cambridge: Cambridge University Press.

Reus-Smit, Christian. 2004d. 'The Politics of International Law'. In *The Politics of International Law*, edited by Christian Reus-Smit, 14–44. Cambridge: Cambridge University Press.

Reus-Smit, Christian. 2011. 'Obligation through Practice'. *International Theory* 3 (2): 339–47.

Risse, Thomas. 2000. '"Let's Argue!": Communicative Action in World Politics'. *International Organization* 54 (1): 1–39.

Risse, Thomas, Stephen C. Ropp, and Kathryn Sikkink, eds. 1999. *The Power of Human Rights: International Norms and Domestic Change*. New York: Cambridge University Press.

Risse, Thomas, Stephen C. Ropp, and Kathryn Sikkink, eds. 2013. *The Persistent Power of Human Rights: From Commitment to Compliance*. Cambridge; New York: Cambridge University Press.

Roberts, Anthea. 2001. 'Traditional and Modern Approaches to Customary International Law: A Reconciliation'. *American Journal of International Law* 95 (4): 757–91.

Ruggie, John Gerard, ed. 1993. *Multilateralism Matters: The Theory and Praxis of an Institutional Form*. New York: Columbia University Press.

Ruggie, John Gerard, ed. 1998. 'What Makes the World Hang Together? Neo-Utilitarianism and the Social Constructivist Challenge'. *International Organization* 52 (4): 855–85.

Rutherford, Kenneth. 1999. 'The Hague and Ottawa Conventions a Model for Future Weapon Ban Regimes?' *The Nonproliferation Review* 6 (3): 36–50.

Rutherford, Kenneth. 2009. 'The Anti-Personnel Landmine Ban Convention: A Non-Hegemonic Regime'. In *Cooperating without America: Theories and Case Studies of Non-Hegemonic Regimes*, edited by Stefan Brem and Kendall Stiles, 123–46. New York: Routledge.

Sandholtz, Wayne. 2007. *Prohibiting Plunder: How Norms Change*. New York: Oxford University Press.

Sandholtz, Wayne, and Kendall Stiles. 2008. *International Norms and Cycles of Change*. New York: Oxford University Press.

Sandler, Todd. 2004. *Global Collective Action*. Cambridge; New York: Cambridge University Press.

Schabas, William. 2004. 'United States Hostility to the International Criminal Court: It's All about the Security Council'. *European Journal of International Law* 15 (4): 701–20.

Schabas, William. 2010. *The International Criminal Court: A Commentary on the Rome Statute*. Oxford: Oxford University Press.

Schabas, William. 2011. 'The Rise and Fall of Complementarity'. In *The International Criminal Court and Complementarity: From Theory to Practice*, edited by Carsten Stahn and Mohamed M. El Zeidy, 150–64. Cambridge; New York: Cambridge University Press.

Scheffer, David. 1999a. 'The United States and the International Criminal Court'. *The American Journal of International Law* 93 (1): 12–22.

Scheffer, David. 2005. 'Article 98(2) of the Rome Statute: America's Original Intent'. *Journal of International Criminal Justice* 3 (2): 333–53.

Schiff, Benjamin N. 2008. *Building the International Criminal Court*. New York: Cambridge University Press.

Schimmelfennig, Frank. 2001. 'The Community Trap: Liberal Norms, Rhetorical Action, and the Eastern Enlargement of the European Union'. *International Organization* 55 (1): 47–80.

Schimmelfennig, Frank. 2005. 'Strategic Calculation and International Socialization: Membership Incentives, Party Constellations, and Sustained Compliance in Central and Eastern Europe'. *International Organization* 59 (04): 827–60.

Schneider, Christina J., and Johannes Urpelainen. 2013. 'Distributional Conflict between Powerful States and International Treaty Ratification'. *International Studies Quarterly* 57 (1): 13–27.

Schroeder, Michael Bluman, and Alana Tiemessen. 2014. 'Transnational Advocacy and Accountability: From Declarations of Anti-Impunity to Implementing the Rome Statute'. In *Implementation and World Politics: How International Norms Change Practice*, edited by Alexander Betts and Phil Orchard, 50–67. Oxford: Oxford University Press.

Scott, Shirley V. 1994. 'International Law as Ideology: Theorizing the Relationship between International Law and International Politics'. *European Journal of International Law* 5 (1): 313–25.

Scott, Shirley V., and Olivia Ambler. 2007. 'Does Legality Really Matter? Accounting for the Decline in US Foreign Policy Legitimacy Following the 2003 Invasion of Iraq'. *European Journal of International Relations* 13 (1): 67–87.

Sewall, Sarah B, and Carl Kaysen, eds. 2000. *The United States and the International Criminal Court: National Security and International Law*. Lanham, MD: Rowman & Littlefield Publishers.

Seymour, Lee J. M. 2014. 'Let's Bullshit! Arguing, Bargaining and Dissembling over Darfur'. *European Journal of International Relations* 20 (3): 571–95.

Shklar, Judith N. 1964. *Legalism: Law, Morals, and Political Trials*. Cambridge, MA: Harvard University Press.

Sikkink, Kathryn. 2008. 'The Role of Consequences, Comparison and Counterfactuals in Constructivist Ethical Thought'. In *Moral Limit and Possibility in World Politics*, edited by Richard Price, 83–111. Cambridge; New York: Cambridge University Press.

Sikkink, Kathryn. 2011. *The Justice Cascade: How Human Rights Prosecutions Are Changing World Politics*. New York: W. W. Norton & Company.

Sikkink, Kathryn, and Hun Joon Kim. 2013. 'The Justice Cascade: The Origins and Effectiveness of Prosecutions of Human Rights Violations'. *Annual Review of Law and Social Science* 9 (1): 269–85.

Simmons, Beth. 1998. 'Compliance with International Agreements'. *Annual Review of Political Science* 1 (1): 75–93.

Simmons, Beth. 2010. 'Treaty Compliance and Violation'. *Annual Review of Political Science* 13 (1): 273–96.

Simmons, Beth A., and Allison Danner. 2010. 'Credible Commitments and the International Criminal Court'. *International Organization* 64 (2): 225–56.

Simmons, Beth A., and Daniel J. Hopkins. 2005. 'The Constraining Power of International Treaties: Theory and Methods'. *American Political Science Review* 99 (4): 623–31.

Simpson, Gerry J. 2004. *Great Powers and Outlaw States: Unequal Sovereigns in the International Legal Order*. Cambridge; New York: Cambridge University Press.

Sinclair, Adriana. 2010. *International Relations Theory and International Law: A Critical Approach*. Cambridge: Cambridge University Press.

Slaughter, Anne-Marie, Andrew S. Tulumello, and Stepan Wood. 1998. 'International Law and International Relations Theory: A New Generation of Interdisciplinary Scholarship'. *The American Journal of International Law* 92 (3): 367–97.

Smidt, Michael L. 2001. 'The International Criminal Court: An Effective Means of Deterrence?' *Military Law Review* 167: 156–240.

Smith-Cannoy, Heather. 2012. *Insincere Commitments: Human Rights Treaties, Abusive States, and Citizen Activism*. Washington, DC: Georgetown University Press.

Snyder, Jack, and Leslie Vinjamuri. 2004. 'Trials and Errors: Principle and Pragmatism in Strategies of International Justice'. *International Security* 28 (3): 5–44.

Spiro, Peter J. 2013. 'Nongovernmental Organizations in International Relations (Theory)'. In *Interdisciplinary Perspectives on International Law and International Relations: The State of the Art*, edited by Jeffrey L. Dunoff and Mark A. Pollack, 223–43. Cambridge: Cambridge University Press.

Stahn, Carsten, ed. 2015. *The Law and Practice of the International Criminal Court*. Oxford; New York: Oxford University Press.

Stahn, Carsten, and Mohamed M. El Zeidy, eds. 2011. *The International Criminal Court and Complementarity: From Theory to Practice*. Cambridge; New York: Cambridge University Press.

Steinberg, Richard H. 2013. 'Wanted—Dead or Alive: Realism in International Law'. In *Interdisciplinary Perspectives on International Law and International Relations: The State of the Art*, edited by Jeffrey L. Dunoff and Mark A. Pollack, 146–72. Cambridge: Cambridge University Press.

Stiles, Kendall. 2009. 'Introduction: Theories of Non-Hegemonic Cooperation'. In *Cooperating without America: Theories and Case Studies of Non-Hegemonic Regimes*, edited by Stefan Brem and Kendall Stiles, 1–20. New York: Routledge.

Stone, Lee. 2011. 'Implementation of the Rome Statute of the International Criminal Court in South Africa'. In *Prosecuting International Crimes in Africa*, edited by Chacha Murungu and Japhet Biegon, 305–30. Pretoria, South Africa: Pretoria University Press.

Struett, Michael J. 2008. *The Politics of Constructing the International Criminal Court: NGOs, Discourse, and Agency*. New York: Palgrave Macmillan.

Sylvan, David, and Stephen Majeski. 1998. 'A Methodology for the Study of Historical Counterfactuals'. *International Studies Quarterly* 42 (1): 79–108.

Tams, Christian J. 2007. 'Enforcement'. In *Making Treaties Work: Human Rights, Environment and Arms Control*, edited by Geir Ulfstein, 391–409. Cambridge: Cambridge University Press.

Tannenwald, Nina. 1999. 'The Nuclear Taboo: The United States and the Normative Basis of Nuclear Non-Use'. *International Organization* 53 (3): 433–68.

Tepe, Daniela. 2011. *The Myth about Global Civil Society: Domestic Politics to Ban Landmines*. New York: Palgrave Macmillan.

Terracino, Julio Bacio. 2007. 'National Implementation of ICC Crimes: Impact on National Jurisdictions and the ICC'. *Journal of International Criminal Justice* 5 (2): 421–40.

Thomas, Ward. 2000. 'Norms and Security: The Case of International Assassination'. *International Security* 25 (1): 105–33.

Thomas, Ward. 2001. *The Ethics of Destruction: Norms and Force in International Relations*. Ithaca, NY: Cornell University Press.

Thompson, Alexander. 2006. 'Coercion through IOs: The Security Council and the Logic of Information Transmission'. *International Organization* 60 (1): 1–34.

Thompson, Alexander. 2013. 'Coercive Enforcement of International Law'. In *Interdisciplinary Perspectives on International Law and International Relations: The State of the Art*, edited by Jeffrey L. Dunoff and Mark A. Pollack, 502–23. Cambridge: Cambridge University Press.

Tiemessen, Alana. 2014. 'The International Criminal Court and the Politics of Prosecutions'. *The International Journal of Human Rights* 18 (4–5): 444–61.

Tomlin, Brian W. 1998. 'On a Fast-Track to a Ban: The Canadian Policy Process'. In *To Walk without Fear: The Global Movement to Ban Landmines*, edited by Maxwell A. Cameron, Robert J. Lawson, and Brian W. Tomlin, 185–211. Toronto: Oxford University Press.

Vagts, Detlev F. 2001. 'Hegemonic International Law'. *American Journal of International Law* 95 (4): 843–8.

Vines, Alex. 1998. 'The Crisis of Anti-Personnel Mines'. In *To Walk without Fear: The Global Movement to Ban Landmines*, edited by Maxwell A. Cameron, Robert J. Lawson, and Brian W. Tomlin, 118–35. Toronto; Oxford: Oxford University Press.

Vinson, Nigel. 1998. 'The Demise of the Anti-Personnel Mine: A Military Perspective'. *The RUSI Journal* 143 (1): 18–23.

von Stein, Jana. 2005. 'Do Treaties Constrain or Screen? Selection Bias and Treaty Compliance'. *American Political Science Review* 99 (4): 611–22.

Wareham, Mary. 1998. 'Rhetoric and Policy Realities in the United States'. In *To Walk without Fear: The Global Movement to Ban Landmines*, 212–47. Toronto; Oxford: Oxford University Press.

Wareham, Mary. 2008. 'Evidence-Based Advocacy: Civil Society Monitoring of the Mine Ban Treaty'. In *Banning Landmines: Disarmament, Citizen Diplomacy, and Human Security*, edited by Jody Williams, Stephen D. Goose, and Mary Wareham, 49–67. Lanham, MD: Rowman & Littlefield Publishers.

Warmington, Valerie, and Celina Tuttle. 1998. 'The Canadian Campaign'. In *To Walk without Fear: The Global Movement to Ban Landmines*, edited by Maxwell A. Cameron, Robert J. Lawson, and Brian W. Tomlin, 48–59. Toronto; Oxford: Oxford University Press.

Wedgwood, Ruth. 1999. 'The International Criminal Court: An American View'. *European Journal of International Law* 10 (1): 93–107.

Wendt, Alexander. 1992. 'Anarchy Is What States Make of It: The Social Construction of Power Politics'. *International Organization* 46 (2): 391–425.

Wendt, Alexander. 1998. 'On Constitution and Causation in International Relations'. *Review of International Studies* 24 (5): 101–18.

Wendt, Alexander. 1999. *Social Theory of International Politics*. Cambridge; New York: Cambridge University Press.

Wendt, Alexander. 2001. 'Driving with the Rearview Mirror: On the Rational Science of Institutional Design'. *International Organization* 55 (4): 1019–49.

Wiener, Antje. 2004. 'Contested Compliance: Interventions on the Normative Structure of World Politics'. *European Journal of International Relations* 10 (2): 189–234.

Wiener, Antje. 2008. *The Invisible Constitution of Politics: Contested Norms and International Encounters*. Cambridge: Cambridge University Press.

Wiener, Antje, and Uwe Puetter. 2009. 'The Quality of Norms Is What Actors Make of It: Critical Constructivist Research on Norms'. *Journal of International Law and International Relations* 5 (1): 1–16.

Wiesbord, Noah. 2013. 'Bargaining Practices: Negotiating the Kampala Compromise for the International Criminal Court'. *Law and Contemporary Problems* 76 (3–4): 85–117.

Wight, Martin. 2004. *Power Politics*. Edited by Hedley Bull and Carsten Holbraad. New York; London: Continuum: Royal Institute of International Affairs.

Williams, Jody, and Stephen D. Goose. 1998. 'The International Campaign to Ban Landmines'. In *To Walk without Fear: The Global Movement to Ban Landmines*, edited by Maxwell A. Cameron, Robert J. Lawson, and Brian W. Tomlin, 20–47. Toronto: Oxford University Press.

Wippman, David. 2004. 'The International Criminal Court'. In *The Politics of International Law*, edited by Christian Reus-Smit, 151–88. Cambridge: Cambridge University Press.

Wippman, David. 2006. 'Exaggerating the ICC'. In *Bringing Power to Justice? The Prospects of the International Criminal Court*, edited by Joanna Harrington, Michael Milde, and Richard Vernon, 99–140. Montreal and Kingston: McGill-Queen's University Press.

Wisotzki, Simone. 2009. 'Negotiating with a Reluctant Hegemon: The Case of the Small Arms and Light Weapons Regime'. In *Cooperating without America: Theories and Case Studies of Non-Hegemonic Regimes*, 21–43. New York: Routledge.

Wohlforth, William C. 2012. 'US Leadership and the Limits of International Institutional Change'. *International Journal* 62 (2): 415–21.

Zidar, Andraz, and Olympia Bekou, eds. 2014. *Contemporary Challenges for the International Criminal Court*. London: British Institute of International and Comparative Law.

Zürn, Michael, and Jeffrey T. Checkel. 2005. 'Getting Socialized to Build Bridges: Constructivism and Rationalism, Europe and the Nation-State'. *International Organization* 59 (04): 1045–79.

Policy Sources (NGO, Governmental, Intergovernmental, and News Reports)

Acheson, Ray, Thomas Nash, and Richard Moyes. 2014. 'A Treaty Banning Nuclear Weapons: Developing a Legal Framework for the Prohibition and Elimination of Nuclear Weapons'. London; New York: Article 36 and Reaching Critical Will. http://www.article36.org/wp-content/uploads/2014/04/AR06_TREATY_REPORT_27.4.14.pdf.

African Union. 2008. 'Speech Delivered by H. E. Mr. Jakaya Mrisho Kikwete, President of the United Republic of Tanzania, on Behalf of the African Union'. Presented at the United Nations General Assembly, 63rd Session, General Debate, New York, 23 September. http://www.un.org/ga/63/generaldebate/pdf/tanzania_en.pdf.

African Union. 2012. 'Press Release No. 002/2012: On the Decisions of Pre-Trial Chamber I of the International Criminal Court (ICC) Pursuant to Article 87(7) of the Rome Statute on the Alleged Failure by the Republic of Chad and the Republic of Malawi to Comply with the Cooperation Requests Issued by the Court with Respect to the Arrest and Surrender of President Omar Hassan Al Bashir of the Republic of Sudan'. https://www.issafrica.org/anicj/uploads/Decisions_of_Pre-Trial_Chamber_I_of_the_ICC.pdf.

African Union Peace and Security Council. 2008. 'Communiqué of the 142nd Meeting of the Peace and Security Council'. Addis Ababa, Ethiopia: African Union. http://www.peaceau.org/en/article/communique-of-the-142nd-meeting-of-the-peace-and-security-council.

American Non-Governmental Organizations Coalition for the International Criminal Court. 2015a. 'Countries Concluding Bilateral Immunity Agreements'. http://www.amicc.org/usicc/bialist.

American Non-Governmental Organizations Coalition for the International Criminal Court. 2015b. 'Reaction to BIAs'. http://www.amicc.org/usicc/biareaction.

Amnesty International. 2008. 'Germany: End Impunity through Universal Jurisdiction'. EUR 23/003/2008. London: Amnesty International. http://www.amnesty.org/en/library/info/EUR23/003/2008/en.

Amnesty International. 2010. 'International Criminal Court: Updated Checklist for Effective Implementation'. IOR 53/009/2010. London: Amnesty International. http://www.amnesty.org/en/library/info/IOR53/009/2010/en.

Amnesty International. 2012. 'Letter from African Civil Society Organizations to Justice Ministers and Attorneys General from African States Parties to the International Criminal Court (AFR 01/007/2012)'. 3 May. http://www.amnesty.org/en/library/info/AFR01/007/2012/en.

Anthony, Ian, and Chris Holland. 2014. 'The Governance of Autonomous Weapons'. In *SIPRI Yearbook 2014: Armaments, Disarmament and International Security*, 423–31. Stockholm; Oxford: Stockholm International Peace Research Institute; Oxford University Press.

Anyoli, Edward. 2010. 'Former LRA Commander Sent to War Court Monday'. *New Vision*, 6 September. http://www.newvision.co.ug/new_vision/news/1283299/lra-commander-sent-war-court.

Appeals Chamber, International Criminal Court. 2011. 'Decision on the Admissibility of the "Appeal of the Government of Kenya against the Decision on the Request for Assistance Submitted on Behalf of the Government of the Republic of Kenya Pursuant to Article 93(10) of the Statute and Rule 194 of the Rules of Procedure and Evidence"'. ICC-01/09-78. The Hague, Netherlands: International Criminal Court. https://www.icc-cpi.int/CourtRecords/CR2011_12079.PDF.

Arab Republic of Egypt. 2010. 'Explanation of Vote on L.8: "Anti-Personnel Land Mines Convention"'. Presented at the United Nations General Assembly First Committee, 65th Session, New York, 28 October. http://reachingcriticalwill.org/images/documents/Disarmament-fora/1com/1com10/eov/L8_Egypt.pdf.

Assembly of States Parties. 2006. *Strengthening the International Criminal Court and the Assembly of States Parties, Annex I: Plan of Action of the Assembly of States Parties for Achieving Universality and Full Implementation of the Rome Statute of the International Criminal Court*. ICC-ASP/5/Res.3. The Hague: International Criminal Court. https://asp.icc-cpi.int/iccdocs/asp_docs/Resolutions/ICC-ASP-ASP5-Res-03-ENG.pdf.

Assembly of States Parties. 2007a. 'Report of the Bureau on Cooperation'. ICC-ASP/6/21. New York: International Criminal Court. https://asp.icc-cpi.int/iccdocs/asp_docs/library/asp/ICC-ASP-6-21_English.pdf.

Assembly of States Parties. 2007b. 'Strengthening the International Criminal Court and the Assembly of States Parties'. Resolution ICC-ASP/6/Res.2. New York: Assembly of States Parties to the International Criminal Court. https://asp.icc-cpi.int/iccdocs/asp_docs/Resolutions/ICC-ASP-ASP6-Res-02-ENG.pdf.

Assembly of States Parties. 2009. 'Report of the Court on International Cooperation and Assistance, Annex I to the Report of the Bureau on Cooperation'. ICC-ASP/8/44. The Hague, Netherlands: International Criminal Court. http://asp.icc-cpi.int/iccdocs/asp_docs/ASP8/ICC-ASP-8-44-ENG.pdf.

Assembly of States Parties. 2010a. *Kampala Declaration*. http://asp.icc-cpi.int/iccdocs/asp_docs/RC2010/RC-4-ENG.pdf.

Assembly of States Parties. 2010b. 'RC/Res.6: The Crime of Aggression'. Assembly of States Parties to the Rome Statute of the International Criminal Court. http://asp.icc-cpi.int/iccdocs/asp_docs/Resolutions/RC-Res.6-ENG.pdf.

Assembly of States Parties. 2011. *Cooperation*. http://asp.icc-cpi.int/iccdocs/asp_docs/ASP10/Resolutions/ICC-ASP-10-Res.2-ENG.pdf.

Assembly of States Parties. 2013a. 'Report of the Bureau on Non-Cooperation'. ICC-ASP/12/34. The Hague, Netherlands: International Criminal Court. http://asp.icc-cpi.int/iccdocs/asp_docs/ASP12/ICC-ASP-12-34-ENG.pdf.

Assembly of States Parties. 2013b. 'Amendments to the Rules of Procedure and Evidence'. Resolution ICC-ASP/12/Res.7. The Hague, Netherlands: International Criminal Court. http://asp.icc-cpi.int/iccdocs/asp_docs/Resolutions/ASP12/ICC-ASP-12-Res7-ENG.pdf.

Assembly of States Parties. 2014a. 'Report of the Bureau on Non-Cooperation'. ICC-ASP/13/40. New York: International Criminal Court. https://asp.icc-cpi.int/iccdocs/asp_docs/ASP13/ICC-ASP-13-40-ENG.pdf.

Assembly of States Parties. 2014b. 'Resolution on Cooperation'. ICC-ASP/13/Res.3. New York: International Criminal Court. http://asp.icc-cpi.int/iccdocs/asp_docs/Resolutions/ASP13/ICC-ASP-13-Res3-ENG.pdf.

Assembly of States Parties. 2015a. 'Press Release: The President of the Assembly Calls on States Parties to Fulfill Their Obligations to Execute the Arrest Warrants against Mr. Al Bashir'. International Criminal Court. https://www.icc-cpi.int/en_menus/icc/press%20and%20media/press%20releases/Pages/pr1117.aspx.

Assembly of States Parties. 2015b. 'ICC-ASP/14/Res.2: Resolution on Article 124'. https://asp.icc-cpi.int/iccdocs/asp_docs/Resolutions/ASP14/ICC-ASP-14-Res2-ENG.pdf.

Assembly of the African Union. 2009. 'Decision on the Meeting of African States Parties to the Rome Statute of the International Criminal Court (ICC)'. Assembly/AU/Dec.245(XIII) Rev.1. Sitre, Libya: African Union Thirteenth Ordinary Session. http://www.au.int/en/sites/default/files/decisions/9560-assembly_en_1_3_july_2009_auc_thirteenth_ordinary_session_decisions_declarations_message_congratulations_motion_0.pdf.

Assembly of the African Union. 2011a. 'Decision on the Implementation of the Decisions of the International Criminal Court'. EX.CL/639(XVIII). Addis Ababa, Ethiopia: African Union Sixteenth Ordinary Session. http://www.au.int/en/sites/

default/files/decisions/9645-assembly_en_30_31_january_2011_auc_assembly_africa.pdf.

Assembly of the African Union. 2011b. 'Decision on the Implementation of the Assembly Decisions on the International Criminal Court'. Assembly/AU/Dec.366(XVII). Malabo, Equatorial Guinea: African Union Seventeenth Ordinary Session. http://www.au.int/en/sites/default/files/decisions/9647-assembly_au_dec_363-390_xvii_e.pdf.

Assembly of the African Union. 2012. 'Decision on the Progress Report of the Commission on the Implementation of the Assembly Decisions on the International Criminal Court (ICC)—Doc. EX.CL/710(XX)'. Assembly/AU/Dec.397(XVIII). Addis Ababa, Ethiopia: African Union Eighteenth Ordinary Session. http://www.au.int/en/sites/default/files/decisions/9649-assembly_au_dec_391_-_415_xviii_e.pdf.

Assembly of the African Union. 2013. 'Decision on Africa's Relationship with the International Criminal Court (ICC)'. Ext/Assembly/AU/Dec.1. Addis Ababa, Ethiopia: Extraordinary Session of the Assembly of the African Union. http://www.au.int/en/sites/default/files/decisions/9655-ext_assembly_au_dec_decl_e_0.pdf.

Assembly of the African Union. 2014. 'Decision on the Progress Report of the Commission on the Implementation of the Decisions of the International Criminal Court'. Assembly/AU/13(XXII). Addis Ababa, Ethiopia: African Union Twenty-Second Ordinary Session. http://www.au.int/en/sites/default/files/decisions/9659-assembly_au_dec_490-516_xxii_e.pdf.

Assembly of the African Union. 2016. 'Decision on the International Criminal Court—Doc. EX.CL/952(XXVIII)'. Assembly/AU/Dec.590(XXVI). Addis Ababa, Ethiopia: African Union Twenty-Sixth Ordinary Session. http://www.au.int/en/sites/default/files/decisions/29514-assembly_au_dec_588_-_604_xxvi_e.pdf.

Avocats Sans Frontières. 2009. 'The Application of the Rome Statute of the International Criminal Court by the Courts of the Democratic Republic of Congo'. Brussels: Avocats Sans Frontières. http://www.asf.be/wp-content/publications/ASF_CaseStudy_RomeStatute_Light_PagePerPage.pdf.

BBC News. 2014a. 'Russia and China Veto UN Move to Refer Syria to ICC'. *BBC News*. 22 May. http://www.bbc.co.uk/news/world-middle-east-27514256.

BBC News. 2014b. 'ICC Halts Darfur War Crime Inquiries'. *BBC News*, 12 December, sec. Africa. http://www.bbc.co.uk/news/world-africa-30458347.

BBC News. 2015. 'South Africa Criticised over Sudan's Omar Al-Bashir's Exit'. *BBC News*. http://www.bbc.co.uk/news/world-africa-33254003.

Bellinger, John B. 2008. 'The United States and the International Criminal Court: Where We've Been and Where We're Going'. Presented at the Remarks to the DePaul University College of Law, Chicago, IL, 25 April. http://2001-2009.state.gov/s/l/rls/104053.htm.

Bolton, John R. 2002. 'International Criminal Court: Letter to UN Secretary General Kofi Annan'. Department of State, United States of America. http://2001-2009.state.gov/r/pa/prs/ps/2002/9968.htm.

Bolton, John R. 2002. 'The United States and the International Criminal Court'. Presented at the Remarks to the Federalist Society, Washington, DC, 14 November. http://2001-2009.state.gov/t/us/rm/15158.htm.

Bosnia and Herzegovina. 1997. 'Statement by Bosnia and Herzegovina'. Presented at the Ottawa Convention Signing Conference, Ottawa, 4 December.

Bosnia and Herzegovina. 2002. 'Statement by Mr. Kusljugić'. S/PV.4568 presented at the United Nations Security Council, 57th year, 4568th Meeting. Agenda Item: The Situation in Bosnia and Herzegovina, New York, 10 July. http://www.un.org/en/sc/meetings/records/2002.shtml.

British Broadcasting Corporation. 2008. 'Uganda Sets up War Crimes Court'. *BBC*, 26 May, sec. Africa. http://news.bbc.co.uk/1/hi/world/africa/7420461.stm.

British Broadcasting Corporation. 2015. 'LRA Commander "to Be Sent to ICC"'. *BBC*, 13 January, sec. Africa. http://www.bbc.co.uk/news/world-africa-30796241.

Canada. 2002. 'Statement by Mr. Heinbecker'. Presented at the United Nations Security Council, 57th year, 4568th meeting. Agenda Item: The Situation in Bosnia and Herzegovina (S/PV.4568), New York, 10 July. http://www.un.org/en/ga/search/view_doc.asp?symbol=S/PV.4568.

Canada. 2009. 'Canadian Statement: Stockpile Destruction—Compliance'. Presented at the Second Review Conference of the Antipersonnel Mine Ban Convention (Cartagena Summit on a Mine-Free World), Cartagena, Colombia, 2 December. http://www.cartagenasummit.org/daily-summaries-and-statements/day-4-wednesday-2-december/.

Canada. 2012. 'Canada Remembers Victims and Condemns Repression on the Anniversary of Syrian Uprising'. Foreign Affairs, Trade and Development. http://www.international.gc.ca/media/aff/news-communiques/2012/03/15a.aspx?lang=eng&view=d.

Canada. 2013. 'Canada's Statement on Compliance'. Presented at the Intersessional Standing Committee Meeting of the Antipersonnel Mine Ban Convention, Geneva, 27 May. http://www.apminebanconvention.org/fileadmin/APMBC/IWP/SC-may13/Speeches-GS/4_COMPLIANCE_-_Canada.pdf.

Canadian Centre for International Justice. 2016. 'Jacques Mungwarere (Rwanda)'. http://www.ccij.ca/cases/mungwarere/.

Central African Republic. 2010. 'Déclaration de La République Centrafricaine à l'occasion de la Conférence de Révision du Statut de Rome de la Cour pénale internationale'. Presented at the First Review Conference of the Rome Statute of the International Criminal Court, Kampala, Uganda, 31 May. https://asp.icc-cpi.int/iccdocs/asp_docs/RC2010/Statements/ICC-RC-gendeba-CAR-FRA.pdf.

Central African Republic. 2014. 'Referral to the ICC Prosecutor for Crimes Allegedly Committed Since 2012'. http://www.icc-cpi.int/iccdocs/otp/2014-05-30-CAR-referral.pdf.

Clinton, William J. 1997. 'Remarks by the President on Land Mines'. Office of the White House Press Secretary, The Roosevelt Room, White House, Washington DC, 17 September. http://www.fas.org/asmp/resources/govern/withdrawal91797.html.

Cluster Munition Coalition. 2014a. 'Cluster Munition Monitor 2014'. Geneva: ICBL-CMC. http://the-monitor.org/index.php/LM/Our-Research-Products/CMM14.

Cluster Munition Coalition. 2014b. 'Australia: Cluster Munition Ban Policy'. 23 August. http://www.the-monitor.org/index.php/cp/display/region_profiles/theme/3246.

Cluster Munition Coalition. 2014c. 'Canada: Cluster Munition Ban Policy'. 26 August. http://www.the-monitor.org/index.php/cp/display/region_profiles/theme/3327.

Cluster Munition Coalition. 2014d. 'United States: Cluster Munition Ban Policy'. 27 August. http://www.the-monitor.org/index.php/cp/display/region_profiles/theme/3974.

Cluster Munition Coalition. 2015. 'Cluster Munition Monitor 2015'. Geneva: ICBL-CMC. http://www.the-monitor.org/en-gb/reports/2015/cluster-munition-monitor-2015.aspx.

Coalition for the International Criminal Court. 2002. 'International Criminal Court Monitor'. 21. New York: CICC. http://www.coalitionfortheicc.org/documents/monitor21.200106.english.pdf.

Coalition for the International Criminal Court. 2004. 'Compilation of Documents on UN Security Council Resolutions 1422/1487'. New York. http://www.iccnow.org/documents/1422DocumentCompilation.pdf.

Coalition for the International Criminal Court. 2006a. 'Summary of Information on Bilateral Immunity Agreements (BIAs) or So-Called "Article 98" Agreements'. http://www.coalitionfortheicc.org/documents/BIAdb_Current.pdf.

Coalition for the International Criminal Court. 2006b. 'Quotes from High Officials Opposing the US Campaign for Bilateral Immunity Agreements'. http://coalitionfortheicc.org/?mod=bia.

Coalition for the International Criminal Court. 2006c. 'Comments by US Officials on the Negative Impact of Bilateral Immunity Agreements (BIAs) and The American Servicemembers' Protection Act (ASPA)'. http://coalitionfortheicc.org/documents/CICCFS-CommentsUSOfficials_BIA-ASPA_current.pdf.

Coalition for the International Criminal Court. 2006d. 'Countries Opposed to Signing a US Bilateral Immunity Agreement (BIA): US Aid Lost in FY04 & FY05 and Threatened in FY06'. http://coalitionfortheicc.org/?mod=bia.

Coalition for the International Criminal Court. 2006e. 'Status of US Bilateral Immunity Agreements (BIAs)'. http://www.coalitionfortheicc.org/documents/CICCFS_BIAstatus_current.pdf.

Coalition for the International Criminal Court. 2008. 'The Serbian Coalition: Advocating for the ICC after Karadžic's Arrest.' In *The Monitor No. 37*. New York: CICC. http://www.coalitionfortheicc.org/documents/monitor37_english.pdf.

Coalition for the International Criminal Court. 2012. 'Chart on the Status of Ratification and Implementation of the Rome Statute and the Agreement on Privileges and Immunities (APIC)'. http://www.coalitionfortheicc.org/documents/Global_Ratificationimplementation_chart_May2012.pdf.

Committee on Alternative Technologies to Replace Antipersonnel Landmines. 2001. 'Alternative Technologies to Replace Antipersonnel Landmines'. Washington, DC: National Research Council, National Academy of Sciences. http://www.nap.edu/catalog/10071/alternative-technologies-to-replace-antipersonnel-landmines.

Council of the European Union. 2001. 'Council Common Position on the International Criminal Court'. http://data.consilium.europa.eu/doc/document/ST-9362-2001-INIT/en/pdf.

Cullinane, Susannah. 2015. 'Ukraine to Ask Hague to Probe "Crimes against Humanity"'. *CNN International*. 26 January. http://www.cnn.com/2015/01/26/europe/ukraine-crisis/index.html.

Democratic Republic of the Congo. 2008. 'Allocution de son excellence, monsieur Emmanuel Luzolo Bambi Lessa, ministre de la justice'. Presented at the Seventh Assembly of States Parties to the Rome Statute of the International Criminal Court, The Hague, Netherlands, 14 November. https://asp.icc-cpi.int/iccdocs/asp_docs/library/asp/ICC-ASP-ASP7-GenDebe-DRC-FRA.pdf.

Democratic Republic of the Congo. 2013. 'Intervention de Monsieur Zénon Mukongo Ngay, Ministre Conseiller et Conseiller Juridique'. Presented at the Twelfth Assembly of States Parties of the Rome Statute of the International Criminal Court, The Hague, Netherlands, 21 November. https://asp.icc-cpi.int/iccdocs/asp_docs/ASP12/GenDeba/ICC-ASP12-GenDeba-DRC-FRA.pdf.

Democratic Socialist Republic of Sri Lanka. 1999. 'Statement by Sri Lanka'. Presented at the First Meeting of the States Parties to the Antipersonnel Mine Ban Convention, Maputo, Mozambique, 3 May.

Democratic Socialist Republic of Sri Lanka. 2004. 'Statement by Sri Lanka'. Presented at the First Review Conference of the Antipersonnel Mine Ban Convention (Nairobi Summit on a Mine-Free World), Nairobi, Kenya, 2 December. http://www.nairobisummit.org/fileadmin/APMBC-RC1/high_level/Sri_Lanka_HLS_RC2004_en.pdf.

Department of State, United States of America. 1998. 'Hidden Killers: The Global Landmine Crisis'. Washington, DC: Bureau of Political-Military Affairs, Office of Humanitarian Demining Programs. http://www.state.gov/www/global/arms/rpt_9809_demine_toc.html.

Department of State, United States of America. 2002. '"On-the-Record" Briefing with the Ambassador-at-Large for War Crimes Pierre-Richard Prosper'. Embassy of the United States of America, London, 20 September. http://www.amicc.org/docs/Prosper9_20_02.pdf.

Department of State, United States of America. 2004a. 'Fact Sheet: New United States Policy on Landmines: Reducing Humanitarian Risk and Saving Lives of United States Soldiers'. Washington, DC: Department of State. http://www.fas.org/asmp/campaigns/landmines/FactSheet_NewUSPolicy_2-27-04.htm.

Department of State, United States of America. 2004b. 'On-the-Record Briefing by Lincoln P. Bloomfield, Jr., Assistant Secretary of State for Political-Military Affairs'. Washington, DC, 27 February. http://2001-2009.state.gov/r/pa/ei/speeches/2004/.

Department of State, United States of America. 2004c. 'Daily Press Briefing by Richard Boucher, Spokesman'. Washington, DC, 23 June. http://www.amicc.org/docs/BoucherJune23_04.pdf.

Department of State, United States of America. 2004d. 'Testimony of Secretary of State Colin L. Powell'. Presented at the Senate Foreign Relations Committee, Washington, DC, 9 September.

Department of State, United States of America. 2010. 'U.S. Engagement with the ICC and the Outcome of the Recently Concluded Review Conference. Special Briefing by Harold Hongju Koh, Legal Advisor U.S. Department of State and Stephen J. Rapp, Ambassador-at-Large for War Crimes Issues'. Washington, DC, 15 June. http://www.state.gov/j/gcj/us_releases/remarks/2010/143178.htm.

Department of State, United States of America. 2012. 'Daily Press Briefing by Victoria Nuland, Spokesperson'. Washington, DC, 13 March. http://www.state.gov/r/pa/prs/dpb/2012/03/185696.htm.

Department of State, United States of America. 2014. 'Daily Press Briefing with Marie Harf'. http://www.state.gov/r/pa/prs/dpb/2014/06/228539.htm#MISCELLANEOUS.

DiCicco, Lucia. 2009. 'The Non-Renewal of the "Nethercutt Amendment" and its Impact on the Bilateral Immunity Agreement (BIA) Campaign'. The American

Non-Governmental Organizations Coalition for the International Criminal Court. http://www.amicc.org/docs/Nethercutt2009.pdf.

Diplomatic Conference for the Adoption of a Convention on Cluster Munitions. 2008. *Convention on Cluster Munitions*. http://clusterconvention.org/files/2011/01/Convention-ENG.pdf#page=2.

Drawbaugh, Kevin. 2007. 'U.S. Senate Panel Backs Law of the Sea Treaty'. *Reuters*, 31 October. http://www.reuters.com/article/idUSN31335584.

Duggal, Sneh. 2012. 'War Crimes Program without Budget Boost for 14 Years'. *Embassy—Canada's Foreign Policy Newspaper*, 18 January. http://www.embassynews.ca/news/2012/01/18/war-crimes-program-without-budget-boost-for-14-years/41111.

European Union. 2012. 'Statement by the High Representative Catherine Ashton Condemning the Continued Repression and Violence in Syria and Marking the Anniversary of the Uprising'. http://www.consilium.europa.eu/uedocs/cms_Data/docs/pressdata/EN/foraff/129013.pdf.

Federal Democratic Republic of Ethiopia. 2001. 'Statement by Mr. Meheret Getahoun, Head of Delegation to the Permanent Mission to the United Nations'. Presented at the Third Meeting of the States Parties to the Antipersonnel Mine Ban Convention, Managua, Nicaragua, 19 September.

Federal Democratic Republic of Nepal. 2006. 'Comprehensive Peace Agreement Held between the Government of Nepal and Communist Party of Nepal (Maoist)'. http://www.reliefweb.int/rw/rwb.nsf/db900SID/VBOL-6VSHK8?OpenDocument.

Federal Democratic Republic of Nepal. 2007. 'Status Paper of Nepal on the National Implementation of the Spirit of Anti-Personnel Mine Ban Convention 1997'. http://www.apminebanconvention.org/fileadmin/APMBC/IWP/SC_april07/speeches-gs/Nepal-23April07.pdf.

Federal Republic of Germany. 2013. 'Statement on Behalf of Germany by Ambassador Pascal Hector, Deputy Director-General for Legal Affairs, Federal Foreign Office, Berlin'. The Hague, Netherlands, 20 November. http://www.icc-cpi.int/en_menus/asp/sessions/general%20debate/Pages/general%20debate%20_%20twelfth%20session.aspx.

Federal Republic of Nigeria. 2004. 'Statement by Mr. Wali'. S/PV.5052 (Resumption 1) presented at the United Nations Security Council, 59th Year, 5052nd Meeting, New York, 6 October. http://www.un.org/en/sc/meetings/.

Federal Republic of Nigeria. 2013. 'Statement by the Leader of Delegation Mr. Mohanned Bello Adoke, SAN, CFR, Honourable Attorney General of the Federation and Minister of Justice'. Presented at the Twelfth Assembly of States Parties of the Rome Statute of the International Criminal Court, The Hague, Netherlands, 21 November. https://asp.icc-cpi.int/iccdocs/asp_docs/ASP12/GenDeba/ICC-ASP12-GenDeba-Nigeria-ENG.pdf.

Federal Republic of Yugoslavia. 2002. 'Statement by H. E. Mr. Dejan Sahovic, Ambassador Extraordinary and Plenipotentiary Permanent Representative of the Federal Republic of Yugoslavia to the United Nations'. Presented at the Preparatory Commission for the International Criminal Court, New York, 1 July.

Fisseha Adugna, Chargé d'affaires, Embassy of Ethiopia, Washington, DC. 1999. 'Ethiopia Responds to the *Times*' Special Report'. *Washington Times*, 3 June.

Friscolanti, Michael. 2011. 'The Truth about Ottawa's Missing War Criminals'. 23 August. http://www.macleans.ca/news/canada/hunting-for-canadas-most-wanted/.

Geneva Academy of International Humanitarian Law and Human Rights. 2013. 'The Arms Trade Treaty (2013)'. Academy Briefing No. 3. Geneva: Geneva Academy. http://www.geneva-academy.ch/docs/publications/Arms%20Trade%20Treaty%203%20WEB%282%29.pdf.

Geneva Call. 2013. 'Deed of Commitment under Geneva Call for Adherence to a Total Ban on Anti-Personnel Mines and for Cooperation in Mine Action'. http://www.genevacall.org/wp-content/uploads/dlm_uploads/2013/12/DoC-Banning-anti-personnel-mines.pdf.

Geneva Call. 2014. 'Annual Report 2013: Protecting Civilians in Armed Conflict'. Geneva: Geneva Call. http://www.genevacall.org/wp-content/uploads/dlm_uploads/2014/06/2013-GenevaCall-Annual-Report.pdf.

Georgia. 2006a. 'Statement by Georgia at ISC Meeting'. Presented at the Intersessional Standing Committee Meetings for the Antipersonnel Mine Ban Convention, Geneva, 8 May.

Georgia. 2006b. 'Statement by Georgia'. Presented at the Seventh Meeting of the States Parties to the Antipersonnel Mine Ban Convention, Geneva, 21 September. http://www.apminebanconvention.org/fileadmin/APMBC/MSP/7MSP/update_day4/Georgia_univ_7MSP_21Sep06.pdf.

Georgia. 2010. 'Statement by Georgia, Presented by H. E. Mr. Alexander Lomaia, Ambassador and Permanent Representative of Georgia to the UN'. Presented at the First Review Conference of the Rome Statute of the International Criminal Court, Kampala, Uganda, 1 June. https://asp.icc-cpi.int/iccdocs/asp_docs/RC2010/Statements/ICC-RC-gendeba-Georgia-ENG.pdf.

Glick, Veronica. 2009. 'An Assessment of US Policy and Action in Relation to the International Criminal Court during the Bush Administration 2001–2009, and Prospects for the Obama Administration's ICC Policy'. New York: The American Non-Governmental Organizations Coalition for the International Criminal Court. http://www.amicc.org/docs/US-ICCpolicy2001-2009.pdf.

Grossman, Marc. 2002. 'American Foreign Policy and the International Criminal Court'. Presented at the Remarks to the Center for Strategic and International Studies, Washington, DC, 6 May. http://2001-2009.state.gov/p/us/rm/9949.htm.

Guardian, The. 2011. 'Canada Pulls out of Kyoto Protocol'. *The Guardian*, 13 December. http://www.theguardian.com/environment/2011/dec/13/canada-pulls-out-kyoto-protocol.

Hashemite Kingdom of Jordan. 2003. 'Statement by Prince Zeid Ra'ad Zeid Al-Hussein'. Presented at the United Nations Security Council, 58th year, 4772nd meeting. Agenda Item: United Nations Peacekeeping (S/PV.4772), New York, 12 June. http://www.un.org/en/ga/search/view_doc.asp?symbol=S/PV.4772.

Hellenic Republic of Greece. 2008. 'Statement by the Permanent Mission of Greece to Geneva'. Presented at the Intersessional Standing Committee Meetings for the Anti-personnel Mine Ban Convention, Geneva, 2 June. http://www.apminebanconvention.org/intersessional-work-programme/june-2008/sd-summary-and-statements/.

Hellenic Republic of Greece. 2010a. 'Statement of the Hellenic Republic of Greece'. Presented at the Intersessional Standing Committee Meetings for the Antipersonnel

Mine Ban Convention, Geneva, 21 June. http://www.apminebanconvention.org/intersessional-work-programme/june-2010/sd-summary-and-statements/.

Hellenic Republic of Greece. 2010b. 'Statement of the Hellenic Republic of Greece'. Presented at the Tenth Meeting of the States Parties to the Antipersonnel Mine Ban Convention, Geneva, 2 December. http://www.apminebanconvention.org/meetings-of-the-states-parties/10msp/what-happened/day-4-thursday-2-december/.

Hellenic Republic of Greece. 2013. 'Statement by Greece at the 13MSP of the Ottawa Convention'. Presented at the Thirteenth Meeting of the States Parties to the Antipersonnel Mine Ban Convention, Geneva, 5 December. http://www.apminebanconvention.org/fileadmin/APMBC/MSP/13MSP/day4/11c_ARTICLE_4_STATES_PARTIES_UPDATES_-_Greece.pdf.

Human Rights Watch. 2001a. 'Making the International Criminal Court Work: A Handbook for Implementing the Rome Statute'. Vol. 13, No. 4. New York: Human Rights Watch. http://www.iccnow.org/documents/HRWhandbook_e.pdf.

Human Rights Watch. 2001b. 'Backgrounder: Landmine Use in Afghanistan'. Human Rights Watch. http://www.hrw.org/legacy/backgrounder/arms/landmines-bck1011.pdf.

Human Rights Watch. 2008. 'Courting History: The Landmark International Criminal Court's First Years'. 1-56432-358-7. New York: Human Rights Watch. http://www.hrw.org/sites/default/files/reports/icc0708webwcover.pdf.

Human Rights Watch. 2009. 'DR Congo: Militia Leader Guilty in Landmark Trial'. http://www.hrw.org/en/news/2009/03/10/dr-congo-militia-leader-guilty-landmark-trial.

Human Rights Watch. 2012a. 'Justice for Serious Crimes before National Courts: Uganda's International Crimes Division'. 1-56432-848-1. New York: Human Rights Watch. http://www.hrw.org/reports/2012/01/15/justice-serious-crimes-national-courts.

Human Rights Watch. 2012b. 'Joint Letter to the Justice Ministers and Attorneys General of the African States Parties to the International Criminal Court Regarding the Proposed Expansion of the Jurisdiction of the African Court of Justice and Human Rights'. 3 May. http://www.hrw.org/news/2012/05/03/joint-letter-justice-ministers-and-attorneys-general-african-states-parties-internat.

Human Rights Watch. 2014a. 'Joint Civil Society Letter on the Draft Protocol on Amendments to the Protocol on the Statute of the African Court on Justice and Human Rights'. 12 May. http://www.hrw.org/news/2014/05/12/joint-civil-society-letter-draft-protocol-amendments-protocol-statute-african-court-.

Human Rights Watch. 2014b. 'Statement Regarding Immunity for Sitting Officials before the Expanded African Court of Justice and Human Rights'. http://www.hrw.org/news/2014/11/13/statement-regarding-immunity-sitting-officials-expanded-african-court-justice-and-hu.

Human Rights Watch. 2014c. 'Human Rights Watch Statement Delivered by Elizabeth Evenson, Senior Counsel, International Justice Program'. Presented at the Thirteenth Assembly of States Parties of the Rome Statute of the International Criminal Court, New York, 10 December. https://asp.icc-cpi.int/iccdocs/asp_docs/ASP13/GenDeba/ICC-ASP13-GenDeba-HRW-ENG.pdf.

Human Security Report Project. 2013. 'Human Security Report 2013: The Decline in Global Violence: Evidence, Explanation, and Contestation'. Vancouver: Human Security Press. http://www.hsrgroup.org/human-security-reports/2013/text.aspx.

ICC Pre-Trial Chamber I. 2009. 'Warrant of Arrest for Omar Hassan Ahmad Al Bashir'. ICC-02/05-01/09. The Hague, Netherlands: International Criminal Court. http://www.icc-cpi.int/iccdocs/doc/doc639078.pdf.

ICC Pre-Trial Chamber I. 2010. 'Second Warrant of Arrest for Omar Hassan Ahmad Al Bashir'. ICC-02/05-01/09. The Hague, Netherlands: International Criminal Court. http://www.icc-cpi.int/iccdocs/doc/doc907140.pdf.

ICC Pre-Trial Chamber I. 2011a. 'Corrigendum to the Decision Pursuant to Article 87(7) of the Rome Statute on the Failure by the Republic of Malawi to Comply with the Cooperation Requests Issued by the Court with Respect to the Arrest and Surrender of Omar Hassan Ahmad Al Bashir'. ICC-02/05-01/09. The Hague, Netherlands: International Criminal Court. http://www.icc-cpi.int/iccdocs/doc/doc1287686.pdf.

ICC Pre-Trial Chamber I. 2011b. 'Decision pursuant to Article 87(7) of the Rome Statute on the Refusal of the Republic of Chad to Comply with the Cooperation Requests Issued by the Court with Respect to the Arrest and Surrender of Omar Hassan Ahmad Al Bashir'. ICC-02/05-01/09. The Hague, Netherlands: International Criminal Court. http://www.icc-cpi.int/iccdocs/doc/doc1384955.pdf.

ICC Pre-Trial Chamber I. 2014. 'Decision on the Non-Compliance by Libya with Requests for Cooperation by the Court and Referring the Matter to the United Nations Security Council'. ICC-01/11-01/11. The Hague, Netherlands: International Criminal Court. http://www.icc-cpi.int/iccdocs/doc/doc1879914.pdf.

ICC Pre-Trial Chamber I. 2016. 'Situation in Georgia: Decision on the Prosecutor's Request for Authorization of an Investigation (ICC-01/15)'. The Hague: International Criminal Court. https://www.icc-cpi.int/CourtRecords/CR2016_00608.PDF.

ICC Pre-Trial Chamber II. 2010. 'Decision Pursuant to Article 15 of the Rome Statute on the Authorization of an Investigation into the Situation in the Republic of Kenya'. ICC-01/09. The Hague, Netherlands: International Criminal Court. http://www.icc-cpi.int/iccdocs/doc/doc854287.pdf.

ICC Pre-Trial Chamber II. 2013. 'Decision on the Non-Compliance of the Republic of Chad with the Cooperation Requests Issued by the Court Regarding the Arrest and Surrender of Omar Hassan Ahmad Al-Bashir'. ICC-02/05-01/09. The Hague, Netherlands: International Criminal Court. http://www.icc-cpi.int/iccdocs/doc/doc1573530.pdf.

ICC Pre-Trial Chamber II. 2014. 'Decision on the Cooperation of the Democratic Republic of the Congo Regarding Omar Al Bashir's Arrest and Surrender to the Court'. ICC-02/05-01/09. The Hague, Netherlands: International Criminal Court. http://www.icc-cpi.int/iccdocs/doc/doc1759849.pdf.

ICC Pre-Trial Chamber II. 2015a. 'Decision on the Prosecutor's Request for a Finding of Non-Compliance against the Republic of the Sudan'. ICC-02/05-01/09. The Hague, Netherlands: International Criminal Court. http://www.icc-cpi.int/iccdocs/doc/doc1919142.pdf.

ICC Pre-Trial Chamber II. 2015b. 'Decision Following the Prosecutor's Request for an Order Further Clarifying That the Republic of South Africa Is under the Obligation to Immediately Arrest and Surrender Omar Al Bashir (ICC-02/05-01/09)'. ICC-02/05-01/09. The Hague: International Criminal Court. https://www.icc-cpi.int/iccdocs/doc/doc1995566.pdf.

ICC Pre-Trial Chamber II. 2016a. 'Decision on the Non-Compliance by the Republic of Djibouti with the Request to Arrest and Surrender Omar Al-Bashir to the Court and Referring the Matter to the United Nations Security Council and the Assembly of the State Parties to the Rome Statute (ICC-02/05-01/09)'. ICC-02/05-01/09. The Hague: International Criminal Court. https://www.icc-cpi.int/CourtRecords/CR2016_04946.PDF.

ICC Pre-Trial Chamber II. 2016b. 'Decision on the Non-Compliance by the Republic of Uganda with the Request to Arrest and Surrender Omar Al-Bashir to the Court and Referring the Matter to the United Nations Security Council and the Assembly of State Parties to the Rome Statute (ICC-02/05-01/09)'. ICC-02/05-01/09. The Hague: International Criminal Court. https://www.icc-cpi.int/CourtRecords/CR2016_04947.PDF.

ICC Registrar. 2014. 'Transmission to Pre-Trial Chamber II of the Observations Submitted by the Democratic Republic of Congo pursuant to the "Decision Requesting Observations on Omar Al-Bashir's Visit to the Democratic Republic of Congo" Dated 3 March 2014. Annex 2 Public'. ICC-02/05-01/09-190-AnxII. The Hague, Netherlands: International Criminal Court. https://www.icc-cpi.int/CourtRecords/CR2014_02813.pdf.

ICC Trial Chamber V(A). 2016. 'Public Redacted Version of: Decision on Defence Applications for Judgments of Acquittal, in the Case of the Prosecutor v. William Samoei Ruto and Joshua Arap Sang (ICC-01/09-01/11)'. ICC-01/09-01/11. The Hague: International Criminal Court. https://www.icc-cpi.int/CourtRecords/CR2016_02617.pdf.

ICC Trial Chamber V(B). 2014. 'Decision on Prosecution's Application for a Finding of Non-Compliance under Article 87(7) of the Statute'. ICC-01/09-02/11-982. The Hague, Netherlands: International Criminal Court. http://www.icc-cpi.int/iccdocs/doc/doc1878157.pdf.

International Bar Association. 2008. 'News Release: IBA Says All States Parties to the ICC Must Adopt Implementing Legislation as a Matter of Urgency'. http://www.iccnow.org/documents/IBA_NEWSRELEASE.pdf.

International Campaign to Ban Landmines. 1999. *Landmine Monitor 1999*. New York: Human Rights Watch. http://www.the-monitor.org/index.php/publications/display?act=submit&pqs_year=1999&pqs_type=lm&pqs_report=&pqs_section=.

International Campaign to Ban Landmines. 2000a. 'Eritrea Country Report 2000'. In *Landmine Monitor*. New York: Human Rights Watch/ICBL. http://www.the-monitor.org/index.php/publications/display?act=submit&pqs_year=2000&pqs_type=lm&pqs_report=eritrea&pqs_section#fn932.

International Campaign to Ban Landmines. 2000b. 'Guinea-Bissau Country Report 2000'. In *Landmine Monitor*. New York: Human Rights Watch/ICBL. http://www.the-monitor.org/index.php/publications/display?url=lm/2000/guinea_bissau.html.

International Campaign to Ban Landmines. 2001a. 'Angola Country Report 2001'. In *Landmine Monitor*. New York: Human Rights Watch/ICBL. www.the-monitor.org/index.php/publications/display?url=lm/2001/angola/.

International Campaign to Ban Landmines. 2001b. 'Rwanda Country Report 2001'. In *Landmine Monitor*. New York: Human Rights Watch/ICBL. http://www.the-monitor.org/index.php/publications/display?url=lm/2001/rwanda/.

International Campaign to Ban Landmines. 2004. 'Landmine Monitor 2004'. New York: Human Rights Watch/ICBL. http://www.the-monitor.org/index.php/LM/Our-Research-Products/Landmine-Monitor.

International Campaign to Ban Landmines. 2007a. 'Israel Country Report'. In *Landmine Monitor*, n.p. New York: Human Rights Watch/ICBL. http://www.the-monitor.org/index.php/publications/display?url=lm/2007/israel.html.

International Campaign to Ban Landmines. 2007b. 'Pakistan Country Report 2007'. In *Landmine Monitor*, n.p. New York: Human Rights Watch/ICBL. http://www.the-monitor.org/index.php/publications/display?url=lm/2007/pakistan.html.

International Campaign to Ban Landmines. 2007c. 'Russian Federation Country Report 2007'. In *Landmine Monitor*, n.p. New York: Human Rights Watch/ICBL. http://www.the-monitor.org/index.php/publications/display?url=lm/2007/russia.html.

International Campaign to Ban Landmines. 2008a. 'Georgia Country Profile'. In *Landmine Monitor*, n.p. New York: Human Rights Watch/ICBL. http://www.the-monitor.org/index.php/publications/display?url=lm/2008/countries/georgia.html.

International Campaign to Ban Landmines. 2008b. 'Landmine Monitor 2008'. Ottawa: ICBL/Mines Action Canada. http://www.the-monitor.org/lm/2008/translations/LMES_2008_07_withMaps.pdf.

International Campaign to Ban Landmines. 2008c. 'Pakistan Country Report 2008'. In *Landmine Monitor*, n.p. New York: Human Rights Watch/ICBL. http://www.the-monitor.org/index.php/publications/display?url=lm/2008/countries/pakistan.html.

International Campaign to Ban Landmines. 2008d. 'Sri Lanka Country Report 2008'. In *Landmine Monitor*, n.p. New York: Human Rights Watch/ICBL. http://www.the-monitor.org/index.php/publications/display?url=lm/2008/countries/sri_lanka.html.

International Campaign to Ban Landmines. 2009a. 'Presentation on States Parties That Were Granted an Extension to their Article 5 Deadlines by the 9th Meeting of States Parties'. Presented at the Intersessional Standing Committee Meetings for the Antipersonnel Mine Ban Convention, Geneva, 27 May. http://www.apminebanconvention.org/intersessional-work-programme/may-2009/mine-clearance-mine-risk-education-and-mine-action-technologies/statements/.

International Campaign to Ban Landmines. 2009b. 'Landmine Monitor 2009'. Ottawa: Mines Action Canada/ICBL. http://www.the-monitor.org/index.php/publications/display?url=lm/2009/.

International Campaign to Ban Landmines. 2009c. 'ICBL Statement on Stockpile Destruction'. Presented at the Second Review Conference of the Antipersonnel Mine Ban Convention (Cartagena Summit on a Mine-Free World), Cartagena, Colombia, 2 December. http://www.cartagenasummit.org/fileadmin/APMBC-RC2/wednesday/2RC-Item9e-2Dec2009-ICBL.pdf.

International Campaign to Ban Landmines. 2011a. 'ICBL Publicly Condemns Reports of Syrian Forces Laying Mines'. http://www.icbl.org/en-gb/news-and-events/news/2011/icbl-publicly-condemns-reports-of-syrian-forces-la.aspx.

International Campaign to Ban Landmines. 2011b. 'World's Newest Country Makes Banning Landmines First International Commitment'. ICBL. http://www.icbl.org/en-gb/news-and-events/news/2011/world%E2%80%99s-newest-country-makes-banning-landmines-fi.aspx.

International Campaign to Ban Landmines. 2012. 'ICBL Urges World to Protest Syria's Use of Landmines'. http://www.icbl.org/en-gb/news-and-events/news/2012/icbl-urges-world-to-protest-syria%E2%80%99s-use-of-landmin.aspx.

International Campaign to Ban Landmines. 2013a. 'Landmine Monitor 2013'. Geneva: ICBL. http://www.the-monitor.org/index.php/publications/display?url=lm/2013/.

International Campaign to Ban Landmines. 2013b. 'South Sudan Country Profile'. http://www.the-monitor.org/index.php/cp/display/region_profiles/theme/4022.

International Campaign to Ban Landmines. 2013c. 'Sudan Country Profile'. http://www.the-monitor.org/index.php/cp/display/region_profiles/theme/3887.

International Campaign to Ban Landmines. 2013d. 'Turkey Country Profile'. ICBL. http://www.the-monitor.org/index.php/cp/display/region_profiles/theme/3939.

International Campaign to Ban Landmines. 2013e. 'Cambodia Country Profile'. ICBL. http://www.the-monitor.org/index.php/cp/display/region_profiles/theme/3320.

International Campaign to Ban Landmines. 2013f. 'Landmine Monitor 2013: United States Country Report'. Geneva: ICBL. http://www.the-monitor.org/index.php/cp/display/region_profiles/theme/3141.

International Campaign to Ban Landmines. 2013g. 'Pakistan Country Profile'. http://www.the-monitor.org/index.php/cp/display/region_profiles/theme/3767.

International Campaign to Ban Landmines. 2013h. 'ICBL Statement during General Exchange of Views'. Presented at the Thirteenth Meeting of the States Parties to the Antipersonnel Mine Ban Convention, Geneva, 2 December. http://www.apminebanconvention.org/fileadmin/APMBC/MSP/13MSP/day1/08_GENERAL_EXCHANGE_OF_VIEWS_-_ICBL.pdf.

International Campaign to Ban Landmines. 2014a. 'ICBL Statement on Compliance'. Presented at the Intersessional Standing Committee Meetings for the Antipersonnel Mine Ban Convention, Geneva, 9 April. http://www.apminebanconvention.org/fileadmin/APMBC/IWP/IM-apr14/3_COMPLIANCE_-_ICBL.pdf.

International Campaign to Ban Landmines. 2014b. '1999–2013 Casualty Trends: States Parties with Significant Numbers of Survivors and Needs'. ICBL. http://archives.the-monitor.org/index.php/LM/Our-Research-Products/Maputo-3rd-Review-Conference/Casualty-trends-1999-2013.

International Campaign to Ban Landmines. 2014c. 'Banning Antipersonnel Mines: A 15-Year Overview of Major Findings, 1999–2014'. http://the-monitor.org/index.php/LM/Our-Research-Products/Maputo-3rd-Review-Conference/Banning-Antipersonnel-Mines-A-15-Year-Overview-of-Major-Findings-1999–2014.

International Campaign to Ban Landmines. 2014d. 'ICBL Statement on Stockpiles and Their Destruction'. Presented at the Third Review Conference of the Antipersonnel Mine Ban Convention (Maputo Summit for a Mine-Free World), Maputo, Mozambique, 23 June. http://www.maputoreviewconference.org/fileadmin/APMBC-RC3/tuesday/07b_DESTROYING_STOCKPILES_-_ICBL.pdf.

International Campaign to Ban Landmines. 2014e. 'Statement on Universalization'. Presented at the Third Review Conference of the Antipersonnel Mine Ban Convention (Maputo Summit for a Mine-Free World), Maputo, Mozambique, 23 June. http://www.maputoreviewconference.org/fileadmin/APMBC-RC3/monday/07a_UNIVERSALIZATION_-_ICBL.pdf.

International Campaign to Ban Landmines. 2014f. 'ICBL Statement on Compliance'. Presented at the Third Review Conference of the Antipersonnel Mine Ban Convention (Maputo Summit for a Mine-Free World), Maputo, Mozambique, 26 June.

http://www.maputoreviewconference.org/fileadmin/APMBC-RC3/thursday/07g_COMPLIANCE_-_ICBL.pdf.

International Campaign to Ban Landmines. 2014g. 'Landmine Monitor 2014'. Geneva: ICBL-CMC. http://the-monitor.org/index.php/LM/Our-Research-Products/Landmine-Monitor/LMM2014/LandmineMonitor2014.

International Campaign to Ban Landmines. 2015. 'Landmine Monitor 2015'. Geneva: ICBL-CMC. http://www.the-monitor.org/media/2152583/Landmine-Monitor-2015_finalpdf.pdf.

International Centre for Criminal Law Reform and Criminal Justice Policy. 2008. 'International Criminal Court: Manual for the Ratification and Implementation of the Rome Statute'. 3rd ed. Vancouver: ICCLR. http://www.iccnow.org/documents/ICC_Manual_-_March_2008_-_ICLR.pdf.

International Committee of the Red Cross. 1997. 'Anti-Personnel Landmines. Friend or Foe?' Geneva: ICRC.

International Committee of the Red Cross. 2004. 'Report on Observations and Conclusions from a Review of the ICRC Study "Anti-Personnel Landmines, Friend or Foe?"' Geneva: ICRC. http://www.icrc.org/eng/assets/files/other/friendfoereportobservations30nov1dec2004.pdf.

International Committee of the Red Cross. 2010. 'ICRC Statement on Stockpile Destruction' Presented at the Tenth Meeting of the States Parties to the Antipersonnel Mine Ban Convention, Geneva, 2 December. http://www.apminebanconvention.org/meetings-of-the-states-parties/10msp/what-happened/day-4-thursday-2-december/.

International Committee of the Red Cross. 2014. 'ICRC Statement on Compliance'. Presented at the Intersessional Standing Committee Meetings for the Antipersonnel Mine Ban Convention, Geneva, 9 April. http://www.apminebanconvention.org/fileadmin/APMBC/IWP/IM-apr14/3_COMPLIANCE_-_ICRC.pdf.

International Criminal Court. 2007. 'Report of the International Criminal Court for 2006/07'. A/62/314. New York: United Nations General Assembly. http://www.icc-cpi.int/NR/rdonlyres/754F8043-22DB-4D78-9F8C-67EFBFC4736A/278567/ICC_Report_to_UN_2006_2007_English.pdf.

International Criminal Court. 2010. 'Delegations to the Review Conference of the Rome Statute of the International Criminal Court (RC/INF.1)'. http://asp.icc-cpi.int/iccdocs/asp_docs/RC2010/RC-INF.1-reissued-ENG-FRA-SPA.pdf.

International Criminal Court. 2011. 'Report of the Court on Cooperation'. ICC-ASP/10/40. New York: Assembly of States Parties to the International Criminal Court. http://asp.icc-cpi.int/iccdocs/asp_docs/ASP10/ICC-ASP-10-40-ENG.pdf.

International Criminal Court. 2013a. 'Report of the Court on Cooperation'. ICC-ASP/12/35. The Hague, Netherlands: Assembly of States Parties to the International Criminal Court. http://asp.icc-cpi.int/iccdocs/asp_docs/ASP12/ICC-ASP-12-35-ENG.pdf.

International Criminal Court. 2013b. 'Report on the Activities of the Court'. ICC-ASP/12/28. The Hague, Netherlands: Twelfth Assembly of States Parties to the International Criminal Court. http://asp.icc-cpi.int/iccdocs/asp_docs/ASP12/ICC-ASP-12-28-ENG.pdf.

International Criminal Court. 2014a. 'Case Information Sheet: The Prosecutor v. Saif Al-Islam Gaddafi (Case No. ICC- 01/11-01/11)'. http://www.icc-cpi.int/iccdocs/PIDS/publications/GaddafiEng.pdf.

International Criminal Court. 2014b. 'Report of the International Criminal Court'. A/69/321. New York: United Nations General Assembly. http://www.icc-cpi.int/iccdocs/presidency/ICC-Rep-UNGA-30-10-2014-Eng.pdf.

International Criminal Court. 2014c. 'Report on the Activities of the International Criminal Court'. ICC-ASP/13/37. New York: Assembly of States Parties to the International Criminal Court. http://asp.icc-cpi.int/iccdocs/asp_docs/ASP13/ICC-ASP-13-37-ENG.pdf.

International Criminal Court. 2015. 'Press Release: Trial Chamber V(B) Terminates the Proceedings (ICC-CPI-20150313-PR1099)'. http://www.icc-cpi.int/en_menus/icc/press%20and%20media/press%20releases/Pages/pr1099.aspx.

Islamic Republic of Afghanistan. 2005. 'Statement by His Excellency Ambassador Ravan Farhadi, Permanent Representative of Afghanistan to the United Nations'. Presented at the 28th Special Session of the United Nations General Assembly to Commemorate the Sixtieth Anniversary of the Liberation of the Nazi Concentration Camps, New York, 24 January.

Islamic Republic of Afghanistan. 2013. 'Statement of H. E. Enayatullah Nabiel, Ambassador of the Islamic Republic of Afghanistan to the Kingdom of the Netherlands'. Presented at the Twelfth Assembly of States Parties of the Rome Statute of the International Criminal Court, The Hague, Netherlands, 21 November. https://asp.icc-cpi.int/iccdocs/asp_docs/ASP12/GenDeba/ICC-ASP12-GenDeba-Afghanistan-ENG.pdf.

Islamic Republic of Afghanistan. 2014. 'Statement by Afghanistan during the Compliance Session'. Presented at the Intersessional Standing Committee Meetings for the Antipersonnel Mine Ban Convention, Geneva, 9 April. http://www.apminebanconvention.org/fileadmin/APMBC/IWP/IM-apr14/3_COMPLIANCE_-_Afghanistan.pdf.

Islamic Republic of Iran. 1998. 'Statement by Dr. Saeid Mirzaei Yengejeh, Representative of Iran'. Presented at the 6th Committee of the United Nations General Assembly, 57th Session. Item 153: Establishment of an International Criminal Court, New York, 22 October.

Islamic Republic of Iran. 2012. 'Explanation of Vote on Draft Resolution Entitled: "Implementation of the Convention on the Prohibition of the Use, Stockpiling, Production and Transfer of Anti-Personnel Mines and on Their Destruction"'. Presented at the United Nations General Assembly First Committee, 67th Session, New York, 5 November. http://reachingcriticalwill.org/images/documents/Disarmament-fora/1com/1com12/eov/L8_Iran.pdf.

Islamic Republic of Pakistan. 1999. 'Statement by Pakistan'. Presented at the First Annual Conference of Parties to the Amended Protocol II of the Convention on Certain Conventional Weapons, Geneva, 17 December.

Islamic Republic of Pakistan. 2007. 'Explanation of Vote on the Resolution Entitled "Implementation of the Convention on the Prohibition of the Use, Stockpiling, Production and Transfer of Anti-Personnel Mines and on Their Destruction" Contained in Document A/C.1/62/L.39'. Presented at the United Nations General Assembly First Committee, 62nd Session, New York, 17 October. http://reachingcriticalwill.org/images/documents/Disarmament-fora/1com/1com07/EOV/L39pakistan.pdf.

Islamic Republic of Pakistan. 2013. 'Explanation of Vote on the Resolution Entitled "Implementation of the Convention on the Prohibition of the Use, Stockpiling, Production and Transfer of Anti-Personnel Mines and on Their Destruction" Contained in Document A/C.1/68/L.3'. Presented at the United Nations General Assembly First Committee, 68th Session, New York, 1 November. http://reachingcriticalwill.org/images/documents/Disarmament-fora/1com/1com13/eov/L3_Pakistan.pdf.

Israel. 1999. 'Statement by Mr. Giora Becher, Director, Arms Control and Disarmament Department, Ministry of Foreign Affairs'. Presented at the First Meeting of the States Parties to the Antipersonnel Mine Ban Convention, Maputo, Mozambique, 3 May.

Italian Republic. 2004. 'Statement by Under-Secretary of Foreign Affairs of Italy, Senator Alfredo Mantica'. Presented at the First Review Conference of the Anti-personnel Mine Ban Convention (Nairobi Summit for a Mine-Free World), Nairobi, Kenya, 2 December. http://www.nairobisummit.org/high-level-segment/overview/.

Italian Republic. 2014. 'Statement on Behalf of the European Union and Its Member States by Professor Mauro Politi, Chair of COJUR-ICC'. Presented at the Thirteenth Assembly of States Parties of the Rome Statute of the International Criminal Court, New York, 10 December. http://asp.icc-cpi.int/iccdocs/asp_docs/ASP13/GenDeba/ICC-ASP13-GenDeba-Italy-EU-ENG.pdf.

Italian Republic and Republic of Zambia. 2009. 'Statement by the Co-Chairs of the Standing Committee on Stockpile Destruction'. Presented at the Second Review Conference of the Antipersonnel Mine Ban Convention (Cartagena Summit on a Mine-Free World), Cartagena, Colombia, 2 December. http://www.cartagenasummit.org/daily-summaries-and-statements/day-4-wednesday-2-december/.

Japan. 1997. 'Statement by Japan'. Presented at the Ottawa Convention Signing Conference, Ottawa, 3 December.

Japan. 2004. 'Statement by Mr. Katsuyuki Kawai, Parliamentary Secretary for Foreign Affairs'. Presented at the First Review Conference of the Antipersonnel Mine Ban Convention (Nairobi Summit for a Mine-Free World), Nairobi, Kenya, 2 December. http://www.nairobisummit.org/fileadmin/APMBC-RC1/high_level/Japan_HLS_RC2004.pdf.

Keaten, Jamey. 2010. 'France to Push for Genocide Panel in Paris Court'. *Associated Press*, 6 January. http://archive.boston.com/news/world/europe/articles/2010/01/06/france_to_push_for_genocide_panel_in_paris_court/.

Kenyans for Peace with Truth and Justice. 2014. 'Statement by the Kenyans for Peace with Truth and Justice'. Presented at the Thirteenth Assembly of States Parties of the Rome Statute of the International Criminal Court, New York, 12 December. https://asp.icc-cpi.int/iccdocs/asp_docs/ASP13/GenDeba/ICC-ASP13-GenDeba-KPTJ-ENG.pdf.

Kingdom of Cambodia. 2008. 'Statement of H. E. Ambassador Sam Sotha, Head of Cambodian Delegation at the Opening of the 9th Meeting of the States Parties to the Mine Ban Convention'. Presented at the Ninth Meeting of the States Parties to the Antipersonnel Mine Ban Convention, Geneva, 24 November. http://www.apminebanconvention.org/fileadmin/APMBC/MSP/9MSP/day1/9MSP-Item10-24Nov2008-Cambodia.pdf.

Kingdom of Cambodia. 2013. 'Statement by Cambodia'. Presented at the Intersessional Standing Committee Meetings for the Antipersonnel Mine Ban Convention,

Geneva, 27 May. http://www.apminebanconvention.org/fileadmin/APMBC/IWP/SC-may13/Speeches-GS/4_COMPLIANCE_-_Cambodia.pdf.

Kingdom of Lesotho. 2014. 'Statement by H. E. Kelebone A. Maope, Ambassador and Permanent Representative of Lesotho to the United Nations, on Behalf of African State Parties to the Rome Statute'. Presented at the Thirteenth Assembly of States Parties of the Rome Statute of the International Criminal Court, New York, 8 December. http://asp.icc-cpi.int/iccdocs/asp_docs/ASP13/GenDeba/ICC-ASP13-GenDeba-Lesotho-AfricanStatesParties-ENG.pdf.

Kingdom of Morocco. 2004. 'Intervention by Ambassador Omar Hilale, Permanent Representative of the Kingdom of Morocco in Geneva and Head of Delegation'. Presented at the First Review Conference of the Antipersonnel Mine Ban Convention (Nairobi Summit on a Mine-Free World), Nairobi, Kenya, 3 December. http://www.nairobisummit.org/fileadmin/APMBC-RC1/other_languages/RC_F_French/high_level/Morocco_HLS_RC2004_fr.pdf.

Kingdom of Norway. 2012. 'Norway Condemns Use of Landmines in Syria'. Ministry of Foreign Affairs. http://www.regjeringen.no/en/archive/Stoltenbergs-2nd-Government/Ministry-of-Foreign-Affairs/Nyheter-og-pressemeldinger/pressemeldinger/2012/landmines_syria.html?id=675079.

Kingdom of Norway. 2013. 'Co-Chair Statement Stockpile Destruction'. Presented at the Thirteenth Meeting of the States Parties to the Antipersonnel Mine Ban Convention, Geneva, 5 December. http://www.apminebanconvention.org/fileadmin/APMBC/MSP/13MSP/day4/11c_ARTICLE_4_-_Norway_as_Co-Chair.pdf.

Kingdom of Thailand. 2008. 'Statement by Mr. Norachit Sinhaseni, Deputy Permanent Secretary, Ministry of Foreign Affairs of the Kingdom of Thailand, on General Exchange of Views (Item 10)'. Presented at the Ninth Meeting of the States Parties to the Antipersonnel Mine Ban Convention, Geneva, 24 November. http://www.apminebanconvention.org/fileadmin/APMBC/MSP/9MSP/day1/9MSP-Item10-24Nov2008-Thailand.pdf.

Kirby, John. 2015. 'Press Statement: Travel of Sudanese President Bashir to South Africa'. United States Department of State. http://www.state.gov/r/pa/prs/ps/2015/06/243793.htm.

Lao People's Democratic Republic. 2007. 'Statement by Dr. Maligna Saignavongs, Director of the National Regulatory Authority for UXO/Mine Action Sector'. Presented at the Eighth Meeting of the States Parties to the Antipersonnel Mine Ban Convention, Dead Sea, Jordan, 18 November. http://www.apminebanconvention.org/fileadmin/APMBC/MSP/8MSP/day1/8MSP-Item11a-18Nov2007-Laos-en.pdf.

Lyons, Amanda, and Michael Reed-Hurtado. 2010. 'Colombia: Impact of the Rome Statute and the International Criminal Court'. ICTJ Briefing. International Center for Transitional Justice. https://www.ictj.org/sites/default/files/ICTJ-Colombia-Impact-ICC-2010-English.pdf.

Malenic, Marina. 2008. 'Vice Chief Tells Senator Army Will Not Procure Victim-Activated Spider'. *Inside the Army*, 26 May.

Maliti, Tom. 2014. 'Kenyan Court of Appeal Suspends Arrest Warrant against Barasa'. *International Justice Monitor*. 29 May. http://www.ijmonitor.org/2014/05/kenyan-court-of-appeal-suspends-arrest-warrant-against-barasa/.

Ministry of Justice, Canada. 2000. *Crimes against Humanity and War Crimes Act.* http://laws-lois.justice.gc.ca/eng/acts/C-45.9/.

Mongolia. 2008. 'Statement by Mr. Gunaajav Batjargal, Deputy Director, Department of Multilateral Cooperation, Ministry of Foreign Affairs and Trade'. Presented at the Ninth Meeting of the States Parties to the Antipersonnel Mine Ban Convention, Geneva, 26 November. http://www.apminebanconvention.org/fileadmin/APMBC/MSP/9MSP/day3/9MSP-Item12a-26Nov2008-Mongolia.pdf.

Netherlands. 2014. 'Statement of the Netherlands on Compliance'. Presented at the Intersessional Standing Committee Meetings for the Antipersonnel Mine Ban Convention, Geneva, 9 April. http://www.apminebanconvention.org/fileadmin/APMBC/IWP/IM-apr14/3_COMPLIANCE_-_Netherlands.pdf.

New Vision. 2010. 'MPs Pass ICC Bill'. 10 March. http://www.newvision.co.ug/new_vision/news/1294489/mps-pass-icc.

New Zealand. 2002. 'Statement by Mr. MacKay'. Presented at the United Nations Security Council, 57th year, 4568th meeting. Agenda Item: The Situation in Bosnia and Herzegovina (S/PV.4568), New York, 10 July. http://www.un.org/en/ga/search/view_doc.asp?symbol=S/PV.4568.

Office of the President of the United States of America. 1998. 'Presidential Decision Directive PDD 64: Humanitarian Demining'. http://fas.org/irp/offdocs/pdd-64.htm.

Office of the President of the United States of America. 2011. 'Notification that approximately 100 U.S. Military Personnel Have Been Deployed to Central Africa to Act as Advisors to Partner Forces against the Lord's Resistance Army and its Leader'. Washington, DC: 112th Congress, 1st Session. http://www.gpo.gov/fdsys/pkg/CDOC-112hdoc64/html/CDOC-112hdoc64.htm.

Office of the President of the United States of America. 2012. 'Fact Sheet: A Comprehensive Strategy and New Tools to Prevent and Respond to Atrocities'. White House, Office of the Press Secretary. https://www.whitehouse.gov/the-press-office/2012/04/23/fact-sheet-comprehensive-strategy-and-new-tools-prevent-and-respond-atro/.

Office of the Prosecutor, International Criminal Court. 2003. 'Annex to the "Paper on Some Policy Issues before the Office of the Prosecutor": Referrals and Communications'. http://www.icc-cpi.int/NR/rdonlyres/278614ED-A8CA-4835-B91D-DB7FA7639E02/143706/policy_annex_final_210404.pdf.

Office of the Prosecutor, International Criminal Court. 2004a. 'Press Release: President of Uganda Refers Situation Concerning the Lord's Resistance Army (LRA) to the ICC'. https://www.icc-cpi.int/pages/item.aspx?name=president+of+uganda+refers+situation+concerning+the+lord_s+resistance+army+_lra_+to+the+icc.

Office of the Prosecutor, International Criminal Court. 2004b. 'Prosecutor Receives Referral of the Situation in the Democratic Republic of Congo'. https://www.icc-cpi.int/Pages/item.aspx?name=prosecutor%20receives%20referral%20of%20the%20situation%20in%20the%20democratic%20republic%20of%20congo.

Office of the Prosecutor, International Criminal Court. 2005. 'Prosecutor Receives Referral Concerning Central African Republic'. https://www.icc-cpi.int/Pages/item.aspx?name=otp%20prosecutor%20receives%20referral%20concerning%20central%20african%20republic.

Office of the Prosecutor, International Criminal Court. 2014a. 'Report on Preliminary Examination Activities 2014'. The Hague, Netherlands: International Criminal Court. http://www.icc-cpi.int/iccdocs/otp/OTP-Pre-Exam-2014.pdf.

Office of the Prosecutor, International Criminal Court. 2014b. 'Press Release: Statement of the Prosecutor of the International Criminal Court, Fatou Bensouda, on the Withdrawal of Charges against Mr. Uhuru Muigai Kenyatta'. The Hague, Netherlands: International Criminal Court. https://www.icc-cpi.int/Pages/item.aspx?name=Adjourn-Kenyatta-05-12-2014.

Office of the Prosecutor, International Criminal Court. 2015. 'Press Release: The Prosecutor of the International Criminal Court, Fatou Bensouda, Opens a Preliminary Examination of the Situation in Palestine'. Press Release ICC-OTP-20150116-PR1083. The Hague, Netherlands: International Criminal Court. http://www.icc-cpi.int/en_menus/icc/press%20and%20media/press%20releases/Pages/pr1083.aspx.

Parliament of the Commonwealth of Australia, Joint Standing Committee on Treaties. 2002. 'The Statute of the International Criminal Court'. 45. Canberra: Commonwealth of Australia. www.coalitionfortheicc.org/documents/AustraliaICCReport45.pdf.

Parliament of Uganda. 2006. *International Criminal Court Bill, 2006*. http://coalitionfortheicc.org/?mod=country&iduct=181.

People's Republic of Bangladesh. 2010. 'Statement by H. E. Mr. Shaflque Ahmed, Honorable Minister Ministry of Law, Justice and Parliamentary Affairs'. Presented at the First Review Conference of the Rome Statute of the International Criminal Court, Kampala, Uganda, 31 May. https://asp.icc-cpi.int/iccdocs/asp_docs/RC2010/Statements/ICC-RC-gendeba-Bangladesh-ENG.pdf.

People's Republic of Bangladesh. 2014. 'Statement by H. E. Mr. Sheikh Mohammad Belal, Ambassador of Bangladesh to the Netherlands and Permanent Representative to the International Criminal Court'. Presented at the Thirteenth Assembly of States Parties of the Rome Statute of the International Criminal Court, New York, 8 December. https://asp.icc-cpi.int/iccdocs/asp_docs/ASP13/GenDeba/ICC-ASP13-GenDeba-Bangladesh-ENG.PDF.

People's Republic of China. 1995. 'Statement by H. E. Ambassador Chen Shiqiu, Representative of China to the Sixth Committee on the Establishment of an International Criminal Court'. Presented at the United Nations General Assembly Sixth Committee, New York, 30 October. http://www.iccnow.org/documents/China1PrepCmt30Oct95.pdf.

People's Republic of China. 1996. 'Statement of the Chinese Delegation'. Presented at the Review Conference of the Convention on Certain Conventional Weapons, Geneva, May.

People's Republic of China. 1999. 'Statement by H. E. Ambassador Shao Guanfu, Head of the Chinese Observer Delegation'. Presented at the First Meeting of the States Parties to the Antipersonnel Mine Ban Convention, Maputo, Mozambique, 4 May.

People's Republic of China. 2002. 'Statement by Mr. Guan Jian, Representative of China'. Presented at the 6th Committee of the United Nations General Assembly, 57th Session. Item 158: Establishment of the International Criminal Court, New York, 15 October.

People's Republic of China. 2003. 'Statement of the Chinese Observer Delegation'. Presented at the Fifth Meeting of the States Parties to the Antipersonnel Mine Ban Convention, Bangkok, Thailand, 19 September. http://www.apminebanconvention.org/fileadmin/APMBC/MSP/5MSP/update_day5/China_5MSP_19_Sept_2003.pdf.

People's Republic of China. 2005. 'Statement by Mr. Wang Guangya'. S/PV.5158 presented at the United Nations Security Council, 60th Year, 5158th Meeting, Agenda Item: Reports of the Secretary-General on the Sudan. S/PV.5158, New York, 31 March. http://www.un.org/en/ga/search/view_doc.asp?symbol=S/PV.5158.

People's Republic of China. 2009. 'Statement by Mr. Xu Hong, Head of the Chinese Delegation'. Presented at the Eighth Assembly of States Parties of the Rome Statute of the International Criminal Court, The Hague, Netherlands, 20 November. https://asp.icc-cpi.int/iccdocs/asp_docs/ASP8/Statements/ICC-ASP-ASP8-GenDeba-China-ENG.pdf.

People's Republic of China. 2010. 'Statement of Chinese Delegation at the General Debate'. Presented at the First Review Conference of the Rome Statute of the International Criminal Court, Kampala, Uganda, 1 June. http://asp.icc-cpi.int/iccdocs/asp_docs/RC2010/Statements/ICC-RC-gendeba-China-ENG.pdf.

People's Republic of China. 2012a. 'Statement of China'. Presented at the Eleventh Assembly of States Parties of the Rome Statute of the International Criminal Court, The Hague, Netherlands, 15 November. http://asp.icc-cpi.int/iccdocs/asp_docs/ASP11/GenDeba/ICC-ASP11-GenDeba-CHN-ENG.pdf.

People's Republic of China. 2012b. 'Statement by the Chinese Observer Delegation'. Presented at the Twelfth Meeting of the States Parties to the Antipersonnel Mine Ban Convention, Geneva, 3 December. http://www.apminebanconvention.org/fileadmin/APMBC/MSP/12MSP/day1/08_GENERAL_EXCHANGE_OF_VIEWS_-_China.pdf.

People's Republic of China. 2013a. 'Statement by Mr. Ma Xinmin, Counsellor of the Department of Treaty and Law of Ministry of Foreign Affairs'. Presented at the Twelfth Assembly of States Parties of the Rome Statute of the International Criminal Court, The Hague, Netherlands, 20 November. http://asp.icc-cpi.int/iccdocs/asp_docs/ASP12/GenDeba/ICC-ASP12-GenDeba-China-ENG.pdf.

People's Republic of China. 2013b. 'Statement by the Chinese Observer Delegation'. Presented at the Thirteenth Meeting of the States Parties to the Antipersonnel Mine Ban Convention, Geneva, 2 December. http://www.apminebanconvention.org/fileadmin/APMBC/MSP/13MSP/day1/08_GENERAL_EXCHANGE_OF_VIEWS_-_China.pdf.

People's Republic of China. 2014a. 'Statement by Madame Dong Zhihua, Counsellor, Dept of Arms Control and Disarmament, MFA China'. Presented at the Third Review Conference of the Antipersonnel Mine Ban Convention (Maputo Summit for a Mine-Free World), Maputo, Mozambique, 26 June. http://www.maputoreviewconference.org/fileadmin/APMBC-RC3/friday/13_HIGH_LEVEL_SEGMENT_-_China.pdf.

People's Republic of China. 2014b. 'Statement by Mr. MA Xinmin, Deputy Director-General of the Department of Treaty and Law of the Ministry of Foreign Affairs'. Presented at the Thirteenth Assembly of States Parties of the Rome Statute of the

International Criminal Court, New York, 8 December. http://asp.icc-cpi.int/iccdocs/asp_docs/ASP13/GenDeba/ICC-ASP13-GenDeba-China-ENG.pdf.

Republic of Angola. 1997. 'Statement by Angola'. Presented at the Ottawa Convention Signing Conference, Ottawa, 3 December.

Republic of Azerbaijan. 2005. 'Azerbaijan and Ottawa Process'. Presented at the Intersessional Standing Committee Meetings for the Antipersonnel Mine Ban Convention, Geneva, 13 June. http://www.apminebanconvention.org/fileadmin/APMBC/IWP/SC_june05/speeches_gs/Azerbaijan_13June05.pdf.

Republic of Azerbaijan. 2008. 'Report under Article 7 of the Convention'. Geneva: United Nations Office at Geneva. www.unog.ch/80256EE600585943/%28httpPages%29/A5378B203CBE9B8CC12573E7006380FA?OpenDocument.

Republic of Belarus. 1997. 'Statement of the Republic of Belarus'. Presented at the Ottawa Convention Signing Conference, Ottawa, 3 December.

Republic of Belarus. 2000. 'Statement by Vladimir F. Malevich, Permanent Representative of the Republic of Belarus to the United Nations Office in Geneva'. Presented at the Second Meeting of the States Parties to the Antipersonnel Mine Ban Convention, Geneva, 11 September.

Republic of Belarus. 2008. 'Statement by Valery Kolesnik, Head of the International Security and Arms Control Department of the Ministry of Foreign Affairs'. Presented at the Intersessional Standing Committee Meetings for the Antipersonnel Mine Ban Convention, Geneva, 2 June. http://www.apminebanconvention.org/intersessional-work-programme/june-2008/sd-summary-and-statements/.

Republic of Belarus. 2010. 'Statement by the Delegation of Belarus'. Presented at the Tenth Meeting of the States Parties to the Antipersonnel Mine Ban Convention, Geneva, 2 December. http://www.apminebanconvention.org/fileadmin/APMBC/MSP/10MSP/day4/10MSP-Item11c-2Dec2010-Belarus-en.pdf.

Republic of Belarus. 2014. 'Statement by the Delegation of the Republic of Belarus on the Implementation of Article 4 of the Convention on the Prohibition of Anti-Personnel Mines'. Presented at the Intersessional Standing Committee Meetings for the Antipersonnel Mine Ban Convention, Geneva, 9 April. http://www.apminebanconvention.org/fileadmin/APMBC/IWP/IM-apr14/7_ARTICLE_4_STATES_MISSED_DEADLINES_-_Belarus.pdf.

Republic of Colombia. 1998. 'Statement by Mr. Valdivieso'. A/53/PV.83 presented at the United Nations General Assembly, 53rd Session, 83rd Meeting, New York, 8 December. http://www.un.org/en/ga/sessions/.

Republic of Colombia. 2010. 'Justice and Peace Law: An Experience of Truth, Justice and Reparation'. RC/ST/PJ/M.1. Kampala, Uganda: Review Conference of the Rome Statute of the International Criminal Court. http://asp.icc-cpi.int/iccdocs/asp_docs/RC2010/Stocktaking/RC-ST-PJ-M.1-ENG.pdf.

Republic of Congo. 2013. 'Déclaration de La République du Congo, Présentée par Monsieur Laurent Tengo, Conseiller Juridique, Administratif et à la Décentralisation du Président de la République'. Presented at the Twelfth Assembly of States Parties of the Rome Statute of the International Criminal Court, The Hague, Netherlands, 12 November. https://asp.icc-cpi.int/iccdocs/asp_docs/ASP12/GenDeba/ICC-ASP12-GenDeba-Congo-FRA.pdf.

Republic of Côte d'Ivoire. 2003. 'Déclaration de reconnaissance de la Compétence de la Cour pénale internationale'. http://www.icc-cpi.int/NR/rdonlyres/CBE1F16B-5712-4452-87E7-4FDDE5DD70D9/279779/ICDE.pdf.

Republic of Côte d'Ivoire. 2010. 'Confirmation de la Déclaration de reconnaissance'. http://www.icc-cpi.int/NR/rdonlyres/498E8FEB-7A72-4005-A209-C14BA374804F/0/ReconCPI.pdf.

Republic of Côte d'Ivoire. 2013. 'Allocution prononcée par monsieur Coulibaly Gnenema, garde des sceaux, ministre de la justice, des droits de l'homme et des libertés publiques de la République de Côte d'Ivoire'. Presented at the Twelfth Assembly of States Parties of the Rome Statute of the International Criminal Court, The Hague, Netherlands, 21 November. https://asp.icc-cpi.int/iccdocs/asp_docs/ASP12/GenDeba/ICC-ASP12-GenDeba-CoteDIvoire-FRA.pdf.

Republic of Croatia. 2002. 'Statement of Croatia'. Presented at the Fourth Meeting of the States Parties to the Antipersonnel Mine Ban Convention, Geneva, 17 September. http://www.apminebanconvention.org/meetings-of-the-states-parties/4msp/daily-summaries-and-statements/update-day-2/.

Republic of Finland. 2002. 'Statement by Finland'. Presented at the Fourth Meeting of the States Parties to the Antipersonnel Mine Ban Convention, Geneva, 18 September. http://www.apminebanconvention.org/meetings-of-the-states-parties/4msp/daily-summaries-and-statements/update-day-3/.

Republic of India. 1998. 'Explanation of Vote by Mr. Dilip Lahiri, Head of Delegation of India, at the Adoption of the Statute of the International Criminal Court'. Presented at the United Nations Diplomatic Conference of Plenipotentiaries on the Establishment of an International Criminal Court, Rome, 17 July. http://legal.un.org/diplomaticconferences/icc-1998/icc-1998.html.

Republic of India. 2008. 'Statement by Prabhat Kumar, Counsellor, Permanent Mission of India to the Conference on Disarmament'. Presented at the Ninth Meeting of the States Parties to the Antipersonnel Mine Ban Convention, Geneva, 24 November. http://www.apminebanconvention.org/fileadmin/APMBC/MSP/9MSP/day1/9MSP-Item10-24Nov2008-India.pdf.

Republic of India. 2011. 'Statement by Mr. Hardeep Singh Puri'. Presented at the United Nations Security Council, 66th year, 6491st meeting. Agenda Item: Peace and Security in Africa. S/PV.6491, New York, 26 February. http://www.un.org/en/ga/search/view_doc.asp?symbol=S/PV.6491.

Republic of India. 2012. 'Statement by India'. Presented at the Twelfth Meeting of the States Parties to the Antipersonnel Mine Ban Convention, Geneva, 3 December. http://www.apminebanconvention.org/fileadmin/APMBC/MSP/12MSP/day1/08_GENERAL_EXCHANGE_OF_VIEWS_-_India.pdf.

Republic of India. 2014a. 'Statement by India'. Presented at the Third Review Conference of the Antipersonnel Mine Ban Convention (Maputo Summit for a Mine-Free World), Maputo, Mozambique, 27 June. http://www.maputoreviewconference.org/fileadmin/APMBC-RC3/friday/13_HIGH_LEVEL_SEGMENT_-_India.pdf.

Republic of India. 2014b. 'Statement by Mr. Siddhartha Nath, First Secretary in the Permanent Mission of India to the Conference on Disarmament'. Presented at the United Nations General Assembly First Committee, 69th Session, thematic debate on Conventional Weapons, New York, 22 October. http://reachingcriticalwill.org/images/documents/Disarmament-fora/1com/1com14/statements/22Oct_India.pdf.

Republic of Indonesia. 1997. 'Statement of the Republic of Indonesia'. Presented at the Ottawa Convention Signing Conference, Ottawa, 3 December.

Republic of Indonesia. 2004. 'Statement by Mr. Bambang S. Basri'. Presented at the Intersessional Standing Committee Meetings for the Antipersonnel Mine Ban Convention, Geneva, 12 February.

Republic of Indonesia. 2010. 'Statement by Mr. Mulya Wirana, Head of Indonesian Delegation'. Presented at the First Review Conference of the Rome Statute of the International Criminal Court, Kampala, Uganda, 1 June. http://asp.icc-cpi.int/iccdocs/asp_docs/RC2010/Statements/ICC-RC-gendeba-Indonesia-ENG.pdf.

Republic of Iraq. 2014. 'Statement by Consulting Engineer Issa Rahim Al-Fayad, Director General, Directorate for Mine Action'. Presented at the Third Review Conference of the Antipersonnel Mine Ban Convention (Maputo Summit for a Mine-Free World), Maputo, Mozambique, 27 June. http://www.maputoreviewconference.org/fileadmin/APMBC-RC3/friday/13_HIGH_LEVEL_SEGMENT_-_Iraq_-_en.pdf.

Republic of Kenya. 2008. 'Final Report of the Commission of Inquiry into the Post Election Violence (CIPEV)'. Nairobi, Kenya. http://reliefweb.int/sites/reliefweb.int/files/resources/15A00F569813F4D549257607001F459D-Full_Report.pdf.

Republic of Kenya. 2011a. 'Application on Behalf of the Government of the Republic of Kenya pursuant to Article 19 of the ICC Statute (ICC-01/09-01/11-19)'. http://www.icc-cpi.int/iccdocs/doc/doc1050005.pdf.

Republic of Kenya. 2011b. 'Request for Assistance on Behalf of the Government of the Republic of Kenya pursuant to Article 93(10) and Rule 194'. ICC-01/09-58. The Hague, Netherlands: International Criminal Court. http://www.icc-cpi.int/iccdocs/doc/doc1062611.pdf.

Republic of Kenya. 2013a. 'Aide Memoire: Kenya and the International Criminal Court'. http://www.coalitionfortheicc.org/documents/AIDE_MEMORIE_KENYA_ICC_(2).pdf.

Republic of Kenya. 2013b. 'Statement by the Hon. Amina Mohammed, CBS, CAV, Cabinet Secretary for Foreign Affairs and International Trade'. Presented at the Twelfth Assembly of States Parties of the Rome Statute of the International Criminal Court, The Hague, Netherlands, 20 November. http://asp.icc-cpi.int/iccdocs/asp_docs/ASP12/GenDeba/ICC-ASP12-GenDeba-Kenya-ENG.pdf.

Republic of Kenya. 2014. 'Statement by Amb. Macharia Kamau, Ambassador/Permanent Representative, Permanent Mission of the Republic of Kenya to the United Nations'. Presented at the Thirteenth Assembly of States Parties of the Rome Statute of the International Criminal Court, New York, 11 December. http://asp.icc-cpi.int/iccdocs/asp_docs/ASP13/GenDeba/ICC-ASP13-GenDeba-Kenya-ENG.PDF.

Republic of Korea. 1997. 'Statement by Korea'. Presented at the Ottawa Convention Signing Conference, Ottawa, 3 December.

Republic of Korea. 2009. 'Explanation of Vote on L.53'. Presented at the United Nations General Assembly First Committee, 64th Session, New York, 30 October. http://reachingcriticalwill.org/images/documents/Disarmament-fora/1com/1com09/eov/ROKL53.pdf.

Republic of Malawi. 2003. 'Statement by Mr. Lamba'. Presented at the United Nations Security Council, 58th year, 4772nd meeting. Agenda Item: United Nations Peacekeeping (S/PV.4772), New York, 12 June. http://www.un.org/en/ga/search/view_doc.asp?symbol=S/PV.4772.

Republic of Mali, Ministry of Justice. 2012. 'Renvoi de la situation au Mali'. http://www.icc-cpi.int/NR/rdonlyres/A245A47F-BFD1-45B6-891C-3BCB5B173F57/0/ReferralLetterMali130712.pdf.

Republic of Mexico. 2005. 'Statement by Mr. Gómez Robledo'. A/60/PV.46 presented at the United Nations General Assembly, 60th Session, 46th Meeting, New York, 8 November. http://www.un.org/en/ga/sessions/.

Republic of Poland. 2007. 'Statement by H. E. Zdzislaw Rapacki, Head of the Polish Observer Delegation'. Presented at the Intersessional Standing Committee Meetings for the Antipersonnel Mine Ban Convention, Geneva, 23 April. http://www.apminebanconvention.org/intersessional-work-programme/april-2007/gs-summary-and-statements/.

Republic of Senegal. 1999. 'Statement Made by the Senegalese Delegation Following Some Allegations Contained in the 1999 Report of ICBL'. Presented at the First Meeting of the States Parties to the Antipersonnel Mine Ban Convention, Maputo, Mozambique, 5 May. http://www.the-monitor.org/index.php/content/view/full/18632.

Republic of Serbia. 2007. 'Statement by H. E. Mr. Pavle Jevremovic'. Presented at the Sixth Assembly of the States Parties of the Rome Statute of the International Criminal Court, New York, 3 December. https://asp.icc-cpi.int/iccdocs/asp_docs/library/asp/Statement_GD_Serbia_EN_6ASP.pdf.

Republic of Serbia. 2013. 'Statement by H. E. Mr. Petar Vico, Ambassador Extraordinary and Plenipotentiary of the Republic of Serbia to the Kingdom of the Netherlands'. Presented at the Twelfth Assembly of States Parties of the Rome Statute of the International Criminal Court, The Hague, Netherlands, 21 November. https://asp.icc-cpi.int/iccdocs/asp_docs/ASP12/GenDeba/ICC-ASP12-GenDeba-Serbia-ENG.pdf.

Republic of South Africa. 2002. *Implementation of the Rome Statute of the International Criminal Court, 2002*. http://www.gov.za/sites/www.gov.za/files/a27-02.pdf.

Republic of South Africa. 2003. 'Statement by Mr. Kumalo'. S/PV.4772 presented at the United Nations Security Council, 58th Year, 4772nd Meeting, Agenda Item: United Nations Peacekeeping, New York, 12 June. http://www.un.org/en/sc/meetings/.

Republic of South Africa. 2013. 'Opening Statement by Mr. J. H. Jeffrey, MP, Deputy Minister of Justice and Constitutional Development'. Presented at the Twelfth Assembly of States Parties of the Rome Statute of the International Criminal Court, The Hague, Netherlands, 20 November. https://asp.icc-cpi.int/iccdocs/asp_docs/ASP12/GenDeba/ICC-ASP12-GenDeba-SouthAfrika-ENG.pdf.

Republic of South Sudan. 2011. 'Statement by Her Excellency Grace Datiro, Deputy Minister of Foreign Affairs'. Presented at the Eleventh Meeting of States Parties to the Antipersonnel Mine Ban Convention, Phnom Penh, Cambodia, 28 November. http://www.apminebanconvention.org/meetings-of-the-states-parties/11msp/what-happened/day-2-monday-28-november/statements/.

Republic of South Sudan. 2013a. 'Report by Deputy Chairperson, National Mine Action Authority, M. Gen Nyang Chol, in the Meetings of the Standing Committees'. Presented at the Intersessional Standing Committee Meetings for the Antipersonnel Mine Ban Convention, Geneva, 27 May. http://www.apminebanconvention.org/fileadmin/APMBC/IWP/SC-may13/Speeches-GS/4_COMPLIANCE_-_South_Sudan.pdf.

Republic of South Sudan. 2013b. 'Statement by South Sudan Regarding Compliance Concerns (Agenda Item 11g)'. Presented at the Thirteenth Meeting of the States Parties to the Antipersonnel Mine Ban Convention, Geneva, 5 December. http://www.apminebanconvention.org/fileadmin/APMBC/MSP/13MSP/day4/11g_COMPLIANCE_CONCERNS_-_South_Sudan.pdf.

Republic of Sudan. 2000. 'Statement of the Republic of Sudan'. Presented at the Second Meeting of the States Parties to the Antipersonnel Mine Ban Convention, Geneva, 11 September.

Republic of Sudan. 2001. 'Statement of the Republic of Sudan'. Presented at the Third Meeting of the States Parties to the Antipersonnel Mine Ban Convention, Managua, Nicaragua, 18 September.

Republic of Sudan. 2004. 'Statement by H. E. Mr. Ibrahim Mahmoud Hamid, Minister of Humanitarian Affairs'. Presented at the First Review Conference of the Antipersonnel Mine Ban Convention (Nairobi Summit on a Mine-Free World), Nairobi, Kenya, 27 November.

Republic of Sudan. 2008. 'Speech by H. E. Mr. Ali Osman Mohamed Taha, Vice-President'. Presented at the United Nations General Assembly, 63rd Session, General Debate, New York, 25 September. http://www.coalitionfortheicc.org/?mod=newsdetail&news=3120.

Republic of Sudan. 2014. 'Sudan's Statement by State Minister of Defence'. Presented at the Third Review Conference of the Antipersonnel Mine Ban Convention (Maputo Summit for a Mine-Free World), Maputo, Mozambique, 27 June. http://www.maputoreviewconference.org/fileadmin/APMBC-RC3/thursday/13_HIGH_LEVEL_SEGMENT_-_Sudan.pdf.

Republic of the Philippines. 1997. 'Statement at the Ottawa Convention Signing Conference'. Presented at the Ottawa Convention Signing Conference, Ottawa, 3 December.

Republic of the Philippines. 2011. 'Statement by H. E. Libran N. Cabactulan, Permanent Representative, Philippine Mission to the United Nations'. Presented at the Tenth Assembly of States Parties of the Rome Statute of the International Criminal Court, New York, 14 December. https://asp.icc-cpi.int/iccdocs/asp_docs/ASP10/Statements/ICC-ASP10-GenDeba-Philippines-ENG.pdf.

Republic of the Philippines. 2013. 'Statement by His Excellency Denis Y. Lepatan, Chargé d'affaires, A.i. and Deputy Permanent Representative, Philippine Mission in Geneva'. Presented at the Thirteenth Meeting of the States Parties to the Antipersonnel Mine Ban Convention, Geneva, 2 December. http://www.apminebanconvention.org/fileadmin/APMBC/MSP/13MSP/day1/08_GENERAL_EXCHANGE_OF_VIEWS_-_Philippines.pdf.

Republic of the Union of Myanmar. 2011. 'Speaking Notes for Myanmar Delegation'. Phnom Penh, Cambodia, 29 November. http://www.apminebanconvention.org/

fileadmin/APMBC/MSP/11MSP/day3/08_GENERAL_EXCHANGE_OF_VIEWS_-_Myanmar.pdf.

Republic of the Union of Myanmar. 2012. 'Statement by Myanmar'. Presented at the Twelfth Meeting of the States Parties to the Antipersonnel Mine Ban Convention, Geneva, 6 December. http://www.apminebanconvention.org/fileadmin/APMBC/MSP/12MSP/day4/10d_UNIVERSALIZATION_-_Myanmar.pdf.

Republic of Tunisia. 2011. 'Statement by the Ambassador and Permanent Representative to the United Nations'. Presented at the Tenth Assembly of States Parties of the Rome Statute of the International Criminal Court, New York, 12 December. https://asp.icc-cpi.int/iccdocs/asp_docs/ASP10/Statements/ICC-ASP10-GenDeba-Tunisia-FRA.pdf.

Republic of Tunisia. 2013. 'Allocution de son excellence monsieur Karim Ben Becher, ambassadeur de la République Tunisienne auprès du Royaume des Pays-Bas'. Presented at the Twelfth Assembly of States Parties of the Rome Statute of the International Criminal Court, The Hague, Netherlands, 20 November. https://asp.icc-cpi.int/iccdocs/asp_docs/ASP12/GenDeba/ICC-ASP12-GenDeba-Tunisia-FRA.pdf.

Republic of Turkey. 2003. 'Statement Delivered by Murat Salim Esenli, Deputy Permanent Representative Permanent Mission of Turkey'. Presented at the Fifth Meeting of the States Parties to the Antipersonnel Mine Ban Convention, Bangkok, Thailand, 17 September. http://www.apminebanconvention.org/en/meetings-of-the-states-parties/5msp/daily-summaries-and-statements/update-day-3/.

Republic of Turkey. 2007a. 'Statement on Universalizing the Convention (Agenda Item 11.A)'. Presented at the Eighth Meeting of the States Parties to the Antipersonnel Mine Ban Convention, Dead Sea, Jordan, 18 November. http://www.apminebanconvention.org/meetings-of-the-states-parties/8msp/what-happened/day-1-sunday-18-november/.

Republic of Turkey. 2007b. 'Statement on Stockpile Destruction (Agenda Item 11.B)'. Presented at the Eighth Meeting of the States Parties to the Antipersonnel Mine Ban Convention, Dead Sea, Jordan, 19 November. http://www.apminebanconvention.org/meetings-of-the-states-parties/8msp/what-happened/day-2-monday-19-november/.

Republic of Turkey. 2008. 'Statement by the Turkish Delegation during the Meeting of the Standing Committee on Stockpile Destruction'. Presented at the Intersessional Standing Committee Meetings for the Antipersonnel Mine Ban Convention, Geneva, 2 June. http://www.apminebanconvention.org/intersessional-work-programme/june-2008/sd-summary-and-statements/.

Republic of Turkey. 2010a. 'Statement by Mr. Ismail Aramaz, Head of the Turkish Delegation'. Presented at the First Review Conference of the Rome Statute of the International Criminal Court, Kampala, Uganda, 1 June. http://asp.icc-cpi.int/iccdocs/asp_docs/RC2010/Statements/ICC-RC-gendeba-Turkey-ENG.pdf.

Republic of Turkey. 2010b. 'Statement of Turkey'. Presented at the Intersessional Standing Committee on the General Status and Operation of the Antipersonnel Mine Ban Convention, Geneva, 21 June. http://www.apminebanconvention.org/intersessional-work-programme/june-2010/.

Republic of Turkey. 2011. 'Statement to the Standing Committee on Stockpile Destruction'. Presented at the Intersessional Standing Committee Meetings for the Antipersonnel Mine Ban Convention, Geneva, 20 June. http://www.apminebanconvention.org/intersessional-work-programme/june-2011/stockpile-destruction/statements/.

Republic of Turkey. 2013. 'Statement by Turkey on Compliance'. Presented at the Intersessional Standing Committee Meeting of the Antipersonnel Mine Ban Convention, Geneva, 27 May. http://www.apminebanconvention.org/fileadmin/APMBC/IWP/SC-may13/Speeches-GS/4_COMPLIANCE_-Turkey.pdf.

Republic of Uganda. 1997. 'Statement by Uganda'. Presented at the Ottawa Convention Signing Conference, Ottawa, 3 December.

Republic of Uganda. 2001. 'The Anti-Personnel Mine Status of Uganda'. Presented at the Third Meeting of the States Parties to the Antipersonnel Mine Ban Convention, Managua, Nicaragua, 18 September.

Republic of Uganda. 2002. 'Statement of the Republic of Uganda'. Presented at the Intersessional Standing Committee Meeting of the Antipersonnel Mine Ban Convention, Geneva, 28 February.

Republic of Uganda. 2006. 'Statement of Uganda Delivered by Ambassador Mirjam Blaak, Head of Delegation'. The Hague, Netherlands, 23 November. http://asp.icc-cpi.int/iccdocs/asp_docs/library/asp/ICC-ASP5_Statement_uganda.pdf.

Republic of Uganda. 2013. 'Statement by the Hon. Frederick Ruhindi, Deputy Attorney General/Minister of State for Justice and Constitutional Affairs of the Republic of Uganda, on Behalf of the African Union'. Presented at the Twelfth Assembly of States Parties of the Rome Statute of the International Criminal Court, The Hague, Netherlands, 21 November. http://asp.icc-cpi.int/iccdocs/asp_docs/ASP12/GenDeba/ICC-ASP12-GenDeba-AU-Uganda-ENG.pdf.

Republic of Yemen. 2013. 'Yemen Response to AP Mines Use in Yemen during 2011'. Presented at the Intersessional Standing Committee Meetings for the Antipersonnel Mine Ban Convention, Geneva, 27 May. http://www.apminebanconvention.org/fileadmin/APMBC/IWP/SC-may13/Speeches-GS/4_COMPLIANCE_-_Yemen.pdf.

Republic of Yemen. 2014. 'Statement by the Permanent Mission of the Republic of Yemen to the Office of the United Nations and Other International Organizations in Geneva'. Presented at the Intersessional Standing Committee Meetings for the Antipersonnel Mine Ban Convention, Geneva, 9 April. http://www.apminebanconvention.org/fileadmin/APMBC/IWP/IM-apr14/Yemen-interim-report-29Mar2014.pdf.

Republic of Zambia. 2013. 'Statement by Zambia during the General Exchange of Views'. Presented at the Thirteenth Meeting of the States Parties to the Antipersonnel Mine Ban Convention, Geneva, 2 December. http://www.apminebanconvention.org/fileadmin/APMBC/MSP/13MSP/day1/08_GENERAL_EXCHANGE_OF_VIEWS_-_Zambia.pdf.

Republic of Zimbabwe. 2000. 'Statement of the Delegation of Zimbabwe'. Presented at the Second Meeting of the States Parties to the Antipersonnel Mine Ban Convention, Geneva, 13 September.

RIA Novosti. 2008. 'Russia Denies Use of Cluster Bombs in Georgia'. http://sputniknews.com/world/20080815/116065270.html.

Ribando, Clare M. 2006. 'Article 98 Agreements and Sanctions on U.S. Foreign Aid to Latin America'. Congressional Research Service Report for Congress. Washington,

DC: Congressional Research Service. http://congressionalresearch.com/RL33337/document.php?study=Article+98+Agreements+and+Sanctions+on+U.S.+Foreign+Aid+to+Latin+America.

Rome Statute of the International Criminal Court. 1998. https://www.icc-cpi.int/resource-library/Documents/RS-Eng.pdf.

Russian Federation. 1996. 'Statement by Grigory V. Berdennikov, Representative of the Russian Federation on Draft Resolution L.46 "International Agreement to Ban Anti-Personnel Landmines" (Agenda Item 71)'. Presented at the United Nations General Assembly First Committee, 51st Session, New York, 7 November.

Russian Federation. 2002. 'Statement by Russia'. Presented at the Fourth Annual Conference of Parties to the Amended Protocol II of the Convention on Certain Conventional Weapons, Geneva, December.

Russian Federation. 2003. 'Statement by Mr. Lavrov'. Presented at the United Nations Security Council, 58th year, 4772nd meeting. Agenda Item: United Nations Peace-keeping. S/PV.4772, New York, 12 June. http://www.un.org/en/ga/search/view_doc.asp?symbol=S/PV.4772.

Russian Federation. 2005. 'Statement by Mr. Denisov'. Presented at the United Nations Security Council, 60th year, 5158th meeting. Agenda Item: Reports of the Secretary-General on the Sudan. S/PV.5158, New York, 31 March. http://www.un.org/en/ga/search/view_doc.asp?symbol=S/PV.5158.

Russian Federation. 2010. 'Statement by H. E. Kirill G. Gevorgyan, Director of the Legal Department of the Ministry of Foreign Affairs of the Russain Federation, Head of the Delegation'. Presented at the First Review Conference of the Rome Statute of the International Criminal Court, Kampala, Uganda, 1 June. http://asp.icc-cpi.int/iccdocs/asp_docs/RC2010/Statements/ICC-RC-gendeba-RussianFederation-ENG.pdf.

Russian Federation. 2014a. 'Statement by Mr. Vladimir Ermakov, Deputy Director of the Department for Nonproliferation and Arms Control of the MFA of Russia, Deputy Head of Delegation'. Presented at the United Nations General Assembly First Committee, 69th Session, New York, 23 October. http://reachingcriticalwill.org/images/documents/Disarmament-fora/1com/1com14/statements/23Oct_Russia.pdf.

Russian Federation. 2014b. 'Statement of the Russian Federation Delivered by Ms. Diana Eloeva, First Secretary of the Legal Department of the Ministry of Foreign Affaires'. Presented at the Thirteenth Assembly of States Parties of the Rome Statute of the International Criminal Court, New York, 12 December. http://asp.icc-cpi.int/iccdocs/asp_docs/ASP13/GenDeba/ICC-ASP13-GenDeba-Russian-ENG.pdf.

Sanger, David E., and Eric Schmitt. 2011. 'U.S. and Allies Seek a Refuge for Qaddafi'. *The New York Times*, 16 April. http://www.nytimes.com/2011/04/17/world/africa/17rebels.html.

Scheffer, David. 1999a. 'The United States and the International Criminal Court'. *The American Journal of International Law* 93 (1): 12–22.

Scheffer, David. 1999b. 'Deterrence of War Crimes in the 21st Century'. Presented at the Twelfth Annual U.S. Pacific Command International Military Operations and Law Conference, Honolulu, Hawaii, 23 February. http://www.iccnow.org/documents/USScheffer23Feb99.pdf.

Second Review Conference of the States Parties to the CCW. 2001. 'Final Declaration'. CCW/Conf.II/2. Geneva: Convention on Certain Conventional Weapons.

https://documents-dds-ny.un.org/doc/UNDOC/GEN/G02/602/61/IMG/G0260261.pdf?OpenElement.

Secretariat of the UNFCCC. 2013. 'An Overview of the Mandates, as Well as the Progress of Work under Institutions, Mechanisms and Arrangements under the Convention'. FCCC/ADP/2013/INF.2. Warsaw, Poland: United Nations Framework Convention on Climate Change, Ad Hoc Working Group on the Durban Platform for Enhanced Action Second session, part three. http://unfccc.int/resource/docs/2013/adp2/eng/inf02.pdf.

Serbia and Montenegro. 2004. 'Statement by Serbia and Montenegro on Universalization'. Presented at the Intersessional Standing Committee Meetings for the Antipersonnel Mine Ban Convention, Geneva, 9 February.

State of Eritrea. 2002. 'Statement by the Eritrean Delegation'. Presented at the Intersessional Standing Committee Meetings for the Antipersonnel Mine Ban Convention, Geneva, 30 January. http://www.apminebanconvention.org/intersessional-work-programme/jan-feb-2002/mine-clearance-statements-and-presentations/.

State of Palestine. 2014a. 'Statement by Dr. Riyad Mansour, Ambassador, Permanent Observer Mission of the State of Palestine to the United Nations'. Presented at the Thirteenth Assembly of States Parties of the Rome Statute of the International Criminal Court, New York, 8 December. http://asp.icc-cpi.int/iccdocs/asp_docs/ASP13/GenDeba/ICC-ASP13-GenDeba-Palestine-ENG.pdf.

State of Palestine. 2014b. 'Declaration Accepting the Jurisdiction of the International Criminal Court'. http://www.icc-cpi.int/iccdocs/PIDS/press/Palestine_A_12-3.pdf.

States Parties to the Antipersonnel Mine Ban Treaty. 2000. 'Declaration of the Second Meeting of the States Parties (APLC/MSP.2/2000/1)'. Geneva. http://www.apminebanconvention.org/meetings-of-the-states-parties/2msp/summary-of-decisions-and-actions/.

States Parties to the Antipersonnel Mine Ban Treaty. 2009. 'Review of the Operation and Status of the Convention on the Prohibition of the Use, Stockpiling, Production and Transfer of Antipersonnel Mines and on their Destruction: 2005–2009'. APLC/CONF/2009/WP.2. Cartagena, Colombia. http://www.cartagenasummit.org/decisions-and-documents/.

States Parties to the Antipersonnel Mine Ban Treaty. 2014a. 'Final Report of the Third Review Conference of the States Parties to the Convention on the Prohibition of the Use, Stockpiling, Production and Transfer of Anti-Personnel Mines and on Their Destruction'. APLC/CONF/2014/CRP.1. Maputo, Mozambique. http://www.maputoreviewconference.org/fileadmin/APMBC-RC3/3RC-Final-report-Jun2014.pdf.

States Parties to the Antipersonnel Mine Ban Treaty. 2014b. 'Maputo Action Plan'. http://www.maputoreviewconference.org/fileadmin/APMBC-RC3/3RC-Maputo-action-plan-adopted-27Jun2014.pdf.

States Parties to the Antipersonnel Mine Ban Treaty. 2014c. 'Review of the Operation and Status of the Convention on the Prohibition of the Use, Stockpiling, Production and Transfer of Anti-Personnel Mines and on their Destruction, 2010–2014'. Maputo, Mozambique. http://www.maputoreviewconference.org/fileadmin/APMBC-RC3/3RC-Draft-review-Convention.pdf.

Swiss Confederation. 2014. 'Statement by Switzerland on Compliance'. Presented at the Intersessional Standing Committee Meetings for the Antipersonnel Mine Ban

Convention, Geneva, 9 April. http://www.apminebanconvention.org/fileadmin/APMBC/IWP/IM-apr14/3_COMPLIANCE_-_Switzerland.pdf.

Syrian Arab Republic. 2002. 'Statement by Mr. Wehbe'. Presented at the United Nations Security Council, 57th year, 4568th meeting. Agenda Item: The Situation in Bosnia and Herzegovina. S/PV.4568 (Resumption 1), New York, 10 July. http://www.un.org/en/ga/search/view_doc.asp?symbol=S/PV.4568(Resumption1).

Transitional Federal Government of Somalia. 2004. 'Statement by H. E. Mr. Ali M. Gedi, the Prime Minister of the Transitional Federal Government of Somalia'. Presented at the First Review Conference of the Antipersonnel Mine Ban Convention (Nairobi Summit for a Mine-Free World), Nairobi, Kenya, 2 December.

Ukraine. 1997. 'Explanation of Vote on Draft Resolution A'. Presented at the United Nations General Assembly, Fifty-second session, 67th Meeting (A/52/PV.67), New York, 9 December. http://research.un.org/en/docs/ga/quick/regular/52.

Ukraine. 2003. 'Statement by the Delegation of Ukraine'. Presented at the Fifth Meeting of the States Parties to the Antipersonnel Mine Ban Convention, Bangkok, Thailand, 16 September. http://www.apminebanconvention.org/fileadmin/APMBC/MSP/5MSP/update_day2/Ukraine_5MSP_16_Sept_2003.pdf.

Ukraine. 2010a. 'Statement of Ambassador Oleksandr Nykonenko, Head of the Delegation, Director-General of the Arms Control—Military and Technical Cooperation Directorate'. Presented at the Intersessional Standing Committee Meetings for the Antipersonnel Mine Ban Convention, Geneva, 21 June. http://www.apminebanconvention.org/intersessional-work-programme/june-2010/sd-summary-and-statements/.

Ukraine. 2010b. 'On Implementation Developments of Ottawa Convention in Ukraine (Article 4)'. Presented at the Tenth Meeting of the States Parties to the Antipersonnel Mine Ban Convention, Geneva, 2 December. http://www.apminebanconvention.org/fileadmin/APMBC/MSP/10MSP/day4/10MSP-Item11c-2Dec2010-Ukraine-en.pdf.

Ukraine. 2014a. 'Declaration of the Verkhovna Rada of Ukraine to the International Criminal Court on the Recognition of the Jurisdiction of the International Criminal Court by Ukraine over Crimes against Humanity, Committed by Senior Officials of the State, Which Led to Extremely Grave Consequences and Mass Murder of Ukrainian Nationals during Peaceful Protests within the Period 21 November 2013–22 February 2014'. http://www.legal-tools.org/doc/1a65fa/.

Ukraine. 2014b. 'Declaration by Ukraine Lodged under Article 12(3) of the Rome Statute'. https://www.legal-tools.org/uploads/tx_ltpdb/Declaration_of_the_Embassy_of_Ukraine_to_the_Kingdom_of_the_Netherlands_on_Recognition_of_the_Jurisdiction_of_the_International_Criminal_Court__ICC__01.pdf.

Ukraine. 2014c. 'Remarks by the Ukrainian Delegation on Compliance with the Provisions of the Ottawa Treaty'. Presented at the Intersessional Standing Committee Meetings for the Antipersonnel Mine Ban Convention, Geneva, 9 April. http://www.apminebanconvention.org/fileadmin/APMBC/IWP/IM-apr14/3_COMPLIANCE_-_Ukraine.pdf.

Ukraine. 2014d. 'Remarks by the Ukrainian Delegation on the Destruction of APLs Stockpiles (Article 4)'. Presented at the Intersessional Standing Committee Meetings for the Antipersonnel Mine Ban Convention, Geneva, 11 April. http://

www.apminebanconvention.org/fileadmin/APMBC/IWP/IM-apr14/7_ARTICLE_4_STATES_PARTIES_MISSED_DEADLINES_-_Ukraine.pdf.

Ukraine. 2015. 'Second Declaration by Ukraine Lodged under Article 12(3) of the Rome Statute'. Minister for Foreign Affairs, Ukraine. https://www.icc-cpi.int/iccdocs/other/Ukraine_Art_12-3_declaration_08092015.pdf.

United Kingdom. 2013. 'Statement of the United Kingdom of Great Britain and Northern Ireland by Iain Macleod, Head of Delegation'. Presented at the Twelfth Assembly of States Parties of the Rome Statute of the International Criminal Court, The Hague, Netherlands, 21 November. http://asp.icc-cpi.int/iccdocs/asp_docs/ASP12/GenDeba/ICC-ASP12-GenDeba-UK-ENG.pdf.

United Kingdom. 2014. 'Statement by Baroness Anelay, Minister of State for the Foreign and Commonwealth Office, United Kingdom of Great Britain and Northern Ireland'. Presented at the Thirteenth Assembly of States Parties of the Rome Statute of the International Criminal Court, New York, 11 December. http://asp.icc-cpi.int/iccdocs/asp_docs/ASP13/GenDeba/ICC-ASP13-GenDeba-UK-ENG.PDF.

United Nations General Assembly. 2013a. *The Arms Trade Treaty*. http://www.un.org/en/ga/search/view_doc.asp?symbol=A/RES/67/234%20B.

United Nations General Assembly. 2013b. *Resolution 68/30: Implementation of the Convention on the Prohibition of the Use, Stockpiling, Production and Transfer of Antipersonnel Mines and on their Destruction*. http://research.un.org/en/docs/ga/quick/regular/68.

United Nations Institute for Disarmament Research. 2008. 'The Humanitarian Impact of Cluster Munitions'. UNIDIR/2008/1. Geneva: UNIDIR. http://www.unidir.org/files/publications/pdfs/the-humanitarian-impact-of-cluster-munitions-335.pdf.

United Nations Security Council. 2002. *Resolution 1422*. http://www.un.org/en/ga/search/view_doc.asp?symbol=S/RES/1422(2002).

United Nations Security Council. 2003a. *Resolution 1487*. http://www.un.org/en/ga/search/view_doc.asp?symbol=S/RES/1487%20(2003).

United Nations Security Council. 2003b. *Resolution 1497*. http://www.un.org/en/ga/search/view_doc.asp?symbol=S/RES/1497%20(2003).

United Nations Security Council. 2005. *Resolution 1593*. http://www.un.org/en/ga/search/view_doc.asp?symbol=S/RES/1593%20(2005).

United Nations Security Council. 2011. *Resolution 1970*. http://www.un.org/en/ga/search/view_doc.asp?symbol=S/RES/1970%20(2011).

United Nations Security Council. 2013a. *Agenda Item: Peace and Security in Africa*. http://www.un.org/en/ga/search/view_doc.asp?symbol=S/PV.7060.

United Nations Security Council. 2013b. 'Security Council Resolution Seeking Deferral of Kenyan Leaders' Trial Fails to Win Adoption, with 7 Voting in Favour, 8 Abstaining.' http://www.un.org/press/en/2013/sc11176.doc.htm.

United Press International. 2010. 'Allegation: Turkey Breaking Landmine Ban'. 16 April. http://www.upi.com/Top_News/World-News/2010/04/16/Allegation-Turkey-breaking-landmine-ban/UPI-19481271424759.

United Republic of Tanzania. 2013. 'Statement by Hon. Mathias M. Chikawe (MP), Minister for Constitutional and Legal Affairs'. Presented at the Twelfth Assembly of States Parties of the Rome Statute of the International Criminal Court, The Hague,

Netherlands, 20 November. http://asp.icc-cpi.int/iccdocs/asp_docs/ASP12/GenDeba/ICC-ASP12-GenDeba-Tanzania-ENG.pdf.

United States Congress. 1992. *National Defense Authorization Act for Fiscal Year 1993. H.R.5005.ENR*. http://thomas.loc.gov/cgi-bin/bdquery/z?d102:HR05006.

United States Congress. 2002. *American Servicemembers' Protection Act of 2002. H.R.4775*. http://www.amicc.org/docs/ASPA_2002.pdf.

United States Congress. 2007. *Consolidated Appropriations Act, 2008. H.R.2764.ENR*. http://www.gpo.gov/fdsys/pkg/PLAW-110publ161/pdf/PLAW-110publ161.pdf.

United States Congress. 2008. *American Servicemembers' Protection Act of 2002 (Amended). H.R.4775*. http://www.amicc.org/docs/ASPA_2008.pdf.

United States of America. 1994a. 'Fact Sheet: U.S. Policy on a Landmine Control Regime'. White House, Office of the Press Secretary. http://clinton6.nara.gov/1994/09/1994-09-26-fact-sheet-us-policy-on-a-landmine-control-regime-a.html.

United States of America. 1994b. 'Remarks by President William Clinton'. Presented at the United Nations General Assembly, Forty-ninth session, New York, 26 September. http://www.presidency.ucsb.edu/ws/index.php?pid=49152&st=united+nations&st1.

United States of America. 1997a. 'Anti-Personnel Landmines: Seeking Support for U.S. Positions at Oslo Conference'. Presented at the Oslo Diplomatic Conference on an International Total Ban on Anti-Personnel Landmines, Oslo, September.

United States of America. 1997b. 'National Statement of the United States'. Ambassador Karl F. Inderfurth, Special Representative to the President and Secretary of State for Global Humanitarian Demining, Ottawa, 4 December.

United States of America. 1999. 'Remarks by the President at Comprehensive Test Ban Treaty Event'. Presented at the White House Office of the Press Secretary, White House East Room, Washington, DC, 6 October.

United States of America. 2000. 'Statement by US President Bill Clinton, Authorizing the US Signing of the Rome Statute of the International Criminal Court'. Camp David, Maryland, 31 December. http://www.iccnow.org/documents/USClintonSigning31Dec00.pdf.

United States of America. 2002a. 'Proposed Text of Article 98 Agreements with the United States'. http://www.coalitionfortheicc.org/documents/USArticle98Agreement1Aug02.pdf.

United States of America. 2002b. 'Statement by Mr. Negroponte'. Presented at the United Nations Security Council, 57th year, 4568th meeting. Agenda Item: The Situation in Bosnia and Herzegovina, New York, 10 July. http://www.un.org/en/ga/search/view_doc.asp?symbol=S/PV.4568.

United States of America. 2005. 'Statement by Mrs. Patterson'. S/PV.5158 presented at the United Nations Security Council, 60th Year, 5158th Meeting, Agenda Item: Reports of the Secretary-General on the Sudan. S/PV.5158, New York, 31 March. http://www.un.org/en/ga/search/view_doc.asp?symbol=S/PV.5158.

United States of America. 2009a. 'Speech to the Assembly of States Parties by Stephen J. Rapp, Ambassador at Large for War Crimes Issues'. Presented at the Eighth Assembly of States Parties of the Rome Statute of the International Criminal Court, The Hague, Netherlands, 19 November. http://asp.icc-cpi.int/iccdocs/asp_docs/ASP8/Statements/ICC-ASP-ASP8-GenDeba-USA-ENG.pdf.

United States of America. 2009b. 'Statement by Ms. DiCarlo'. Presented at the United Nations Security Council, 64th year, 6230th meeting. Agenda Item: Reports of the Secretary-General on the Sudan. S/PV.6230, New York, 4 December. http://www.un.org/en/ga/search/view_doc.asp?symbol=S/PV.6230.

United States of America. 2010a. 'Statement by Stephen J. Rapp, U.S. Ambassador-at-Large for War Crimes'. Presented at the First Review Conference of the Rome Statute of the International Criminal Court, Kampala, Uganda, 1 June. http://asp.icc-cpi.int/iccdocs/asp_docs/RC2010/Statements/ICC-RC-gendeba-USA-ENG.pdf.

United States of America. 2010b. 'Statement at the Review Conference of the International Criminal Court by Harold Hongju Koh, Legal Adviser, U.S. Department of State'. Presented at the First Review Conference of the Rome Statute of the International Criminal Court, Kampala, Uganda, 4 June. http://www.state.gov/s/l/releases/remarks/142665.htm.

United States of America. 2010c. 'Closing Intervention at the Review Conference of the International Criminal Court by Harold Hongju Koh, Legal Advisor, U.S. Department of State'. Presented at the First Review Conference of the Rome Statute of the International Criminal Court, Kampala, Uganda, 11 June. http://www.state.gov/s/l/releases/remarks/143218.htm.

United States of America. 2011a. 'Statement by Steven Costner, United States Delegation'. Presented at the Eleventh Meeting of the States Parties to the Antipersonnel Mine Ban Convention, Phnom Penh, Cambodia, 1 December. http://www.apminebanconvention.org/fileadmin/APMBC/MSP/11MSP/day5/10d_UNIVERSALIZATION_-_USA.pdf.

United States of America. 2011b. 'Statement by Ambassador Stephen Rapp'. Presented at the Tenth Assembly of States Parties of the Rome Statute of the International Criminal Court, New York, 14 December. http://asp.icc-cpi.int/iccdocs/asp_docs/ASP10/Statements/ICC-ASP10-GenDeba-USA-ENG.pdf.

United States of America. 2012. 'Statement by Steven Costner, the United States Delegation'. Presented at the Twelfth Meeting of the States Parties to the Antipersonnel Mine Ban Convention, Geneva, 6 December. http://www.apminebanconvention.org/fileadmin/APMBC/MSP/12MSP/day4/10d_UNIVERSALIZATION_-_United_States_of_America.pdf.

United States of America. 2013. 'Statement by Steven Costner, United States Delegation'. Presented at the Thirteenth Meeting of the States Parties to the Antipersonnel Mine Ban Convention, Geneva, 5 December. http://www.apminebanconvention.org/fileadmin/APMBC/MSP/13MSP/day4/11d_UNIVERSALIZATION_-_United_States_of_America.pdf.

United States of America. 2014a. 'Statement by Ambassador Griffiths, United States Embassy Maputo'. Presented at the Third Review Conference of the Antipersonnel Mine Ban Treaty (Maputo Summit for a Mine-Free World), Maputo, Mozambique, 27 June. http://www.maputoreviewconference.org/fileadmin/APMBC-RC3/friday/13_HIGH_LEVEL_SEGMENT_-_United_States.pdf.

United States of America. 2014b. 'Fact Sheet: Changes to U.S. Anti-Personnel Landmine Policy'. White House, Office of the Press Secretary. http://www.whitehouse.gov/the-press-office/2014/09/23/fact-sheet-changes-us-anti-personnel-landmine-policy.

United States of America. 2014c. 'Explanation of Vote before the Vote, on Item L.5/Rev.1 (Agenda Item 96(o)), "Implementation of the Convention on the Prohibition of the Use, Stockpiling, Production, and Transfer of Anti-Personnel Mines and on their Destruction" by Ms. Katharine C. Crittenberger, Adviser, Delegation of the United States of America'. Presented at the United Nations General Assembly First Committee, 69th Session, New York, 3 November. http://reachingcriticalwill.org/images/documents/Disarmament-fora/1com/1com14/eov/L5Rev1_US.pdf.

United States of America. 2014d. 'Intervention of the United States Observer Delegation by Ambassador-at-Large for Global Criminal Justice Stephen Rapp'. Presented at the Thirteenth Assembly of States Parties of the Rome Statute of the International Criminal Court, New York, 11 December. http://asp.icc-cpi.int/iccdocs/asp_docs/ASP13/GenDeba/ICC-ASP13-GenDeba-USA-ENG.pdf.

United States of America General Accountability Office. 2002. 'Military Operations: Information on U.S. Use of Land Mines in the Persian Gulf War'. GAO-02-1003. Washington, DC: General Accountability Office. http://www.gao.gov/products/GAO-02-1003.

United States of America Permanent Mission to the United Nations and other International Organizations in Geneva. 2012. 'Annual Report in Accordance with Article 13, Paragraph 4 of Amended Protocol II to the Convention on Certain Conventional Weapons'. 015/12. Geneva: Convention on Certain Conventional Weapons. http://www.unog.ch/80256EDD006B8954/(httpAssets)/AD0E2FD6365586DFC12579D300589B45/$file/United_States_APII_NAR_30_March_2012.pdf.

Vienna Convention on the Law of Treaties. 1969. https://treaties.un.org/doc/Publication/UNTS/Volume%201155/volume-1155-I-18232-English.pdf.

Watt, Nicholas, and Richard Norton-Taylor. 2011. 'Muammar Gaddafi Could Stay in Libya, William Hague Concedes'. *The Guardian*, 25 July. http://www.theguardian.com/world/2011/jul/25/gaddafi-libya-william-hague-plan.

York, Geoffrey. 2001. 'Russia Flouts Land-Mine Vow'. *The Globe & Mail*, 4 June. https://groups.yahoo.com/neo/groups/chechnya-sl/conversations/topics/16450.

Index